Acing the New SAT I Math

Greenhall Publishing
Thousand Oaks, CA

Copyright © 2004 by Greenhall Publishing

This edition published by Greenhall Publishing

Greenhall Publishing
Thousand Oaks, CA 91360
http://greenhallpublishing.com

Cover Design by Hespenheide Design

Printed by Delta Printing Solutions
Printed and bound in the United States

ISBN 0-9754753-0-4

To the students...

If you're reading this, you are on your way to a better score on the new SAT I math! Below are guidelines for getting the most out of this book, as well as information about changes to the math section of the SAT I.

How to use this book

Math Tutorial

Each of the twenty chapters in this book teaches a particular group of mathematical concepts you need to know for the SAT I. The concepts are taught using key terms – listed and explained at the beginning of each chapter – along with illustrations and diagrams.

Next to the key terms and illustrations you will find sample questions, with complete solutions, that demonstrate the application of the concepts you have just learned. Keep a pencil and sheet of paper handy and follow along, working out the sample questions for yourself – this will help you later in solving the practice problems.

Exercise Sets

Each chapter includes a set of practice problems, followed with answers and explanations, to ensure that you master the material.

Practice Tests

At the end of the book you will find one PSAT and two SAT I practice tests. For the maximum benefit, these should be taken under realistic testing-center conditions – timed and free from outside distractions.

Study Timetable

As with any test, students will see the best results by studying consistently over at least several weeks before the exam date, rather than trying to cram and learn "test tricks" in a day or two.

Students studying an hour a day over two months should be more than able to finish all the exercises in this book. The clear subject organization by chapter means you can focus your efforts and spend more time on topics you are struggling with. While chapters can be broken up over a couple sessions, students should finish each practice test in one uninterrupted sitting.

About the New SAT I

Content

Starting in spring of 2005, the math portion of the SAT I will cover three years of high school math. The SAT currently tests students on Geometry and Algebra I material; for the new exam students must also be familiar with material typically taught in Algebra II classes. Quantitative comparison questions will be eliminated.

The math portion of the new SAT I will consist of three sections – two 25-minute sections and one 20-minute section, for a total of 70 minutes in math testing. (Tests may also include one experimental math section, which does not count toward your score.)

The new PSAT/NMSQT (to be released in October 2004) will also include the new topics, although the SAT I will test for these concepts at a higher level. Quantitative comparison questions will be eliminated from the PSAT as well.

The math portion of the new PSAT/NMSQT will consist of two sections – each 25 minutes, for a total of 50 minutes in math testing.

Math questions on the SAT I and PSAT fall into two main categories: multiple choice (with five answer choices given) and student produced response questions. Student produced response questions, commonly referred to as "grid-ins," require students to formulate their own answers, then enter the numeric values into a special grid.

Calculators

Students may use a four-function, scientific, or graphing calculator during the SAT I exam (calculators with a QWERTY keyboard are not allowed). Use of a calculator is highly recommended, though all of the problems can be solved without one. Becoming comfortable with your calculator during test preparation will help you use this tool to solve problems more quickly and efficiently during the actual exam.

Scoring

Scores on the math portion of the SAT I range from 200 to 800. An average score on the math section is about 500, but this can vary with each individual test. Consult the College Board Web site (www.collegeboard.com) for further specifics.

Signing Up for the SAT

Students can register online for the SAT at the College Board Web site. Students can also pick up registration packets at their high schools and sign up via snail mail. Generally the registration deadlines are a little over a month before the actual testing date. Late registrations incur additional fees.

This book was written to be a straightforward study guide for the SAT I math. There are no shortcuts or gimmicks, but taking the time to work through this book should leave you feeling confident and well prepared for the test.

Good luck!

Table of Contents

Part A – Math Review

Part B – Practice Tests

Part A
Math Review

I. Arithmetic and Algebra

1. Properties of Numbers

Key Terms / Illustrations   Examples

---

1. Number Line

Numbers can be pictured as points on a horizontal line called a number line.

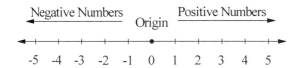

☑ On the SAT, number lines are drawn to scale. You will be expected to make reasonable approximations of the coordinate of the point.

☑ The distances between tick marks on a number line can be integers, fractions, or decimals.

2. Integers

Positive integers, negative integers, and zero make up the set of integers.

{ **positive integers** } = { 1, 2, 3, $\cdots$ }

{ **negative integers** } = { $\cdots$ $-5, -4, -3, -2, -1$ }

{ **integers** } = { $\cdots$ $-3, -2 -1, 0, 1, 2, 3,$ $\cdots$ }

{ **whole numbers** } = { $0, 1, 2, 3, \cdots$ }

☑ **Zero** is neither positive nor negative.

3. **Consecutive integers** are numbers obtained by counting by ones from any integer.

$$\ldots -3, -2, -1, 0, 1, 2, \ldots$$

n, $n+1$, $n+2$, $n+3$, ...
represents consecutive integers, where n is any integer.

Example 1 ◻ **Number line**

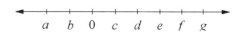

On the number line above, the marks are equally spaced. If $g - a = 28$ what is the value of $f - b$?

Solution ◻

Since the figure is drawn to scale and g is 8 units to the right of a, the distance between each space is $28 \div 7 = 4$. Therefore the coordinate of f is 16 and the coordinate of b is -4.

The value of $f - b = 16 - (-4) = 20$.   Answer

Example 2 ◻ **Finding positive integers for a two variable equation.**

$2x + 5y = 18$, and x and y are positive integers. What is the value of x?

Solution ◻

Choose the first few positive integers for x-values and make substitutions for the given equation. Construct a table of values.

x	1	2	3	4
y	3.2	2.8	2.4	2

Both x and y are positive integers when x equals 4 and y equals 2.

Therefore the value of x is 4.   Answer

Key Terms / Illustrations   Examples

4. **Consecutive even integers** are numbers obtained by counting by twos from any even integer.

   $...-4,-2,0,2,4,6...$

5. **Consecutive odd integers** are numbers obtained by counting by twos from any odd integer.

   $...-3,-1,1,3,5...$

   Thus
   n, $n+2$, $n+4$, $n+6$, ...,
   represents consecutive even integers if n is even, and consecutive odd integers if n is odd.

6. A **prime number** is an integer greater than 1 whose only factors are 1 and itself.

   The first ten prime numbers are :

   2, 3, 5, 7, 11, 13, 17, 19, 23, 29

7. When you write a number as a product of prime numbers, you are writing the **prime factorization** of the number.

8. A **composite number** is a whole number that has factors other than 1 and itself.

   ☑ **1** is neither a prime nor a composite number.

9. The product of a real number and an integer is called a **multiple** of the real number.

10. The **greatest common factor** (GCF) is the largest exact divisor of two or more numbers.

11. The **least common multiple** (LCM) is the smallest whole number that is a multiple of two or more whole numbers.

Example 3 □ **Finding consecutive even integers**

If the sum of 4 consecutive even integers is x, what is the smallest of the 4 consecutive even integers in terms of x ?

Solution □
Let n = the smallest of the 4 consecutive even integers.

$$n+(n+2)+(n+4)+(n+6)=x$$
$$4n+12=x$$
$$4n=x-12$$

$$n=\frac{x-12}{4} \text{ or } \frac{x}{4}-3 \quad \text{Answer}$$

Example 4 □ **Prime factorization**

Find the prime factorization of 60.

Solution □

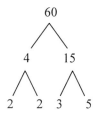

$$60=2\cdot2\cdot3\cdot5=2^2\cdot3\cdot5 \quad \text{Answer}$$

Example 5 □ **GCF and LCM of two numbers**

Find the GCF and LCM of 24 and 60.

Solution □

Write the prime factorization of each number.
$24=2\cdot2\cdot2\cdot3=2^3\cdot3$
$60=2\cdot2\cdot3\cdot5=2^2\cdot3\cdot5$

The common prime factors are 2 and 3.
The smallest power of 2 is 2^2.
The smallest power of 3 is 3.
GCF $=2^2\cdot3=12$ Answer

The greatest power of 2 is 2^3.
The greatest power of 3 is 3.
The greatest power of 5 is 5.
LCD $=2^3\cdot3\cdot5=120$ Answer

12. Remainders

If a positive integer a is divided by another positive integer b, and leaves a remainder of r, then a is r more than a multiple of b.

$a = b + r$
$a = 2b + r$
$a = 3b + r$ and so on ....

Dividend $=$ Quotient $\times$ Divisor $+$ Remainder

☑ Use your calculator to find the quotient and remainder of a number. For example, to find the remainder when 60 is divided by 7, $60 \div 7 =$ 8.5714...
Then we know that the quotient is 8.
The remainder is $60 - 8 \times 7 = 4$.

$60 = 8 \cdot 7 + 4$

13 Decimals

Place value chart

$\Leftarrow$ decimal point	tenths	hundredths	thousandths	ten-thousandths
•	$\dfrac{1}{10}$	$\dfrac{1}{100}$	$\dfrac{1}{1,000}$	$\dfrac{1}{10,000}$

14. Rounding Decimals

To round a decimal to the desired place, locate the digit in that place, then

a) if the digit to the right is 5 or more round up,
b) if the digit to the right is 4 or less round down,
c) drop all digits to the right of the desired place.

Example 6 □ **Multiple of a number**

How many of the positive integers less than 50 are 3 less than a multiple of 8?

Solution □

8, 16, 24, 32, 40, 48, 56 $\Leftarrow$ multiples of 8
5, 13, 21, 29, 37, 45, 53 $\Leftarrow$ 3 less than a
                                multiple of 8
There are 6 integers.   Answer

Example 7 □ **Remainder**

If a divided by 9 leaves a remainder of 5, and a is greater than 9, what is the remainder when a is divided by 4?

Solution □

Since a is 5 more than a multiple of 9,
$a = 9 + 5$
$a = 2 \cdot 9 + 5$
$a = 3 \cdot 9 + 5$ and so on ...

If a is 14, the remainder when 14 is divided by 4 is 2. If a is 23, the remainder when 23 is divided by 4 is 3. Therefore the remainder cannot be determined from the information given.

Example 8 □ **Rounding Decimals**

Round 42.937 to the nearest
a) tenth   b) hundredth

Solution □

a) Locate the digit in the tenths place.
42.⬚9⬚37   Since the digit to the right is less than 5, round down. Drop all the digits to the right of the tenths place.

42.9   Answer

b) Locate the digit in the hundredths place.
42.9⬚3⬚7   Since the digit to the right is more than 5, round up. Drop all the digits to the right of the hundredths place.

42.94   Answer

15. Divisibility Rules

A number is **divisible by 2** if it has a ones digit of 0, 2, 4, 6, or 8.

A number is **divisible by 3** if the sum of the digits is divisible by 3.

A number is **divisible by 4** if the last two digits form a number divisible by 4.

A number is **divisible by 5** if the ones digit is 0 or 5.

A number is **divisible by 6** if the number is divisible by 2 and 3.

A number is **divisible by 8** if the last three digits form a number divisible by 8.

A number is **divisible by 9** if the sum of the digits is divisible by 9.

A number is **divisible by 10** if the ones digit is 0.

16 Odd and Even

$\text{Odd} + \text{Odd} = \text{Even}$	$\text{Odd} \times \text{Odd} = \text{Odd}$
$\text{Even} + \text{Even} = \text{Even}$	$\text{Even} \times \text{Even} = \text{Even}$
$\text{Odd} + \text{Even} = \text{Odd}$	$\text{Odd} \times \text{Even} = \text{Even}$

17. Order of Operations

$$10 - 2 \cdot 7 + (11 - 5)^2 \div 3$$

1. **Parentheses** $= 10 - 2 \cdot 7 + 6^2 \div 3$
2. **Exponents** $= 10 - 2 \cdot 7 + 36 \div 3$
3. **Multiplication** $= 10 - 14 + 36 \div 3$
4. **Division** $= 10 - 14 + 12$
5. **Addition** $= -4 + 12$
6. **Subtraction** $= 8$

Example 9 □ **Roman numeral problem**

If a and b are integers and $a - b = 2$, which of the following must be true?

  I. $a + b$ is even
  II. $b - a$ is negative
  III. $a + b$ is greater than 2

(A) I only
(B) II only
(C) III only
(D) I and II only
(E) I, II, and III only

Solution □

*This type of question is referred to as the **Roman numeral answer format**. For these type of questions evaluate each statement seperately and decide whether each statement is true or false.*

Statement I : If $a - b = 2$, is $a + b$ always even?

Method 1 : Pick numbers which make $a - b = 2$.

If $a = 5$ and $b = 3$, then $a + b = 8$, which is even.
If $a = 4$ and $b = 2$, then $a + b = 6$, which is even.

Method 2 : Solve the equation.

$$a - b = 2 \implies a = b + 2$$
$$a + b = (b + 2) + b \qquad \text{Make substitution.}$$
$$= 2b + 2 = 2(b + 1)$$

Two times a number is always even. Therefore $a + b$ is even, and Roman numeral I is true. Circle I.

Statement II : Is $b - a$ always negative?

$$a - b = 2 \qquad\qquad\qquad \text{Given}$$
$$b - a = -(a - b) = -(2) \qquad \text{Make substitution.}$$

Roman numeral II is true. Circle II.

Statement III : Is $a + b$ always greater than 2?

Pick negative numbers which make $a - b = 2$.
Let $a = -3$ and $b = -5$,
then $a + b = -3 + (-5) = -8$
Roman numeral III is false. Do not circle III.

Therefore choice (D) is correct.

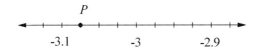

1. On the number line above, the marks are equally spaced. What is the coordinate of P ?

   (A) -3.75 (B) -3.125 (C) -3.09

   (D) -3.075 (E) -3.050

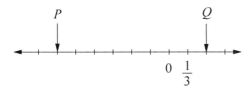

2. On the number line above, the marks are equally spaced. What is the average of P and Q ?

   (A) $-\dfrac{10}{3}$ (B) $-\dfrac{5}{2}$ (C) $-\dfrac{5}{3}$

   (D) $-\dfrac{5}{6}$ (E) $-\dfrac{2}{3}$

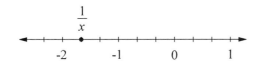

3. On the number line above, the marks are equally spaced. The value of x is most nearly equal to

   (A) -1.8
   (B) -1.5
   (C) -0.8
   (D) -0.6
   (E) -0.4

4. Kay purchased $500 worth of stock. If each share of stock was worth either $30 or $50, which of the following CANNOT be the number of shares purchased?

   (A) 8
   (B) 10
   (C) 12
   (D) 14
   (E) 16

5. If the product of six integers is an odd integer, exactly how many of the six integers must be odd?

   (A) 1
   (B) 2
   (C) 3
   (D) 5
   (E) 6

6. If a and b are positive integers, each greater than 1, and $7(a-3)=11(b-1)$, what is the least possible value of $a+b$?

   (A) 8
   (B) 12
   (C) 22
   (D) 27
   (E) 33

7. If n is an integer divisible by 8 but not by 6, then which of the following CANNOT be an integer?

   (A) $\dfrac{n}{2}$ (B) $\dfrac{n}{3}$ (C) $\dfrac{n}{7}$

   (D) $\dfrac{n}{8}$ (E) $\dfrac{n}{10}$

8. S is the sum of 4 consecutive integers, the smallest of which is n. In terms of S, what is the sum of four consecutive integers of which the greatest is n?

   (A) $S - 12$

   (B) $S - 10$

   (C) $S + 10$

   (D) $S + 12$

   (E) $S - 6$

9. If j and k are integers and $j + 2k = 3$, then $2j + k$ must be

   (A) even

   (B) odd

   (C) a multiple of 2

   (D) a multiple of 3

   (E) positive

10. What is the least prime number greater than 61?

    (A) 63

    (B) 67

    (C) 71

    (D) 73

    (E) 77

11. For which of the following pairs of integers is the greatest common factor subtracted from the least common multiple of the integers the greatest?

    (A) 5, 8

    (B) 10, 15

    (C) 7, 21

    (D) 9, 12

    (E) 39, 3

12. The greatest integer of a set of consecutive integers is 19. If the sum of the integers is –20, how many integers are in this set?

    (A) 20

    (B) 21

    (C) 38

    (D) 39

    (E) 40

13. If r is an integer, and the remainder of $3r + 4$ divided by 7 is r, what is a possible value of r?

    (A) 3

    (B) 4

    (C) 5

    (D) 6

    (E) 7

14. If x is an integer and $x^2 + 2x - 1$ is even, which of the following must be odd?

   (A) x

   (B) $x + 1$

   (C) $x - 1$

   (D) $x^2 - 1$

   (E) $x^2 + x$

15. If x and y are positive integers such that $xy = 1000$, and if neither x nor y is a multiple of 10, then $x + y =$

   (A) 254

   (B) 133

   (C) 125

   (D) 70

   (E) 65

16. If an integer n is divisible by 4, 5, and 6, what is the next integer divisible by these numbers?

   (A) $n + 20$

   (B) $n + 24$

   (C) $n + 30$

   (D) $n + 45$

   (E) $n + 60$

17. If m is an even integer and n is an odd integer, which of the following statements could be true?

   I. mn is an odd integer

   II. $\dfrac{m}{n}$ is an even integer

   III. $\dfrac{m}{2} + n$ is an odd integer

   (A) None

   (B) I only

   (C) II only

   (D) II and III only

   (E) I, II, and III

18. If a and b are even integers which of the following could be an odd integer?

   I. $\dfrac{a}{b}$

   II. $a(b-1)$

   III. $\dfrac{a+b}{2}$

   (A) I only

   (B) II only

   (C) I and III only

   (D) II and III only

   (E) I, II and III

1. Let m be the greatest integer less than 256 that is divisible by 6, and let n be the smallest integer greater than 256 that is divisible by 9. What is the value of $m + n$?

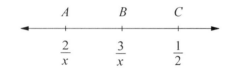

2. On the number line above, if $AB = BC$ what is the value of x?

3. What is the least of three consecutive integers whose product is 120?

4. What is the least positive integer k for which $18k$ is the cube of an integer?

$$753T4$$

5. If the five-digit number above is divisible by 4 and 9, what is the value of T?

6. If p and r are different prime numbers, how many positive factors of p^2r are there?

7. If $3x + 8y = 25$ and x and y are positive integers, what is the value of $x + y$?

Answer Key

<u>Multiple Choice Questions</u>

1. D	2. E	3. D	4. A	5. E
6. C	7. B	8. A	9. D	10. B
11. A	12. E	13. C	14. A	15. B
16. E	17. D	18. C		

<u>Grid-In Questions</u>

1. 513	2. 8	3. 4	4. 12	5. 8
6. 6	7. 5			

<u>Note:</u> Throughout the book, the symbol " $\Rightarrow$ " is used to indicate that one step of an equation implies the next step of the equation.

Answers and Explanations

<u>Multiple Choice Questions</u>

1. D

The marks are equally spaced. The distance between the marks is 0.025. Therefore the coordinate of P is $-3 - 0.075 = -3.075$.

2. E

Since the distance between the marks is $\frac{1}{3}$, the coordinate of P is -2 and the coordinate of Q is $\frac{2}{3}$.

The average of P and $Q = \dfrac{-2 + 2/3}{2} = \dfrac{-4/3}{2} = -\dfrac{2}{3}$.

3. D

The coordinate of $\dfrac{1}{x}$ is $-1\dfrac{2}{3}$. Therefore $\dfrac{1}{x} = -1\dfrac{2}{3}$

$\Rightarrow \dfrac{1}{x} = -\dfrac{5}{3} \Rightarrow -5x = 3$ (cross product) $\Rightarrow$

$x = -\dfrac{3}{5}$ or $x = -0.6$.

4. A

Answers for this type of question can be found easily by finding the <u>minimum</u> and <u>maximum</u> number of stocks that can be bought.

The minimum number of stocks that can be bought is when all the stocks are \$50 denominations, which is $\dfrac{500}{50} = 10$ stocks.

The maximum number of stocks that can be bought is when all the stocks are \$30 denominations, which is $\dfrac{500}{30} \approx 16.7 \Rightarrow 16$ stocks.

5. E

If the product of six integers is an odd integer, there cannot be any even integers. All six integers must be odd.

6. C

$7(a-3) = 11(b-1) \Rightarrow$
$(a-3) = 11$ and $(b-1) = 7$.

Therefore $a = 14$ and $b = 8$.
$a + b = 14 + 8 = 22$

7. B

Since n is an integer divisible by 8, n is a multiple of 8: 8, 16, 24, 32, 40, 48, 56, ….
But n is not divisible by 6, so n cannot be

24, 48, …. Therefore n is not divisible by 3, and $\dfrac{n}{3}$

cannot be an integer.

8. A

S is the sum of 4 consecutive integers, the <u>smallest</u> of which is n. $\Rightarrow S = n + (n+1) + (n+2) + (n+3)$
$\Rightarrow S = 4n + 6 \Rightarrow 4n = S - 6$

Let T equal the sum of four consecutive integers, the <u>greatest</u> of which is n.

$\Rightarrow T = (n-3) + (n-2) + (n-1) + n$
$\Rightarrow T = 4n - 6$ (make substitution, $4n = S - 6$)
$\Rightarrow T = (S-6) - 6 = S - 12$

9. D

$j + 2k = 3 \Rightarrow j = 3 - 2k$
$2j + k = 2(3 - 2k) + k = 6 - 4k + k = 6 - 3k$
$= 3(2-k)$. Since k is an integer, $(2-k)$ is also an integer and $3(2-k)$ must be a multiple of 3.

10. B

11. A

Numbers	LCM $-$ GCF
5, 8	$40 - 1 = 39$
10, 15	$30 - 5 = 25$
7, 21	$21 - 7 = 14$
9, 12	$36 - 3 = 33$
39, 3	$39 - 3 = 36$

12. E

The set of consecutive integers is
$\{-20, -19, -18, ..., -1, 0, 1, 2, ..., 18, 19\}$
The greatest integer is 19 and their sum is -20.

$\underbrace{-20}_{1\ number}, \underbrace{-19, -18, ..., -2, -1}_{19\ numbers}, \underbrace{0}_{1\ number}, \underbrace{1, 2, ..., 18, 19}_{19\ numbers}$

Altogether there are 40 numbers.

13. C

To find the value of r, let's test each answer choice. Choice (A): If $r = 3$, $3r + 4 = 3(3) + 4 = 13$. When 13 is divided by 7 the remainder is 6. Since the remainder is not 3, this is not the correct answer.

Choice (B): If $r = 4$, $3r + 4 = 3(4) + 4 = 16$. When 16 is divided by 7 the remainder is 2. Since the remainder is not 4, this is not the correct answer.

Choice (C): If $r = 5$, $3r + 4 = 3(5) + 4 = 19$. When 19 is divided by 7 the remainder is 5.

Choice (C) is correct.

14. A

Let's test out some values of x which make $(x^2 + 2x - 1)$ even. If $x = 1$, all the answer choices except (A) become even.
If $x = 3$, $(x^2 + 2x - 1)$ is even, and again all the answer choices except (A) become even.

15. B

Let's make a table of values.

value	x	y	xy
1	1	1000	1000
2	2	500	1000
4	4	250	1000
5	5	200	1000
8	8	125	1000 ← neither x nor y is a multiple of 10

$x + y = 8 + 125 = 133$

16. E

The smallest integer n that is divisible by 4, 5, and 6 is the LCM of 4, 5, and 6.
$4 = 2^2$
$5 = 5$
$6 = 2 \cdot 3$
LCM $= 2^2 \cdot 5 \cdot 3 = 60$

Therefore n is a multiple of 60, and the next larger integer divisible by these numbers is $n + 60$.

17. D

Pick an even number for m and an odd number for n. Let's try $m = 2$ and $n = 3$.

   I. $mn = 2 \cdot 3 = 6$; even times odd is always even.
      Roman numeral I is not true.

   II. $\dfrac{m}{n} = \dfrac{2}{3}$ is not an integer. Let's try $m = 6$, then

      $\dfrac{m}{n} = \dfrac{6}{3}$ is an even integer.
      Roman numeral II could be true.

   III. $\dfrac{m}{2} + n = \dfrac{2}{2} + 3 = 4$, which is not an odd integer.

      Let's try $m = 4$. Then $\dfrac{m}{2} + n = \dfrac{4}{2} + 3 = 5$, which is an odd integer.
      Roman numeral III could be true.

18. C

Pick numbers. Let's try $a = 4$ and $b = 2$.

   I. $\dfrac{a}{b} = \dfrac{4}{2} = 2$, which is not an odd integer.

      Let's try $a = 6$. Then $\dfrac{a}{b} = \dfrac{6}{2} = 3$, which is an

      odd integer.
      Roman numeral I could be true.

   II. Since a is even, $a(b-1)$ is always an even integer.
      Roman numeral II is not true.

   III. $\dfrac{a+b}{2} = \dfrac{4+2}{2} = 3$, which is an odd integer.
      Roman numeral III could be true.

Grid-In Questions

1. 513

When 256 is divided by 6, the quotient is 42 and the remainder is 4. $\Rightarrow$ $42 \times 6 = 252$ is the greatest integer less than 256 that is divisible by 6, so $m = 252$.

When 256 is divided by 9, the quotient is 28 and the remainder is 4. $\Rightarrow$ $29 \times 9 = 261$ is the smallest integer greater than 256 that is divisible by 9, so $n = 261$.

Therefore $m + n = 252 + 261 = 513$

2. 8

$AB = BC \Rightarrow \dfrac{1}{2} - \dfrac{3}{x} = \dfrac{3}{x} - \dfrac{2}{x}$

Multiply both sides of the equation by $2x$.

$2x(\dfrac{1}{2} - \dfrac{3}{x}) = 2x(\dfrac{3}{x} - \dfrac{2}{x}) \Rightarrow x - 6 = 6 - 4$

$x = 8$

3. 4

Trial and error is the best way to find the answer here. Pick numbers: 3, 4, and 5 $\Rightarrow 3 \cdot 4 \cdot 5 = 60$.
Try 4, 5, and 6 $\Rightarrow 4 \cdot 5 \cdot 6 = 120$.

Therefore the least of the three consecutive integers is 4.

4. 12

We need to find the prime factorization of 18.
$18k = 2 \cdot 3 \cdot 3 \cdot k$
The least positive integer k for which $18k$ is the cube of an integer $\Rightarrow$
$18k = 2 \cdot 3 \cdot 3 \cdot k = 2^3 \cdot 3^3 \Rightarrow k = 2^2 \cdot 3 = 12$

Check: $18k = 18 \times 12 = 216 = 6^3$

5. 8

If a number is divisible by 9, then the sum of the digits is divisible by 9.
$7 + 5 + 3 + T + 4 = 19 + T$
Since T is a digit, T cannot be more than 9.
$19 + T$ must be a multiple of 9. $\Rightarrow T = 8$

If a number is divisible by 4, then the last two digits of the number form a number divisible by 4.
84 is also is divisible by 4.

6. 6

Pick numbers. Let $p = 2$ and $r = 3$, then
$p^2 r = 2^2 \cdot 3 = 12$
The positive factors of 12 are 1, 2, 3, 4, 6, and 12.
There are 6 factors.

Let $p = 5$ and $r = 7$, then
$p^2 r = 5^2 \cdot 7$

The positive factors of $5^2 \cdot 7$ are 1, 5, 7, 25, 35 and 175.
There are 6 factors.
There are always 6 different factors of $p^2 r$, if p and r are prime numbers.

7. 5

We need to make a table of values.

$$3x + 8y = 25$$

value	x	y
	1	$11/4$ (not an integer)
	2	$19/8$ (not an integer)
	3	2

So $x = 3$ and $y = 2$ are solutions for the given equation, and $x + y = 3 + 2 = 5$.

2. Fractions (Rational Expressions)

Key Terms / Illustrations   Examples

1. Fractions meaning division

Phrase	Fractional Expression
A number divided by 6	$\dfrac{x}{6}$
The quotient of a number and 3	$\dfrac{n}{3}$

2. Fractions meaning parts of a whole

Phrase	Fractional Expression
Nine members out of 25	$\dfrac{9}{25}$
Three quarters out of one dollar	$\dfrac{75}{100}$ or $\dfrac{3}{4}$

3. Zero Numerators

The value of a fraction is zero if the numerator is zero.

$$\frac{0}{n} = 0 \quad \text{(where } n \neq 0 \text{)}$$

4. Zero Denominators

A number divided by zero is undefined.

$\dfrac{n}{0}$ is **undefined**.

5. Lowest Common Denominator (LCD)

To find a Least Common Denominator
1) Factor each denominator into primes.
2) Find the product of the greatest power of each prime factor.

Example 1 □ **Fractions meaning parts of a whole**

Charlotte painted $\dfrac{3}{8}$ of her room in the morning and she painted $\dfrac{1}{2}$ of the remaining portion in the afternoon. What fraction of her room is painted?

Solution □

Let x = total work, then $\dfrac{3}{8}x$ is the work done in the morning.

$$x - \frac{3}{8}x = \frac{5}{8}x \qquad \text{Remaining work}$$

$$\frac{1}{2} \times \frac{5}{8}x = \frac{5}{16}x \qquad \text{Work done in the afternoon}$$

$$\frac{3}{8}x + \frac{5}{16}x = \frac{11}{16}x \qquad \text{Total amount of work done}$$

$$\frac{\text{finished part}}{\text{total work}} = \frac{11/16\,x}{x}$$

$$= \frac{11}{16} \qquad \text{Answer}$$

Example 2 □ **Finding the LCD**

Find the LCD of $\dfrac{2}{9x+18}$ and $\dfrac{5}{3x^2-12}$.

Solution □

Factor each denominator into primes.

$$9x + 18 = 9(x+2) = 3^2(x+2)$$

$$3x^2 - 12 = 3(x^2-4) = 3(x+2)(x-2)$$

Find the product of the greatest power of each prime factor.

LCD is $3^2(x+2)(x-2)$.   Answer

6. Simplifying Fractions

  (1) Factor the numerator and denominator.
  (2) Cancel the common factors.

7. Binomials that are negatives of each other

  Binomials such as $(a-b)$ and $(b-a)$ are negatives
  of each other.
  Hence $a - b = -(b - a)$

8. Addition and Subtraction Rule for Fractions

$$\frac{a}{c} + \frac{b}{c} = \frac{a+c}{c}$$

$$\frac{a}{c} - \frac{b}{c} = \frac{a-b}{c}$$

9. Multiplication and Division Rule for Fractions

$$\frac{a}{b} \cdot \frac{c}{d} = \frac{ac}{bd}$$

$$\frac{a}{b} \div \frac{c}{d} = \frac{a}{b} \cdot \frac{d}{c} = \frac{ad}{bc}$$

10. Mixed Expressions

  The sum or difference of a polynomial and a
  fraction is called a mixed expression.

  For example $2 + \frac{3}{x}$ and $x - \frac{3}{8}$ are mixed
  expressions.

11. Rules of Reciprocals

  1) The product of two reciprocals is 1.
  $$a \cdot \frac{1}{a} = 1, \qquad \frac{a}{b} \cdot \frac{b}{a} = 1$$

  2) To divide by a number, multiply by its reciprocal.
  $$a \div b = a \cdot \frac{1}{b}, \qquad a \div \frac{b}{c} = a \cdot \frac{c}{b} = \frac{ac}{b}$$

Example 3 □   Simplifying a mixed expression

Simplify $3 + \frac{1}{x}$.

Solution □

$$3 + \frac{1}{x}$$

$$= \frac{3}{1} + \frac{1}{x} \qquad \text{Write the whole number as a fraction}$$

whose denominator is 1.

$$= \frac{3}{1} \cdot \frac{x}{x} + \frac{1}{x} \qquad \text{Multiplication property of 1 } (\frac{x}{x} = 1)$$

$$= \frac{3x}{x} + \frac{1}{x} \qquad \text{Multiply.}$$

$$= \frac{3x+1}{x} \qquad \text{Add the numerators.}$$

**Example 4 □   Finding the reciprocal of a mixed
                    expression**

Find the reciprocal of $r + \frac{1}{3}$.

Solution □

$$r + \frac{1}{3}$$

$$= \frac{r}{1} + \frac{1}{3} \qquad \text{Write the polynomial as a fraction}$$

whose denominator is 1.

$$= \frac{r}{1} \cdot \frac{3}{3} + \frac{1}{3} \qquad \text{Multiplication property of 1 } (\frac{3}{3} = 1)$$

$$= \frac{3r}{3} + \frac{1}{3} \qquad \text{Multiply.}$$

$$= \frac{3r+1}{3} \qquad \text{Add the numerators.}$$

The reciprocal is $\frac{3}{3r+1}$.

12. Solving Rational Equations

1) Multiply by LCD of each fraction in the equation.

2) Cross multiplying can be used only when each side of the equation is written as a single fraction.

13. Complex Fractions

A complex fraction is a fraction whose numerator or denominator contains one or more fractions.

To simplify complex fractions
1) Simplify the numerator and denominator.
2) Express the fraction as a quotient using the ÷ sign.
3) Multiply by the reciprocal of the divisor.

Example 6 □ **Simplifying complex fractions**

Add $\dfrac{1}{2/3}+\dfrac{2}{3/5}$.

Solution □

$$\dfrac{1}{2/3}+\dfrac{2}{3/5}$$

$$=1\div\frac{2}{3}+2\div\frac{3}{5} \qquad \text{Express the fraction as a quotient using } \div \text{ sign.}$$

$$=1\times\frac{3}{2}+2\times\frac{5}{3} \qquad \text{Multiply by the reciprocal of the divisor.}$$

$$=\frac{3}{2}+\frac{10}{3} \qquad \text{Simplify.}$$

$$=\frac{3}{2}\cdot\frac{3}{3}+\frac{10}{3}\cdot\frac{2}{2} \qquad \text{LCD is 6.}$$

$$=\frac{9}{6}+\frac{20}{6}=\frac{29}{6} \qquad \text{Answer}$$

Example 5 □ **Solving equations by cross multiplying**

Solve $\dfrac{3}{x-2}=\dfrac{5}{x+4}$.

Solution □

$$\frac{3}{x-2}=\frac{5}{x+4}$$

$3(x+4)=5(x-2)$ Cross multiply.

$3x+12=5x-10$ Distributive property

$-2x+12=-10$ Subtract $5x$ from both sides.

$-2x=-22$ Subtract 12 from both sides.

$x=11$ Divide both sides by -2 .

Example 7 □ **Simplifying complex fractions**

Simplify $\dfrac{2}{1-\dfrac{1}{a}}$

Solution □

$$\frac{2}{1-\frac{1}{a}}=\frac{2}{1\cdot\frac{a}{a}-\frac{1}{a}} \qquad \text{Multiplication property of 1}$$

$$=\frac{2}{\frac{a-1}{a}} \qquad \text{Add the numerators.}$$

$$=2\div\frac{a-1}{a} \qquad \text{Express the fraction as a quotient using } \div \text{ sign.}$$

$$=2\times\frac{a}{a-1} \qquad \text{Multiply by the reciprocal of the divisor.}$$

$$=\frac{2a}{a-1} \qquad \text{Answer}$$

1. Which of the following is equal to $\dfrac{42+3n}{6}$?

    (A) $\dfrac{7+3n}{6}$

    (B) $\dfrac{7+n}{2}$

    (C) $7+3n$

    (D) $42+\dfrac{n}{2}$

    (E) $7+\dfrac{1}{2}n$

2. If $p=k-1$ and $q=\dfrac{p+1}{p-1}$, then k CANNOT equal which of the following?

    (A)   1

    (B) -1

    (C)   2

    (D) -2

    (E)   0

3. If $0.14x=2.8$, what is the value of $\dfrac{1}{x}$?

    (A) 2

    (B) .2

    (C) .5

    (D) .05

    (E) .005

4. The number that is $\dfrac{1}{3}$ of 42 is what fraction of 63?

    (A) $\dfrac{2}{7}$

    (B) $\dfrac{3}{5}$

    (C) $\dfrac{1}{2}$

    (D) $\dfrac{2}{9}$

    (E) $\dfrac{2}{3}$

5. If n pounds of sugar is divided equally among 8 people, each person gets 3.5 pounds. If one person does not want any sugar, how much sugar can be given to each of the others?

    (A) 3

    (B) 4

    (C) 4.5

    (D) 5

    (E) 6

6. If $\dfrac{n\cdot n}{n+n}-\dfrac{1}{x}=0$ $(n\cdot x\neq 0)$, then $x=$

    (A) $\dfrac{n}{2}$

    (B) $\dfrac{2}{n}$

    (C) $\dfrac{1}{2n^2}$

    (D) $\dfrac{1}{2n}$

    (E) $2n$

7. If $\dfrac{r}{3}+\dfrac{s}{11}=\dfrac{39}{33}$, where r and s are positive integers, what is the value of $r+s$?

   (A) 2

   (B) 3

   (C) 5

   (D) 9

   (E) 11

8. If $y=\dfrac{k}{x}$ $(xy \neq 0)$, which of the following is equivalent to $\dfrac{k-x}{1-y}$?

   (A) $-x$

   (B) $-k$

   (C) 1

   (D) x

   (E) k

9. On a number line, point P has coordinate $-\dfrac{1}{3}$ and Q has coordinate 3. What is the coordinate of the point that is located $\dfrac{2}{5}$ of the way from P to Q?

   (A) 1

   (B) $\dfrac{5}{3}$

   (C) 2

   (D) $\dfrac{7}{3}$

   (E) $\dfrac{8}{3}$

10. There are oranges, apples, and peaches in a basket of fruit. Of the fruit, $\dfrac{1}{3}$ are oranges, $\dfrac{2}{5}$ of the remaining fruit are apples, and 12 are peaches. How many apples are in the basket?

    (A) 5   (B) 7   (C) 8

    (D) 10   (E) 14

11. During a basketball game the Lancers scored 16 points in the first quarter, $\dfrac{2}{7}$ of their total score in the second quarter, $\dfrac{1}{4}$ of their total score in the third quarter, and the remaining 10 points in the fourth quarter. What is the total of number of points the Lancers scored?

    (A) 48

    (B) 53

    (C) 56

    (D) 60

    (E) 65

12. If p, q, r, and s are positive numbers such that $p=\dfrac{r}{s-r}$ and $q=\dfrac{r}{s}$, what is q in terms of p?

    (A) $\dfrac{1}{1+p}$

    (B) $\dfrac{p}{1+p}$

    (C) $1+\dfrac{1}{p}$

    (D) $1+p$

    (E) $p-1$

1. If a gas tank presently contains 15 liters of gas and is 3/8 full, how many additional liters of gas are needed to fill up the tank?

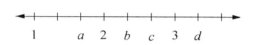

2. The marks on the number line above are equally spaced and the numbers 1, a, 2, b, c, 3, and d are shown. What is the value of $(c+d)-(a+b)$?

3. If $\dfrac{-3}{x+2} = \dfrac{1}{x-2}$, what is the value of x?

4. If $\dfrac{a}{b} = 2$, $\dfrac{b}{c} = 6$, and $\dfrac{c}{d} = 18$, then $\dfrac{ac}{b^2} - \dfrac{bd}{c^2} =$

5. If $\dfrac{1}{a} + \dfrac{1}{b} = 3$ and $a = \dfrac{3}{8}$, what is the value of b?

6. What is the value of $\dfrac{r}{t}$, if r is $\dfrac{3}{4}$ of s and s is $\dfrac{2}{5}$ of t?

7. Find the value of $1 + \dfrac{1}{2 - \dfrac{1}{1 - \dfrac{1}{3}}}$.

8. David used $\dfrac{1}{9}$ of his monthly salary for groceries and $\dfrac{1}{4}$ of the remaining money for his car payment. He also paid twice as much for rent as for his car payment. If David has $600 left after paying for groceries, his car payment, and rent, how much is his monthly salary?

Answer Key

<u>Multiple Choice Questions</u>

1. E	2. C	3. D	4. D	5. B
6. B	7. C	8. A	9. A	10. C
11. C	12. B			

<u>Grid-In Questions</u>

1. 25	2. 2	3. 1	4. 0	5. 3
6. 3/10	7. 3	8. 2700		

Answers and Explanations

<u>Multiple Choice Questions</u>

1. E

$$\frac{42+3n}{6}=\frac{42}{6}+\frac{3n}{6}=7+\frac{1}{2}n$$

2. C

$$q=\frac{p+1}{p-1}$$

$$=\frac{(k-1)+1}{(k-1)-1} \qquad \text{Make substitution. } (p=k-1)$$

$$=\frac{k}{k-2} \qquad \text{Simplify.}$$

Since the denominator cannot be zero, k cannot equal 2.

3. D

$$.14x=2.8 \;\Rightarrow\; x=\frac{2.8}{.14}=20$$

$$\frac{1}{x}=\frac{1}{20}=.05$$

4. D

$$\frac{1}{3}\text{ of }42 \;\Rightarrow\; \frac{1}{3}\times 42=14$$

$$14\text{ is what fraction of }63? \;\Rightarrow\; \frac{14}{63}=\frac{2}{9}$$

5. B

$$\frac{n}{8}=3.5 \;\Rightarrow\; n=28$$

If one person does not want any sugar, then 7 people will share the sugar.

$$28\div 7=4$$

6. B

$$\frac{n\cdot n}{n+n}-\frac{1}{x}=0 \;\Rightarrow\; \frac{n^2}{2n}-\frac{1}{x}=0 \;\Rightarrow\; \frac{n}{2}-\frac{1}{x}=0$$

$$\Rightarrow\; \frac{n}{2}=\frac{1}{x} \;\Rightarrow\; nx=2 \text{ (cross product)}$$

$$\Rightarrow\; x=\frac{2}{n}$$

7. C

$$\frac{r}{3}+\frac{s}{11}=\frac{39}{33} \;\Rightarrow\; \frac{r\cdot 11}{3\cdot 11}+\frac{s\cdot 3}{11\cdot 3}=\frac{39}{33}$$

$$\frac{11r}{33}+\frac{3s}{33}=\frac{39}{33} \;\Rightarrow\; \frac{11r+3s}{33}=\frac{39}{33}$$

$$\Rightarrow\; 11r+3s=39$$

Make a table of values.

	$11r+3s=39$	
value	r	s
	1	$28/3$ (not an integer)
	2	$17/3$ (not an integer)
	3	2 ← correct answer

So $r=3$ and $s=2$ are solutions for the given equation, and $r+s=3+2=5$.

8. A

$$\frac{k-x}{1-y} = \frac{k-x}{1-\frac{k}{x}}$$ Make substitutions. ($y = \frac{k}{x}$)

$$= \frac{(k-x)\cdot x}{(1-\frac{k}{x})\cdot x}$$ Multiply x on the top and bottom.

$$= \frac{(k-x)\cdot x}{(x-k)} = \frac{(k-x)\cdot x}{-(k-x)} = -x$$

9. A

The distance between P and Q

$$= 3 - (-\frac{1}{3}) = 3 + \frac{1}{3} = \frac{10}{3}$$

$$\frac{2}{5} \text{ of } PQ = \frac{2}{5} \times \frac{10}{3} = \frac{4}{3}$$

The coordinate of the point that is located $\frac{2}{5}$ of

the way from P to Q is $-\frac{1}{3} + \frac{4}{3} = 1$

10. C

Let x = the total number of fruits in the basket

Then $\frac{1}{3}x$ = the number of oranges,

$\frac{2}{3}x$ = the number of remaining fruits, and

$\frac{2}{5} \times \frac{2}{3}x = \frac{4}{15}x$ is the number of apples.

$$\underbrace{\frac{1}{3}x}_{\substack{\text{number of}\\\text{oranges}}} + \underbrace{\frac{4}{15}x}_{\substack{\text{number of}\\\text{apples}}} + \underbrace{12}_{\substack{\text{number}\\\text{of}\\\text{peaches}}} = \underbrace{x}_{\substack{\text{the total}\\\text{number}\\\text{of fruits}}}$$

$$\Rightarrow \frac{9}{15}x + 12 = x \Rightarrow \frac{6}{15}x = 12 \Rightarrow x = 30$$

The number of apples $= \frac{4}{15}x = \frac{4}{15}(30) = 8$.

11. C

Let x = the total number of points the Lancers scored

$$\underbrace{16}_{\text{1st quarter}} + \underbrace{\frac{2}{7}x}_{\text{2nd quarter}} + \underbrace{\frac{1}{4}x}_{\text{3rd quarter}} + \underbrace{10}_{\text{4th quarter}} = \underbrace{x}_{\text{total score}}$$

$$26 + \frac{15}{28}x = x$$

$$\Rightarrow \frac{13}{28}x = 26 \Rightarrow x = 56$$

12. B

$$p = \frac{r}{s-r}$$
$$\Rightarrow p(s-r) = r$$
$$\Rightarrow ps - pr = r$$
$$\Rightarrow ps = r + pr$$
$$\Rightarrow ps = r(1+p) \Leftrightarrow \frac{r}{s} = \frac{p}{1+p}$$

Therefore $q = \frac{r}{s} = \frac{p}{1+p}$.

Grid-In Questions

1. 25

Let x = the total capacity of the gas tank in liters.

Then $\frac{3}{8}x = 15 \Rightarrow x = 15 \times \frac{8}{3} = 40$

Since the gas tank is 3/8 full, we need $\frac{5}{8}$ more to

fill up the gas tank.

$\frac{5}{8} \times 40 = 25$

2. 2

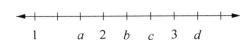

$$1 \qquad a \quad 2 \quad b \quad c \quad 3 \quad d$$

The distance between each mark is $\dfrac{1}{3}$.

So $a = 1\dfrac{2}{3}$, $b = 2\dfrac{1}{3}$, $c = 2\dfrac{2}{3}$, and $d = 3\dfrac{1}{3}$.

$(c+d) - (a+b) = (2\dfrac{2}{3} + 3\dfrac{1}{3}) - (1\dfrac{2}{3} + 2\dfrac{1}{3})$

$= 6 - 4 = 2$

3. 1

$\dfrac{-3}{x+2} = \dfrac{1}{x-2} \;\Rightarrow\; -3(x-2) = 1(x+2)$

$\Rightarrow\; -3x + 6 = x + 2 \;\Rightarrow\; -4x = -4 \;\Rightarrow\; x = 1$

4. 0

$\dfrac{b}{c} = 6 \;\Rightarrow\; \dfrac{c}{b} = \dfrac{1}{6}$

$\dfrac{c}{d} = 18 \;\Rightarrow\; \dfrac{d}{c} = \dfrac{1}{18}$

$\dfrac{ac}{b^2} - \dfrac{bd}{c^2}$

$= \dfrac{a}{b} \cdot \dfrac{c}{b} - \dfrac{b}{c} \cdot \dfrac{d}{c}$

$= 2 \cdot \dfrac{1}{6} - 6 \cdot \dfrac{1}{18} = \dfrac{1}{3} - \dfrac{1}{3} = 0$

5. 3

$a = \dfrac{3}{8} \;\Rightarrow\; \dfrac{1}{a} = \dfrac{8}{3}$

$\dfrac{1}{a} + \dfrac{1}{b} = 3 \;\Rightarrow\; \dfrac{8}{3} + \dfrac{1}{b} = 3$

$\Rightarrow\; \dfrac{1}{b} = 3 - \dfrac{8}{3} = \dfrac{1}{3} \;\Rightarrow\; b = 3$

6. $\dfrac{3}{10}$

r is $\dfrac{3}{4}$ of $s \;\Rightarrow\; r = \dfrac{3}{4}s$

s is $\dfrac{2}{5}$ of $t \;\Rightarrow\; s = \dfrac{2}{5}t$

$r = \dfrac{3}{4}s = \dfrac{3}{4} \cdot \dfrac{2}{5}t = \dfrac{3}{10}t$

$\Rightarrow\; \dfrac{r}{t} = \dfrac{3}{10}$

7. 3

$1 + \cfrac{1}{2 - \cfrac{1}{1 - \cfrac{1}{3}}} = 1 + \cfrac{1}{2 - \cfrac{1}{\left(\frac{2}{3}\right)}} = 1 + \cfrac{1}{2 - \cfrac{3}{2}}$

$= 1 + \cfrac{1}{\frac{1}{2}} = 1 + 2 = 3$

8. 2700

Let x = David's total monthly salary, then

grocery costs $= \dfrac{1}{9}x$

remaining salary $= x - \dfrac{1}{9}x = \dfrac{8}{9}x$

car payment $= \dfrac{1}{4} \cdot \dfrac{8}{9}x = \dfrac{2}{9}x$

rent $= 2 \cdot \dfrac{2}{9}x = \dfrac{4}{9}x$

$\underbrace{\dfrac{1}{9}x}_{\substack{\text{grocery}\\\text{costs}}} + \underbrace{\dfrac{2}{9}x}_{\text{car payment}} + \underbrace{\dfrac{4}{9}x}_{\text{rent}} + \underbrace{600}_{\text{remaining}} = \underbrace{x}_{\substack{\text{total}\\\text{salary}}}$

$\dfrac{7}{9}x + 600 = x \;\Rightarrow\; 600 = \dfrac{2}{9}x$

$\Rightarrow\; x = 600 \cdot \dfrac{9}{2} = 2700$

3. Ratios and Proportions

1. A **ratio** is a comparison between two numbers. The ratio of two numbers a and b can be written in three ways.

   a to b

   $a : b$

   $\dfrac{a}{b}$ $(b \neq 0)$

2. If two values are in the ratio of $a : b$, then the two numbers can be represented as **ax** and **bx**, where x is a positive integer.

3. A **proportion** is an equation stating that two ratios are equal.

   The proportions can be written in several different ways.

   $a : b = c : d$ reads "a is to b as c is to d"

   $\dfrac{a}{b} = \dfrac{c}{d}$ reads "a divided by b equals c divided by d"

4. **Cross-Multiplying Property**

   If $\dfrac{a}{b} = \dfrac{c}{d}$, then $ad = bc$

5. **Direct Variation**

   y **varies directly** as x if, for a constant k, $y = kx$.

   The number k is called the **constant of variation**.

   ☑ A proportion can be used to solve direct variation problems.

   $$\left\{ \begin{array}{l} y_1 = kx_1 \\ y_2 = kx_2 \end{array} \right\} \Rightarrow \left\{ \dfrac{x_1}{y_1} = \dfrac{1}{k}, \ \dfrac{x_2}{y_2} = \dfrac{1}{k} \right\} \Rightarrow \dfrac{x_1}{y_1} = \dfrac{x_2}{y_2}$$

Example 1 □ Ratio of two fractions

Express the ratio $1\dfrac{3}{4}$ to $2\dfrac{1}{2}$ in simplest form.

Solution □

$$\dfrac{1\frac{3}{4}}{2\frac{1}{2}} = \dfrac{\frac{7}{4}}{\frac{5}{2}} = \dfrac{\frac{7}{4} \times 4}{\frac{5}{2} \times 4} = \dfrac{7}{10}$$

The ratio is $\dfrac{7}{10}$, 7 to 10, or 7 : 10.   Answer

Example 2 □ Ratio of angles in a triangle

Three angles of a triangle are in the ratio of 3 : 5 : 7. Find the measure of each angle.

Solution □

The measure of each angle of the triangle can be represented as $3x$, $5x$, and $7x$.

$$3x + 5x + 7x = 180$$
$$15x = 180$$
$$x = 12$$

the measure of three angles are

$3x = 3 \cdot 12 = 36$, $5x = 5 \cdot 12 = 60$, and $7x = 7 \cdot 12 = 84$ Answer

---

Example 3 □ Ratios in square units

If 2 inches is equivalent to 5 centimeters, how many square centimeters are there in 1 square inch?

Solution □

2 inches = 5 centimeters

$1 \ in = \dfrac{5}{2} cm$ Divide both sides by 2.

$(1 \ in)^2 = (\dfrac{5}{2} cm)^2$ Square both sides.

$1 \ in^2 = \dfrac{25}{4} cm^2$ Answer

6. Inverse Variation

y **varies inversely** as x if, for a constant k, $xy = k$ or $y = \dfrac{k}{x}$.

The number k is called the **constant of variation**.

☑ A proportion can be used to solve inverse variation problems.

$$\left.\begin{cases} x_1 y_1 = k \\ x_2 y_2 = k \end{cases}\right\} \Rightarrow x_1 y_1 = x_2 y_2$$

Dividing each side by $y_1 y_2$, we have the

following proportion, $\dfrac{x_1}{y_2} = \dfrac{x_2}{y_1}$.

For meshed gears, the number of teeth and the number of revolutions vary inversely.

$$\dfrac{r_1}{t_2} = \dfrac{r_2}{t_1} \Leftrightarrow r_1 t_1 = r_2 t_2$$

7. Unit Price = $\dfrac{\text{Price}}{\text{Number of Units}}$

Example 4 □ Direct variation

If y varies directly as x, and $y = 18$ when $x = 4$, find y when $x = 10$.

Solution □

$y = kx$	Direct variation
$18 = k(4)$	$y = 18$ when $x = 4$.
$k = \dfrac{18}{4} = \dfrac{9}{2}$	Solve for k.
$y = \dfrac{9}{2}x$	Substitute $\dfrac{9}{2}$ for k.
$y = \dfrac{9}{2}(10) = 45$	Answer

Example 5 □ Inverse variation

If y varies inversely as x, and $y = \dfrac{1}{3}$ when $x = 24$, find y when $x = 10$.

Solution □

$$xy = k \Rightarrow k = (24)(\tfrac{1}{3}) = 8 \Rightarrow xy = 8$$

$$(10)y = 8 \Rightarrow y = \dfrac{8}{10} = \dfrac{4}{5} \qquad \text{Answer}$$

Example 6 □ Unit price

If 12 grams of coffee costs x dollars and each gram makes y cups of coffee, what is the cost of one cup of coffee?

Solution □

Unit price $= \dfrac{x \text{ dollars}}{12 \text{ grams}}$.

The cost of each gram of coffee is $\dfrac{x}{12}$ dollars, and that makes y cups of coffee.

Therefore the cost of 1 cup of coffee is

$$\dfrac{x/12 \text{ dollars}}{y \text{ cups}} = \dfrac{x}{12y} \text{ dollars.} \qquad \text{Answer}$$

1. The ratio of 8 to 27 is equal to the ratio of 12 to what number?

   (A) 18

   (B) 36

   (C) 40.5

   (D) 42

   (E) 48.5

2. The ratio of boys to girls in a school is 6 to 7. If there are 798 boys in the school what is the total number of students in the school?

   (A) 1729

   (B) 1690

   (C) 1625

   (D) 1560

   (E) 1482

3. The sum of two numbers is 15 and the ratio of the two numbers is −4. What is the product of the two numbers?

   (A) −25

   (B) −50

   (C) −75

   (D) −100

   (E) −125

4. In a certain room the ratio of males to females is 4 to 5. After 8 males enter the room, the ratio of males to females is 6 to 5. What is the total number of people in the room before the additional males enter the room?

   (A) 27

   (B) 36

   (C) 45

   (D) 54

   (E) 63

5. The tennis balls in a bag are either white or yellow. If the ratio of white balls to yellow balls is $\dfrac{3}{10}$, which of the following could not be the number of balls in the bag?

   (A) 26

   (B) 39

   (C) 42

   (D) 52

   (E) 65

6. A tree is 8 feet tall now and grows 8 inches each year. In how many years from now will the tree reach a height of 30 feet?

   (A) 27

   (B) 33

   (C) 45

   (D) 52

   (E) 65

7. A car is traveling at a constant rate of x miles per hour. How many miles has the car traveled in y minutes?

(A) $60xy$

(B) $\dfrac{60x}{y}$

(C) $\dfrac{xy}{60}$

(D) $\dfrac{y}{60x}$

(E) $\dfrac{x}{60y}$

8. Jason and Donny painted a room and received $300. To complete the painting job Jason spent 4 hours 25 minutes and Donny spent 2 hours 15 minutes. If they split the $300 in proportion to the amount of time each spent painting, how much did Donny receive?

(A) $101.25

(B) $110.75

(C) $118.00

(D) $123.00

(E) $128.00

9. If 3 identical robots can assemble 3 machine parts in 3 hours, then 300 identical robots can assemble 300 machine parts in how many hours?

(A) 3 hours

(B) 10 hours

(C) 30 hours

(D) 100 hours

(E) 300 hours

10. The length of a large picture is 18 inches and its width is 12 inches. If each dimension is reduced by x inches to make the ratio of length to width 5 to 3, what is the value of x?

(A) 6

(B) 5

(C) 4

(D) 3

(E) 2

11. If Aaron reads x pages of a science fiction book in m minutes, what is the number of pages Aaron reads in $30m$ seconds?

(A) $\dfrac{1}{2}x$

(B) x

(C) $2x$

(D) $3x$

(E) $30x$

12. A faulty watch gains 3 minutes per hour. If the watch is set to the correct time at 8:00 a.m., what is the correct time when the faulty watch shows 10:00 p.m. on the same day?

(A) 9:32 p.m.

(B) 9:26 p.m.

(C) 9:24 p.m.

(D) 9:20 p.m.

(E) 9:18 p.m.

13. Cement, gravel, and sand are mixed by weight in the ratio of 4:7:9, respectively. How many tons of cement are there in 9 tons of the mixture?

   (A) 1.2

   (B) 1.5

   (C) 1.8

   (D) 2

   (E) 2.5

14. If a person is born every 5 seconds and a person dies every 12 seconds, then how many seconds does it take for the population to grow by one person?

   (A) 7 sec

   (B) $8\frac{4}{7}$ sec

   (C) $10\frac{5}{7}$ sec

   (D) $11\frac{3}{7}$ sec

   (E) 14 sec

15. The intensity of light, L, varies inversely as the square of the distance, d, between the source of the light and the object illuminated. If for a certain light source, the intensity of light is 12 at a distance of 3 meters, what will be the intensity of light at a distance of 9 meters from the light source?

   (A) $\frac{4}{3}$

   (B) $\frac{8}{3}$

   (C) 4

   (D) 8

   (E) 36

1. A machine produces 735 tapes in $5\frac{1}{4}$ hours. What fraction of the 735 tapes was produced in one hour?

2. A wall that measures 14 feet by 9 feet needs to be painted. If one gallon of paint is needed for each 12 square feet of wall, how many gallons of paint is needed for the entire wall?

3. If a person can save $168 in 4 weeks, in how many weeks can the person save 4.5 times this amount, saving at the same rate?

4. The distance an object falls from rest is directly proportional to the square of the length of time it has fallen. If an object falls 144 ft in 3 seconds, how far will it fall in 4 seconds?

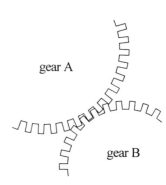

gear A

gear B

5. In the figure above gear A, which has 40 teeth, drives gear B, which has 30 teeth. If gear A makes 75 revolutions, how many revolutions does gear B make?

6. If $\frac{3}{4}$ quart of lemonade concentrate is mixed with $6\frac{2}{3}$ quarts of water to make lemonade for 40 people, how many quarts of lemonade concentrate are needed to make the same lemonade for 24 people?

7. The real numbers a and b are positive, and the ratio of a to b is 16 times the ratio of b to a. What is the value of $\frac{a}{b}$?

Answer Key

<u>Multiple Choice Questions</u>

1. C	2. A	3. D	4. B	5. C
6. B	7. C	8. A	9. A	10. D
11. A	12. D	13. C	14. B	15. A

<u>Grid-In Questions</u>

1. 4/21   2. 10.5   3. 18   4. 256   5. 100

6. 9/20   7. 4

Answers and Explanations

<u>Multiple Choice Questions</u>

1. C

$$\frac{8}{27} = \frac{12}{x} \Rightarrow 8x = 27 \cdot 12 \Rightarrow x = 40.5$$

2. A

Let g = the number of girls
$$\frac{6}{7} = \frac{798}{g} \Rightarrow 6g = 7 \cdot 798 \Rightarrow g = 931$$
The total number of students $= 798 + 931 = 1729$.

3. D

$x + y = 15$ and
$$\frac{x}{y} = -4 \Rightarrow x = -4y$$
$-4y + y = 15$ Substitution
$-3y = 15 \Rightarrow y = -5$
$x = -4y = -4(-5) = 20$ Substitution
$x \cdot y = 20 \cdot (-5) = -100$

4. B

Let m = the number of males
Let f = the number of females
$$\frac{m}{f} = \frac{4}{5} \Rightarrow 5m = 4f$$

After 8 males enter the room, the ratio of males to females is 6 to 5. $\Rightarrow \frac{m+8}{f} = \frac{6}{5}$
$\Rightarrow 5(m+8) = 6f \Rightarrow 5m + 40 = 6f$
$\Rightarrow 4f + 40 = 6f$ (Substitution, $5m = 4f$)
$\Rightarrow 40 = 2f \Rightarrow f = 20$
$\Rightarrow 5m = 4f \Rightarrow 5m = 4 \cdot 20 \Rightarrow m = 16$
$m + f = 16 + 20 = 36$

5. C

Since the ratio of white balls to yellow balls is $\frac{3}{10}$,
$3x$ represents the number of white balls and $10x$ represents the number of yellow balls.

The total number of balls in the bag equals $13x$.
Therefore the total number of balls in the bag must be a multiple of 13.
The number 42 is the only number which is not a multiple of 13.

6. B

Let x = the number of years it will take the tree to reach a height of 30 feet

8 feet $+ (\frac{8}{12}$ feet$) \cdot x = 30$ feet (1 foot = 12 inches)
$\Rightarrow (\frac{8}{12}$ feet$) \cdot x = 22$ feet $\Rightarrow \frac{8}{12}x = 22$
$\Rightarrow x = 22 \cdot \frac{12}{8} = 33$

7. C

$$\frac{x \text{ miles}}{1 \text{ hour}} = \frac{\boxed{\text{number of miles traveled}}}{y \text{ minutes}}$$

$\Rightarrow \dfrac{x \text{ miles}}{60 \text{ minutes}} = \dfrac{\boxed{\text{number of miles traveled}}}{y \text{ minutes}}$

$x \cdot y = 60 \cdot \boxed{\text{number of miles traveled}}$
(Cross Multiplication)

$\boxed{\text{number of miles traveled}} = \dfrac{xy}{60}$

8. A

Total time = Jason's hours + Donny's hours
= 4 hr 25 min + 2 hr 15 min
= 6 hr 40 min

The amount Donny received

$= 300 \times \dfrac{2 \text{ hr } 15 \text{ min}}{6 \text{ hr } 40 \text{ min}} = 300 \times \dfrac{2\frac{1}{4} \text{ hr}}{6\frac{2}{3} \text{ hr}}$

$= 300 \times \dfrac{9/4}{20/3} = 300 \times \dfrac{9}{4} \cdot \dfrac{3}{20} = 101.25$

9. A

3 robots can assemble 3 parts in 3 hours
$\Rightarrow$ 1 robot can assemble 1 part in 3 hours
$\Rightarrow$ 300 robots can assemble 300 parts in 3 hours

10. D

new length = $18 - x$
new width = $12 - x$

$\dfrac{18-x}{12-x} = \dfrac{5}{3} \Rightarrow 3(18-x) = 5(12-x)$

$54 - 3x = 60 - 5x \Rightarrow 2x = 6$
$\Rightarrow x = 3$

11. A

Let y = the number of pages Aaron can read in $30m$ seconds

$\dfrac{x \text{ pages}}{m \text{ minutes}} = \dfrac{y \text{ pages}}{30m \text{ seconds}}$

$\Rightarrow \dfrac{x \text{ pages}}{60m \text{ seconds}} = \dfrac{y \text{ pages}}{30m \text{ seconds}}$

$\Rightarrow 60my = 30mx \Rightarrow y = \dfrac{1}{2}x$

12. D

The time elapsed between a faulty clock's readings of 8:00 a.m. and 10:00 p.m. on the same day comes to 14 hours, or 840 min.

Let x = time elapsed between a good clock's readings of 8:00 a.m. and 10:00 p.m. on the same day.

Set up a proportion.
$\dfrac{\text{time elapsed by a faulty clock}}{\text{time elapsed by a good clock}} = \dfrac{63 \text{ minutes}}{60 \text{ minutes}}$

$\dfrac{840}{x} = \dfrac{63}{60} \Rightarrow 63x = 60 \cdot 840$

$x = 800$ minutes = 13 hr 20 min
Therefore the correct time is 9:20 pm.

13. C

The ratio of cement, gravel, and sand is 4:7:9
$\Rightarrow 4x$ = the number of tons of cement
$\quad 7x$ = the number of tons of gravel
$\quad 9x$ = the number of tons of sand

total weight = $4x + 7x + 9x = 20x$

Let y = the # of tons of cement in the mixture.
Set up a proportion.
$\dfrac{4x}{20x} = \dfrac{y}{9} \Rightarrow \dfrac{1}{5} = \dfrac{y}{9} \Rightarrow 5y = 9$

$\Rightarrow y = \dfrac{9}{5} = 1.8$

14. B

A person is born every 5 seconds
$\Rightarrow$ 12 persons are born per minute

A person dies every 12 seconds
$\Rightarrow$ 5 persons die per minute

Every minute the population grows by 7 persons.
Therefore it takes $\dfrac{60 \text{ seconds}}{7} = 8\dfrac{4}{7}$ seconds
for the population to grow by one person.

15. A

$$\underset{\substack{\text{the intensity} \\ \text{of light}}}{\underbrace{L}} = \underset{\substack{\text{varies inversely as the} \\ \text{square of the distance}}}{\underbrace{\dfrac{k}{d^2}}}$$

$12 = \dfrac{k}{3^2}$ ($L = 12$ when $d = 3$)

$\Rightarrow k = 12 \cdot 9 = 108$

$L = \dfrac{108}{d^2}$ (Replace k with 108.)

When $d = 9$, $L = \dfrac{108}{9^2} = \dfrac{108}{81} = \dfrac{4}{3}$

Grid-In Questions

1. $\dfrac{4}{21}$

The number of tapes produced in one hour

$= 735 \div 5\dfrac{1}{4} = 735 \div \dfrac{21}{4} = 735 \times \dfrac{4}{21} = 140$

$\dfrac{140}{735} = \dfrac{4}{21}$

2. 10.5

Area of the wall $= 14 \times 9 = 126 \text{ ft}^2$
$126 \div 12 = 10.5$

3. 18

$4 \times 4.5 = 18$

4. 256

Let d = the distance an object falls
Let t = the length of time

The distance an object falls from rest is directly proportional to the square of the length of time it takes to fall $\Rightarrow d = kt^2$, where k is the constant of variation.

To find the value of k, substitute corresponding

values in the equation and solve for k.

$144 = k \cdot 3^2 \Rightarrow k = 16$
So the equation is $d = 16t^2$.
Use this equation to find the distance.
$d = 16 \cdot 4^2 = 256$

5. 100

For meshed gears, the number of teeth and the number of revolutions vary inversely. Therefore

$\dfrac{r_1}{t_2} = \dfrac{r_2}{t_1} \Rightarrow \dfrac{75}{30} = \dfrac{r_2}{40} \Rightarrow 30 \cdot r_2 = 75 \cdot 40$

$\Rightarrow r_2 = 100$

6. $\dfrac{9}{20}$

In this question " $6\dfrac{2}{3}$ quarts of water" was unnecessary information.

Let x = the number of quarts of lemonade
    concentrate needed for 24 people

$\dfrac{3/4 \text{ qts}}{40 \text{ people}} = \dfrac{x \text{ qts}}{24 \text{ people}}$

$\Rightarrow \dfrac{3}{4} \times 24 = 40x \Rightarrow 18 = 40x$

$\Rightarrow x = \dfrac{18}{40} = \dfrac{9}{20}$

7. 4

The ratio of a to b is 16 times the ratio of b to a

$\Rightarrow \dfrac{a}{b} = 16 \times \dfrac{b}{a}$

$\dfrac{a}{b}(\dfrac{a}{b}) = (16 \times \dfrac{b}{a})\dfrac{a}{b}$ Multiply $\dfrac{a}{b}$ on both sides.

$\dfrac{a^2}{b^2} = 16$ Simplify.

$\dfrac{a}{b} = \pm 4$ Find square roots.

Since the numbers a and b are positive,

$\dfrac{a}{b} = +4$.

4. Averages

Key Terms / Illustrations   Examples

1. **Mean** $= \dfrac{\text{The sum of the values in a set of data}}{\text{The number of values in a set of data}}$

☑ The sum of the values
  $=$ mean $\times$ the number of values

2. **Median** : The median of a set of data is the middle
  value.

☑ If there are two middle values, the median is the
  mean of the two values.

3. **Mode** : The mode of a set of data is the value that
  appears most frequently.

☑ Some sets of data have more than one mode, and
  others have no mode.

  In the set of data {5, 6, 8, 10, 15}, there is no mode
  since each number appears only once.

  In the set of data {8, 9, 9, 13, 15, 15, 22}, the modes
  are 9 and 15, since both numbers appear twice.

4. **Range** : The range in a set of data is the difference
  between the greatest and the least values
  of the data.

5. **Weighted Average** of 2 groups

$$= \dfrac{\left\{\begin{array}{c}\text{Sum of the values}\\\text{of group 1}\end{array}\right\} + \left\{\begin{array}{c}\text{Sum of the values}\\\text{of group 2}\end{array}\right\}}{\text{Total number of persons}}$$

* Sum of the values of group 1 $=$
  Mean of group 1 $\times$ Number of persons in group 1.

* Sum of the values of group 2 $=$
  Mean of group 2 $\times$ Number of persons in group 2.

Example 1 □ **Finding mean, median, mode, and
range.**

Test Scores	Number of students
67	1
75	3
87	2
91	2

The test scores of 8 students are shown above. Find
the mean, median, mode, and range of the scores.

Solution □

To find the mean, median, mode, and range
of the scores, arrange all the scores in order.

67, 75, 75, 75, 87, 87, 91, 91

$\text{Mean} = \dfrac{67+75+75+75+87+87+91+91}{8} = 81$

$\text{Median} = \dfrac{75 + 87}{2} = 81$

$\text{Mode} = 75$

$\text{Range} = 91 - 67 = 24$

Example 2 □ **Weighted average**

In a geometry class there are 8 boys and 12 girls. If
the average test score of the class is 84 and the
boys' average score is 81, what is the girls' average
score?

Solution □

Let $x =$ Girls' average

$84 = \dfrac{(81 \times 8) + (x \times 12)}{8 + 12}$ Use weighted average.

                           formula.

$84 = \dfrac{648 + 12x}{20}$ Simplify.

$84 \times 20 = 648 + 12x$ Multiply by 20 on both sides.

$1680 = 648 + 12x$ Simplify.

$x = 86$ Answer

1. If the average (arithmetic mean) of 7 and x is equal to the average of 1, 11, and x, what is the value of x?

   (A) 1

   (B) 2

   (C) 3

   (D) 4

   (E) 5

2. If x is the average (arithmetic mean) of the three numbers 3, 8, and n, what is the value of n in terms of x?

   (A) $x + 11$

   (B) $3x - 11$

   (C) $x - 11$

   (D) $\dfrac{x - 11}{3}$

   (E) $\dfrac{x - 5}{3}$

3. The average (arithmetic mean) of two numbers is $\dfrac{1}{2}x + 1$. If one of the numbers is x, what is the other number?

   (A) $x + 1$

   (B) $x + 2$

   (C) $x - 1$

   (D) 1

   (E) 2

4. If the average (arithmetic mean) of 5 consecutive odd integers is x, what is the median of these 5 integers in terms of x?

   (A) $x - 2$

   (B) x

   (C) $x + 2$

   (D) $5x - 5$

   (E) $5x$

5. The average (arithmetic mean) of thirteen numbers is 22. After one of the numbers is removed, the average of the remaining numbers is 23. What number has been removed?

   (A) 1

   (B) 10

   (C) 12

   (D) 13

   (E) 15

6. The Lees invested $6,300 in a stock when the price per share was $15, and $4,480 in a bond when the price per share was $8. What was the average (arithmetic mean) price per share purchased of the combined stocks and bonds?

   (A) $10.25

   (B) $11

   (C) $11.85

   (D) $13

   (E) $13.40

7. If the average (arithmetic mean) of 2, a and b is $2x$, what is the average of a and b in terms of x?

   (A) $2x - 1$

   (B) $2x - 2$

   (C) $3x - 1$

   (D) $3x - 2$

   (E) $4x - 1$

8. The average (arithmetic mean) of a set of 8 numbers is n and the average of the 4 greatest numbers in the set is 7.5. What is the average of the other 4 numbers in terms of n?

   (A) $n - 2$

   (B) $2n - 30$

   (C) $8n - 30$

   (D) $2n - 7.5$

   (E) $4n - 15$

9. If x, y, and z represent three numbers where $z = y - 5$ and $y = x + 1$, what is the value when the median of the three numbers is subtracted from the average (arithmetic mean) of the numbers?

   (A) -1

   (B) 0

   (C) 1

   (D) 2

   (E) 3

10. In a history class the average (arithmetic mean) test score of the 12 boys was 81 and the average score of the girls was 87. If the average score of the whole class is 84.6, how many girls are in the class?

   (A) 14   (B) 15   (C) 16

   (D) 17   (E) 18

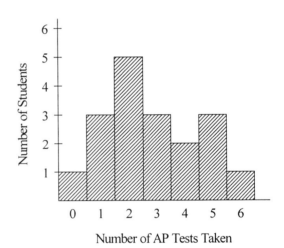

Number of AP Tests Taken

11. The graph above depicts a survey of 18 senior students in a high school. The number of AP tests taken by each student last May ranges from zero to six. Which of the following is true of the survey results?

   I. The average (arithmetic mean) number of tests taken by each student was more than 3.

   II. The mode of the number of tests taken by each student was 3.

   III. The median number of tests taken by each student was 2.5.

   (A) I only

   (B) II only

   (C) III only

   (D) II and III only

   (E) I, II, and III

1. If the average (arithmetic mean) of m, n, and -1 is 0, what is the value of $m+n$?

2. If the average (arithmetic mean) of n, $n-3$, $2n+1$, $3n-5$, and $5n+11$ is 8, what is the median of these numbers?

3. If the average (arithmetic mean) of 3 different positive integers is greater than 50 and less than 60, what is the greatest possible value of one of these integers?

4. The average (arithmetic mean) of p, q, and r is 15, and the average of q and r is 7. What is the value of p?

5. The average (arithmetic mean) test score for all the students in a class is 84. The average score of the m boys in the class was 79, while that of the n girls was 87. What is the ratio of m to n?

6. A student has an average (arithmetic mean) score of 86 points for 4 previous tests. What is the total score this student needs in the next two tests, in order to have an average of 90 for all 6 tests?

7. The average (arithmetic mean) of a set of n integers is 14 and the average of these n integers and 30 is 16. What is the value of n?

8. A car travels 50 miles per hour for 4 hours and then travels 65 miles per hour for x more hours. If the average speed for the entire trip was 57 miles per hour, what is the value of x?

Answer Key

Multiple Choice Questions

1. C 2. B 3. E 4. B 5. B

6. B 7. C 8. D 9. A 10. E

11. C

Grid-In Questions

1. 1 2. 4 3. 176 4. 31 5. 3/5

6. 196 7. 7 8. 3.5

Answers and Explanations

Multiple Choice Questions

1. C

$$\frac{7+x}{2}=\frac{1+11+x}{3} \Rightarrow \frac{7+x}{2}=\frac{12+x}{3}$$
$$\Rightarrow 3(7+x)=2(12+x) \Rightarrow 21+3x=24+2x$$
$$\Rightarrow x=3$$

2. B

$$x=\frac{3+8+n}{3} \Rightarrow 3x=11+n \Rightarrow n=3x-11$$

3. E

Let the other number $= n$

$\frac{x+n}{2}=\frac{1}{2}x+1$ Avg. of two numbers is $\frac{1}{2}x+1$.

$2(\frac{x+n}{2})=2(\frac{1}{2}x+1)$ Multiply 2 on both sides.

$x+n=x+2$ Distribute.

$n=2$ Subtract 2 on both sides.

4. B

Let $n, n+2, n+4, n+6$, and $n+8$ be 5 consecutive odd integers.

Then $\frac{n+(n+2)+(n+4)+(n+6)+(n+8)}{5}=x$.

$\frac{5n+20}{5}=x \Rightarrow n+4=x \Rightarrow n=x-4$

Since the median of these 5 integers is $n+4$,
$n+4=(x-4)+4=x$.

5. B

Let the removed number $= x$.

If the average of 13 numbers is 22, then the sum of the 13 numbers is $13\times22=286$.
If the average of 12 numbers is 23, then the sum of the 12 numbers is $12\times23=276$.

$286-x=276 \Rightarrow x=10$

6. B

The number of stocks $=\frac{6300}{15}=420$.

The number of bonds $=\frac{4480}{8}=560$.

The average price per share purchased

$=\frac{\text{total amount}}{\text{the \# of stocks + the \# of bonds}}$

$=\frac{6300+4480}{420+560}=\frac{10780}{980}=11$

7. C

$\frac{2+a+b}{3}=2x \Rightarrow 2+a+b=6x$
$\Rightarrow a+b=6x-2$

The average of a and b equals $\frac{a+b}{2}$.

$\frac{a+b}{2}=\frac{6x-2}{2}$ (by substitution)
$=3x-1$

8. D

The sum of 8 numbers equals $8n$.
The sum of the 4 greatest numbers equals
$7.5 \times 4 = 30$.
Therefore the sum of the other 4 numbers equals
$8n - 30$.

The average of the other 4 numbers
$= \dfrac{8n - 30}{4} = 2n - 7.5$.

9. A

$y = x + 1$,
$z = y - 5 = (x + 1) - 5 = x - 4$

$\qquad x - 4, x, x + 1$
The three numbers above are listed from the least to the greatest. Therefore the median is x.

The average of the 3 numbers
$= \dfrac{(x - 4) + x + (x + 1)}{3} = \dfrac{3x - 3}{3} = x - 1$

Average $-$ median $= (x - 1) - x = -1$.

10. E

Let $g = $ the number of girls in the class.

Weighted Average of 2 groups

$= \dfrac{\left\{ \begin{array}{c} \text{Sum of the values} \\ \text{of group 1} \end{array} \right\} + \left\{ \begin{array}{c} \text{Sum of the values} \\ \text{of group 2} \end{array} \right\}}{\text{Total number of persons}}$

$= \dfrac{(12 \times 81) + g \times 87}{12 + g} = 84.6$
$12 \times 81 + 87g = 84.6(12 + g)$
$972 + 87g = 1015.2 + 84.6g$
$2.4g = 43.2 \Rightarrow g = 18$

11. C

To find the mean, median, and mode of the number of tests taken by each student, first put all of the numbers in order.

0, 1, 1, 1, 2, 2, 2, 2, 2, 3, 3, 3, 4, 4, 5, 5, 5, 6

Mean $= \dfrac{0 \cdot 1 + 1 \cdot 3 + 2 \cdot 5 + 3 \cdot 3 + 4 \cdot 2 + 5 \cdot 3 + 6 \cdot 1}{18}$

$\qquad = \dfrac{51}{18} \approx 2.83$

Therefore Roman numeral I is false.

Since the number 2 appears most frequently, the mode is 2.

Therefore Roman numeral II is false.

There are two middle values: 2(the 9th number) and 3(the 10th number). The median is the mean of these two values.

Median $= \dfrac{2 + 3}{2} = 2.5$

Therefore Roman numeral III is true.

Grid-In Questions

1. 1

$\dfrac{m + n + (-1)}{3} = 0 \Rightarrow m + n + (-1) = 0$
$\Rightarrow m + n = 1$

2. 4

$\dfrac{n + (n - 3) + (2n + 1) + (3n - 5) + (5n + 11)}{5} = 8$
$\Rightarrow n + (n - 3) + (2n + 1) + (3n - 5) + (5n + 11) = 40$
$\Rightarrow 12n + 4 = 40 \Rightarrow n = 3$

Therefore the five numbers are 3, 0, 7, 4, and 26.
Arrange the five numbers in order.
0, 3, 4, 7, and 26.
The median of this set of numbers is 4.

3. 176

Let the 3 different positive integers be $a, b,$ and c, where c is the greatest.
The average of the 3 different positive integers is greater than 50 and less than 60.

$$50 < \frac{a+b+c}{3} < 60$$
$$\Rightarrow 150 < a+b+c < 180$$

The value of c is greatest when the values of a and b are the least. That is, when $a = 1$ and $b = 2$.

$$a+b+c < 180 \Rightarrow 1+2+c < 180 \Rightarrow c < 177$$
$$\Rightarrow c = 176$$

4. 31

$$\frac{p+q+r}{3} = 15 \Rightarrow p+q+r = 45$$

$$\frac{q+r}{2} = 7 \Rightarrow q+r = 14$$

$$p+q+r = 45$$
$$p+14 = 45 \qquad \text{Substitution } (q+r = 14)$$
$$p = 31$$

5. $\dfrac{3}{5}$

Weighted Average of 2 groups

$$= \frac{\left\{\begin{array}{c}\text{Sum of the values} \\ \text{of group 1}\end{array}\right\} + \left\{\begin{array}{c}\text{Sum of the values} \\ \text{of group 2}\end{array}\right\}}{\text{Total number of persons}}$$

$$84 = \frac{79m + 87n}{m+n} \Rightarrow 84(m+n) = 79m + 87n$$
$$\Rightarrow 84m + 84n = 79m + 87n \Rightarrow 5m = 3n$$
$$\Rightarrow \frac{m}{n} = \frac{3}{5}$$

6. 196

The student's total score for the 4 previous tests is 86×4, or 344.
In order to have an average of 90 for all 6 tests, this student needs 90×6, or 540, points total.

So the total score he needs on the next two tests is $540 - 344$, or 196.

7. 7

If the average of a set of n integers is 14, then the sum of n integers is $14n$.

The average of a set of n integers and 30 is 16
$$\Rightarrow \frac{\text{sum of the terms}}{\text{number of the terms}} = \frac{14n+30}{n+1} = 16$$
$$\Rightarrow 14n + 30 = 16(n+1) \Rightarrow 14n + 30 = 16n + 16$$
$$\Rightarrow 14 = 2n \Rightarrow n = 7$$

8. 3.5

The distance traveled at 50 miles per hour for 4 hours is 50×4, or 200 miles.
The distance traveled at 65 miles per hour for x hours is $65x$ miles

$$\text{Average speed } = \frac{\text{total distance}}{\text{total time}}$$

$$= \frac{200 + 65x}{4+x} = 57$$

$$\Rightarrow 200 + 65x = 57(4+x)$$
$$\Rightarrow 200 + 65x = 57 \times 4 + 57x$$
$$\Rightarrow 8x = 28 \Rightarrow x = 3.5$$

5. Percents

Key Terms / Illustrations   Examples

1. **Percent** is a ratio that compares a number to 100. Percent means " hundredths" or "per hundred."

2. **Percent Increase** $= \dfrac{\text{Amount of Increase}}{\text{Original Amount}}$

3. **Percent Decrease** $= \dfrac{\text{Amount of Decrease}}{\text{Original Amount}}$

4. Translating verbal phrases into algebraic expressions:

Verbal Phrase	Algebraic Expression
A number increased by 12 percent.	$n + 0.12n = 1.12n$
A number increased by 200 percent.	$n + 2n = 3n$
A number decreased by 25 percent.	$n - 0.25n = 0.75n$
What is 14 % of 25?	$n = 0.14 \times 25$
What percent of 8 is 6?	$\dfrac{n}{100} \times 8 = 6$
9 is what percent of 24?	$9 = \dfrac{n}{100} \times 24$
120 % of what is 42?	$1.2 \times n = 42$

Example 1 ⊓ Percents, decimals, and fractions

Fractional notation	Decimal notation	Percent Notation
7/100	.07	7 %
3/20	.15	15 %
7/8	.875	87.5 %

Example 2 □ Percent increase

The temperature increased from 60° F to 72° F. Find the percent increase in temperature.

Solution □

$$\text{Percent increase} = \frac{72 - 60}{60} = \frac{12}{60} = 0.2 \;\Rightarrow\; 20\%$$

Example 3 □ Percent increase and decrease combined

The quantities x and y are positive. If x is decreased by 8 percent and y is increased by 25 percent, then the product of x and y is increased by what percent?

Solution □

original value		new value
x	$\Rightarrow$	$x - .08x = .92x$
y	$\Rightarrow$	$y + .25y = 1.25y$
$x \cdot y$	$\Rightarrow$	$(.92x) \cdot (1.25y) = 1.15xy$

Therefore the product of x and y is increased by 15 percent.

5. **Simple Interest Formula**

$$I = P \cdot r \cdot t$$
where

I = Interest
P = Principal (Initial Amount)
r = Interest Rate
t = Number of Years

6. **Profit** = Selling price – Cost

Example 4 □   **Simple interest**

What is the total interest earned on $2,500 invested for 2 years 6 months at 9 percent simple annual interest?

Solution □

$$I = P \cdot r \cdot t$$
$$= (\$2,500) \cdot (0.09) \cdot (2.5)$$
$$= \$562.50 \hspace{2cm} \text{Answer}$$

Example 5 □   **Amount left in terms of a percent**

A pizza is sliced into n equal pieces. If a person eats one piece, what percent of the pizza is left, in terms of n?

Solution □

$(1 - \dfrac{1}{n})$ Amount of pizza left after one slice is eaten.

$= 100(1 - \dfrac{1}{n})\%$ Write the fraction as a percent.

or $100(\dfrac{n-1}{n})\%$ Answer

1. Which of the following is equivalent to .003 percent of 4?

    (A) .012

    (B) .0012

    (C) .00012

    (D) .000012

    (E) .0000012

2. $0.40\% =$

    (A) $\dfrac{1}{400}$

    (B) $\dfrac{1}{250}$

    (C) $\dfrac{1}{40}$

    (D) $\dfrac{1}{25}$

    (E) $\dfrac{2}{5}$

3. If Kevin's monthly salary of $2,850 is 75 percent of Paul's monthly salary, what is Paul's monthly salary?

    (A) $2,137.50

    (B) $3,120.25

    (C) .$3,350

    (D) $3,650

    (E) $3,800

4. If 125 percent of x is 80, and x is n percent of 400, then $n =$

    (A) 12.5

    (B) 16

    (C) 18.5

    (D) 24

    (E) 40

5. In a bookcase, there were 10 history books. When the number of books increases by x percent, the new number of history books is 24. What is the value of x?

    (A) 41%

    (B) 58%

    (C) 70%

    (D) 120%

    (E) 140%

6. The sale price of a computer is $468 after a 35% discount has been given. What was the original price of the computer?

    (A) $620

    (B) $650

    (C) $680

    (D) $720

    (E) $750

7. A video game with a list price of x dollars is first discounted by 15%, and then by an additional 12%. What is the final sale price of the video game, in terms of x?

(A) $0.73x$

(B) $0.748x$

(C) $0.75x$

(D) $0.765x$

(E) $0.78x$

8. The value of a stock increased from $40 to $52. What is the percent increase in value?

(A) 12%

(B) 19%

(C) 25%

(D) 30%

(E) 32%

9. There are a total of n pairs of shoes in a store and all the shoes in the store are either black or brown. If there are m pairs of brown shoes in the store, then in terms of m and n, what percent of the shoes in the store are black?

(A) $\dfrac{m}{n}\%$

(B) $\dfrac{100m}{n}\%$

(C) $\dfrac{n-m}{n}\%$

(D) $(1-\dfrac{100m}{n})\%$

(E) $100\,(1-\dfrac{m}{n})\%$

10. What is the total interest earned on x dollars invested for 18 months at 8 percent simple annual interest?

(A) $0.12x$

(B) $0.128x$

(C) $0.144x$

(D) $1.2x$

(E) $1.44x$

11. There are 2,000 bicycles in a store and 20 percent of the bicycles in the store are blue. On Monday 5 percent of the blue bicycles in the store are sold, and on Tuesday 5 percent of the remaining blue bicycles are sold. How many bicycles are sold in the two days?

(A) 36

(B) 39

(C) 40

(D) 42

(E) 44

12. A chemist mixes 15 liters of 40 percent acid solution and 25 liters of 20 percent acid solution. What percent of the mixture is acid?

(A) 22.5%

(B) 25%

(C) 27.5%

(D) 30%

(E) 32.5%

13. The numbers *a, b,* and *c* are positive and *a* equals 3.2*bc.* If *b* is increased by 150 percent and *c* is decreased by 60 percent, then *a* is

 (A) increased by 90%

 (B) increased by 10%

 (C) unchanged

 (D) decreased by 40%

 (E) decreased by 30%

14. The price of a package of 4 pens is $8.00 and the same pens are sold at $2.50 each. If Alex bought three packages of pens rather than buying 12 pens individually, the amount he saved on the 12 pens is what percent of the amount he paid?

 (A) 6%

 (B) 20%

 (C) 25%

 (D) 30%

 (E) 35%

15. At a certain concert all tickets are equally priced. A survey showed that decreasing the price of these tickets by 10 percent would increase the number of tickets sold by 20 percent. If each concert ticket is discounted by 10 percent, what is the percent increase in the amount of money received from the sale of tickets?

 (A) 8%

 (B) 10%

 (C) 12%

 (D) 15%

 (E) It cannot be determined from the information given.

1. If 300 percent of 0.18 is equivalent to 20 percent of *b*, then *b* is equal to what number?

2. A number *n* is 25 less than 120 percent of itself. What is the value of *n*?

3. Five people contributed $9,000 each toward the purchase of a sailboat. If they ended up paying $38,500 plus 8 percent sales tax for the sailboat, how much money should be refunded to each person?

4. A bag contains red, blue, green, and yellow marbles. Of these marbles, 32 percent are red, 30 percent are blue, 20 percent are green, and 27 marbles are yellow. How many marbles are in the bag?

5. If this year's enrollment in Mesa School District is 6000, and enrollment is 20 percent higher than last year, what was last year's enrollment in Mesa School District?

6. There are 800 students in a school and 45% of the students are male. If 30 percent of the male students and 25 percent of the female students play a varsity sport, how many students play a varsity sport?

7. A store used to sell a radio for $72, which is 50 percent more than the wholesale cost. At a special holiday sale, the price of the radio was 20 percent less than the wholesale cost. What was the special sale price of the radio?

8. By what percent is 4.5×10^5 greater than 9×10^4?

Answer Key

Multiple Choice Questions

1. B	2. B	3. E	4. B	5. E
6. D	7. B	8. D	9. E	10. A
11. B	12. C	13. C	14. C	15. A

Grid-In Questions

1. 2.7	2. 125	3. 684	4. 150
5. 5000	6. 218	7. 38.4	8. 400

Answers and Explanations

Multiple Choice Questions

1. B

0.03 percent of $4 = 0.0003 \times 4 = 0.0012$

2. B

$0.40\% = 0.4 \times \dfrac{1}{100} = \dfrac{4}{10} \times \dfrac{1}{100}$

$= \dfrac{4}{1000} = \dfrac{1}{250}$

3. E

Let x = Paul's monthly salary

$2850 = 0.75x \implies x = \dfrac{2850}{0.75} = 3800$

4. B

$\underbrace{1.25x}_{125\% \text{ of } x} = 80 \implies x = \dfrac{80}{1.25} = 64$

$\underbrace{x}_{x \text{ is}} = \underbrace{\dfrac{n}{100}}_{n\%} \times \underbrace{400}_{\text{of } 400} \implies x = 4n$

$\implies n = \dfrac{x}{4} = \dfrac{64}{4} = 16$

5. E

$\underbrace{10 + (10 \times \dfrac{x}{100})}_{10 \text{ increased by } x\% \text{ of } 10} \underbrace{= 24}_{\text{is } 24}$

$\implies 10 + \dfrac{10x}{100} = 24 \implies \dfrac{x}{10} = 14 \implies x = 140$

6. D

Let x = the original price of the computer

$\underbrace{468}_{\substack{\text{price after} \\ \text{discount}}} = \underbrace{x}_{\substack{\text{original} \\ \text{price}}} - \underbrace{.35x}_{\substack{35\% \text{ of} \\ \text{original price}}}$

$\implies 468 = .65x \implies x = \dfrac{468}{.65} = 720$

7. B

$\underbrace{x - 0.15x}_{\substack{\text{discounted} \\ \text{by 15 percent}}} = \underbrace{0.85x}_{\substack{\text{new price after} \\ 15\% \text{ discount}}}$

$\underbrace{.85x}_{\substack{\text{new} \\ \text{price}}} \underbrace{-.12 \times .85x}_{\substack{\text{new price is} \\ \text{discounted} \\ \text{additional 12\%}}} = \underbrace{0.748x}_{\text{final price}}$

8. D

$\text{Percent Increase} = \dfrac{\text{Amount of Increase}}{\text{Original Amount}}$

$= \dfrac{52 - 40}{40} = \dfrac{12}{40} = \dfrac{3}{10} \implies 30\%$

9. E

Total number of shoes $= n$
The number of brown shoes $= m$
The number of black shoes $= n - m$

The fraction of black shoes in the store $= \dfrac{n-m}{n}$

The percent of black shoes in the store

$= (\dfrac{n-m}{n}) \times 100\% = (\dfrac{n}{n} - \dfrac{m}{n}) \times 100\%$

$= (1 - \dfrac{m}{n}) \times 100\%$ or $100(1 - \dfrac{m}{n})$ %

10. A

$I = P \cdot r \cdot t$

$I = x \cdot (0.08) \cdot (1\dfrac{1}{2})$ $\Leftarrow$ 18 months equals $1\dfrac{1}{2}$ year

$I = 0.12x$

11. B

Total number of blue bicycles $= 2000 \times 0.2 = 400$
On Monday 400×0.05, or 20, blue bicycles are sold.
The number of remaining blue bicycles is $400 - 20$, or 380.
On Tuesday 380×0.05, or 19, blue bicycles are sold.
Therefore 20 + 19, or 39, blue bicycles are sold in two days.

12. C

The percent of acid

$= \dfrac{\text{the amount of acid in the solution}}{\text{total amount}} \times 100\%$

$= \dfrac{(15 \times 0.4) + (25 \times 0.2)}{15 + 25} \times 100\%$

$= \dfrac{6+5}{40} \times 100\% = \dfrac{11}{40} \times 100\% = 27.5\%$

13. C

Given: $a = 3.2bc$

If b is increased by 150 %, it becomes $b + 1.5b$, or $2.5b$.
If c is decreased by 60 %, it becomes $c - 0.6c$, or $0.4c$.
Multiplying these new values gives
$a = 3.2(2.5b \times 0.4c) = 3.2(bc)$

Therefore the value is unchanged.

You can also solve this problem by picking numbers. (When you pick numbers, always pick easy-to-use numbers.)

Let $b = 4$, $c = 10$, then
$a = 3.2bc = 3.2(4)(10) = 128$
4 increased by 150% $\rightarrow$ $4 + 4 \times 1.5 = 10$
10 decreased by 60% $\rightarrow$ $10 - 10 \times 0.6 = 4$
$a = 3.2bc = 3.2(10)(4) = 128$

Therefore the value is unchanged.

14. C

The cost of three packages of pens
$= 3 \times \$8.00 = \$24.00$
The cost of 12 pens bought individually
$= 12 \times \$2.50 = \$30.00$
amount saved $= 30 - 24 = 6$

$\dfrac{\text{amount saved}}{\text{the cost of 3 packages of pens}} = \dfrac{6}{24}$

$= \dfrac{1}{4} = 0.25 \Rightarrow 25\%$

15. A

Let x = regular price of the tickets
Let y = the number tickets sold at regular price
Then xy = the total amount received from the sale of tickets at the original price

If the price of tickets decreases by 10 percent, the new price of tickets will be $x - 0.1x$, or $0.9x$.
If the number of tickets sold increases by 20 % the new number sold will be $y + 0.2y$, or $1.2y$.

Amount of money received from the sale of tickets at the lower price $= (0.9x)(1.2y) = 1.08xy$.
So, the total amount is increased by 8 percent.

Grid-In Questions

1. 2.7

$$\underbrace{3}_{300\% } \times \underbrace{0.18}_{of\ \ 0.18} \underbrace{=}_{is} \underbrace{0.2b}_{20\%\ of\ b}$$

$$\Rightarrow\ 0.54 = .2b\ \Rightarrow\ b = \frac{.54}{.2} = 2.7$$

2. 125

A number n is 25 less than 120 percent of itself.
$\Rightarrow\ n = 1.2n - 25$
$\Rightarrow\ .2n = 25\ \Rightarrow\ n = 125$

3. 684

Total amount contributed from five people
$= \$9000 \times 5 = \$45000$
The price of the sail boat
$= \$38,500 + 0.08 \times \$38,500 = \$41,580$
The total amount that should be refunded is
$45,000 - 41,580$, or $3,420$.

$3,420 \div 5 = 684$

4. 150

Let $x = $ the total number of marbles in the bag

$$\underbrace{0.32x}_{red} + \underbrace{0.3x}_{blue} + \underbrace{0.2x}_{green} + \underbrace{27}_{yellow} = \underbrace{x}_{total}$$
$\Rightarrow\ 0.82x + 27 = x\ \Rightarrow\ 0.18x = 27$
$\Rightarrow\ x = 150$

5. 5000

Let $x = $ last year's enrollment in Mesa School
　　　　District

$$\underbrace{\text{This year's enrollment}}_{6000}\ \underbrace{\text{is}}_{=}$$
$$\underbrace{\text{20\% higher than last year's enrollment.}}_{x+0.2x}$$
$\Rightarrow\ 6000 = 1.2x\ \Rightarrow\ x = 5000$

6. 218

The number of male students $= 800 \times 0.45 = 360$.
The number of female students $= 800 - 360 = 440$.

$$\underbrace{0.3 \times 360}_{30\%\ of\ males} + \underbrace{0.25 \times 440}_{25\%\ of\ females}$$
$= 108 + 110 = 218$

7. 38.4

Let $x = $ the wholesale cost

$72 = x + 0.5x$
($72 is 50% more than the wholesale cost.)
$\Rightarrow\ 72 = 1.5x\ \Rightarrow\ x = 48$

Special holiday sale price $= 48 - 0.2 \times 48 = 38.4$
(Special holiday sale price was 20% less than the
 wholesale cost.)

8. 400

$$4.5 \times 10^5 = 9 \times 10^4 + \underbrace{\frac{x}{100}(9 \times 10^4)}_{x\%\ more\ than\ 9 \times 10^4}$$

$$4.5 \times 10^5 = 9 \times 10^4 (1 + \frac{x}{100})$$

$$\frac{4.5 \times 10^5}{9 \times 10^4} = 1 + \frac{x}{100}$$

$$5 = 1 + \frac{x}{100}\ \Rightarrow\ \frac{x}{100} = 4\ \Rightarrow\ x = 400$$

6. Exponents and Radical Expressions

Key Terms / Illustrations

Examples

1. $a^n = \underbrace{a \cdot a \cdot a \cdots\cdots a}_{n \text{ factors of } a}$

The number a is the **base**,
and the number n is the **exponent**.
The expression a^n is called a **power**.

Example 1 □ **Expression as a product of powers**

$$5 \cdot a \cdot a \cdot b \cdot b \cdot b = 5a^2 b^3$$

2. **Properties of Exponents**

Products of Powers $\quad a^m \cdot a^n = a^{m+n}$

Quotients of Powers $\quad \dfrac{a^m}{a^n} = a^{m-n}$

Power of a Power $\quad \left(a^m\right)^n = a^{m \cdot n}$

Power of a Product $\quad (a \cdot b)^n = a^n \cdot a^n$

Power of a Quotient $\quad (\dfrac{a}{b})^n = \dfrac{a^n}{b^n}$

Negative Exponent $\quad a^{-n} = \dfrac{1}{a^n} \quad (a \neq 0)$

$(\dfrac{a}{b})^{-n} = (\dfrac{b}{a})^n \quad (ab \neq 0)$

Zero Exponent $\quad a^0 = 1 \; (a \neq 0)$

$(-1)^n = 1$ if n is an even integer
$(-1)^n = -1$ if n is an odd integer

Example 2 □ **Properties of exponents**

Products of Powers
$$3^2 \cdot 3^4 = 3^{2+4} = 3^6$$
$$x^{-2} \cdot x^5 = x^{-2+5} = x^3$$

Quotients of Powers
$$\dfrac{4^7}{4^3} = 4^{7-3} = 4^4$$
$$\dfrac{x^{-3}}{x^{-5}} = x^{-3-(-5)} = x^2$$

Power of a Power $\quad (3^2)^5 = 3^{2 \cdot 5} = 3^{10}$

Power of a Product
$$(2 \cdot 5)^3 = 2^3 \cdot 5^3$$
$$3^x \cdot 4^x = (3 \cdot 4)^x = 12^x$$

Power of a Quotient $\quad (\dfrac{2}{3})^4 = \dfrac{2^4}{3^4} = \dfrac{16}{81}$

$$(\dfrac{-3x}{y^2})^2 = \dfrac{(-3x)^2}{(y^2)^2} = \dfrac{(-3)^2 (x)^2}{y^4} = \dfrac{9x^2}{y^4}$$

Negative Exponent $\quad 3^{-2} = \dfrac{1}{3^2} = \dfrac{1}{9}$

$$(\dfrac{4}{3})^{-2} = (\dfrac{3}{4})^2 = \dfrac{3^2}{4^2} = \dfrac{9}{16}$$

Zero Exponent $\quad 12^0 = 1$
$$(2xy^3)^0 = 1$$

3. Definition of **Square Root**

For any real numbers a and b, if $a^2 = b$,
then $a = \pm\sqrt{b}$.

Example 3 □ **Simplifying exponents**

Simplify $4^{3x} \cdot 8^x$.

4. Definition of **Cube Root**

For any real numbers a and b, if $a^3 = b$,
then $a = \sqrt[3]{b}$.

Solution □

$$4^{3x} \cdot 8^x = (2^2)^{3x} \cdot (2^3)^x = 2^{6x} \cdot 2^{3x} = 2^{9x} \qquad \text{Answer}$$

5. Properties of Radicals

For any positive real numbers a and b,

$$\sqrt{ab} = \sqrt{a}\sqrt{b} = a^{\frac{1}{2}}b^{\frac{1}{2}}$$

$$\sqrt[3]{ab} = \sqrt[3]{a}\sqrt[3]{b} = a^{\frac{1}{3}}b^{\frac{1}{3}}$$

$$\sqrt{\frac{a}{b}} = \frac{\sqrt{a}}{\sqrt{b}} = \frac{a^{\frac{1}{2}}}{b^{\frac{1}{2}}}$$

$$\sqrt{a^m} = (a^m)^{\frac{1}{2}} = a^{\frac{m}{2}}$$
$$\sqrt[3]{a^m} = (a^m)^{\frac{1}{3}} = a^{\frac{m}{3}}$$

6. A number is in **scientific notation** when it is in the form $a \times 10^n$, where $1 \le a < 10$ and n is an integer.

Example 5 □   Square roots, cube roots

$$\sqrt{49} = 7, \qquad -\sqrt{36} = -6$$

$$\sqrt[3]{27} = 3, \qquad \sqrt[3]{-8} = -2$$

If $x^2 = 25$ then $x = \pm 5$

If $x^3 = -125$ then $x = -5$

Example 6 □   **Simplifying radicals**

$$\sqrt{32} = \sqrt{16 \cdot 2} = \sqrt{16}\sqrt{2} = 4\sqrt{2}$$

$$\sqrt[3]{16x^3} = \sqrt[3]{16}\sqrt[3]{x^3} = \sqrt[3]{2^3 \cdot 2} \cdot x$$
$$= \sqrt[3]{2^3}\sqrt[3]{2} \cdot x = 2x\sqrt[3]{2}$$

$$\sqrt{\frac{36}{25}} = \frac{\sqrt{36}}{\sqrt{25}} = \frac{6}{5}$$

$$\sqrt{5^3} = (5^3)^{\frac{1}{2}} = 5^{\frac{3}{2}} = 5^{1+\frac{1}{2}} = 5 \cdot 5^{\frac{1}{2}} = 5\sqrt{5}$$

$$\sqrt[3]{4^4} = (4^4)^{\frac{1}{3}} = 4^{\frac{4}{3}} = 4^{1+\frac{1}{3}} = 4 \cdot 4^{\frac{1}{3}} = 4\sqrt[3]{4}$$

Example 4 □   **Scientific notation**

Write each number in scientific notation.

1) $56,700 = 5.67 \times 10,000 = 5.67 \times 10^4$

2) $0.0000175 = 1.75 \times 10^{-5}$

3) $152,000 \times 0.003 = (1.52 \times 10^5) \times (3 \times 10^{-3})$
$$= 4.56 \times 10^2$$

Example 7 □   **Solving a radical equation**

Solve $\sqrt{2x+1} - 3 = 4$.

Solution □

$\sqrt{2x+1} - 3 = 4$	Original equation
$\sqrt{2x+1} = 7$	Add 3 to both sides.
$(\sqrt{2x+1})^2 = 7^2$	Square both sides.
$2x+1 = 49$	Simplify.
$2x = 48$	Subtract 1 from both sides.
$x = 24$	Answer

1. If $3^{n+1} = 81$, what is the value of n?

   (A) 1

   (B) 2

   (C) 3

   (D) 4

   (E) 5

2. $5^{3x} \cdot 5^{4x} =$

   (A) 25^{7x}

   (B) 25^{12x}

   (C) 5^{7x}

   (D) 5^{12x}

   (E) 5^{12x^2}

3. If a and b are positive numbers, which of the following is equal to $\sqrt{a^3} + \sqrt{ab^2}$?

   (A) $\sqrt{a(a^2 + b^2)}$

   (B) $a(\sqrt{a} + \sqrt{b})$

   (C) ab

   (D) $a\sqrt{a+b}$

   (E) $(a+b)\sqrt{a}$

4. If $x^2 = 45$, which of the following could be true?

   (A) $5 < x < 6$

   (B) $7 < x < 8$

   (C) $-6 < x < -5$

   (D) $-7 < x < -6$

   (E) $-8 < x < -7$

5. If $\sqrt[3]{8} = \sqrt{x}$, what is the value of x?

   (A) 2

   (B) 4

   (C) 6

   (D) 12

   (E) 16

6. $\sqrt{0.0009x^8} =$

   (A) $0.003x^6$

   (B) $0.003x^4$

   (C) $0.03x^6$

   (D) $0.03x^4$

   (E) $0.09x^4$

7. If x and y are positive, and $x > y$, then
$\sqrt{x^2 + 2xy + y^2} + \sqrt{x^2 - 2xy + y^2} =$

(A) $2(x^2 + y^2)$

(B) $2(x + y)$

(C) $2\sqrt{x^2 + y^2}$

(D) $2x$

(E) $2y$

8. If $x \neq 0$, then $\sqrt{25x^4} \div x =$

(A) $5x$

(B) $5x^2$

(C) $5x^3$

(D) $25x^2$

(E) $25x^3$

9. If $8^{\frac{4}{3}} \cdot 8^{-\frac{8}{3}} = \dfrac{1}{2^m}$, what is the value of m?

(A) $-\dfrac{4}{3}$

(B) -4

(C) $-\dfrac{32}{9}$

(D) $\dfrac{4}{3}$

(E) 4

10. If $m = \dfrac{4}{5}$ and $n = 2$, then $(m\sqrt{5})^n - (n^2 - m^2) =$

(A) 2

(B) $-\dfrac{4}{25}$

(C) $-\dfrac{4}{5}$

(D) -2

(E) 0

11. Which of the following is equal to 0.0000083?

(A) 83×10^{-6}

(B) 8.3×10^{-5}

(C) $(8 \times 10^{-7}) + (3 \times 10^{-6})$

(D) $(80 \times 10^{-7}) + (3 \times 10^{-6})$

(E) $(8 \times 10^{-6}) + (3 \times 10^{-7})$

12. What is the least integer value of n for which
$\dfrac{1}{3^n} < 0.002$?

(A) 3

(B) 4

(C) 5

(D) 6

(E) 7

13. If $4^a = b$, then $8b =$

(A) 32^a

(B) 2^{5+a}

(C) 2^{3+2a}

(D) 2^{6a}

(E) 2^{3+a}

14. $(3^x + 3^x + 3^x) \cdot 3^x =$

(A) 3^{4x} (B) 3^{3x^2} (C) 3^{x^4}

(D) 3^{2x+1} (E) 9^{x^2}

15. If $\sqrt{-x} - \dfrac{1}{6} = \dfrac{1}{3}$, what is the value of x?

(A) $-\dfrac{1}{4}$

(B) $\dfrac{1}{4}$

(C) $-\dfrac{1}{2}$

(D) $\dfrac{1}{2}$

(E) There is no real number solution.

16. If $z > 0$ and $\dfrac{\sqrt{z}}{\sqrt{3}} = \dfrac{3\sqrt{3}}{\sqrt{z}}$, then $z =$

(A) 1

(B) $\sqrt{3}$

(C) 3

(D) 9

(E) 27

17. If $rs > 0$, $\dfrac{r^2}{s}\sqrt{\dfrac{s}{r^3}} =$

(A) $\dfrac{1}{\sqrt{r}}$ (B) $\sqrt{\dfrac{r}{s}}$ (C) $\dfrac{1}{\sqrt{rs}}$

(D) $\dfrac{r}{\sqrt{s}}$ (E) $\dfrac{1}{r\sqrt{s}}$

18. If $a > 0$ and $\dfrac{a^m}{a^n} = 1$, what is the value of $m - n$?

(A) 1

(B) -1

(C) 0

(D) $\sqrt{2}$

(E) It cannot be determined from the information given.

19. If $xy \neq 0$, then $\dfrac{(-2xy^2)^3}{4x^4y^5} =$

(A) $-2x$

(B) $-\dfrac{xy}{2}$

(C) $-\dfrac{2}{x}$

(D) $-\dfrac{2y}{x^2}$

(E) $-\dfrac{2y}{x}$

20. What is the greatest positive integer n for which 2^n is a factor of 20^9?

(A) 9

(B) 12

(C) 16

(D) 18

(E) 20

21. If $x^{12} = 32n^4$ and $x^9 = 4n$, then $x =$

(A) $2n$

(B) $2\sqrt[3]{n}$

(C) $4\sqrt{n}$

(D) 2

(E) It cannot be determined from the information given.

22. If m and n are positive integers, then $3^{2m} \cdot 4^{(m+n)} =$

(A) 12^{3m+n}

(B) $12^{3m} \cdot 4^n$

(C) $36^m \cdot 4^n$

(D) $6^{3m} \cdot 4^n$

(E) $12^{3m} + 4^n$

23. If $4x^{-1} = 3$, what is the value of $(3x)^{-\frac{1}{2}}$?

(A) $\dfrac{1}{4}$

(B) $\dfrac{1}{3}$

(C) $\dfrac{1}{2}$

(D) 3

(E) 4

1. If $785,000 \times 0.004 = 3.14 \times 10^n$, what is the value of n?

4. If $a^4 \cdot a^9 = a^n \cdot a^n$, what is the value of n?

2. If $2 \times 5^4 + 5 \times 5^2 = a \times 5^4$, what is the value of a?

5. If $\sqrt{x-8} = 2\sqrt{5}$, what is the value of x?

3. If $5^{x-2} = 25^2$, what is the value of x?

6. If $12^{99} - 12^{97} = 12^{97} \times n$, what is the value of n?

7. If $60^{120} \div 120^{60} = x^{60}$, what is the value of x?

10. If $8x^{10} = 27x^7$ and $x \neq 0$, then $x =$

8. If x and y are positive integers, and $12^3 = 2^x \cdot 3^y$, what is the value of $x + y$?

11. If $a^n \times 3^n = 6^{2n}$, what is the value of a?

9. If $a^{\frac{3}{4}} = 8$, what is the value of $a^{-\frac{1}{2}}$?

12. If $2^{-x} \cdot 6^x = 9$, what is the value of x?

Answer Key

Multiple Choice Questions

1. C	2. C	3. E	4. D	5. B
6. D	7. D	8. A	9. E	10. B
11. E	12. D	13. C	14. D	15. A
16. D	17. B	18. C	19. E	20. D
21. A	22. C	23. C		

Grid-In Questions

1. 3	2. 2.2	3. 6	4. 6.5	5. 28
6. 143	7. 30	8. 9	9. 1/4	10. 3/2
11. 12	12. 2			

Answers and Explanations

Multiple Choice Questions

1. C

$$3^{n+1} = 81 \Rightarrow 3^{n+1} = 3^4 \Rightarrow n+1 = 4$$
$$\Rightarrow n = 3$$

2. C

$$5^{3x} \cdot 5^{4x} = 5^{3x+4x} = 5^{7x}$$

3. E

$$\sqrt{a^3} + \sqrt{ab^2} = \sqrt{a^2 \cdot a} + \sqrt{a}\sqrt{b^2}$$
$$= a\sqrt{a} + \sqrt{a} \cdot b = (a+b)\sqrt{a}$$

4. D

$$x^2 = 45 \Rightarrow x = \pm\sqrt{45} \approx \pm 6.7$$

5. B

$$\sqrt[3]{8} = \sqrt{x} \Rightarrow \sqrt[3]{2^3} = \sqrt{x} \Rightarrow 2 = \sqrt{x}$$
$$\Rightarrow x = 4$$

6. D

$$\sqrt{0.0009x^8} = \sqrt{(0.03x^4)^2} = 0.03x^4$$

7. D

$$\sqrt{x^2 + 2xy + y^2} + \sqrt{x^2 - 2xy + y^2}$$
$$= \sqrt{(x+y)^2} + \sqrt{(x-y)^2}$$
$$= (x+y) + (x-y) \text{ (since } x > 0, y > 0, \text{ and } x > y)$$
$$= 2x$$

8. A

$$\sqrt{25x^4} \div x = \sqrt{(5x^2)^2} \div x = 5x^2 \div x = 5x$$
$$\sqrt{(5x^2)^2} \div x = 5x^2 \div x = 5x$$

9. E

$$8^{\frac{4}{3}} \cdot 8^{-\frac{8}{3}} = \frac{1}{2^m} \Rightarrow (2^3)^{\frac{4}{3}} \cdot (2^3)^{-\frac{8}{3}} = \frac{1}{2^m}$$
$$\Rightarrow 2^{3 \times \frac{4}{3}} \cdot 2^{3 \times -\frac{8}{3}} = \frac{1}{2^m} \Rightarrow 2^4 \cdot 2^{-8} = \frac{1}{2^m}$$
$$\Rightarrow 2^{-4} = \frac{1}{2^m} \Rightarrow \frac{1}{2^4} = \frac{1}{2^m} \Rightarrow m = 4$$

10. B

$$m = \frac{4}{5} \text{ and } n = 2,$$
$$(m\sqrt{5})^n - (n^2 - m^2)$$
$$= (\frac{4}{5}\sqrt{5})^2 - \left[2^2 - (\frac{4}{5})^2\right] = (\frac{16}{25} \cdot 5) - (4 - \frac{16}{25})$$
$$= \frac{80}{25} - (\frac{100}{25} - \frac{16}{25}) = \frac{80}{25} - \frac{84}{25} = -\frac{4}{25}$$

11. E

$$0.0000083 = 0.000008 + 0.0000003$$
$$= 8 \times 10^{-6} + 3 \times 10^{-7}$$

12. D

$$\frac{1}{3^n} < 0.002$$

Use your calculator to find the value of n.

Try $n = 5$, then $\dfrac{1}{3^5} = \dfrac{1}{243} \approx 0.004 > 0.002$.

Try $n = 6$, then $\dfrac{1}{3^6} = \dfrac{1}{729} \approx 0.0014 < 0.002$.

Therefore 6 is the smallest integer possible.

13. C

$$4^a = b$$
$$8b = 8 \cdot 4^a = 2^3 \cdot (2^2)^a = 2^3 \cdot 2^{2a} = 2^{3+2a}$$

14. D

$$(3^x + 3^x + 3^x) \cdot 3^x$$
$$= (3 \cdot 3^x) \cdot 3^x = 3^{1+x} \cdot 3^x = 3^{1+2x}$$

15. A

$$\sqrt{-x} - \frac{1}{6} = \frac{1}{3} \implies \sqrt{-x} = \frac{1}{3} + \frac{1}{6}$$

$$\implies \sqrt{-x} = \frac{1}{2} \implies (\sqrt{-x})^2 = (\frac{1}{2})^2$$

$$\implies -x = \frac{1}{4} \implies x = -\frac{1}{4}$$

16. D

$$\frac{\sqrt{z}}{\sqrt{3}} = \frac{3\sqrt{3}}{\sqrt{z}} \text{ and } z > 0$$
$$\sqrt{z} \cdot \sqrt{z} = \sqrt{3} \cdot 3\sqrt{3} \text{ (cross product)}$$
$$\implies z = 9$$

17. B

$$\frac{r^2}{s}\sqrt{\frac{s}{r^3}} = \frac{r^2}{s} \cdot \frac{\sqrt{s}}{\sqrt{r^3}} = \frac{r^2}{s} \cdot \frac{\sqrt{s}}{r\sqrt{r}}$$

$$= \frac{r \cdot \cancel{r}}{\sqrt{s} \cdot \cancel{\sqrt{s}}} \cdot \frac{\cancel{\sqrt{s}}}{\cancel{r}\sqrt{r}} = \frac{r}{\sqrt{s}\sqrt{r}}$$

$$= \frac{\sqrt{r}}{\sqrt{s}} = \sqrt{\frac{r}{s}}$$

18. C

$$\frac{a^m}{a^n} = 1 \implies a^{m-n} = 1 \implies a^{m-n} = a^0$$
$$\implies m - n = 0$$

19. E

$$\frac{(-2xy^2)^3}{4x^4y^5} = \frac{(-2)^3 x^3 y^6}{4x^4 y^5} = \frac{-8x^3 y^6}{4x^4 y^5}$$

$$= \frac{-2y}{x}$$

20. D

Find the prime factorization of 20^9.
$$20^9 = (2^2 \times 5)^9 = 2^{18} \cdot 5^9$$

Therefore 18 is the greatest positive integer n for which 2^n is a factor of 20^9.

21. A

$$x^{12} = 32n^4 \text{ and } x^9 = 4n$$

$$\frac{x^{12}}{x^9} = \frac{32n^4}{4n} = 8n^3$$

$$\implies x^3 = 8n^3$$
$$\implies x = 2n$$

22. C

$$3^{2m} \cdot 4^{(m+n)} = 3^{2m} \cdot (2^2)^{(m+n)} = 3^{2m} \cdot 2^{2m+2n}$$
$$= 3^{2m} \cdot 2^{2m} \cdot 2^{2n} = (3 \cdot 2)^{2m} \cdot 2^{2n} = 6^{2m} \cdot (2^2)^n$$
$$= (6^2)^m \cdot (4)^n = 36^m \cdot 4^n$$

23. C

$$4x^{-1} = 3 \implies 4 \cdot \frac{1}{x} = 3 \implies \frac{4}{x} = 3$$
$$\implies 4 = 3x \implies x = \frac{4}{3}$$
$$(3x)^{-\frac{1}{2}} = (3 \cdot \frac{4}{3})^{-\frac{1}{2}} = (4)^{-\frac{1}{2}}$$
$$= \frac{1}{(4)^{\frac{1}{2}}} = \frac{1}{2}$$

Grid-In Questions

1. 3

$$785,000 \times 0.004 = 3.14 \times 10^n \implies$$
$$3140 = 3.14 \times 10^n \implies n = 3$$

2. 2.2

$$2 \times 5^4 + 5 \times 5^2 = a \times 5^4$$

Use calculator.
$$1250 + 125 = a \times 625$$
$$\implies 1375 = 625a$$
$$\implies a = \frac{1375}{625} = 2.2$$

3. 6

$$5^{x-2} = 25^2 \implies 5^{x-2} = (5^2)^2$$
$$\implies 5^{x-2} = 5^4 \implies x - 2 = 4 \implies x = 6$$

4. 6.5

$$a^4 \cdot a^9 = a^n \cdot a^n$$
$$\implies a^{4+9} = a^{n+n}$$
$$\implies 13 = 2n \implies n = 6.5$$

5. 28

$$\sqrt{x-8} = 2\sqrt{5}$$
$$(\sqrt{x-8})^2 = (2\sqrt{5})^2 \qquad \text{Square both sides.}$$
$$x - 8 = 2^2 \cdot 5 \qquad \text{Simplify.}$$
$$x = 28$$

6. 143

$$12^{99} - 12^{97} = 12^{97} \times n$$
$$12^{97}(12^2 - 1) = 12^{97} \times n \qquad \text{Factor.}$$
$$\implies 12^2 - 1 = n$$
$$\implies n = 143$$

7. 30

$$60^{120} \div 120^{60} = x^{60}$$
$$60^{120} \div 120^{60} = \frac{60^{60} \cdot 60^{60}}{(2 \cdot 60)^{60}} = \frac{60^{60} \cdot \cancel{60^{60}}}{2^{60} \cdot \cancel{60^{60}}}$$
$$= \frac{60^{60}}{2^{60}} = (\frac{60}{2})^{60} = 30^{60}$$
$$\implies 30^{60} = x^{60} \implies x = 30$$

8. 9

$$12^3 = 2^x \cdot 3^y$$
$$12^3 = (2^2 \cdot 3)^3 = 2^6 \cdot 3^3$$
$$\implies 2^6 \cdot 3^3 = 2^x \cdot 3^y$$
$$\implies x = 6, \ y = 3$$
$$\implies x + y = 6 + 3 = 9$$

9. $\dfrac{1}{4}$

$a^{\frac{3}{4}} = 8 \Rightarrow (a^{\frac{3}{4}})^{\frac{4}{3}} = (8)^{\frac{4}{3}}$

$\Rightarrow \ a = (8)^{\frac{4}{3}} \Rightarrow \ a = (2^3)^{\frac{4}{3}}$

$\Rightarrow \ a = 2^4 = 16$

$a^{-\frac{1}{2}} = (16)^{-\frac{1}{2}} = (2^4)^{-\frac{1}{2}} = 2^{-2}$

$\qquad = \dfrac{1}{2^2} = \dfrac{1}{4}$

10. $\dfrac{3}{2}$

$8x^{10} = 27x^7$

$\dfrac{8x^{10}}{x^7} = \dfrac{27x^7}{x^7}$ Divide both sides by x^7.

$8x^3 = 27$ Simplify.

$\dfrac{8x^3}{8} = \dfrac{27}{8}$ Divide both sides by 8.

$x^3 = \dfrac{27}{8}$ Simplify.

$x = \sqrt[3]{\dfrac{27}{8}}$ Find the cube root.

$\qquad = \dfrac{\sqrt[3]{27}}{\sqrt[3]{8}} = \dfrac{3}{2}$

11. 12

$a^n \times 3^n = 6^{2n}$

$6^{2n} = (2 \cdot 3)^{2n} = 2^{2n} \cdot 3^{2n} = (2^2)^n \cdot 3^{n+n}$

$\qquad = 4^n \cdot 3^n \cdot 3^n = (4 \cdot 3)^n \cdot 3^n$

$\qquad = 12^n \cdot 3^n$

Therefore $a^n \times 3^n = 12^n \cdot 3^n$

$\qquad \Rightarrow \ a = 12$

12. 2

$2^{-x} \cdot 6^x = 9$

$\dfrac{1}{2^x} \cdot 6^x = 9$

$\dfrac{6^x}{2^x} = 9$

$(\dfrac{6}{2})^x = 9$

$(3)^x = 9$

$\Rightarrow \ x = 2$

7. Polynomials and Factoring

Key Terms / Illustrations

Examples

---

1. FOIL

To multiply two binomials, you can use both left and right Distributive Properties.

$$(ax+b)(cx+d) = \overbrace{(ax)(cx)}^{\text{First}} + \overbrace{(ax)d}^{\text{Outer}} + \overbrace{b(cx)}^{\text{Inner}} + \overbrace{bd}^{\text{Last}}$$

Factored Form   F   O   I   L   Trinomial Form

$(x+2)(x+3) = x^2 + 3x + 2x + 6 = x^2 + 5x + 6$

$(2x-1)(x+3) = 2x^2 + 6x - x - 3 = 2x^2 + 5x - 3$

Example 1 □ FOIL

If $(x+\frac{1}{x})^2 = 4$, then $x^2 + \frac{1}{x^2} =$

Solution □

$$(x+\frac{1}{x})^2 = (x+\frac{1}{x})(x+\frac{1}{x}) = x^2 + x\cdot\frac{1}{x} + \frac{1}{x}\cdot x + (\frac{1}{x})^2$$

$$= x^2 + 2 + \frac{1}{x^2} = 4$$

Therefore $x^2 + \frac{1}{x^2} = 2$ Answer

---

2. Special Products

$(x+y)(x-y) = x^2 - y^2$ **Difference of Two Squares**

$(x+y)^2 = x^2 + 2xy + y^2$ **Perfect Square Trinomial**

$(x-y)^2 = x^2 - 2xy + y^2$ **Perfect Square Trinomial**

Example 2 □ Special products

If $x^2 + y^2 = 8$ and $xy = -2$, then $(x-y)^2 =$

Solution □

$$(x-y)^2 = x^2 - 2xy + y^2 = (x^2 + y^2) - 2xy$$

$$= 8 - 2(-2) = 12$$ Answer

---

3. Factoring Polynomials

a) Factoring a Perfect Square Trinomial

$$4x^2 - 12x + 9 = (2x)^2 - 2(2x)(3) + 3^2$$

$$= (2x-3)^2$$

b) Factoring a Difference of Two Squares

$$25a^2 - 16 = (5a)^2 - 4^2$$

$$= (5a+4)(5a-4)$$

c) Factoring out a Common Monomial

$$12x^3 + 36x^2 + 27x = 3x(4x^2 + 12x + 9)$$

$$= 3x(2x+3)^2$$

d) Factoring a Quadratic Trinomial of the Form
$x^2 + bx + c$, when c is positive.

$x^2 - 5x + 6 = (x - \boxed{?})(x - \boxed{?})$ Find factors of 6

$= (x-2)(x-3)$ whose sum is −5.

Example 3 □ Factoring and zero product property

The product of two consecutive positive integers is 12 more than 5 times the smaller number. Find the larger number.

Solution □

Let $x =$ the first of the integers, then
$x + 1 =$ the second integer.

$$\underbrace{x(x+1)}_{\text{The product}} \underset{=}{\text{is}} \underbrace{5x + 12}_{\substack{\text{12 more than 5 times} \\ \text{the smaller number.}}}$$

$x^2 + x = 5x + 12$ Distributive property

$x^2 - 4x - 12 = 0$ Write in standard form.

$(x+2)(x-6) = 0$ Factor.

$x + 2 = 0$ or $x - 6 = 0$ Zero product property

$x = -2$ or $x = 6$ Solve for x.

Since x is a positive number, $x = 6$.
The larger number is $x + 1 = 7$.   Answer

e) **Factoring a Quadratic Trinomial of the Form**
$x^2 + bx + c$, when c is negative.

$$x^2 - x - 12 = (x - \boxed{?})(x - \boxed{?}) \qquad \text{Find factors of } -12$$
$$= (x + 3)(x - 4) \qquad \text{whose sum is } -1.$$

f) **Factoring When Leading Coefficient Is Not 1**

$$2x^2 + 7x - 4 = (2x - \boxed{?})(x + \boxed{?})$$

      Guess   **Check**
$$(2x + 1)(x - 4) = 2x^2 - 7x - 4$$
$$(2x - 4)(x + 1) = 2x^2 - 2x - 4$$
$$(2x - 1)(x + 4) = 2x^2 + 7x - 4 \leftarrow \text{Correct}$$

g) **Factoring by Grouping**

$$x^3 - 2x^2 + 5x - 10 \qquad \text{Group into two}$$
$$= x^2(x - 2) + 5(x - 2) \qquad \text{binomials and find}$$
$$= (x^2 + 5)(x - 2) \qquad \text{the GCF of each.}$$

4. **Zero Product Property**

For all real numbers a and b, $a \cdot b = 0$ if and only if
$a = 0$ or $b = 0$.
*(A product of factors is equal to zero if and only if
one or more of the factors is zero.)*

5. **The Quadratic Formula**

The solutions of the quadratic equation

$$ax^2 + bx + c = 0 \text{ are } \quad x = \frac{-b \pm \sqrt{b^2 - 4ac}}{2a}$$

6. If $ax^2 + bx + c = px^2 + qx + r$, then
$a = p$, $b = q$, and $c = r$.

7. If $ax^2 + by^2 = 0$, where $a \neq 0$, $b \neq 0$, then
$x = 0$, and $y = 0$.

Example 4 □   If $x^2 + kx + 4 = (x - 2)^2$ for all values
             of x, what is the value of k?

Solution □

    Since $x^2 + kx + 4 = (x - 2)^2$
$$x^2 + kx + 4 = x^2 - 4x + 4$$
$$k = -4 \qquad \text{Answer}$$

Example 5 □   If $x^2 + 2y^2 = 0$, what is the value of
             $x + y$?

Solution □

    Since $x^2 \geq 0$ and $y^2 \geq 0$, the only values of
        x^2 and y^2 for which $x^2 + 2y^2 = 0$ are
        $x^2 = y^2 = 0$ or $x = y = 0$.

      Therefore $x + y = 0$.   Answer

Example 6 □   **Simplifying a fraction**

       Simplify $\dfrac{2a - a^2}{5a^3 - 10a^2}$.

Solution □

$$\frac{2a - a^2}{5a^3 - 10a^2}$$

$$= \frac{a(2 - a)}{5a^2(a - 2)} \qquad \text{Factor the numerator and}$$
                  denominator.

$$= \frac{a(-1)(a - 2)}{5a^2(a - 2)} \qquad (2 - a) = (-1)(a - 2)$$

$$= \frac{\cancel{a}(-1)\cancel{(a-2)}}{5\cancel{a} \cdot a \cancel{(a-2)}} \qquad \text{Cancel the common factor.}$$

$$= -\frac{1}{5a}$$

1. $(\dfrac{a+b}{2})^2 - (\dfrac{a-b}{2})^2 =$

(A) ab

(B) $-ab$

(C) b^2

(D) $\dfrac{2ab+b^2}{2}$

(E) $ab+b^2$

2. If $x = -3$, then $3x^2 - 2x + 6 =$

(A) -15

(B) -9

(C) 9

(D) 27

(E) 39

3. If $x^2 - 2xy + y^2 = 9$, what is one possible value of $(x-y)^3$?

(A) 3

(B) 9

(C) 12

(D) 27

(E) 36

4. If $x^2 + x - 6 = 0$ and $x^2 + 3x - 10 = 0$, then $x =$

(A) -5

(B) -3

(C) 2

(D) 3

(E) 5

5. If $(x+y)^2 = 25$ and $xy = 7$, what is the value of $x^2 + y^2$?

(A) 10

(B) 11

(C) 18

(D) 32

(E) 39

6. $3x^2 + 12x - 15 =$

(A) $(3x-5)(x+3)$

(B) $(3x+5)(x-3)$

(C) $3(x-5)(x+1)$

(D) $3(x+5)(x-1)$

(E) $3(x+5)(x-3)$

Exercises (Multiple Choice)

7. $(5-x)(x-5) =$

(A) $25 - x^2$

(B) $x^2 - 25$

(C) $-x^2 - 25$

(D) $(x-5)^2$

(E) $-(x-5)^2$

8. $a^2 - (a+b)^2 =$

(A) $-b^2$

(B) $-b(2a+b)$

(C) $b(2a+b)$

(D) $(a-b)^2$

(E) $-2ab + b^2$

9. $\dfrac{x(x-1)+x-1}{x^2-1} =$

(A) $\dfrac{1}{x+1}$

(B) $\dfrac{1}{x-1}$

(C) $\dfrac{x+1}{x-1}$

(D) $\dfrac{x-1}{x+1}$

(E) 1

10. If $x > 0$ and $3x - 2 = \dfrac{5}{3x+2}$, then $x =$

(A) 1

(B) 2

(C) 3

(D) 4

(E) 5

11. The square of a positive number is 24 more than twice the number. What is the number?

(A) 14

(B) 12

(C) 10

(D) 8

(E) 6

12. If $x = 5$ is one solution to the equation $x^2 - rx - 21 = 0$, then $r =$

(A) $\dfrac{4}{5}$

(B) 1

(C) 3

(D) 5

(E) 7

70 • Polynomials and Factoring

13. $(\sqrt{3}-2)^2 =$

   (A) -1

   (B) 1

   (C) $-7+4\sqrt{3}$

   (D) $7-4\sqrt{3}$

   (E) $-1+4\sqrt{3}$

14. If $(x-5)(x-s)=x^2-rx+10$, what is the value of $r+s$?

   (A) 5

   (B) 7

   (C) 9

   (D) 10

   (E) 12

15. Which of the following equals $1+2x-(1+2x)x$?

   (A) $(1+2x)(1-x)$

   (B) $(1-2x)^2$

   (C) $-x(1+2x)$

   (D) $1-2x^2$

   (E) $x(1-2x)$

16. What is the value of x, if $rx+sx=3$ and $r+s=\dfrac{1}{3}$?

   (A) 1

   (B) 3

   (C) 9

   (D) 27

   (E) It cannot be determined from the information given.

17. If $(x+\dfrac{1}{x})^2=9$, then $(x-\dfrac{1}{x})^2 =$

   (A) 3

   (B) 5

   (C) 7

   (D) 9

   (E) It cannot be determined from the information given.

18. If $\dfrac{x}{6}-\dfrac{2}{x}=\dfrac{2}{3}$, what is the value of x?

   (A) -6

   (B) -2

   (C) 2

   (D) 2 or -6

   (E) 6 or -2

19. If $x^2 + x - 2 \neq 0$ and

$$\frac{x^2 + 1}{x^2 + x - 2} - \frac{x}{x + 2} = \frac{ax + b}{x^2 + x - 2}, \quad \text{what is the value}$$

of $a + b$?

(A) 1

(B) 2

(C) 3

(D) 4

(E) 6

20. If $x(x - 4)(x + 3) \neq 0$, then

$$\frac{x^2 + 2x - 3}{x - 4} \div \frac{x + 3}{x^2 - 4x} =$$

(A) $x + 1$

(B) $\dfrac{x + 1}{x - 1}$

(C) $\dfrac{x - 1}{x + 1}$

(D) $x^2 - x$

(E) $x^2 - 1$

21. Which of the following equations have (has) two or more real number solutions?

$$\text{I. } x + 1 = 0$$
$$\text{II. } x^2 + x = 0$$
$$\text{III. } x^3 + 4x = 0$$

(A) I only

(B) II only

(C) III only

(D) I and II only

(E) I, II, and III

1. If $(x+y)^2 = 10$ and $xy = -2$, what is the value of $x^2 + y^2$?

2. If x and y are positive integers, $x^2 - y^2 = 35$, and $x^2 + 2xy + y^2 = 49$, what is the value of $x - y$?

3. The height, in feet, of a falling object is modeled by $h = -16t^2 + 32t + 60$ where t is the time in seconds. What is the height of the object after falling three seconds?

4. If $(51)(47)$ is expressed as $(0.1n+2)(0.1n-2)$, where $n > 0$, what is the value of n?

5. If $s > 0$ and $4x^2 - rx + 9 = (2x - s)^2$, what is the value of $r - s$?

6. If $(x^2 + x + 2)(x + 3) = ax^3 + bx^2 + cx + d$ for all values of x, what is the value of $a + b + c + d$?

7. If $y = x^2 - 6x + 9$, what is the least value of y?

10. If $x = \sqrt{-2x + 35}$, what is the value of x?

8. If $4x^2 + 3y^2 = 0$, what is the value of $x + y$?

9. If $\sqrt{n} + \sqrt[3]{n} = 12$, what is the value of n?

Answer Key

<u>Multiple Choice Questions</u>

1. A	2. E	3. D	4. C	5. B
6. D	7. E	8. B	9. E	10. A
11. E	12. A	13. D	14. C	15. A
16. C	17. B	18. E	19. B	20. D
21. B				

<u>Grid-In Questions</u>

1. 14	2. 5	3. 12	4. 490	5. 9
6. 16	7. 0	8. 0	9. 64	10. 5

Answers and Explanations

<u>Multiple Choice Questions</u>

1. A

$$(\frac{a+b}{2})^2 - (\frac{a-b}{2})^2 = \frac{(a+b)^2}{2^2} - \frac{(a-b)^2}{2^2}$$

$$= \frac{a^2+2ab+b^2}{4} - \frac{a^2-2ab+b^2}{4}$$

$$= \frac{a^2+2ab+b^2-a^2+2ab-b^2}{4}$$

$$= \frac{4ab}{4} = ab$$

2. E

$x = -3$, then
$3x^2 - 2x + 6 = 3(-3)^2 - 2(-3) + 6$
$= 3(9) + 6 + 6 = 39$

3. D

$x^2 - 2xy + y^2 = 9 \Rightarrow (x-y)^2 = 9$
$\Rightarrow x - y = \pm\sqrt{9} = \pm 3$
If $x - y = 3$, $(x-y)^3 = 3^3 = 27$

4. C

$x^2 + x - 6 = 0 \Rightarrow (x-2)(x+3) = 0$
The solutions are $x = 2, -3$.

$x^2 + 3x - 10 = 0 \Rightarrow (x+5)(x-2) = 0$
The solutions are $x = 2, -5$.

To find the solutions of two equations joined with "***and***," find the values of the variable which make both equations true.
Therefore the solution is $x = 2$.

5. B

$(x+y)^2 = 25 \Rightarrow x^2 + 2xy + y^2 = 25$
Since $xy = 7$, $x^2 + 2(7) + y^2 = 25$.
$x^2 + y^2 = 25 - 14 = 11$

6. D

$3x^2 + 12x - 15$
$= 3(x^2 + 4x - 5)$ Factor out the GCF.
$= 3(x + \boxed{?})(x + \boxed{?})$ Find factors of -5 whose sum is $+4$.
$= 3(x+5)(x-1)$ $-5 = (-1)(5)$, $-1 + 5 = 4$

7. E

$(5-x)(x-5)$
$= -(x-5)(x-5)$ $5 - x = -(x-5)$
$= -(x-5)^2$

8. B

$a^2 - (a+b)^2$
$= a^2 - (a^2 + 2ab + b^2)$
$= a^2 - a^2 - 2ab - b^2$
$= -2ab - b^2 = -b(2a+b)$

9. E

$$\frac{x(x-1)+x-1}{x^2-1} = \frac{x^2-x+x-1}{x^2-1}$$
$$= \frac{x^2-1}{x^2-1} = 1$$

10. A

$$3x-2 = \frac{5}{3x+2}$$
$$(3x-2)(3x+2) = \frac{5}{3x+2}(3x+2)$$
(multiply "$3x+2$" on both sides)
$$9x^2-4=5 \implies 9x^2=9 \implies x^2=1$$
$$\implies x=\pm 1$$

Since $x>0$, $x=1$ is the solution.

11. E

$$\underbrace{x^2}_{\substack{\text{The square} \\ \text{of a number}}} \underbrace{=}_{\text{is}} \underbrace{2n+24}_{\substack{\text{24 more than} \\ \text{twice the number.}}}$$

$$x^2-2n-24=0 \text{ (standard form)}$$
$$(x-6)(x+4)=0 \text{ (factor)}$$
$$x=6 \text{ or } x=-4$$

Since the number is positive, $x=6$ is the solution.

12. A

Since $x=5$ is one solution to the equation, substitute 5 for x.
$$x^2-rx-21=0$$
$$5^2-r\cdot5-21=0$$
$$25-5r-21=0 \implies 4-5r=0$$
$$\implies r=\frac{4}{5}$$

13. D

$$(\sqrt{3}-2)^2 = (\sqrt{3}-2)(\sqrt{3}-2)$$
$$= 3-2\sqrt{3}-2\sqrt{3}+4$$
$$= 7-4\sqrt{3}$$

14. C

$$(x-5)(x-s) = x^2-rx+10$$
$$x^2-(5+s)x+5s = x^2-rx+10$$
(Match the left and right sides of the equation)
$$\implies x^2=x^2, \ 5+s=r, \ 5s=10$$
$$\implies s=2 \text{ and } r=7$$
$$r+s=7+2=9$$

15. A

$$1+2x-(1+2x)x = (1+2x)\cdot1-(1+2x)x$$
$$= (1+2x)(1-x) \text{ ("}1+2x\text{" is a common factor.)}$$

16. C

$$rx+sx=3 \implies (r+s)x=3$$
$$\implies \frac{1}{3}x=3 \text{ (since } r+s=\frac{1}{3})$$
$$\implies x=9$$

17. B

$$(x+\frac{1}{x})^2=9 \implies (x+\frac{1}{x})(x+\frac{1}{x})=9$$
$$\implies x\cdot x+x\cdot\frac{1}{x}+\frac{1}{x}\cdot x+\frac{1}{x}\cdot\frac{1}{x}=9$$
$$\implies x^2+2+\frac{1}{x^2}=9 \implies x^2+\frac{1}{x^2}=7$$

$$(x-\frac{1}{x})^2 = (x-\frac{1}{x})(x-\frac{1}{x}) = x^2-2+\frac{1}{x^2}$$
$$= (x^2+\frac{1}{x^2})-2 = 7-2=5$$

18. E

$$\frac{x}{6}-\frac{2}{x}=\frac{2}{3}$$ LCD of given equation is $6x$.
$$6x(\frac{x}{6}-\frac{2}{x})=6x(\frac{2}{3})$$ Multiply both sides by $6x$.
$$x^2-12=4x$$ Simplify.

$x^2 - 4x - 12 = 0$ Subtract $4x$ from both sides.
$(x-6)(x+2) = 0$ Factor.
$x - 6 = 0$ or $x + 2 = 0$
$\quad x = 6 \qquad x = -2$

The solutions are 6 and -2.

19. B

$$\frac{x^2+1}{x^2+x-2} - \frac{x}{x+2} = \frac{ax+b}{x^2+x-2}$$

$$\frac{x^2+1}{(x+2)(x-1)} - \frac{x}{x+2} = \frac{ax+b}{(x+2)(x-1)}$$

Factor the denominators. The LCD is $(x+2)(x-1)$.
Multiply both sides by $(x+2)(x-1)$ and simplify.

$x^2 + 1 - x(x-1) = ax + b$

$x^2 + 1 - x^2 + x = ax + b$

$x + 1 = ax + b \implies a = 1$ and $b = 1$

Therefore $a + b = 1 + 1 = 2$

20. D

$$\frac{x^2+2x-3}{x-4} \div \frac{x+3}{x^2-4x}$$

$$= \frac{x^2+2x-3}{x-4} \times \frac{x^2-4x}{x+3}$$

$$= \frac{(x+3)(x-1)}{x-4} \times \frac{x(x-4)}{x+3}$$

$$= x(x-1) = x^2 - x$$

21. B

I. $x + 1 = 0 \implies x = -1$
There is only one solution.
Roman Numeral I is not true.

II. $x^2 + x = 0 \implies x(x+1) = 0$
$\implies x = 0$ or $x = -1$

There are two solutions.
Therefore Roman Numeral II is true.

III. $x^3 + 4x = 0 \implies x(x^2+4) = 0$
$\implies x = 0$ or $x^2 + 4 = 0$
But since $x^2 + 4 = 0 \implies x^2 = -4$,
there is no real solution for the equation $x^2 + 4 = 0$.
The equation $x^3 + 4x = 0$ has only one real number solution.
Roman Numeral III is not true.

Grid-In Questions

1. 14

$(x+y)^2 = 10$ Original equation
$x^2 + 2xy + y^2 = 10$ FOIL
$x^2 + 2(-2) + y^2 = 10$ Substitution ($xy = -2$)
$x^2 - 4 + y^2 = 10$ Simplify.
$x^2 + y^2 = 14$ Add 4 on both sides.

2. 5

$x^2 + 2xy + y^2 = 49 \implies (x+y)^2 = 49$
$\implies x + y = \pm\sqrt{49} = \pm 7$

Since x and y are positive integers, $x + y = +7$.
$x^2 - y^2 = 35 \implies (x+y)(x-y) = 35$
$\implies 7(x-y) = 35$ (substitute: $x + y = 7$)
$\implies x - y = 5$

3. 12

$h = -16t^2 + 32t + 60$ Original equation
$h = -16(3)^2 + 32(3) + 60$ Substitution ($t = 3$)
$h = -144 + 96 + 60$ Simplify.
$\quad = 12$

4. 490

$$(51)(47)$$
$$= (49+2)(49-2)$$
$$= (0.1n+2)(0.1n-2)\Big\} \implies 49 = 0.1n$$
$$n = 490$$

5. 9

$$4x^2 - rx + 9 = (2x - s)^2$$
$$\implies 4x^2 - rx + 9 = 4x^2 - 4sx + s^2 \text{ (FOIL)}$$
$$\implies r = 4s \text{ and } 9 = s^2 \text{ (Match the left and right sides}$$
$$\text{of the equation.)}$$

$$\implies s = \pm 3 \text{ but } s > 0, \implies s = 3$$
$$r = 4s = 4(3) = 12$$
$$r - s = 12 - 3 = 9$$

6. 16

$$(x^2 + x + 2)(x + 3) = ax^3 + bx^2 + cx + d$$
$$(x^2 + x + 2)(x + 3) = x^3 + x^2 + 2x + 3x^2 + 3x + 6$$
$$= x^3 + 4x^2 + 5x + 6$$

Therefore
$$ax^3 + bx^2 + cx + d = x^3 + 4x^2 + 5x + 6$$
$$\implies a = 1, b = 4, c = 5, \text{ and } d = 6.$$
$$a + b + c + d = 1 + 4 + 5 + 6 = 16$$

7. 0

Method I

$$y = x^2 - 6x + 9 = (x - 3)^2$$
Since $(x - 3)^2 \geq 0$, the least value occurs when
$x - 3 = 0$.

Therefore the least value of y equals zero.

Method II

Use your graphing calculator.

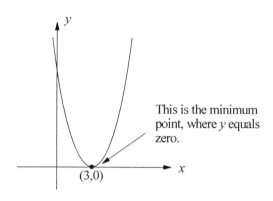

This is the minimum point, where y equals zero.

8. 0

$$4x^2 + 3y^2 = 0 \implies x = 0, y = 0$$
$$x + y = 0 + 0 = 0$$

9. 64

If $\sqrt{n} + \sqrt[3]{n} = 12$, then both $\sqrt{n}$ and $\sqrt[3]{n}$ must be integers. So n has to be a square of an integer and, at the same time, a cube of an integer.

number	square of a number	cube of a number
1	1	1
2	4	8
3	9	27
4	16	64
5	25	
6	36	
7	49	
8	64	

10. 5

$$x = \sqrt{-2x + 35}$$
$$(x)^2 = (\sqrt{-2x + 35})^2 \text{ (Square both sides.)}$$
$$x^2 = -2x + 35$$
$$x^2 + 2x - 35 = 0$$
$$(x + 7)(x - 5) = 0$$
$$x = -7 \text{ or } x = 5$$

Try checking each x-value in the original equation.
$x = 5$ works, but $x = -7$ does not.
Thus the equation has 5 as its solution.

8. Solving Equations

1. Verbal Phrases into Algebraic Expressions

Verbal Phrase	Algebraic Expression
The *sum* of 3 and a number	$x + 3$
Six *more than* a number	$n + 6$
A number *increased by* 12	$x + 12$
The *difference* of n and 5	$n - 5$
Nine *less than* a number	$x - 9$
A number *decreased by* 7	$n - 7$
The *product* of 8 and a number	$8x$
Three fifths *of* a number	$\dfrac{3}{5}x$
Twice a number	$2x$
The *quotient* of a number and 6	$\dfrac{n}{6}$

2. Solving an Equation

Verbal Sentence	Equation
14 less than a number equals 56.	$n - 14 = 56$
Twice a number, increased by 7 is 17.	$2x + 7 = 17$
Two-thirds of a number is 18.	$\dfrac{2}{3}x = 18$
If 5 is added to one-half of a number, the result is 49.	$\dfrac{1}{2}x + 5 = 49$
A number n exceeds m by 10.	$n = m + 10$

3. Distributive Property

For all real numbers *a, b,* and *c*

$$a(b + c) = ab + ac$$
$$a(b - c) = ab - ac$$

Example 1 □ Verbal phrase to algebraic expression

Write each expression algebraically.

a. Three times the sum of a number and 7
b. The product of 6 and 5 less than a number
c. 12 less than the quotient of a number and 4
d. 9 less than twice a number, multiplied by 8
e. A number increased by 4, multiplied by 3 less than the number

Solution □

a. $3(x + 7)$ b. $6(n - 5)$

c. $\dfrac{n}{4} - 12$ d. $8(2x - 9)$

e. $(n + 4)(n - 3)$

Example 2 □ Solving equations

One number is 4 times another number. If their sum is -15, what is the smaller of the numbers?

Solution □

Let x be a number, then $4x$ is the other number.

$$
\begin{aligned}
x + 4x &= -15 &&\text{Their sum is } -15. \\
5x &= -15 \\
x &= -3 &&\Leftarrow \text{ one number} \\
4x = 4(-3) &= -12 &&\Leftarrow \text{ 4 times the other number}
\end{aligned}
$$

Since -12 is smaller than -3, the answer is -12.

Example 3 □ Distributive property

Simplify $-2(x + 3) - 3(x - 5)$

Solution □

$$
\begin{aligned}
&-2(x + 3) - 3(x - 5) &&\text{Given} \\
&= -2x - 6 - 3x + 15 &&\text{Distributive property} \\
&= -5x + 9 &&\text{Answer}
\end{aligned}
$$

4. Absolute Value

The absolute value of a number is the distance on a number line between the graph of the number and the origin.

Because it is a measure of distance, the absolute value of a number is always positive (or zero).

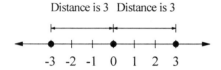

Distance is 3   Distance is 3

$|-3| = 3$ The absolute value of -3 is 3.

$|3| = 3$ The absolute value of 3 is 3.

5. Systems of Linear Equations with Two Variables

To solve a system of two linear equations by the **substitution method**
1. Solve one equation for either variable.
2. Substitute this equation into the second equation.

To solve a system of two linear equations by the **elimination method**
1. Multiply one or both equations by a number to obtain new coefficients for x (or y) that are opposites.
2. Add the equations and solve.

6. Solving systems of two equations with three variables.

☑ On the SAT, you may find questions with two equations with three variables, and you will be asked to solve for the variables. For this type of question, solutions can be found either by adding the two equations or by subtracting one equation from the other.

7. Literal Equations

A literal equation is an equation that uses more than one letter as a variable. You can solve a literal equation for any one of its letters.

Example 4 □   Absolute Value Equation

If $x = -5$ and $y = 3$, then $3|x| - 2|y| =$

Solution □

$3|x| - 2|y| = 3|-5| - 2|3| = 15 - 6 = 9$

Example 5 □   Absolute Value Equation

Solve $|x - 3| + 4 = 16$.

Solution □

$$|x - 3| + 4 = 16$$
$$|x - 3| = 12 \qquad \text{Subtract 4 from both sides.}$$
$$x - 3 = 12 \quad \text{or} \quad x - 3 = -12$$
$$x - 3 + 3 = 12 + 3 \quad \text{or} \quad x - 3 + 3 = -12 + 3$$
$$x = 15 \quad \text{or} \quad x = -9$$

The equation has two solutions: 15 and -9. Check these solutions by substituting each into the original equation.

Example 6 □   Substitution Method

Solve the linear system.
$$x - y = 2$$
$$2x + y = 7$$

Solution □

$$y = 7 - 2x \qquad \text{Solve the second equation for } y.$$
$$x - y = 2 \qquad \text{First equation}$$
$$x - (7 - 2x) = 2 \qquad \text{Substitute } (7 - 2x) \text{ for } y.$$
$$3x - 7 = 2 \qquad \text{Simplify.}$$
$$3x = 9 \qquad \text{Add 7 to both sides.}$$
$$x = 3 \qquad \text{Solve for } x.$$

$$3 - y = 2 \qquad \text{Substitute 3 for } x.$$
$$y = 1 \qquad \text{Solve for } y.$$

The solution is (3, 1).

Example 7 □   **Elimination Method**

Solve the linear system.

$$3x - 2y = 5$$
$$x + 4y = 4$$

Solution □

$3x - 2y = 5$	First equation
$6x - 4y = 10$	Multiply by 2.
$+ \mid x + 4y = 4$	Second equation
$7x = 14$	Add equations.
$x = 2$	Solve for x.

$3(2) - 2y = 5$	Substitute 2 for x.
$-2y = -1$	Subtract 6 from both sides.
$y = \dfrac{1}{2}$	Solve for y.

The solution is $(2, \dfrac{1}{2})$

Example 8 □   **Finding solutions by adding the two equations.**

If $2x - y = 4$ and $3y + 2z = 10$, what is the value of $x + y + z$?

Solution □

$2x - y = 4$	First equation
$+ \mid 3y + 2z = 10$	Second equation
$2x - y + 3y + 2z = 14$	Add the two equations.
$2x + 2y + 2z = 14$	Simplify.

$2(x + y + z) = 14$	Factor.
$x + y + z = 7$	Answer

Example 9 □   **Finding solutions by subtracting one equation from the other.**

If $a - b + c = 5$ and $2a + 3c = 23$, what is the value of $a + b + 2c$?

Solution □

Subtract first equation from second equation.

$$(2a + 3c) - (a - b + c) = 23 - 5$$
$$a + b + 2c = 18 \qquad \text{Answer}$$

Example 10 □   **Solving literal equations for a specified variable**

Solve the formula $P = 2L + 2W$ for L.

Solution □

$P = 2L + 2W$	Given
$P - 2W = 2L$	Subtract $2W$ from both sides.
$\dfrac{P - 2W}{2} = L$	Divide both sides by 2.

Example 11 □   **Solving literal equations for a specified variable**

Solve the formula $\dfrac{r}{r+1} = s$ for r.

Solution □

$\dfrac{r}{r+1} = s$	Given
$r = s(r + 1)$	Multiply both sides by $(r + 1)$.
$r = sr + s$	Distributive property
$r - sr = s$	Subtract sr from both sides.
$r(1 - s) = s$	Distributive property
$r = \dfrac{s}{1 - s}$	Divide both sides by $(1 - s)$.

1. If $a + 3 = 14$, then $2a - 6 =$

   (A) 7

   (B) 14

   (C) 16

   (D) 18

   (E) 22

2. If $x = 1 - y$ and $3x = 8 - 5y$, what is the value of x?

   (A) -2

   (B) $-\dfrac{3}{2}$

   (C) $-\dfrac{1}{2}$

   (D) $\dfrac{5}{2}$

   (E) 5

3. If $a = -2$, then $2a^3 - (2a)^3 =$

   (A) -80

   (B) -48

   (C) 16

   (D) 48

   (E) 80

4. If $\dfrac{x}{y} = 1$, then $x - y =$

   (A) 0

   (B) 1

   (C) x

   (D) $2x$

   (E) $-2y$

5. Two adult tickets and one student ticket cost $9.95, while one adult ticket and three student tickets cost $11.10. What is the cost of one student ticket?

   (A) $1.75

   (B) $2.25

   (C) $2.45

   (D) $3.25

   (E) $3.75

6. If $w = \dfrac{x}{3}$, $x = 3y$, $4y = z$, and $z \neq 0$, then $\dfrac{w}{z} =$

   (A) $\dfrac{1}{4}$

   (B) $\dfrac{1}{3}$

   (C) $\dfrac{1}{2}$

   (D) 2

   (E) 3

One half of a number n increased by 10 is the same as four less than twice the number.

7. Which of the following equations represents the statement above?

   (A) $\dfrac{1}{2}(n + 10) = 2(n + 4)$

   (B) $\dfrac{1}{2}n + 10 = 2(n - 4)$

   (C) $\dfrac{1}{2}n + 10 = 2n - 4$

   (D) $\dfrac{1}{2}n + 10 = 2 - 4n$

   (E) $\dfrac{1}{2}(n + 10) = 2n - 4$

Questions 8-9 refer to the following information.

A sales clerk for an appliance store receives monthly pay of $1400, plus 6% commission on the revenue from appliances sold.

8. Which of the following expressions gives the total monthly income of a sales clerk, in dollars, if the amount sold is x?

(A) $1400 + 0.06 \times 1400$

(B) $1400 \times 0.06 + x$

(C) $(1400 + x) \times 0.06$

(D) $1400 + 0.06x$

(E) $1400 \times 0.06x$

9. Which of the following graphs could show the total income of the sales clerk?

(A)

(B)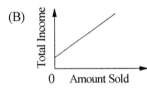

(C)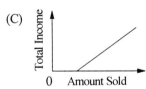

(D)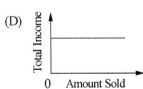

(E)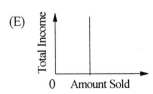

10. If a is b less than one-half of c, what is b in terms of a and c?

(A) $\frac{1}{2}c - a$

(B) $\frac{1}{2}c + a$

(C) $a - \frac{1}{2}c$

(D) $c - 2a$

(E) $2a - c$

x	- - -	8	- - -	20	- - -
y	- - -	1	- - -	10	- - -

11. In the table above, 8 and 20 of the x-values correspond to 1 and 10 of the y-values, respectively. Which of the following linear equations could be used to find the relation between x-values and y-values?

(A) $y = x - 7$

(B) $y = x - 10$

(C) $y = -\frac{3}{4}x + 5$

(D) $y = \frac{3}{4}x - 5$

(E) $y = \frac{3}{4}x$

12. One number is 3 more than twice another number, and their sum is -15. What is the lesser of the two numbers?

(A) -3

(B) -6

(C) -7

(D) -9

(E) -12

13. If $\dfrac{(n-2)180}{n} = g$, then which of the following gives the value of n in terms of g?

(A) $\dfrac{1}{2} - 180g$

(B) $\dfrac{g-180}{360}$

(C) $\dfrac{g}{360} - 2$

(D) $180g - \dfrac{1}{2}$

(E) $\dfrac{360}{180-g}$

14. If $a - b = 8$ and $2b + c = 5$, what is the value of $a + b + c$?

(A) 3

(B) 6.5

(C) 11

(D) 13

(E) It cannot be determined from the information given.

15. If $y = kx$, which of the following is equal to ky?

(A) $\dfrac{y}{x}$

(B) $\dfrac{x}{y}$

(C) kx^2

(D) ky^2

(E) k^2x

16. In the equation $V = \dfrac{1}{3}\pi r^2 h$, if the value of r is doubled and the value of h is halved, what happens to the value of V?

(A) V is not changed.

(B) V is halved.

(C) V is doubled.

(D) V is tripled.

(E) V is multiplied by 4.

17. If $1 - \dfrac{bx-1}{a-x} = 0$ and $a - x \neq 0$, then which of the following gives the value of x in terms of a and b?

(A) $\dfrac{b-1}{a-1}$

(B) $\dfrac{a+1}{b+1}$

(C) $\dfrac{b-1}{a}$

(D) $\dfrac{a-1}{b}$

(E) $\dfrac{a+1}{b}$

18. If $2c - a = 3b$ and $3a - b = 5c$, then $c =$

   (A) $2b$

   (B) $4b$

   (C) $6b$

   (D) $8b$

   (E) $10b$

21. If $b - a = c - b = d - c$, which of the following is equal to $d - b$?

   (A) $d + a$

   (B) $b + a$

   (C) $c + a$

   (D) $c - a$

   (E) $b - c$

19. If $x = r + s$, $y = t - r$, and $z = s - t$, then $x + y + z =$

   (A) 0

   (B) $2r$

   (C) $2s$

   (D) $2t$

   (E) It cannot be determined from the information given.

22. If $3|5 - x| = 24$, what is the value of x?

   (A) 3 or −3

   (B) 3 or −13

   (C) 3 or 13

   (D) −3 or 13

   (E) −3 or −13

20. If Kelly gives 3 marbles to Joe, then Joe has twice as many marbles as Kelly. If instead Joe gives one marble to Kelly, then they will have an equal number of marbles. How many marbles did Kelly originally have?

   (A) 7

   (B) 8

   (C) 9

   (D) 10

   (E) 11

1. The quotient of a number and five equals nine less than one half of the number. What is the number?

2. If $2a = b$ and $b = 3c + 14$, what is the value of a when $c = 6$?

3. How much greater than $a - 3$ is $a + 7$?

4. If $x + 5 \neq 0$, for what integer value of x is
$$\frac{3}{x+5} - \frac{x+2}{4} = \frac{3}{10} - \frac{7}{4}?$$

5. If $7x - 2y = 15$ and $y = 2x - 3$, what is the value of x?

6. If $a \cdot b \cdot c = 64$ and $b \cdot c \cdot d = 0$, what is the value of $4d$?

1. Subtract 3 from a number n.
2. Divide by 4.
3. Add 5.
4. Multiply by 6.

7. When the sequence of operations above has been completed in order, the result is 42. What is the value of n?

8. The sum of two numbers a and b is 12, and the number a is 5 more than b. What is the value of a?

9. If $a = -5$ and $b = 2$, then $\left|a^2 - b^2\right| - 2|a| =$

10. When a number n is divided by $\dfrac{2}{3}$, the result is the same as when 6 is added to n. What is the value of $\dfrac{2}{3}n$?

11. If $r + s + t = 19$ and $r + s - t = 13$, what is the value of t?

12. The price of brand A computer is \$500 more than the price of brand B computer. If \$300 were to be discounted from the price of each computer, then brand A computer would cost 1.5 times as much as brand B computer. What is the price of brand A computer?

Answer Key

Multiple Choice Questions

1. C 2. B 3. D 4. A 5. C

6. A 7. C 8. D 9. B 10. A

11. D 12. D 13. E 14. D 15. E

16. C 17. B 18. E 19. C 20. E

21. D 22. D

Grid-In Questions

1. 30 2. 16 3. 10 4. 5 5. 3

6. 0 7. 11 8. 8.5 9. 11 10. 8

11. 3 12. 1800

Answers and Explanations

Multiple Choice Questions

1. C

$a + 3 = 14 \implies a = 11$
$2a - 6 = 2(11) - 6 = 22 - 6 = 16$

2. B

$x = 1 - y \implies y = 1 - x$
$3x = 8 - 5y$ 2nd equation
$3x = 8 - 5(1 - x)$ Substitution ($y = 1 - x$)
$3x = 8 - 5 + 5x$ Distribute.
$-2x = 3$ Simplify.
$x = -\dfrac{3}{2}$ Divide by –2.

3. D

$a = -2$, then
$2a^3 - (2a)^3 = 2(-2)^3 - (2(-2))^3$

$= 2(-8) - (-4)^3 = -16 - (-64)$
$= -16 + 64 = 48$

4. A

$\dfrac{x}{y} = 1 \implies y(\dfrac{x}{y}) = 1(y)$ (Multiply y on both sides.)
$\implies x = y$

$x - y = y - y = 0$

5. C

Let x = the cost of an adult ticket
Let y = the cost of a student ticket

$2x + y = 9.95$
$x + 3y = 11.1$
Multiply the second equation by -2, then add to the first equation.

$-2x - 6y = -22.2$
$+ \ \underline{2x + \ y = 9.95}$
$\qquad -5y = -12.25$

$\implies y = 2.45$

6. A

$w = \dfrac{x}{3}$ $x = 3y$, $4y = z$, and $z \neq 0$,

$\dfrac{w}{z} = \dfrac{\frac{1}{3}x}{4y} = \dfrac{\frac{1}{3}(3y)}{4y} = \dfrac{y}{4y} = \dfrac{1}{4}$

7. C

$\underset{\substack{\text{one half of}\\\text{a number } n}}{\dfrac{1}{2}n}$ $\underset{\substack{\text{increased}\\\text{by 10}}}{+10}$ $\underset{\substack{\text{is the}\\\text{same as}}}{=}$ $\underset{\substack{\text{4 less than twice}\\\text{the number}}}{2n-4}$

8. D

Let x = the revenue from the appliances sold
Then $0.06x$ = the amount of commission

Total monthly income
= monthly pay + commission
= $1,400 + 0.06x$

9. B

Let y = total monthly income
Then $y = 0.06x + 1400$.
The slope of the graph is 0.06 and the y-intercept is 1,400.

Answer choice is B, since it is the only graph with a positive y-intercept, and the income increases as the amount of sales increases.

10. A

$$\underset{a \text{ is}}{\underset{\downarrow}{a}} = \underset{\underbrace{\frac{1}{2}c - b}_{\substack{b \text{ less than} \\ \text{one-half of } c}}}{} \Rightarrow b = \frac{1}{2}c - a$$

11. D

Since the equation is a linear equation, we can start with $y = mx + b$.
When $x = 8$, $y = 1 \Rightarrow 1 = m(8) + b$.
When $x = 20$, $y = 10 \Rightarrow 10 = m(20) + b$.

Subtract the first equation from the second.

$$
\begin{array}{r}
10 = 20m + b \\
- \lfloor 1 = 8m + b \\
\hline
9 = 12m
\end{array}
$$

$$\Rightarrow m = \frac{9}{12} = \frac{3}{4}$$

Substitute the value of m into the first equation.

$$1 = 8(\frac{3}{4}) + b \Rightarrow 1 = 6 + b \Rightarrow b = -5$$

So the linear equation is $y = \frac{3}{4}x - 5$.

12. D

Let x = one number
Let y = another number

$$x = 2y + 3$$
$$x + y = -15$$

Substitute $(2y + 3)$ for x into the second equation.
$(2y + 3) + y = -15 \Rightarrow$
$3y + 3 = -15 \Rightarrow 3y = -18 \Rightarrow$
$y = -6$
Substitute the value of y into the first equation.
$x = 2(-6) + 3 = -9$

Since $-9 < -6$, -9 is the answer.

13. E

$\dfrac{(n-2)180}{n} = g$	Original equation
$\not{n}\dfrac{(n-2)180}{\not{n}} = g \cdot n$	Multiply n on both sides.
$(n-2)180 = gn$	Simplify.
$180n - 360 = gn$	Distributive Property
$180n - gn = 360$	Simplify.
$n(180 - g) = 360$	Distributive Property
$n = \dfrac{360}{180 - g}$	Divide both sides by 180-g.

14. D

Add two equations.

$$
\begin{array}{r}
a - b = 8 \\
+ \lfloor 2b + c = 5 \\
\hline
a - b + 2b + c = 8 + 5
\end{array}
$$

$$\Rightarrow a + b + c = 13$$

15. E

$y = kx$	Original equation
$k \cdot y = k(kx)$	Multiply k on both sides.
$ky = k^2x$	$k \cdot k = k^2$

16. C

$$V = \frac{1}{3}\pi r^2 h$$

The value of r is doubled and the value of h is halved.

$$\text{New } V = \frac{1}{3}\pi (2r)^2 (\frac{1}{2}h) = \frac{1}{3}\pi (4r^2)(\frac{1}{2}h)$$

$$= \frac{1}{3}\pi (2r^2 h) = 2\left[\frac{1}{3}\pi r^2 h\right] = 2V$$

Therefore V is doubled.

17. B

$$1 - \frac{bx-1}{a-x} = 0 \implies 1 = \frac{bx-1}{a-x}$$

$\implies a - x = bx - 1$ (Multiply $a-x$ on both sides.)

$\implies a + 1 = bx + x$

$\implies a + 1 = x(b+1) \implies x = \frac{a+1}{b+1}$

18. E

$2c - a = 3b$ and $3a - b = 5c$

Solve the first equation for a.
$a = 2c - 3b$

Substitute a into the second equation.
$3(2c - 3b) - b = 5c$

$\implies 6c - 9b - b = 5c \implies 6c - 10b = 5c$

$\implies c = 10b$

19. C

Add all three equations.
$$x = r + s$$
$$y = t - r$$
$$+ \ \underline{|\ z = s - t}$$
$$x + y + z = (r+s) + (t-r) + (s-t)$$

$\implies x + y + z = 2s$

20. E

Let k and j be the number of marbles Kelly and Joe had, respectively, before any transaction.

If Kelly gives 3 marbles to Joe, then Kelly has $(k-3)$ marbles and Joe has $(j+3)$ marbles. After the transaction Joe has twice as many marbles as Kelly.

$\implies \ 2(k-3) = j + 3$ (First equation)

If, instead, Joe gives one marble to Kelly, then they will have an equal number of marbles.

$\implies \quad \underbrace{j-1}_{\substack{\text{Joe has }(j\text{-}1) \\ \text{marbles after} \\ \text{he gives one} \\ \text{to Kelly.}}} = \underbrace{k+1}_{\substack{\text{Kelly has }(k\text{+}1) \\ \text{marbles after} \\ \text{Joe gives one} \\ \text{to him.}}}$ (Second equation)

Simplify the first equation.
$j = 2k - 9$

Substitute $(2k-9)$ for j into the second equation.
$(2k-9) - 1 = k + 1$

$\implies 2k - 10 = k + 1$

$\implies k = 11$

21. D

$b - a = c - b = d - c$

$\implies b - a = d - c$

$\implies d = b - a + c$

$\implies d - b = c - a$

22. D

$$3|5 - x| = 24$$
$$\frac{3|5-x|}{3} = \frac{24}{3} \qquad \text{Divide both sides by 3.}$$
$$|5 - x| = 8$$

$5 - x = 8$	or	$5 - x = -8$
$5 - 5 - x = 8 - 5$	or	$5 - 5 - x = -8 - 5$
$-x = 3$	or	$-x = -13$
$x = -3$	or	$x = 13$

Grid-In Questions

1. 30

$$\underbrace{\frac{n}{5}}_{\substack{\text{the quotient of} \\ \text{a number and 5}}} \underbrace{=}_{\text{equals}} \underbrace{\frac{1}{2}n}_{\substack{\text{one half of} \\ \text{a number}}} \underbrace{-9}_{\text{nine less than}}$$

$$\Rightarrow \frac{1}{5}n - \frac{1}{2}n = -9 \Rightarrow -\frac{3}{10}n = -9$$

$$\Rightarrow n = 30$$

2. 16

$2a = b$ and $b = 3c + 14$.
If $c = 6$, $b = 3c + 14 = 3(6) + 14 = 32$.
$2a = b = 32 \Rightarrow a = 16$

3. 10

$(a + 7) - (a - 3) = a + 7 - a + 3 = 10$

4. 5

$$\frac{3}{x+5} - \frac{x+2}{4} = \frac{3}{10} - \frac{7}{4}$$

If we look at both sides of the equation carefully, we can match $x + 5$ and 10 to each other, and $x + 2$ and 7 to each other.

$$\left. \begin{array}{l} x + 2 = 7 \\ x + 5 = 10 \end{array} \right\} \Rightarrow x = 5$$

5. 3

$7x - 2y = 15$
$y = 2x - 3$

Substitute $(2x - 3)$ for y into the first equation.
$7x - 2(2x - 3) = 15 \Rightarrow 7x - 4x + 6 = 15$
$\Rightarrow 3x + 6 = 15 \Rightarrow 3x = 9 \Rightarrow x = 3$

6. 0

If $a \cdot b \cdot c = 64$, $a \neq 0, b \neq 0$, and $c \neq 0$.
If $b \cdot c \cdot d = 0$ and $b \cdot c \neq 0$, then d must be zero.

$4d = 4(0) = 0$

7. 11

1) Subtract 3 from a number $n \Rightarrow n - 3$

2) Divide by 4 $\Rightarrow \dfrac{n-3}{4}$

3) Add 5 $\Rightarrow \dfrac{n-3}{4} + 5$

4) Multiply by 6 $\Rightarrow (\dfrac{n-3}{4} + 5) \times 6$

5) The result is 42 $\Rightarrow (\dfrac{n-3}{4} + 5) \times 6 = 42$

$$\Rightarrow (\frac{n-3}{4} + 5) = 7 \qquad \text{Divide both sides by 6.}$$

$$\Rightarrow \frac{n-3}{4} = 2 \qquad \text{Subtract 5 from both sides.}$$

$$\Rightarrow n - 3 = 8 \qquad \text{Multiply by 4 on both sides.}$$
$$\Rightarrow n = 11 \qquad \text{Add 3 on both sides.}$$

8. 8.5

$$\underbrace{a + b}_{\substack{\text{the sum of} \\ a \text{ and } b}} \underbrace{=}_{\text{is}} \underbrace{12}_{12} \qquad \underbrace{a}_{a} \underbrace{=}_{\text{is}} \underbrace{b+5}_{5 \text{ more than } b}$$

Solve the first equation for b.
$b = 12 - a$
Substitute $(12 - a)$ for b into the second equation.
$a = (12 - a) + 5 \Rightarrow a = 17 - a$
$\Rightarrow 2a = 17 \Rightarrow a = 8.5$

9. 11

$a = -5$ and $b = 2$

$$\left|a^2 - b^2\right| - 2|a| = \left|(-5)^2 - 2^2\right| - 2|-5|$$

$$= |25 - 4| - 2 \cdot 5$$

$$= 21 - 10 = 11$$

10. 8

$$n \div \frac{2}{3} = n + 6 \implies n \times \frac{3}{2} = n + 6$$

$$2(n \times \frac{3}{2}) = 2(n + 6) \implies 3n = 2n + 12$$

$$\implies n = 12$$

$$\frac{2}{3}n = \frac{2}{3}(12) = 8$$

11. 3

Subtract the second equation from the first.

$$r + s + t = 19$$
$$- \underline{\left| \; r + s - t = 13 \right.}$$
$$2t = 6$$
$$\implies t = 3$$

12. 1800

Let a = the price of brand A computer
Let b = the price of brand B computer

$$a = b + 500$$
$$a - 300 = 1.5(b - 300)$$

Solve the first equation for b.

$$b - a = 500$$

Substitute $(a - 500)$ for b into the second equation.

$$a - 300 = 1.5(a - 500 - 300)$$
$$a - 300 = 1.5(a - 800) \implies a - 300 = 1.5a - 1200$$
$$900 = 0.5a \implies a = 1800$$

9. Word Problems

Key Terms / Illustrations

Examples

---

1. A Linear Equation Model for a Real-Life Situation

Linear equations can be used to model many types of real life situations such as cost problems, and business and economic situations.

Illustration

1) A linear model for phone charges

The cost of an overseas call is $1.25 for the first three minutes and $0.12 for each additional minute.

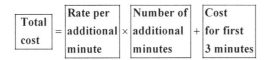

Total cost of long distance call $= y$
Cost for first three minutes $= 1.25$
Rate per additional minute $= 0.12$
Total number of minutes $= x$
Number of additional minutes $= x - 3$

Linear model : $\quad y = 0.12(x-3)+1.25$

2) A linear model for projected sales

In 1990, sales revenue of a company was $1,200.000. During the next 10 years, its annual sales increased by $540,000 per year.

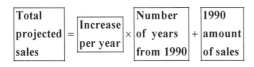

Total projected annual sales $= y$
1990 sales $= 1,200,000$
Increase per year $= 540,000$
Number of years from 1990 $= x$

Linear model : $\quad y = 540,000x + 1,200,000$

Example 1 □   A linear function as a model

In 1990 a house was purchased for $140,000. In 1998 it was sold at $207,000. Assuming that the value of house increased at a constant rate,

(a) find a linear equation that models this situation,

(b) draw a graph, and

(c) estimate the price of the house in the year 2003.

Solution □

Let x = the number of years from 1990, and
y = the price of the house in thousands of dollars.

(a) The following two points are on the line.
(0, 140) and (8, 207)

$y = mx + b$ Linear equation
$140 = m(0) + b$ When $x = 0$, $y = 140$

$$m = \frac{y_2 - y_1}{x_2 - x_1} = \frac{207 - 140}{8 - 0} = \frac{67}{8} = 8.375$$

$y = 8.375x + 140$ Answer

(b)

(c)

$y = 8.375(13) + 140$ $x = 13$ in the year 2003.

$= 248.875$ or $248,875.00   Answer

Word Problems • 93

2. Motion Problems

Distance = Rate $\times$ Time

$$d = r \cdot t \quad \Rightarrow \quad t = \frac{d}{r}$$

$$\Rightarrow \quad r = \frac{d}{t}$$

Average speed $= \dfrac{\textbf{Total distance}}{\textbf{Total time}}$

There are three types of motion problems :

1) **Motion in the same direction.**
2) **Motion in opposite directions.**
3) **Round trip.**

Each is solved using a chart, a sketch, and the formula.

Example 2 □   Motion in the same direction

Jason can run 8m/sec and Mary 7.5 m/sec. On a 200 meter race track, how many meters will Mary have left to run after Jason completes running?

Solution □

Let x = the distance Mary has run when Jason completes the track.

	Rate	Time	Distance
Jason	8	200 / 8	200
Mary	7.5	x / 7.5	x

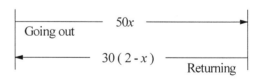

At the moment Jason finishes running, his time equals Mary's time for distance x.

$$\frac{200}{8} = \frac{x}{7.5}$$

$8x = 7.5 \times 200$	Cross product
$x = 187.5$	Simplify.

The distance left $= 200 - 187.5$
$ = 12.5$ meters   Answer

Example 3 □   Round trip

Carl drove from his home to the beach at a speed of 50 mph and returned home along the same route at a speed of 30 mph. If his total driving time for the trip was 2 hours, how many minutes did it take him to drive from his home to the beach?

Solution □

Let x = the time in hours it took for Carl to drive to the beach.
Then $2 - x$ = the time spent for the return trip.

	Rate	Time	Distance
Going out	50	x	$50x$
Returning	30	$2 - x$	$30 (2 - x)$

$50x = 30(2 - x)$	The distance out is the same as the distance back.
$50x = 60 - 30x$	Distributive property
$80x = 60$	Add $30x$ on both sides.
$x = \dfrac{60}{80} = \dfrac{3}{4}$ hour	
or 45 minutes Answer	

3. Mixture Problems

1) Mixture of two different brands

Cost of one brand = Number of units × Price

Cost of mixture = Cost of brand A + Cost of brand B

2) Mixture of two different solutions

Amount of acid
= Amount of solution × Percentage of acid

Percentage of solution
$$= \frac{\text{Amount of acid}}{\text{Total amount of solution}}$$

4. Cost, Profit, and Value Problems

Total value = number of items × value per item

Profit = Selling cost − Buying cost

5. Work Problems

Work rate × Time = Work done

The part of a job that can be completed in one unit of time is called the work rate. The fractional parts of a job must have a sum of 1.

6. Age Problems

To represent an age x years ago, subtract x from present age.

To represent an age x years from now, add x to the present age.

Example 4 □   Mixture of two different brands

In a store raisins sell for $3.00 per pound and nuts sell for $4.50 per pound. How many pounds of each should be mixed together to obtain 12 pounds of a mixture worth $4.00 per pound?

Solution □

Let x = number of pounds of raisins.
Then $12 - x$ = number of pounds of nuts.

	Pounds	Price	Cost
Raisins	x	3.00	$3x$
Nuts	$12 - x$	4.50	$4.5(12-x)$
Mixture	12	4.00	48

Cost of raisins + cost of nuts = cost of mixture
$$3x + 4.5(12 - x) = 48$$
$$\Rightarrow \ x = 4$$
4 lbs of raisins and 8 lbs of nuts should be mixed together.   Answer

---

Example 5 □   Mixture of two different solutions

A chemist has one solution that is 40% acid and another solution that is 30% acid. How many liters of each solution must be added to produce 40 liters of a solution that is 36% acid?

Solution □
Let x = # of liters of 40% acid solution to be added.
Then $40 - x$ = # of liters of 30% acid solution to be added.

	Amount of solution	Acid Percentage	Total amount of acid
Solution A	x	0.4	$0.4x$
Solution B	$40 - x$	0.3	$0.3(40-x)$
Mixture	40	0.36	14.4

Amount of acid in solution A + Amount of acid in solution B = Amount of acid in the mixture

$$0.4x + 0.3(40 - x) = 0.36 \times 40$$
$$\Rightarrow \ x = 24$$

24 liters of 40% solution and 16 liters of 30% solution should be added.   Answer

Example 6 □   Cost and profit

At a music store, the owner purchased x compact discs for \$6.50 each, and he sold all but 19 of them for \$12.00 each. If he made a profit of \$564.00 from the compact discs, what is the value of x ?

Solution □

Selling cost $= (x - 19) \times 12$
Buying cost $= 6.5x$

Profit = Selling cost − Buying cost

$$564 = (x - 19) \times 12 - 6.5x$$
$$= 12x - 228 - 6.5x$$
$$= 5.5x - 228$$
$$792 = 5.5x$$
$$x = 144 \qquad \text{Answer}$$

Example 7 □   Work problem

Mike can finish a certain job in 6 days and Bob can do it in 4 days. How long will it take them to finish the job if they work together?

Solution □

Mike's work rate $= \dfrac{1}{6}$,   Bob's work rate $= \dfrac{1}{4}$.

Let x = number of days required to finish the job.

	Work rate	Time	Amount of work done
Mike	1 / 6	x	$x / 6$
Bob	1 / 4	x	$x / 4$

$\dfrac{1}{6}x + \dfrac{1}{4}x = 1$ Part of job Mike does plus part of job Bob does equals the whole job.

$12\left(\dfrac{1}{6}x + \dfrac{1}{4}x\right) = 12(1)$ Multiply 12 on both sides.

$\qquad 2x + 3x = 12$ Simplify.
$\qquad\qquad 5x = 12$ Simplify.
$\qquad\qquad x = \dfrac{12}{5}$ days   Answer

Example 8 □   Age problem

Jose is 8 and his mother is 33. How long will it be before he is half as old as she?

Solution □

	Age now	Age x years later
Jose	8	$8 + x$
Mother	33	$33 + x$

x years later Jose will be half as old as his mother.

$$8 + x = \frac{1}{2}(33 + x)$$
$$2(8 + x) = 33 + x$$
$$16 + 2x = 33 + x$$
$$x = 17 \text{ years} \qquad\qquad \text{Answer}$$

Questions 1-2 refer to the following information.

The cost of a long distance call is $1.25 for the first three minutes and $.15 for each additional minute.

1. Which of the following equations gives the total cost of a phone call, y, in terms of the number of minutes, x?

(A) $y = 0.15x + 1.25$

(B) $y = 1.25x + 0.15$

(C) $y = 0.15(x - 3) + 1.25$

(D) $y = 1.25(x - 3) + 0.15$

(E) $y = 0.15x + (3 - 1.25)$

2. If an x minute phone call costs $4.70, what is the value of x?

(A) 14

(B) 16

(C) 18

(D) 20

(E) 26

3. To join Ace Gym one must pay a $180 membership fee plus dues of $35 per month. To join Best Gym one must pay a $300 membership fee plus dues of $23 per month. After how many months would the total cost of joining either gym be the same?

(A) 6

(B) 8

(C) 9

(D) 10

(E) 12

4. The Apex Car Rental company charges a flat fee of $20.00 per day plus $0.45 per mile to rent a car. The Jason Car Rental company charges a flat fee of $32.00 per day plus $0.29 per mile to rent a car. If a car is rented for three days, at how many miles would the rental charges of the two companies be the same?

(A) 75

(B) 120

(C) 175

(D) 225

(E) 250

5. Manny bought x candies at a price of 70 cents each. If he sold all but k candies at a price of $1.25, and made a profit of p dollars, which of the following represents p in terms of x and k?
(Profit = selling price – buying cost)

(A) $p = 0.55x - 1.25k$

(B) $p = 1.25x - 1.25k$

(C) $p = 1.25x - 0.7k$

(D) $p = 55x - 12.5k$

(E) $p = 1.25x - 70k$

6. At a bagel shop the first 6 bagels purchased cost 55 cents apiece, and additional bagels cost c cents apiece. If a customer paid $5.70 for 12 bagels, what is the value of c?

(A) 25

(B) 30

(C) 35

(D) 40

(E) 45

7. Two motorcycles leave the same place at the same time for a weekend trip to the same destination. Motorcycle *A* travels at 64 mph and motorcycle *B* travels at 68 mph for the entire trip. If motorcycle *A* arrived at the destination 15 minutes after motorcycle *B*, how many miles long is the trip?

(A) 256

(B) 272

(C) 280

(D) 292

(E) 308

8. Mike can average 12 meters per second on his bike and Maria can average 10.5 meters per second on her bike. If they race on a 1500-meter course, how many meters will Maria have left to bike after Mike completes the course?

(A) 125

(B) 187.5

(C) 250

(D) 312.5

(E) 375

9. A car averages 18 miles per gallon of gas in city driving and 27 miles per gallon of gas in highway driving. What is the total number of gallons of gas needed to drive 6*x* miles in the city and 18*x* miles on the highway?

(A) *x*

(B) 2*x*

(C) 3*x*

(D) 3.5*x*

(E) 4.5*x*

10. Two trains travel in opposite directions from the same station. The first train travels 20 miles an hour faster than the second, but it starts 1 hour and 30 minutes after the second train. Five hours after the second train starts, the trains are 512 miles apart. What is the speed of the first train in miles per hour?

(A) 48

(B) 52

(C) 64

(D) 68

(E) 72

11. At a museum, Yumiko bought 3 student tickets and 2 adult tickets for $29.00. At the same museum Sandy bought 5 student tickets and 4 adult tickets for $54.00. How much did Yumiko spend just for student tickets?

(A) $4.00

(B) $8.50

(C) $12.00

(D) $15.0

(E) $17.40

12. Victor invests part of his $5000 in a savings account that pays 6.5% annual simple interest, and the rest in bonds that pay 11% annual simple interest. If Victor's total income in one year from these investments is $460, how much money is invested in bonds?

(A) 1500

(B) 2500

(C) 3000

(D) 3500

(E) 4000

13. Gary can load the truck in 3 hours. If Gary and his brother work together, they can load the truck in 2 hours. How long would it take his brother alone to load the truck?

    (A) 1.5

    (B) 3

    (C) 4.5

    (D) 6

    (E) 7.5

14. At a music shop a customer bought 10 cassettes and CDs at $9.00 per cassette and $14.00 per CD. If x is the number of CDs and the customer paid d dollars for the cassettes and CDs, which of the following represents x in terms of d?

    (A) $x = d - 90$

    (B) $x = d - 5$

    (C) $x = 0.2d + 5$

    (D) $x = 0.2d - 18$

    (E) $x = 0.2d + 18$

15. Water flows into an empty 50-gallon tank through a fill pipe at the rate of 4 gallons per minute, and flows out of the tank through a drain pipe at the rate of x gallons per minute. If both pipes were opened at the same time and the empty tank filled in exactly 20 minutes, what is the value of x?

    (A) 1

    (B) 1.5

    (C) 2

    (D) 2.5

    (E) 3

16. Soomi's mother was 26 years old when Soomi was born. Seven years ago she was 3 times Soomi's age. What is the sum of their ages now?

    (A) 46

    (B) 52

    (C) 56

    (D) 62

    (E) 66

17. A chemist has 18 liters of a solution that is 40% acid. She wants to add x liters of a solution that is 25% acid, to make a solution that is 30% acid. Which of the following equations could she use in order to find the value of x?

    (A) $\dfrac{0.4x + 0.25x}{18 + x} = 0.3$

    (B) $\dfrac{7.2 + 0.25x}{18 + x} = 0.3$

    (C) $\dfrac{7.2 + 0.25x}{18} = 0.3$

    (D) $\dfrac{18 + 0.25x}{18 + x} = 0.3$

    (E) $\dfrac{0.4x + 0.25x}{18 + 7.2} = 0.3$

1. Two groups of people began a 9-mile hike near the lake at the same time. When group *A* finished the hike, group *B* was 1.4 miles behind them. If it took 4 hours for group *A* to finish the hike, what was the difference in the groups' hiking rates, in miles per hour, for those 4 hours?

2. A car travels the first 42 miles of a trip at a speed of 56 miles per hour. How fast must the car travel for the remaining 51 miles of the trip for the total travel time to be 1 hour 30 minutes?

3. A large container can be filled with four times as much water as a medium size container, or nine times as much as a small size container. If *x* small containers and *x* large containers are needed to fill a water tank that could be filled with 120 medium size containers, what is the value of *x*?

4. Mickey can finish a job in 15 hours and Minnie can do the same job in 12 hours. What part of the job can they finish by working together for 3 hours?

5. A car travels for 30 minutes at an average speed of 40 miles per hour. If the car travels *x* more miles at an average speed of 50 miles per hour, and the overall average speed is 45 miles per hour, what is the value of *x*?

6. Jean has $8 more than Sara. Together Jean and Sara have $55 more than Mike, who has half as much money as Jean. How much money does Sara have?

Answer Key

<u>Multiple Choice Questions</u>

1. C	2. E	3. D	4. D	5. A
6. D	7. B	8. B	9. A	10. E
11. C	12. C	13. D	14. D	15. B
16. E	17. B			

<u>Grid-In Questions</u>

1. 0.35	2. 68	3. 27	4. 9/20	5. 25
6. 34				

Answers and Explanations

<u>Multiple Choice Questions</u>

1. C

If the total number of minutes equals x, then $(x-3)$ is the number of additional minutes.

total cost of a phone call $\quad$ cost for the first 3 minutes $\quad$ cost for each additional minute $\quad$ number of additional minutes

$$y = 1.25 + 0.15 \cdot (x-3)$$

2. E

$4.70 = 0.15(x-3)+1.25$
$4.70 = 0.15x - 0.45 + 1.25$
$4.70 = 0.15x + 0.8$
$3.9 = 0.15x$
$x = 26$

3. D

Let x = the number of months after which the cost of membership at the two gyms is the same.

$35x + 180 = 23x + 300$
$12x = 120$
$x = 10$

4. D

Let x = the number of miles for which the two companies' rental charges are the same.

$$\underbrace{20 \times 3 + 0.45x}_{\substack{\text{Apex Car Rental's} \\ \text{rental charge for 3 days}}} = \underbrace{32 \times 3 + 0.29x}_{\substack{\text{Jason Car Rental's} \\ \text{rental charge for 3 days}}}$$

$\Rightarrow 60 + 0.45x = 96 + 0.29x$
$\Rightarrow 0.16x = 36 \Rightarrow x = 225$

5. A

Selling price $= 1.25(x-k)$
Buying cost $= 0.7x$

Profit = selling price − buying cost
$p = 1.25(x-k) - 0.7x$
$p = 1.25x - 1.25k - 0.7x$
$p = 0.55x - 1.25k$

6. D

$$\underbrace{6}_{\text{1st 6 bagels}} \times \underbrace{0.55}_{\substack{\text{price of} \\ \text{1st 6 bagels}}} + \underbrace{6c}_{\substack{\text{additional 6 bagels} \\ \text{costs } c \text{ cents each}}} = \underbrace{5.70}_{\text{total price}}$$

$3.3 + 6c = 5.7$
$\Rightarrow c = 0.4 \Rightarrow 40$ cents

7. B

distance = rate × time
$\quad d = r \cdot t$

Let x = motorcycle A's time, then
$x - \frac{1}{4}$ = motorcycle B's time (15min. = $\frac{1}{4}$ hr.)

	rate	× time	= distance
motorcycle A	64	x	$64x$
motorcycle B	68	$(x-\frac{1}{4})$	$68(x-\frac{1}{4})$

Both motorcycles traveled the same distance.

$64x = 68(x-\frac{1}{4}) \Rightarrow 64x = 68x - 17$

$$\Rightarrow x = \frac{17}{4}$$

The distance traveled $= 64x = 64(\frac{17}{4}) = 272$.

8. B

The time it took Mike to complete the race equals $\frac{1500 \text{ meters}}{12 \text{ meters/sec}}$, or 125 seconds.

The distance Maria had traveled when Mike completed the course equals 10.5×125, or 1312.5 meters.

The distance left to bike $= 1500 - 1312.5 = 187.5$.

9. A

The number of gallons of gas needed to drive $6x$ miles in the city $= \frac{6x}{18} = \frac{1}{3}x$.

The number of gallons of gas needed to drive $18x$ miles on the highway $= \frac{18x}{27} = \frac{2}{3}x$.

Total $= \frac{1}{3}x + \frac{2}{3}x = x$.

10. E

Let $x = $ speed of the second train, then $x + 20 = $ speed of the first train.

	rate	$\times$ time	$=$ distance
first train	$x + 20$	$(5 - 1.5)$	$3.5\,(x + 20)$
second train	x	5	$5x$

$\xleftarrow{\quad 5x \quad} \bullet \xrightarrow{\quad 3.5(x+20) \quad}$

512 miles

$3.5(x + 20) + 5x = 512$
$\Rightarrow 8.5x + 70 = 512 \Rightarrow x = 52$
Speed of the first train $= 52 + 20 = 72$

11. C

Let $x = $ the price of a student ticket.
Let $y = $ the price of an adult ticket.

$3x + 2y = 29$
$5x + 4y = 54$

Multiply the first equation by -2, then add to the second equation.

$\begin{array}{l} (-2)3x + (-2)2y = (-2)29 \\ + \underline{\quad 5x + \quad 4y = 54 \quad} \\ \quad -1x \qquad = -4 \end{array} \Bigg\} \Rightarrow x = 4$

Yumiko bought 3 student tickets. $3 \times \$4.00 = \$12.00$

12. C

Let $x = $ the amount invested in bonds, then $(5000 - x) = $ the amount invested in savings.

$0.11x + 0.065(5000 - x) = 460$
$\Rightarrow 0.11x + 325 - 0.065x = 460$
$\Rightarrow 0.045x + 325 = 460$
$\Rightarrow 0.045x = 135 \Rightarrow x = 3000$

13. D

Gary's work rate $= \frac{1}{3}$.

Let his brother's work rate $= \frac{1}{x}$.

	workrate $\times$	time $=$	amount of work done
Gary	$\frac{1}{3}$	2	$2(\frac{1}{3})$
His brother	$\frac{1}{x}$	2	$2(\frac{1}{x})$

$\underbrace{2(\frac{1}{3})}_{\substack{\text{amount of work done} \\ \text{by Gary in 2 hours}}} + \underbrace{2(\frac{1}{x})}_{\substack{\text{amount of work done} \\ \text{by his brother in 2 hours}}} = \underbrace{1}_{\substack{\text{amount of work} \\ \text{to finish job}}}$

$3x(\frac{2}{3}) + 3x(\frac{2}{x}) = 3x \cdot 1$ (Multiply by $3x$ on both sides.)
$2x + 6 = 3x \Rightarrow x = 6$

14. D

If x is the number of CDs sold, then $10 - x$ is the number of cassettes sold.

$$\underbrace{14x}_{\substack{x \text{ CDs} \\ \text{for \$14 each}}} + \underbrace{9(10 - x)}_{\substack{(10-x) \text{ cassettes} \\ \text{for \$9 each}}} = \underbrace{d}_{\text{total}}$$

$\Rightarrow \ 14x + 90 - 9x = d \ \Rightarrow \ 5x + 90 = d$

$\Rightarrow \ 5x = d - 90 \ \Rightarrow \ x = \dfrac{1}{5}(d - 90)$

$\Rightarrow \ x = \dfrac{1}{5}d - 18 \ \Rightarrow \ x = 0.2d - 18$

15. B

	rate	×	time	=	amount
flow in	4		20		4×20
flow out	x		20		$20x$

$$\underbrace{4 \times 20}_{\substack{\text{the total number} \\ \text{of gallons of water} \\ \text{which flows in in} \\ \text{20 minutes}}} - \underbrace{20x}_{\substack{\text{the total number} \\ \text{of gallons of water} \\ \text{which flows out in} \\ \text{20 minutes}}} = \underbrace{50}_{\substack{\text{the total number} \\ \text{of gallons of water} \\ \text{in the tank after 20} \\ \text{minutes}}}$$

$80 - 20x = 50 \ \Rightarrow \ -20x = -30$
$\Rightarrow \ x = 1.5$

16. E

Let x = Soomi's age now, then
$x + 26$ = her mother's age now.

	age now	age 7 years ago
Soomi	x	$x - 7$
Her mother	$x + 26$	$(x + 26) - 7$

Seven years ago Soomi's mother was 3 times Soomi's age.
$\Rightarrow \ x + 19 = 3(x - 7)$
$\Rightarrow \ x + 19 = 3x - 21 \ \Rightarrow \ 40 = 2x$
$\Rightarrow \ x = 20$
$\Rightarrow$ Mother's age $= 20 + 26 = 46$

$20 + 46 = 66$

17. B

The amount of acid in 18 liters of solution
$= 18 \times 0.4 = 7.2$

The amount of acid in x liters of solution
$= x \times 0.25 = 0.25x$

Acid percentage of solution

$= \dfrac{\text{Amount of acid}}{\text{Total amount of solution}}$

$$\underbrace{0.3}_{\substack{\text{percentage of} \\ \text{acid in solution}}} = \dfrac{\underbrace{7.2}_{\substack{\text{amount of acid} \\ \text{in 18 L solution}}} + \underbrace{0.25x}_{\substack{\text{amount of acid} \\ \text{in } x \text{ L solution}}}}{\underbrace{18 + x}_{\text{total amount of solution}}}$$

Grid-In Questions

1. 0.35 or $\dfrac{7}{20}$

Rate of group $A = \dfrac{9 \text{ miles}}{4 \text{ hours}}$

The distance traveled by group B in 4 hours
$= 9 - 1.4 = 7.6 \text{ miles}$.

Rate of group $B = \dfrac{7.6 \text{ miles}}{4 \text{ hours}}$

The difference in their rates in miles per hour
$= \dfrac{9}{4} - \dfrac{7.6}{4} = \dfrac{1.4}{4} = 0.35$

2. 68

$d = r \cdot t \ \Rightarrow \ t = \dfrac{d}{r}$

Let r = speed during the second part of the trip.

$$1\frac{1}{2} = \frac{42}{56} + \frac{51}{r}$$

total time   time for the   time for the
1st part of trip   2nd part of trip

$$\Rightarrow \frac{3}{2} = \frac{3}{4} + \frac{51}{r} \Rightarrow 4r(\frac{3}{2}) = 4r(\frac{3}{4} + \frac{51}{r})$$
$$\Rightarrow 6r = 3r + 204 \Rightarrow 3r = 204 \Rightarrow r = 68$$

3. 27

Let m = the capacity of the medium container, then
   $4m$ = the capacity of the large container, and

$\frac{4m}{9}$ = the capacity of the small container.

$$x(\frac{4m}{9}) + x(4m) = 120(m)$$

amount of water in   amount of water in   amount of water in
x small containers x large containers   120 medium containers

$$m(\frac{4}{9}x + 4x) = 120\,m$$

$$4\frac{4}{9}x = 120 \Rightarrow \frac{40}{9}x = 120$$

$$\Rightarrow x = \frac{9}{40}(120) = 27$$

4. $\frac{9}{20}$

Mickey's work rate = $\frac{1}{15}$

Minnie's work rate = $\frac{1}{12}$

	work rate ×	time =	amount of work done
Mickey	$\frac{1}{15}$	3	$3(\frac{1}{15})$
Minnie	$\frac{1}{12}$	3	$3(\frac{1}{12})$

$$3(\frac{1}{15}) + 3(\frac{1}{12}) = \frac{1}{5} + \frac{1}{4}$$
$$= \frac{4}{20} + \frac{5}{20} = \frac{9}{20}$$

5. 25

$$\text{Average speed} = \frac{\text{total distance}}{\text{total time}}$$

$$45 = \frac{(\frac{1}{2} \times 40) + (x)}{\frac{1}{2} + \frac{x}{50}}$$

the distance traveled   the distance traveled
during the 1st part of trip   during the 2nd part of trip

the time for the   the time for the
1st part of trip   2nd part of trip

$$45 = \frac{20 + x}{\frac{1}{2} + \frac{x}{50}} \Rightarrow 45(\frac{1}{2} + \frac{x}{50}) = 20 + x$$

$$22.5 + 0.9x = 20 + x \Rightarrow 2.5 = 0.1x$$
$$\Rightarrow x = 25$$

6. 34

Let x = Sara's money, then
$x + 8$ = Jean's money, and
$\frac{1}{2}(x + 8)$ = Mike's money.

$$x + (x + 8) = \frac{1}{2}(x + 8) + 55$$

$$2x + 8 = \frac{1}{2}x + 4 + 55 \Rightarrow \frac{3}{2}x = 51$$

$$\Rightarrow x = \frac{2}{3} \times 51 = 34$$

10. Inequalities

Key Terms / Illustrations   Examples

1. Transitive Property of Inequality

For all real numbers a, b, and c:

If $a < b$ and $b < c$, then $a < c$.

2. Addition and Subtraction Properties of Inequality

For all real numbers a, b, and c:

If $a < b$,
then $a + c < b + c$ and
$a - c < b - c$

3. Multiplication Properties of Inequality

For all real numbers a, b, and c:

If $a < b$ and c is *positive*, then $ac < bc$

If $a < b$ and c is *negative*, then $ac > bc$

☑ When you <u>multiply</u> or <u>divide</u> each side of an inequality <u>by a negative number</u>, you must change the direction of the inequality symbol.

4. For all *positive* numbers a, b, and c :

If $a \leq b \leq c$,
then $\dfrac{1}{c} \leq \dfrac{1}{b} \leq \dfrac{1}{a}$

5. For all real numbers m, M, n, and N :

If $m \leq x \leq M$, and $n \leq y \leq N$, then

$$\underset{\substack{\text{minimum} \\ \text{value of } x}}{m} - \underset{\substack{\text{maximum} \\ \text{value of } y}}{N} \leq x - y \leq \underset{\substack{\text{maximum} \\ \text{value of } x}}{M} - \underset{\substack{\text{minimum} \\ \text{value of } y}}{n}$$

Example 1 □   Transitive property of inequality

If $c < b$, $c > a$, $d < b$, and $a > e$, which of the five variables in the inequalities is greatest?

Solution □

$$\left. \begin{cases} c < b \\ c > a \Leftrightarrow a < c \\ a > e \Leftrightarrow e < a \end{cases} \right\} \Rightarrow e < a < c < b \quad \text{and} \quad d < b$$

Therefore b is greatest.   Answer

Example 2 □   Solving inequalities

If $9 - 2x > 1 - x$ and $3 - x < -3.5$, what is the integer value of x?

Solution □

$$9 - 2x > 1 - x$$

$9 - 9 - 2x > 1 - 9 - x$	Subtract 9 from both
$-2x > -8 - x$	sides and simplify.
$-2x + x > -8 - x + x$	Add x to both sides and
$-x > -8$	simplify.
$(-1)(-x) < (-1)(-8)$	Multiply both sides by -1
	& reverse the inequality.
$x < 8$	Simplify.

$3 - x < -3.5$	
$3 - 3 - x < -3.5 - 3$	Subtract 3 from both
$-x < -6.5$	sides and simplify.
$(-1)(-x) > (-1)(-6.5)$	Multiply both sides by -1
$x > 6.5$	& reverse the inequality.

Since x is an integer and $6.5 < x < 8$, x equals 7.   Answer

6. Conjunction and Disjunction

1) A sentence formed by joining two sentences with the word ***and*** is called a **conjunction.**

☑ If $x > 2$ ***and*** $x < 7$, the conjunction is true for all values of x between 2 and 7. It is usually written as $2 < x < 7$.

2) A sentence formed by joining two sentences with the word ***or*** is called a **disjunction.**

☑ If $x < 2$ ***or*** $x > 7$, the disjunction is true for all values of x less than 2 or greater than 7.

7. Quadratic Inequalities

1) If $(x+1)(x-1) \leq 0$, then the solution set is $\{x \mid -1 \leq x \leq 1\}$.

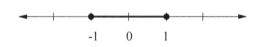

2) If $(x+1)(x-1) \geq 0$, then the solution set is $\{x \mid x \leq -1 \text{ or } x \geq 1\}$.

Example 3 □ Solving inequalities

If $4x - 3$ is greater than 12 and less than 120, how many integer values of x are there?

Solution □

$$12 < 4x - 3 < 120$$
$$15 < 4x < 123 \qquad \text{Add 3 to each expression}$$
$$3.75 < x < 30.75 \qquad \text{Divide each expression by 4.}$$

The integer values of x are 4, 5, 6, . . . 29, 30.
$30 - 4 = 26$.
Add 1 to 26.

There are 27 integers.   Answer

· ·

Example 4 □ Finding possible maximum value(s)

If $11 \leq x \leq 15$ and $3 \leq y \leq 8$, what is the greatest possible value of $\dfrac{1}{x-y}$?

Solution □

$$11 - 8 \leq x - y \leq 15 - 3$$
$$3 \leq x - y \leq 12$$
$$\Rightarrow \frac{1}{12} \leq \frac{1}{x-y} \leq \frac{1}{3}$$

The greatest value of $\dfrac{1}{x-y}$ is $\dfrac{1}{3}$.   Answer

8. Absolute Value Inequalities

1) The inequality $|x| \le 1$ is equivalent to $-1 \le x \le 1$.

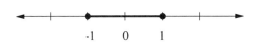

2) The inequality $|x| \ge 1$ is equivalent to $x \le -1$ or $x \ge 1$.

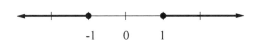

9. If $0 < x < 1$, then $x^3 < x^2 < x$.

If $-1 < x < 0$, then $x < x^3 < x^2$.

Example 5 □ **Solving a quadratic inequality**

Find and graph the solution set of $x^2 + 2x < 3$.

Solution □

$x^2 + 2x < 3$

$x^2 + 2x - 3 < 0$ Rewrite the inequality so that 0 is on the right side.

$(x+3)(x-1) < 0$ Factor completely.

The solution set is $\{x \mid -3 < x < 1\}$.   Answer

Example 6 □ **Solving an absolute value inequality**

Solve $|x-2| > 4$.

Solution □

$|x-2| > 4$

$\Rightarrow x-2 < -4$ or $x-2 > 4$

$\Rightarrow x < -2$ or $x > 6$ Answer

The product of 7 and a number n is no less than 91.

1. Which of the following inequalities represents the statement above?

   (A) $7n < 91$

   (B) $7n \le 91$

   (C) $7n \ge 91$

   (D) $7 + n < 91$

   (E) $7 + n \ge 91$

2. At a county fair the admission is $5.00 and each ride costs $0.60. If you go to the fair with $10.00, what is the maximum number of rides you can go on?

   (A) 6

   (B) 8

   (C) 10

   (D) 12

   (E) 14

3. If $ab^2c^3 < 0$, which of the following products must be negative?

   (A) ab

   (B) a^2c

   (C) ac^2

   (D) ab^2

   (E) a^3c

4. The sum of two positive integers is less than 25, and the product of the two integers is greater than 140. Which of the following could be one of the integers?

   (A) 7

   (B) 9

   (C) 11

   (D) 15

   (E) 18

5. If $x < 5$, which of the following is not possible?

   (A) $x^2 < 25$

   (B) $25 < x^2$

   (C) $x^2 = 25$

   (D) $-x < -5$

   (E) $0 < -x$

6. Which of the following is the graph of $|x + 2| \le 3$?

   (A)

   (B)

   (C)

   (D)

   (E)

7. Kay lives eight miles from the library and her friend lives five miles from Kay's house. Which of the following is not a possible distance between the library and Kay's friend's house?

   (A) 3

   (B) 5

   (C) 8

   (D) 12

   (E) 14

8. If $x \le 10$ and $y \ge -10$, then which of the following must be true?

   (A) $x + y \le 0$

   (B) $x - y \le 20$

   (C) $x + y \ge 20$

   (D) $x - y \ge 20$

   (E) $x + y \ge 0$

9. For which of the following ordered pairs (x, y) is $y > x - 4$ and $x + y < 5$?

   (A) $(0, 2)$

   (B) $(0, -5)$

   (C) $(5, 3)$

   (D) $(4, -2)$

   (E) $(3, 3)$

10. If $b = \dfrac{2a - 1}{a}$ and $a > 1$, then which of the following could be equal to b?

    (A) $\dfrac{1}{5}$

    (B) $\dfrac{3}{5}$

    (C) $\dfrac{8}{5}$

    (D) $\dfrac{16}{5}$

    (E) $\dfrac{27}{5}$

11. If x is an integer and $x^2 < 50$, what is the greatest possible value of $7 - x$?

    (A) 0

    (B) 2

    (C) 6

    (D) 7

    (E) 14

12. If $-1 < ab < 0$, then which of the following could be true?

    (A) $a > 1$ and $b < -1$

    (B) $a < -1$ and $b > 1$

    (C) $a < 0$ and $b < 0$

    (D) $a < 1$ and $b > -1$

    (E) $a < -1$ and $b < -1$

13. Which of the following is the graph of $\frac{1}{3}x - 1 > 0$

   or $\frac{1}{2}x - 1 \le -3$?

   (A)

   (B)

   (C)

   (D)

   (E)

15. Which of the following is equivalent to $x^2 < -2x$?

   (A) $x < 0$

   (B) $x < 2$

   (C) $x < -2$ or $0 < x$

   (D) $-2 < x < 0$

   (E) $-2 < x < -1$

16. Which of the following is equivalent to $x^2 - 1 \ge 8$?

   (A) $x \ge 3$

   (B) $x \ge 9$

   (C) $x \ge -3$ or $x \le 3$

   (D) $-3 \le x \le 3$

   (E) $x \le -3$ or $x \ge 3$

14. If a and b are numbers on the number line above, which of the following must be true?

   I. $\dfrac{b}{a} < 0$

   II. $\dfrac{1}{a} < -1$

   III. $b - a > 0$

   (A) I only

   (B) II only

   (C) I and II only

   (D) I and III only

   (E) I, II, and III

17. If $-5 \le a \le 1$ and $-4 \le b \le -1$, then what is the minimum value of $\dfrac{a}{b}$?

   (A) -5

   (B) -1

   (C) $-\dfrac{1}{4}$

   (D) 0

   (E) $\dfrac{5}{4}$

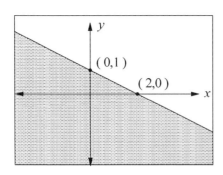

18. Which of the following inequalities represents the graph above?

   (A) $x + 2y \geq 2$

   (B) $x - 2y \leq 2$

   (C) $x - 2y \geq 2$

   (D) $x + 2y \leq 2$

   (E) $x + y \geq 1$

19. If $x < -3$ and $y + 10 = 2x$, which of the following must be true?

   (A) $x + 3 > 0$

   (B) $y + 10 > 0$

   (C) $x + y > 0$

   (D) $x < y$

   (E) $y < -16$

20. Which of the following is the graph of
$$\frac{x^2 - 4}{x} \leq 0 ?$$

   (A)

   (B)

   (C)

   (D)

   (E)

21. Which of the following is the solution set for
$$\left| -3x + 7 \right| - 2 > 6 ?$$

   (A) $\{x : x > -\frac{1}{3}\}$

   (B) $\{x : x < -\frac{1}{3} \text{ or } x > 5\}$

   (C) $\{x : x < -5 \text{ or } x > \frac{1}{3}\}$

   (D) $\{x : -\frac{1}{3} < x < 5\}$

   (E) $\{x : -5 < x < \frac{1}{3}\}$

1. For what integer value of x is $4x - 2 > 17$ and $3x + 5 < 24$?

2. If $a = 10$ and $b = 20$, what is one possible value of x for which $\frac{1}{b} < x < \frac{1}{a}$?

3. If x is a positive integer and $1.2 < \frac{x + 0.5}{x - 0.5} < 1.4$, what is one possible value of x?

4. If $-2 < n < -1$, what is the value of $(7 + \frac{1}{2}n)$ rounded to the nearest whole number?

5. If $\frac{1}{4}x - 1 \le -x + 5$, what is the greatest possible value of x?

6. The number of students in a geometry class is four-fifths of the number of students in a Spanish class. The total number of students in both classes is not more than 54. What is the greatest possible number of students in the Spanish class?

7. At a sporting goods store, Kay paid $86.00 for a pair of shoes and a pair of pants. The pants cost less than two-thirds of what the shoes cost. What is the minimum price of the shoes to the nearest dollar?

8. If $\left|\frac{3}{4}x - 2\right| < 1$ and x is an integer, what is one possible value of x?

Answer Key

<u>Multiple Choice Questions</u>

1. C	2. B	3. E	4. C	5. D
6. C	7. E	8. B	9. A	10. C
11. E	12. D	13. B	14. D	15. D
16. E	17. B	18. D	19. E	20. C
21. B				

<u>Grid-In Questions</u>

1. 5 or 6 2. $\dfrac{1}{20} < x < \dfrac{1}{10}$ 3. $3 < x < 5.5$ 4. 6
5. 4.8 6. 30 7. 52 8. 2 or 3

Answers and Explanations

<u>Multiple Choice Questions</u>

1. C

$$\underbrace{7 \cdot n}_{\substack{\text{the product of 7} \\ \text{and a number } n}} \quad \underbrace{\geqq}_{\text{no less than}} \quad 91$$

"No less than" is the same as "greater than or equal to"

2. B

Let x = the number of rides you can go on, then $0.6x$ = the cost of the rides.

$$\underbrace{5}_{\text{admission}} \quad \underbrace{+\ 0.6x}_{\substack{\text{plus the cost} \\ \text{for the rides}}} \quad \underbrace{\leqq}_{\substack{\text{cannot be} \\ \text{more than}}} \quad \underbrace{10}_{\text{10 dollars}}$$

$\Rightarrow \ 0.6x \leq 5 \ \Rightarrow \ \dfrac{0.6}{0.6}x \leq \dfrac{5}{0.6}$

$\Rightarrow \ x \leq \dfrac{5}{0.6} \approx 8.3$

Therefore the maximum number of rides is 8.

3. E

Given $ab^2c^3 = (ac)b^2c^2 < 0$.

Since b^2c^2 cannot be negative, $a \cdot c$ is negative. Try each of the answer choices.

Choice (E): $a^3c = \underbrace{a^2}_{\text{positive}} \cdot \underbrace{(ac)}_{\text{negative}} < 0$, which is negative.

4. C

Let the two integers be x and y, and try each of the answer choices to find out possible values of x and y.

Make a table of values.

x	y	sum	product	
7	17	24	119	
9	15	24	135	
11	13	24	143	← the sum is no greater than 24 and the product is more than 140
15	9	24	135	
18	6	24	108	

Therefore the integer could be 11 or 13.

5. D

Given: $x < 5$.

Choice (A): If $x = 4$, then $x^2 < 25$. It is possible.

Choice (B): If $x = -6$, then $25 < x^2$. It is possible.

Choice (C): If $x = -5$, then, $x^2 = 25$. It is possible.

Choice (D): Given $x < 5$, multiply by -1 on both sides. Then, $-x > -5$. (When you multiply both sides by a negative number, you reverse the inequality.) It is <u>not possible</u>.

Choice (E): If $x = -1$, then $-x = 1$, which is greater than zero. It is possible.

6. C

$$|x+2| \le 3 \iff$$

$-3 \le x+2 \le 3$ The inequality is equivalent to $|x+2| \le 3$.

$-5 \le x \le 1$ Subtract 2 from each side.

The graph is

     -5   1

7. E

Kay's home

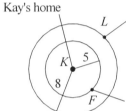

L Library is somewhere on this circle.

Friend's home is somewhere on this circle.

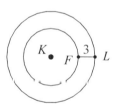

Smallest distance is 8-5, or 3 miles.

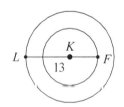

Greatest distance is 8+5, or 13 miles.

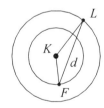

Any distance between 3 and 13 is possible.

8. B

$y \ge -10$ Given inequality

$(-1)y \le (-1)(-10)$ Multiply both sides by -1 and reverse the inequality.

$-y \le 10$ Simplify.

$\underline{+\ |x \le 10}$ Given inequality

$-y + x \le 10 + 10$ Add the two inequalities.

$x - y \le 20$ Simplify.

9. A

Plug the values given for each answer choice into the equations.

$y > x - 4$ and $x + y < 5$

Choice (A) : (0, 2) $2 > 0 - 4$. True

                       $0 + 2 < 5$. True

Choice (B) : (0, –5) $-5 > 0 - 4$. Not true

                       $0 + (-5) < 5$. True

Choice (C) : (5, 3) $3 > 5 - 4$. True

                       $5 + 3 < 5$. Not true

Choice (D) : (4, –2) $-2 > 4 - 4$. Not true

                       $4 + (-2) < 5$. True

Choice (E) : (3, 3) $3 > 3 - 4$. True

                       $3 + 3 < 5$. Not true

10. C

Given: $b = \dfrac{2a-1}{a}$ and $a > 1$

Choice (A) : If $b = \dfrac{2a-1}{a} = \dfrac{1}{5}$,

$5(2a-1) = 1 \cdot a$ (Cross multiplication)

$10a - 5 = a \implies a = \dfrac{5}{9} < 1$. Not true, since $a > 1$.

Choice (B) : If $b = \dfrac{2a-1}{a} = \dfrac{3}{5}$, $5(2a-1) = 3a$

$\implies a = \dfrac{5}{7} < 1$. Not true, since $a > 1$.

Choice (C) : If $b = \dfrac{2a-1}{a} = \dfrac{8}{5}$, $5(2a-1) = 8a$

$\implies a = \dfrac{5}{2} > 1$. True, since $a > 1$.

11. E

$$x^2 < 50 \Rightarrow x^2 - 50 < 0$$
$$\Rightarrow (x+\sqrt{50})(x-\sqrt{50}) < 0$$
$$\Rightarrow -\sqrt{50} < x < \sqrt{50}$$

Since x is an integer, the minimum value of x is -7 and the maximum value of x is 7. The value of $(7-x)$ is at a maximum when x is -7.

$$7-(-7)=14$$

12. D

Choice (A) : If $a > 1$ and $b < -1$, then $ab < -1$.

Choice (B) : If $a < -1$ and $b > 1$, then $ab < -1$.

Choice (C) : If $a < 0$ and $b < 0$, then $ab > 0$.

Choice (D) : Since $a < 1$ and $b > -1$,

let $a = \frac{1}{2}$ and $b = -\frac{1}{2}$.

Then $ab = (\frac{1}{2})(-\frac{1}{2}) = -\frac{1}{4}$,

which is true.

13. B

$$\frac{1}{3}x - 1 > 0 \Rightarrow \frac{1}{3}x > 1 \Rightarrow x > 3$$
$$\frac{1}{2}x - 1 \le -3 \Rightarrow \frac{1}{2}x \le -2 \Rightarrow x \le -4$$

The graph is

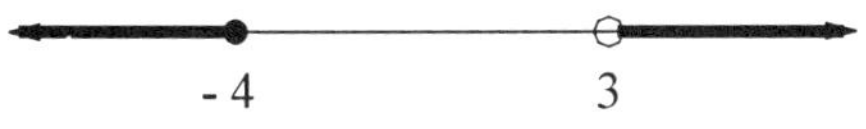

14. D

From the given number line, we can approximate the values of a and b. Plug in $-\frac{3}{2}$ as the value of a and $\frac{1}{3}$ as the value of b, for each of the given statements.

I. $\frac{b}{a} < 0 \Rightarrow \frac{1/3}{-3/2} = -\frac{2}{9} < 0$. True

II. $\frac{1}{a} < -1 \Rightarrow \frac{1}{-3/2} < -1 \Rightarrow -\frac{2}{3} < -1$. Not true

III. $b - a > 0 \Rightarrow \frac{1}{3} - (-\frac{3}{2}) > 0 \Rightarrow \frac{1}{3} + \frac{3}{2} > 0$. True

15. D

$$x^2 < -2x$$
$$\Rightarrow x^2 + 2x < 0$$
$$\Rightarrow x(x+2) < 0$$
$$\Rightarrow -2 < x < 0$$

16. E

$$x^2 - 1 \ge 8$$
$$\Rightarrow x^2 - 9 \ge 0$$
$$\Rightarrow (x+3)(x-3) \ge 0$$
$$\Rightarrow x \le -3 \text{ or } x \ge 3$$

17. B

Given $-5 \le a \le 1$ and $-4 \le b \le -1$. Since b is always negative, a has to be positive to get the minimum value of $\frac{a}{b}$.

Try some different values for a and b.

a	b	a/b	
0	-4	0	
1	-4	$-1/4$	
1	-1	-1	$\leftarrow \frac{a}{b}$ is at a minimum.

18. D

The equation of the line in slope-intercept form is $y = -\dfrac{1}{2}x + 1$. In standard form, the equation of the same line is $x + 2y = 2$.

Eliminate answer choices (B), (C), and (E) because their equations do not represent the line of the graph shown.

Let's use $(0,0)$ as a test point to see whether the point belongs to the graph of the inequality.

Choice (A): $x + 2y \geq 2$ $0 + 2(0) \geq 2$. Not true

Choice (D): $x + 2y \leq 2$ $0 + 2(0) \leq 2$. True

19. E

$y + 10 = 2x$	Given equation
$x = \dfrac{1}{2}y + 5$	Solve for x.
$x < -3$	Given inequality
$\dfrac{1}{2}y + 5 < -3$	Substitution
$\dfrac{1}{2}y < -8$	Subtract 5 from both sides.
$y < -16$	Multiply by 2 on both sides.

20. C

Given: $\dfrac{x^2 - 4}{x} \leq 0$.

$\dfrac{(x+2)(x-2)}{x} \leq 0$ Factor the numerator.

The three linear factors are zero for $x = 2$, $x = -2$, and $x = 0$. These three numbers divide the real-number line into four intervals.

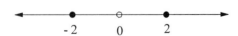

$$\begin{array}{ccc} \bullet & \circ & \bullet \\ -2 & 0 & 2 \end{array}$$

Test values on each part of the number line to check the result.

Try $x = -3$. $\dfrac{(-3)^2 - 4}{-3} \leq 0$ True

Try $x = -1$. $\dfrac{(-1)^2 - 4}{-1} \leq 0$ False

Try $x = 1$. $\dfrac{(1)^2 - 4}{1} \leq 0$ True

Try $x = 3$. $\dfrac{(3)^2 - 4}{3} \leq 0$ False

And $x = 0$ is the excluded value.

So, $x \leq -2$ or $0 < x \leq 2$.

21. B

$$|-3x + 7| - 2 > 6$$
$$|-3x + 7| - 2 + 2 > 6 + 2$$
$$|-3x + 7| > 8$$

$$-3x + 7 < -8 \qquad \text{or} \qquad -3x + 7 > 8$$
$$-3x + 7 - 7 < -8 - 7 \qquad \text{or} \qquad -3x + 7 - 7 > 8 - 7$$
$$-3x < -15 \qquad \text{or} \qquad -3x > 1$$

$$\dfrac{-3x}{-3} > \dfrac{-15}{-3} \qquad \text{or} \qquad \dfrac{-3x}{-3} < \dfrac{1}{-3}$$

(When you divide each side of an inequality by a negative number, you must change the direction of the inequality symbol.)

$$x > 5 \qquad \text{or} \qquad x < -\dfrac{1}{3}$$

Grid-In Questions

1. 5 or 6

$$4x - 2 > 17 \implies 4x > 19 \implies x > \frac{19}{4} = 4.75 \text{ and}$$

$$3x + 5 < 24 \implies 3x < 19 \implies x < \frac{19}{3} \approx 6.33$$

5 and 6 are the two integers greater than 4.75 and less than 6.33.

2. $\frac{1}{20} < x < \frac{1}{10}$

$a = 10$ and $b = 20$

$$\frac{1}{b} < x < \frac{1}{a} \implies \frac{1}{20} < x < \frac{1}{10} \text{ or } 0.05 < x < 0.1$$

Any fraction or decimal between $\frac{1}{20}$ and $\frac{1}{10}$ is a good answer.

3. $3 < x < 5.5$

Given: $1.2 < \frac{x + 0.5}{x - 0.5} < 1.4$. Multiply by $(x - 0.5)$ to each expression. The expression $(x - 0.5)$ is positive since x is a positive integer.

$$1.2(x - 0.5) < \frac{(x + 0.5)(x - 0.5)}{(x - 0.5)} < 1.4(x - 0.5)$$

$1.2x - 0.6 < x + 0.5 < 1.4x - 0.7$
To solve the above inequality we need to break it into two inequalities.

$1.2x - 0.6 < x + 0.5$ and $x + 0.5 < 1.4x - 0.7$

$1.2x - 0.6 < x + 0.5 \implies 0.2x < 1.1 \implies x < 5.5$

$x + 0.5 < 1.4x - 0.7 \implies 1.2 < 0.4x \implies 3 < x$

By combining the two inequalities we have $3 < x < 5.5$.

Any number greater than 3 and less than 5.5 is a good answer.

4. 6

$-2 < n < -1$	Given
$-1 < \frac{1}{2}n < -\frac{1}{2}$	Multiply by $\frac{1}{2}$ on each side.
$7 - 1 < 7 + \frac{1}{2}n < 7 - \frac{1}{2}$	Add 7 on each side.
$6 < 7 + \frac{1}{2}n < 6.5$	Simplify.

Therefore $(7 + \frac{1}{2}n)$ rounded to the nearest whole number is 6.

5. 4.8

$\frac{1}{4}x - 1 \le -x + 5$	Given
$\frac{1}{4}x - 1 + (x + 1) \le -x + 5 + (x + 1)$	
	Add $(x + 1)$ on both sides.
$\frac{5}{4}x \le 6$	Simplify.
$\frac{4}{5}(\frac{5}{4}x) \le \frac{4}{5}(6)$	Multiply by $\frac{4}{5}$ on both sides.
$x \le \frac{24}{5} = 4.8$	Simplify.

Therefore the greatest possible value of x is 4.8.

6. 30

Let $x =$ the number of students in the Spanish class.
Then $\frac{4}{5}x =$ the number of students in the geometry class.

$$\underbrace{x + \frac{4}{5}x}_{\substack{\text{The total number of} \\ \text{students in both classes}}} \quad \underbrace{\le}_{\substack{\text{is not} \\ \text{more than}}} \quad \underbrace{54}_{54}$$

$$\implies \frac{9}{5}x \le 54 \implies x \le 54(\frac{5}{9}) = 30$$

The greatest possible number of students in the Spanish class is 30.

7. 52

Let x = the cost of the shoes.
Let y = the cost of the pants.

$$\underbrace{x + y = 86}_{\substack{\text{The cost of shoes} \\ \text{and pants is } \$86}} \quad \Rightarrow \quad y = 86 - x$$

$$\underbrace{y}_{\substack{\text{The pants} \\ \text{cost}}} \quad \underbrace{\leq}_{\text{less than}} \quad \underbrace{\tfrac{2}{3}x}_{\tfrac{2}{3} \text{ the cost of the shoes}}$$

$$86 - x < \frac{2}{3}x \quad \text{(Substitution)}$$

$$\Rightarrow \ 86 < \frac{5}{3}x \ \Rightarrow \ 86(\frac{3}{5}) < x \ \Rightarrow \ 51.6 < x$$

The minimum price of the shoes to the nearest dollar is $52.

8. 2 or 3

$$\left| \frac{3}{4}x - 2 \right| < 1$$

$$\Rightarrow \ -1 < \frac{3}{4}x - 2 < 1$$

$$\Rightarrow \ 1 < \frac{3}{4}x < 3$$

$$\Rightarrow \ \frac{4}{3} < x < 4$$

Since x is an integer, x is 2 or 3.

11. Functions and Graphs

Key Terms / Illustrations   Examples

1. A **relation** is a set of ordered pairs (x, y).

2. The **domain** of a relation is the set of all x-values from the ordered pairs.

3. The **range** of a relation is the set of all y-values from the ordered pairs.

4. A **mapping diagram** shows how each member of the domain is paired with each member of the range.

   A mapping diagram, below, illustrates a relation determined by a rule: $\{(-3,1),(0,7),(1,9)\}$.

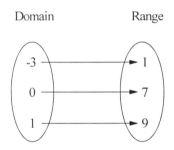

5. A **function** is a special type of relation in which each element of the domain is paired with exactly one element from the range.

6. **Linear Function**

   A function f is a linear function if it can be written in the form $f(x) = mx + b$, where m and b are constants.

   The graph of the linear function is a nonvertical straight line with slope m and y-intercept b.

☑ In the definition of a linear function, m or b may be zero. If $m = 0$, then $f(x) = b$. The graph is a horizontal line.

Example 1 □   **Finding the domain and the range**

Find the domain and range of each function.

a) $y = \sqrt{x-2}$

b) $\{(-3,1),(-1,4),(2,-5),(6,11)\}$

c) $y = \dfrac{1}{x-1}$

Solution □

(a) $y = \sqrt{x-2}$

   $x - 2 \geq 0$ The expression under a square root must be non-negative.

   $x \geq 2$

   Domain $= \{x : x \geq 2\}$ or $[2, \infty)$

   $y \geq 0$ The expression $\sqrt{x-2}$ is always non-negative.

   Range $= \{y : y \geq 0\}$ or $[0, \infty)$

(b) The domain of the relation is $\{-3, -1, 2, 6\}$, which is the set of all the first coordinates from the ordered pairs.

   The range of the relation is $\{-5, 1, 4, 11\}$, which is the set of all the second coordinates from the ordered pairs.

(c) Since division by 0 is not possible, the denominator $x - 1$ can never be 0. Thus, x can never equal 1. The domain of f is $(-\infty, 1) \cup (1, \infty)$.

   Since the expression $\dfrac{1}{x-1}$ cannot equal 0, the range of f is $(-\infty, 0) \cup (0, \infty)$.

7. Quadratic Function

A function f is a quadratic function if it can be written in the form $f(x) = ax^2 + bx + c$, where a, b, and c are constants and $a \neq 0$.

8. Standard Form of a Quadratic Function

$$f(x) = a(x-h)^2 + k$$

The vertex of the graph of f is the point (h, k), and its line of symmetry is $x = h$.

9. Functional Notation and Evaluation

If x is an element of the domain of a function, the output value that corresponds to x is usually denoted by $f(x)$. The symbol $f(x)$ is read "f of x" and is called the **value of f at x**.

☑ Equations that represent functions are often written in functional notation. The equation $y = 3x - 8$ can be written as $f(x) = 3x - 8$. The symbol $f(x)$ replaces the y. Letters other than f can be used to represent a function. For example, the equation can also be written as $g(x) = 3x - 8$.

Illustration

Let f be the function defined $f(x) = x^2 - 4$.

$f(-2) = (-2)^2 - 4 = 0$ -2 is substituted for x.

$f(0) = (0)^2 - 4 = -4$ 0 is substituted for x.

$f(\frac{1}{2}) = (\frac{1}{2})^2 - 4$ $\frac{1}{2}$ is substituted for x.

$= \frac{1}{4} - 4 = -\frac{15}{4}$

$f(t) = t^2 - 4$ t is substituted for x.

$f(a-1) = (a-1)^2 - 4$ $(a-1)$ is substituted for x.

$= a^2 - 2a + 1 - 4$

$= a^2 - 2a - 3$

Example 2 □ **Finding functional values**

If $f(x) = x^2 - bx + 7$ and $f(3) = 4$, what is the value of $f(-3)$?

Solution □

$f(3) = (3)^2 - b(3) + 7 = 4$
$\Rightarrow 9 - 3b + 7 = 4 \Rightarrow 3b = 12$
$\Rightarrow b = 4$
$\Rightarrow f(x) = x^2 - 4x + 7$

$f(-3) = (-3)^2 - 4(-3) + 7 = 28$ Answer

Example 3 □ **Finding functional values**

For all real numbers m, let $f(m) = 2 - m$. What is the value of $f(f(2))$?

Solution □

$f(m) = 2 - m$
$f(2) = 2 - (2) = 0$ Replace m with 2.
$f(f(2)) = f(0)$ $f(2) = 0$
$= 2 - 0$ Replace m with 0.
$= 2$ Answer

Example 4 □ **Finding functional values**

Let $f(x) = x^2 + 6$. If r is a positive number and $f(4r) - f(2r) = 3$, what is the value of r?

Solution □

$f(4r) - f(2r) = 3$
$[(4r)^2 + 6] - [(2r)^2 + 6] = 3$
$\Rightarrow 12r^2 = 3 \Rightarrow r^2 = \frac{1}{4} \Rightarrow r = \pm\frac{1}{2}$

Since r is positive, $r = \frac{1}{2}$.   Answer

10. **The Domain and Range of Six Basic Functions and Their Graphs**

(1) $f(x) = x$

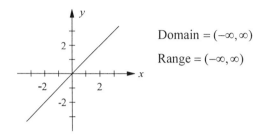

Domain $= (-\infty, \infty)$

Range $= (-\infty, \infty)$

The domain and range of f is the set of all real numbers.

(2) $f(x) = x^2$

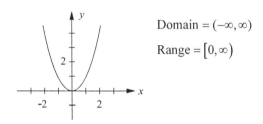

Domain $= (-\infty, \infty)$

Range $= [0, \infty)$

The domain of f is the set of all real numbers, and the range of f is the set of all numbers y such that $y \geq 0$.

(3) $f(x) = \sqrt{x}$

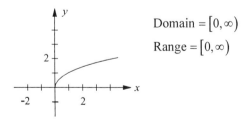

Domain $= [0, \infty)$

Range $= [0, \infty)$

The domain of f is the interval $x \geq 0$, since the expression under a square root has to be nonnegative. The range of the function is all numbers $f(x)$ such that $f(x) \geq 0$, since the expression $\sqrt{x}$ is always nonnegative.

(4) $f(x) = |x|$

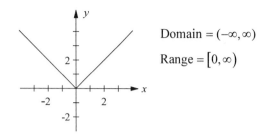

Domain $= (-\infty, \infty)$

Range $= [0, \infty)$

The domain of f is the set of all real numbers, and the range of f is the set of all numbers y such that $y \geq 0$.

(5) $f(x) = \dfrac{1}{x}$

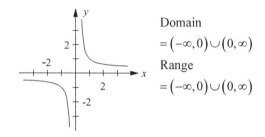

Domain $= (-\infty, 0) \cup (0, \infty)$

Range $= (-\infty, 0) \cup (0, \infty)$

The domain of the rational function is the set of all real numbers except those for which the denominator is zero. The range of the function is the set of all real numbers except for $f(x) = 0$, (or $y = 0$), since the expression $\dfrac{1}{x}$ cannot equal zero.

(6) $f(x) = x^3$

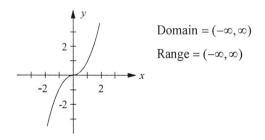

Domain $= (-\infty, \infty)$

Range $= (-\infty, \infty)$

Both the domain and range of f are the set of all real numbers.

11. Graphs of Quadratic Equations

The graph of $y = ax^2 + bx + c$ is a **parabola**.

(1) The **vertex** has an x-coordinate of $-b/2a$.

(2) The **axis of symmetry** is the vertical line $x = -\dfrac{b}{2a}$.

(3) If a is positive the parabola opens up, and the function has **minimum value** at $x = -\dfrac{b}{2a}$.

(4) If a is negative the parabola opens down, and the function has **maximum value** at $x = -\dfrac{b}{2a}$.

(5) As the value of $|a|$ increases, the graph becomes **narrower**.

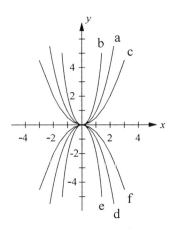

a. $y = x^2$ b. $y = 2x^2$ c. $y = \dfrac{1}{2}x^2$

d. $y = -x^2$ e. $y = -2x^2$ f. $y = -\dfrac{1}{2}x^2$

Example 5 □   **Finding the domain and range, line of symmetry, vertex, and minimum value of a quadratic function**

Find the line of symmetry, vertex, minimum value, domain, and range of a quadratic function $f(x) = x^2 - 2x - 8$.

Solution □

For this quadratic function, $a = 1$, $b = -2$, and $c = -8$.

The line of symmetry is $x = -\dfrac{b}{2a} = -\dfrac{-2}{2(1)} = 1$.

The y-coordinate of the vertex is therefore $f(1) = (1)^2 - 2(1) - 8 = -9$.

The vertex is located at the point $(1, -9)$.

The minimum value of the function is -9. ($f(x)$ is at a minimum at the vertex.)

The graph of the function $f(x) = x^2 - 2x - 8$ is shown below.

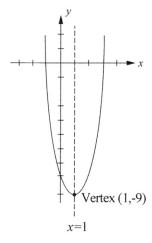

Vertex (1,-9)

$x=1$

Domain $= (-\infty, \infty)$
Range $= [-9, \infty)$

12. Transformations of Functions
(*h* and *k* are positive real numbers)

Original graph: $\qquad$ $y = f(x)$

Horizontal shifts
h units to the **right**: $\qquad$ $y = f(x - h)$
h units to the **left**: $\qquad$ $y = f(x + h)$

Vertical shifts
k units **downward**: $\qquad$ $y = f(x) - k$
k units **upward**: $\qquad$ $y = f(x) + k$

Reflections
about the *x*-axis: $\qquad$ $y = -f(x)$
about the *y*-axis: $\qquad$ $y = f(-x)$

Illustration

Original graph: $\qquad$ $y = x^2$

Horizontal shifts
2 units to the **right**: $\qquad$ $y = (x - 2)^2$
2 units to the **left**: $\qquad$ $y = (x + 2)^2$

Vertical shifts
3 units **downward**: $\qquad$ $y = x^2 - 3$
3 units **upward**: $\qquad$ $y = x^2 + 3$

Reflections
about the *x*-axis: $\qquad$ $y = -x^2$
about the *y*-axis: $\qquad$ $y = (-x)^2 = x^2$

Example 6 □ **Transformations of functions**

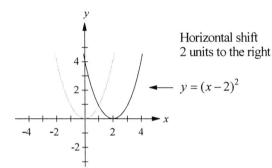

Horizontal shift
2 units to the right
$y = (x - 2)^2$

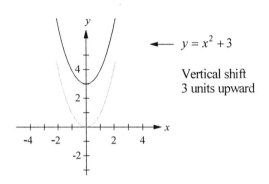

$y = x^2 + 3$

Vertical shift
3 units upward

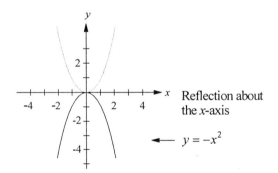

Reflection about
the *x*-axis
$y = -x^2$

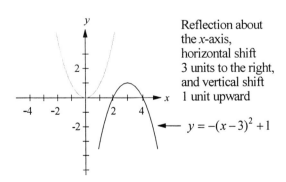

Reflection about
the *x*-axis,
horizontal shift
3 units to the right,
and vertical shift
1 unit upward
$y = -(x - 3)^2 + 1$

x	-3	4
y	3	-11

1. What are the domain and range of the relation shown in the table above?

   (A) Domain : $\{-3,3\}$; Range : $\{4,-11\}$

   (B) Domain : $\{-3,4\}$; Range : $\{3,-11\}$

   (C) Domain : $\{4,-11\}$; Range : $\{-3,3\}$

   (D) Domain : $\{3,-11\}$; Range : $\{-3,4\}$

   (E) Domain : $\{-3,-11\}$; Range : $\{3,4\}$

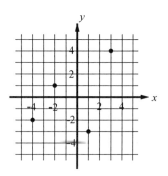

2. What is the domain of the relation graphed above?

   (A) $\{-3,-2,1,4\}$

   (B) $\{-4,-1,-2,1\}$

   (C) $\{1,-3,3,4\}$

   (D) $\{-4,-2,1,3\}$

   (E) $\{$all the integers$\}$

3. If $f(x) = ax(x-3)$ and $f(-2) = 5$, what is the value of a?

   (A) $-\dfrac{1}{2}$ (B) $\dfrac{1}{2}$ (C) 1

   (D) 2   (E) –2

4. If $g(x) = 2x^2 + bx + 5$ and $g(1) = 4$, what is the value of $g(-1)$?

   (A) 1

   (B) 2

   (C) 4

   (D) 7

   (E) 10

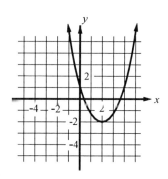

5. What is the range of the function graphed above?

   (A) $\{y : y \le -2\}$

   (B) $\{y : y \le 0\}$

   (C) $\{y : y \ge 0\}$

   (D) $\{y : y \ge -2\}$

   (E) $\{$all real numbers$\}$

6. For all values of x, let $f(x)$ be defined as

$f(x) = \dfrac{2^x - 1}{5}$. If $f(4) = m$, then $f(m) =$

(A) $\dfrac{3}{5}$

(B) 1

(C) $\dfrac{7}{5}$

(D) 3

(E) 4

7. If $f(x) = \sqrt{2 - x}$, then which of the following is the domain of f?

(A) $\{x : x \neq 2\}$

(B) $\{x : x \leq 2\}$

(C) $\{x : x \geq 2\}$

(D) $\{x : x \geq 0\}$

(E) $\{x : x \leq 0\}$

8. For all values of x and y, let $f(x, y)$ be defined

as $f(x, y) = \dfrac{1 + x}{1 - y}$, where $y \neq 1$. If $f(a, 3) = \dfrac{5}{2}$,

what is the value of a?

(A) -6

(B) -5

(C) -3

(D) 5

(E) 6

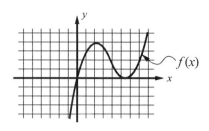

9. If the graph above represents $f(x)$, which of the following graphs represents $-f(x)$?

(A)

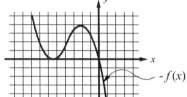

(B)

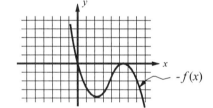

(C)

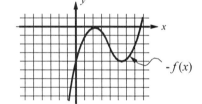

(D)

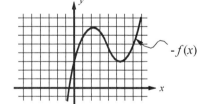

(E)

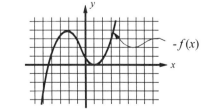

10. If $f(x) = x^2 + bx + c$ for all x, and if $f(2) = 0$,
    then $2b + c =$

    (A) −4

    (B) −2

    (C) 0

    (D) 2

    (E) 4

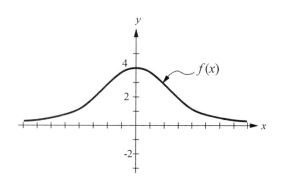

11. The figure above shows the graph of $f(x)$.
    Which of the following is the range of $f(x)$?

    (A) $\{y : y \le 4\}$

    (B) $\{y : y \ge 4\}$

    (C) $\{y : 0 < y \le 4\}$

    (D) $\{y : y \ne 0\}$

    (E) $\{y : -\infty < y < \infty\}$

12. Which of the following is the graph of
    $y = (x-3)^2 + 1$?

(A)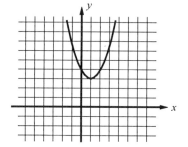

(B)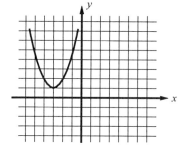

(C)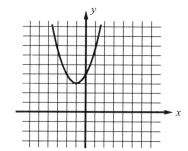

(D)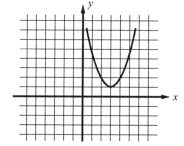

(E)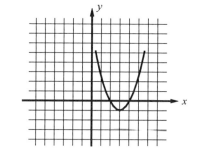

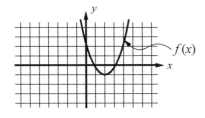

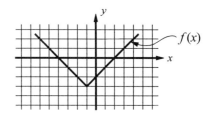

13. If the figure above shows the graph of $f(x)$, which of the following graphs represents the graph of $f(x-2)$?

14. If the figure above shows the graph of $f(x)$, which of the following graphs represents the graph of $f(x+1)-2$?

(A)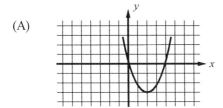

(A)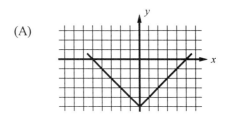

(B)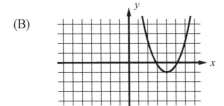

(B)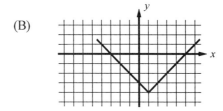

(C)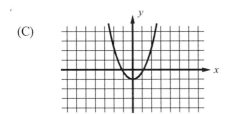

(C)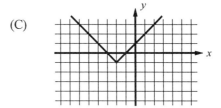

(D)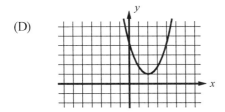

(D)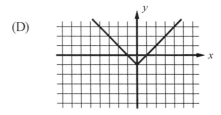

(E)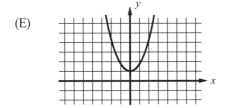

(E)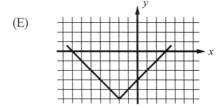

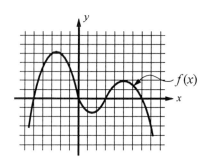

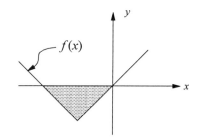

15. The figure above shows the graph of $f(x)$. For what values of x are the values of $f(x)$ positive?

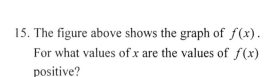

    (A) $-5 < x < 0$

    (B) $0 < x < 3$

    (C) $-5 < x < 7$

    (D) $-5 < x < 0$ or $3 < x < 7$

    (E) all values of x

17. In the figure above, the area of the shaded region, bounded by the graph of $y = f(x)$ and the x-axis, is 9. What is the area of the region bounded by the graph of $y = f(x-7)$ and the x-axis ?

    (A) 2

    (B) 7

    (C) 9

    (D) 16

    (E) It cannot be determined from the information given.

16. If $f(x)$ is a linear function, and $f(3) = -3$ and $f(-3) = 7$, then $f(x) =$

    (A) $-\dfrac{2}{3}x - 1$

    (B) $-2x + 1$

    (C) $\dfrac{2}{3}x - 5$

    (D) $2x - 9$

    (E) $\dfrac{2}{3}x - 1$

18. For all nonzero real numbers x, let $f(x) = x^2 + 1$ and $g(x) = x^2 - 1$. If a is a real number, which of the following equals $f(a+1)$?

    (A) $g(a) + 2$

    (B) $g(a+1) + a$

    (C) $g(a+1) + 2$

    (D) $f(a-1) + 2$

    (E) $f(a) + f(1)$

19. If $f(x) = \sqrt{x+3}$ and $g(x) = x^2 + 4$, what is the value of $g(f(3))$?

(A) 4

(B) $\sqrt{6} + 4$

(C) 7

(D) 10

(E) $13\sqrt{6}$

20. If $f(x) = x^2 - 2$ for $-1 \le x \le 3$, then which of the following sets is the range of f?

(A) $\{y: -3 \le y \le 4\}$

(B) $\{y: -2 \le y \le 4\}$

(C) $\{y: -1 \le y \le 1\}$

(D) $\{y: -1 \le y \le 7\}$

(E) $\{y: -2 \le y \le 7\}$

Exercises (Grid-In)

1. If $f(x) = \frac{1}{2}x^2 - 4$, what is the value of $f(4) - f(2)$?

x	-2	-1	0	1	2
y	7	k	1	-2	-5

5. In the table above, if $f(x)$ is a linear function, what is the value of k?

2. For a function $f(x) = \sqrt{x-3}$, the domain is $\{x : x \geq k\}$. What is the value of k?

6. For all integers a and b, let $g(x)$ be defined as $g(x) = \frac{3}{2-x}$. If $g(\frac{1}{a}) = 2$, what is the value of a?

3. If $f(x) = 2^x - 2^{-x}$, what is the value of $f(2)$?

7. For all integers x, let $f(x) = \frac{\sqrt{x}}{2}$ when x is a positive integer and $f(x) = \frac{\sqrt[3]{x}}{3}$ when x is a negative integer. What is the value of $f(81) - f(-27)$?

4. If $f(x) = 3x + 1$ and $f(x+h) - f(x) = 6$, what is the value of h?

Answer Key

Multiple Choice Questions

1. B	2. D	3. B	4. E	5. D
6. C	7. B	8. A	9. B	10. A
11. C	12. D	13. B	14. E	15. D
16. C	17. C	18. C	19. D	20. E

Grid-In Questions

1. 4	2. 3	3. 15/4	4. 2	5. 4
6. 2	7. 5.5			

Answers and Explanations

Multiple Choice Questions

1. B

The domain is the set of all x-values and the range is the set of all y-values.

2. D

The x-coordinates of the points are -4, -2, 1, and 3.

3. B

$f(x) = ax(x-3)$ and $f(-2) = 5$
$f(-2) = a(-2)(-2-3) = 10a = 5$
$\Rightarrow a = \dfrac{1}{2}$

4. E

$g(x) = 2x^2 + bx + 5$ and $g(1) = 4$
$g(1) = 2(1)^2 + b(1) + 5 = 2 + b + 5 = 7 + b$

$\Rightarrow 7 + b = 4 \Rightarrow b = -3$
$\Rightarrow g(x) = 2x^2 - 3x + 5$

$g(-1) = 2(-1)^2 - 3(-1) + 5 = 2 + 3 + 5 = 10$

5. D

We read from the graph that the range is all numbers y such that $y \geq -2$. In other words, the range of the function is the interval $[-2, \infty)$.

6. C

$f(x) = \dfrac{2^x - 1}{5}$ and $f(4) = m$
$f(4) = \dfrac{2^4 - 1}{5} = \dfrac{16 - 1}{5} = \dfrac{15}{5} = 3$
$\Rightarrow m = 3$
$f(m) = f(3) = \dfrac{2^3 - 1}{5} = \dfrac{8 - 1}{5} = \dfrac{7}{5}$

7. B

The expression under a square root must be nonnegative.

$2 - x \geq 0 \Rightarrow 2 \geq x$

8. A

$f(x, y) = \dfrac{1 + x}{1 - y}$

$f(a, 3) = \dfrac{1 + a}{1 - 3} = \dfrac{1 + a}{-2} = \dfrac{5}{2}$

$\Rightarrow 2(1 + a) = (-2) \cdot 5 \Rightarrow 2 + 2a = -10$
$\Rightarrow a = -6$

9. B

The graph of the new function $y = -f(x)$ is the **reflection about the x-axis** of the graph of $y = f(x)$.

10. A

$f(x) = x^2 + bx + c$ and $f(2) = 0$

$f(2) = 2^2 + b(2) + c = 0$
$\Rightarrow 4 + 2b + c = 0 \Rightarrow 2b + c = -4$

11. C

We read from the graph that the range is all numbers y such that $0 < y \le 4$.

12. D

The vertex of the graph of $y = (x-3)^2 + 1$ is the point $(3,1)$.

13. B

The graph of the new function $f(x-2)$ is the graph of $f(x)$ shifted horizontally 2 units to the right.

14. E

The graph of the new function $f(x+1) - 2$ is the graph of $f(x)$ shifted horizontally 1 unit to the left, and vertically down 2 units.

15. D

The values of $f(x)$ are positive when the graph of $f(x)$ is above the x-axis.

$\Rightarrow -5 < x < 0$ or $3 < x < 7$

16. C

If $f(x)$ is a linear function, then $f(x) = mx + b$.

$f(3) = m(3) + b = -3$
$f(-3) = m(-3) + b = -7$

$3m + b = -3$ (First equation simplified)
$-3m + b = -7$ (Second equation simplified)

Add the two equations.
We get $2b = -10 \Rightarrow b = -5$

Make a substitution into the first equation.
$3m + (-5) = -3 \Rightarrow m = \dfrac{2}{3}$

Therefore $f(x) = \dfrac{2}{3}x - 5$

17. C

The graph of the new function $f(x-7)$ is the graph of $f(x)$ shifted horizontally 7 units to the right. Therefore, the area of the region bounded by the graph of $y = f(x-7)$ and the x-axis is the same as the area of the shaded region bounded by the graph of $f(x)$.

18. C

$f(x) = x^2 + 1$ and $g(x) = x^2 - 1$
$f(a+1) = (a+1)^2 + 1 = a^2 + 2a + 2$

(A) $g(a) + 2 = (a^2 - 1) + 2 = a^2 + 1$

(B) $g(a+1) + a = (a+1)^2 - 1 + a = a^2 + 3a$

(C) $g(a+1) + 2 = (a+1)^2 - 1 + 2 = a^2 + 2a + 2$

Choice (C) is correct.

19. D

$$f(x) = \sqrt{x+3} \text{ and } g(x) = x^2 + 4$$

$f(3) = \sqrt{3+3} = \sqrt{6}$ 3 is substituted for x.

$g(f(3)) = g(\sqrt{6})$ $f(3) = \sqrt{6}$

$\quad = (\sqrt{6})^2 + 4$ $\sqrt{6}$ is substituted for x.

$\quad = 6 + 4 = 10$

20. E

Given : $f(x) = x^2 - 2$. Use graphing calculator. The graph shows that f is at a minimum when $x = 0$, and f is at a maximum when $x = 3$.

$f(0) = (0)^2 - 2 = -2$ and $f(3) = (3)^2 - 2 = 7$.

The range of f is $\{y : -2 \le y \le 7\}$.

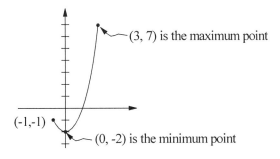

(3, 7) is the maximum point

(-1,-1)

(0, -2) is the minimum point

Grid-In Questions

1. 4

$$f(x) = \frac{1}{2}x^2 - 4$$

$$f(4) - f(2) = \left[\frac{1}{2}(4)^2 - 4\right] - \left[\frac{1}{2}(2)^2 - 2\right]$$
$$= (8 - 4) - (2 - 2) = 4$$

2. 3

The expression under a square root must be nonnegative. Therefore $x - 3 \ge 0$.

$\Rightarrow x \ge 3 \Rightarrow k = 3$

3. $\dfrac{15}{4}$

$$f(x) = 2^x - 2^{-x}$$

$$f(2) = 2^2 - 2^{-2} = 4 - \frac{1}{2^2} = 4 - \frac{1}{4} = \frac{15}{4}$$

4. 2

$$f(x) = 3x + 1$$

$$f(x+h) - f(x) = [3(x+h)+1] - (3x+1) = 6$$

$$3x + 3h + 1 - 3x - 1 = 6$$
$$\Rightarrow 3h = 6 \Rightarrow h = 2$$

5. 4

$f(x)$ is a linear function, and when x increases by 1, y decreases by 3.

$$\Rightarrow k = 4$$

6. 2

$$g(x) = \frac{3}{2-x} \qquad g(\frac{1}{a}) = \frac{3}{2 - \frac{1}{a}} = 2$$

$$\Rightarrow 3 = 2 \cdot (2 - \frac{1}{a}) \Rightarrow 3 = 4 - \frac{2}{a}$$

$$\Rightarrow \frac{2}{a} = 1 \Rightarrow a = 2$$

7. 5.5

$f(x) = \dfrac{\sqrt{x}}{2}$ when x is a positive integer.

$f(x) = \dfrac{\sqrt[3]{x}}{3}$ when x is a negative integer.

$$f(81) = \frac{\sqrt{81}}{2} = \frac{9}{2} = 4.5$$

$$f(-27) = \frac{\sqrt[3]{-27}}{3} = \frac{\sqrt[3]{(-3)^3}}{3} = \frac{-3}{3} = -1$$

$$f(81) - f(-27) = 4.5 - (-1) = 5.5$$

II. Geometry

12. Coordinate Geometry

Key Terms / Illustrations   Examples

1. Quadrants

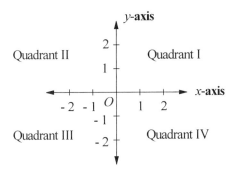

A coordinate plane is composed of the **x-axis** and the **y-axis**, which meet at the **origin** (0,0). The axes divide the plane into four parts called **quadrants.**

2. Slope = $\dfrac{\text{Vertical Change}}{\text{Horizontal Change}}$

The slope m of a line passing through the points (x_1, y_1) and (x_2, y_2) is $m = \dfrac{y_2 - y_1}{x_2 - x_1}$.

3. The Slope of a Line and its Direction

a. A line with **positive slope** rises from left to right.

b. A line with **negative slope** falls from left to right.

c. A line with **zero slope** is horizontal.

d. A line with **undefined slope** is vertical. (where $x_1 = x_2$)

4. Two lines are **parallel** if their slopes, m_1 and m_2, are equal.
$$m_1 = m_2$$

5. Two non-vertical lines are **perpendicular** if their slopes, m_1 and m_2, are negative reciprocals of each other.
$$m_1 \cdot m_2 = -1$$

Example 1 □ **Quadrants**

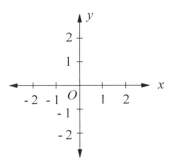

In the figure above, points $(7, y)$ and $(x, -3)$, not shown, are in quadrants IV and III, respectively. In which quadrant is point (x, y)?

Solution □

If point $(7, y)$ is in quadrant IV, y is negative.
If point $(x, -3)$ is in quadrant III, x is negative.

Therefore (x, y) is in quadrant III.   Answer

Example 2 □ **Lines with positive, negative, and zero slopes**

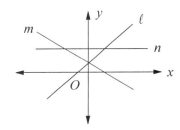

In the figure above, three lines ℓ, m, and n have slopes a, b, and c, respectively. Order the slopes from the least to the greatest.

Solution □

b is negative since the line falls from left to right.
a is positive since the line rises from left to right.
c is zero since the line is horizontal.

Therefore $b < c < a$.   Answer

6. Equations of Lines

a. Slope-Intercept Form

$y = mx + b$, where b is the y-intercept.

b. Point-Slope Form

$y - y_1 = m(x - x_1)$, where (x_1, y_1) are the coordinates of a point on the line.

c. Standard Form

$Ax + By = C$, where A, B, and C are integers.

d. Vertical Line

$x = a$, where a is the x-intercept.

e. Horizontal Line

$y = b$, where b is the y-intercept.

7. The x-intercept is the value of x when $y = 0$.

The y-intercept is the value of y when $x = 0$.

8. Distance Formula

The distance between the points (x_1, y_1) and (x_2, y_2) is given by

$$d = \sqrt{(x_2 - x_1)^2 + (y_2 - y_1)^2}$$

9. Midpoint Formula

The midpoint M between (x_1, y_1) and (x_2, y_2) is

$$M\left(\frac{x_1 + x_2}{2}, \frac{y_1 + y_2}{2}\right)$$

Example 3 □ Finding the x-intercept, y-intercept, and slope of a line

Find the x-intercept, y-intercept, and slope of the line $2x + 5y = 10$.

Solution □

$2x + 5y = 10$	Original equation
$2x + 5(0) = 10$	Substitute 0 for y.
$x = 5$	Solve for x.
The x-intercept is 5.	Answer

$2x + 5y = 10$	Original equation
$2(0) + 5y = 10$	Substitute 0 for x.
$y = 2$	Solve for y.
The y-intercept is 2.	Answer

$2x + 5y = 10$	Original equation
$5y = -2x + 10$	Subtract $2x$.
$y = -\frac{2}{5}x + 2$	Divide by 5.

The slope of the line is $-\frac{2}{5}$. Answer

Example 4 □ Finding the distance and the endpoint

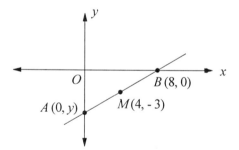

In the figure above, $M(4, -3)$ is the midpoint of segment AB. Find the value of y and the length of $\overline{AB}$.

Solution □

$$(4, -3) = \left(\frac{0+8}{2}, \frac{y+0}{2}\right) = \left(4, \frac{y}{2}\right)$$

$$\Rightarrow -3 = \frac{y}{2} \quad \Rightarrow y = -6 \quad \text{Answer}$$

Since $A(0, -6)$, $B(8, 0)$

$$AB = \sqrt{(8-0)^2 + (0-(-6))^2} = \sqrt{64 + 36}$$

$$= \sqrt{100} = 10 \qquad \text{Answer}$$

10. Standard Equation of a Circle

The equation of a circle with center at (h, k) and a radius of r units is
$(x-h)^2 + (y-k)^2 = r^2$.

Center	Radius	Equation of Circle
$(0,0)$	5	$x^2 + y^2 = 25$
$(-2,3)$	$\sqrt{6}$	$(x+2)^2 + (y-3)^2 = 6$
(h, k)	r	$(x-h)^2 + (y-k)^2 = r^2$

11. Line of Symmetry

If line ℓ is a line of **reflection** for P and its image R, then ℓ is a perpendicular bisector of $\overline{PR}$.
Point Q is the midpoint of $\overline{PR}$ and $PQ = QR$.
Line ℓ is called a line of symmetry.

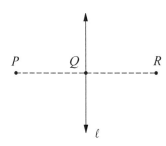

12. Rotations

On the coordinate plane, a point $P(3, 2)$ is rotated $90°$, $-90°$ and $180°$ about the center of rotation $O(0,0)$. The points Q, R, and S are the rotation images of point P.

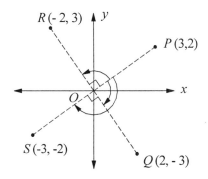

Example 5 □ Endpoint on a circle

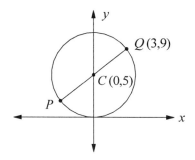

In the circle above, C is the center of the circle and $\overline{PQ}$ is a diameter. What is the coordinate of point P ?

Solution □

The center of the circle is at $(0,5)$. Point Q is Located 3 units to the right and 4 units up from the center. Therefore point P is 3 units to the left and 4 units down from the center.
The coordinate of point P is $(-3,1)$.   Answer

Example 6 □ Reflection

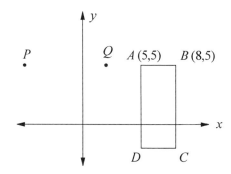

In the figure above, $ABCD$ is a rectangle. If point A and P are symmetric about the y-axis, and point B and point Q are symmetric about line AD, what is the length of segment PQ (not shown)?

Solution □

Since A and P are symmetric about the y-axis, P has coordinates of $(-5, 5)$. Since B and Q are symmetric about line AD, $QA = AB = 3$. Therefore Q has coordinates of $(2, 5)$.
The length of segment PQ is 7.   Answer

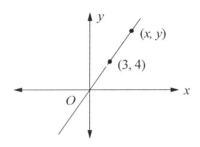

1. In the figure above, if $y = 10$ what is the value of x?

(A) 6.5   (B) 7.5   (C) 8

(D) 8.5   (E) 9

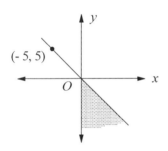

2. Of the following pairs of coordinates, which point lies inside the shaded region?

(A) $(6, -5)$ (B) $(5, -4)$ (C) $(4, -3)$

(D) $(3, -2)$ (E) $(2, -3)$

3. The slope of a line containing the points $(s, 2)$ and $(4, t)$ is $-\dfrac{1}{2}$. What is the value of $\dfrac{s}{t}$?

(A) 2   (B) 1   (C) -1

(D) $\dfrac{1}{2}$ (E) -2

4. Which of the following is the equation of the line whose slope is 2 and passes through $(-3, 1)$?

(A) $y = 2x - 3$ (B) $y = 2x + 1$

(C) $y = 2x + 5$ (D) $y = 2x - 5$

(E) $y = 2x + 7$

5. Which of the following descriptions is NOT true for the graph of the equation $6x - 2y = 12$?

(A) It is parallel to the graph of the equation $y = 3x - 1$.

(B) It is perpendicular to the graph of the equation $y = \dfrac{1}{3}x + 1$.

(C) The point $(1, -3)$ lies on it.

(D) The x-intercept is 2.

(E) The y-intercept is -6.

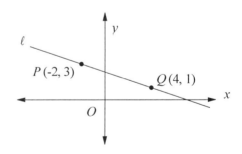

6. In the figure above, P, Q, and R (not shown) are points on line ℓ. If the coordinates of R are $(25, r)$, what is the value of r?

(A) -3 (B) -4 (C) -5

(D) -6 (E) -7

Questions <u>7–8</u> refer to the following coordinate system.

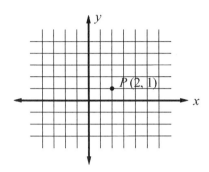

7. Line ℓ (not shown) contains point P and has slope 3. Which of the following points is on line ℓ?

(A) $(1, -2)$ (B) $(5, 2)$ (C) $(4, 6)$

(D) $(-1, 0)$ (E) $(3, 3)$

8. Point Q (not shown) is located by beginning at P, moving 1 unit up, and reflecting over the y-axis. What is the slope of line segment PQ?

(A) 4   (B) $\frac{1}{4}$ (C) $-\frac{1}{4}$

(D) $-\frac{1}{2}$ (E) -4

9. A line is perpendicular to the y-axis and passes through $(3, -2)$. What is the equation of the line?

(A) $y = 3x$ (B) $y = -2x$

(C) $y = -2$ (D) $x = 3$

(E) $y = -\frac{2}{3}$

Questions <u>10–11</u> refer to the following coordinate system.

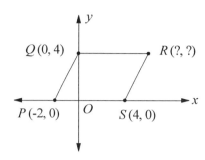

10. In the figure above, P, Q, R, and S are the vertices of a parallelogram. What are the coordinates of R?

(A) $(6, 4)$ (B) $(5, 4)$ (C) $(4, 6)$

(D) $(4, 4)$ (E) $(7, 4)$

11. What is the coordinate of the midpoint of segment PR (not shown)?

(A) $(3.5, 2)$ (B) $(2.5, 2)$ (C) $(2, 3)$

(D) $(3, 2)$ (E) $(2, 2)$

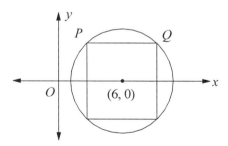

12. In the figure above, a rectangle is inscribed in a circle whose equation is $(x - 6)^2 + y^2 = 25$. Which of the following are possible coordinates of P and Q?

(A) $(2, 3), (9, 3)$ (B) $(2, 3), (10, 3)$

(C) $(4, 4), (7, 4)$ (D) $(4, 5)(8, 5)$

(E) $(4, 4)(6, 4)$

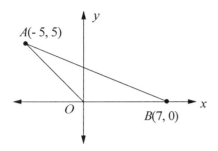

13. In the figure above, what is the perimeter of triangle AOB ?

    (A) 25   (B) $20+5\sqrt{2}$ (C) $18+5\sqrt{2}$

    (D) $12+5\sqrt{2}$ (E) 22

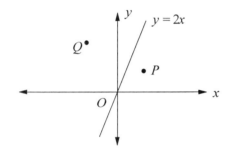

14. If a line through $\overline{PQ}$ (not shown) is perpendicular to $y = 2x$, what is the slope of the line that passes through points P and Q?

    (A) –2   (B) –1   (C) $-\dfrac{1}{2}$

    (D) $\dfrac{1}{2}$ (E) 1

15. The coordinates of the midpoint of line segment PQ are $(-3, 2)$. If the coordinates of point P are $(2, -3)$, what are the coordinates of point Q ?

    (A) (–8, 7)   (B) (–8 , 5)   (C) (–5 , 5)

    (D) (–5 , 7)   (E) (–1 , 5)

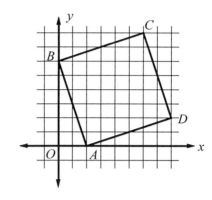

16. In the figure above, the grid consists of unit squares and A, B, C, and D are points of intersection on the grid. What is the area of square $ABCD$?

    (A) 60   (B) 54   (C) 49

    (D) 40   (E) 36

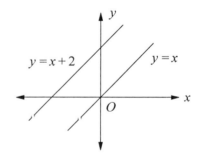

17. In the rectangular coordinate system above, what is the shortest distance between the lines $y = x$ and $y = x + 2$?

    (A) 1   (B) $\dfrac{\sqrt{2}}{2}$ (C) $\sqrt{2}$

    (D) 2   (E) $2\sqrt{2}$

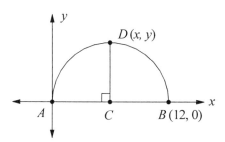

1. In the semicircle above, $\overline{AB}$ is a diameter and $\overline{CD}$ is a radius. What is the value of $x + y$?

2. If the points $A(-1,1)$, $B(5,1)$, and $C(5,4)$ are vertices of a triangle, what is the area of the triangle?

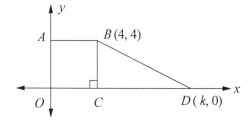

3. In the figure above, if the area of square $OABC$ is equal to the area of $\triangle BCD$, what is the value of k?

4. The coordinates of the midpoint of line segment AB are $(2, 3)$ and the coordinates of point A are $(-1,1)$. If the coordinates of point B are (s,t) what is the value of $s + t$?

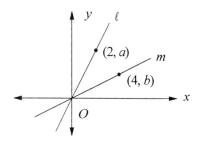

5. In the figure above, the slope of line ℓ is 2 and the slope of line m is $\frac{1}{2}$. What is the value of $a - b$?

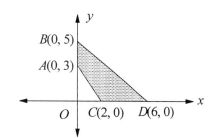

6. In the coordinate system above, what is the area of the shaded region?

7. If the *x*-intercept of a line is −4 and the *y*-intercept of the same line is 6, what is the slope of the line?

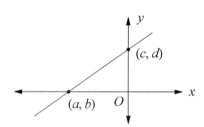

8. In the coordinate plane above, what is the value of $b + c$?

9. In the coordinate plane above, segment *OA* is rotated clockwise through an angle of 90° to position $\overline{OB}$ (not shown). What is the value of *x*?

<u>Questions 10–11</u> refer to the following coordinate system.

10. In the rectangular coordinate system above, △*OAB* is an isosceles right triangle with *AB* = *OB*. What is the value of *y* ?

11. In the coordinate plane above, what is the area of △*OAB* ?

Answer Key

Multiple Choice Questions

1. B	2. E	3. A	4. E	5. B
6. D	7. A	8. C	9. C	10. A
11. E	12. B	13. B	14. C	15. A
16. D	17. C			

Grid-In Questions

1. 12	2. 9	3. 12	4. 10	5. 2
6. 12	7. 3/2	8. 0	9. 4	10. 8
11. 17				

Answers and Explanations

Multiple Choice Questions

1. B

The slope of the line is $\frac{4}{3}$ and $y = 10$.

$$\text{slope} = \frac{y_2 - y_1}{x_2 - x_1} = \frac{10-4}{x-3} = \frac{4}{3} \implies \frac{6}{x-3} = \frac{4}{3}$$

$\implies 4(x-3) = 18 \implies 4x - 12 = 18 \implies 4x = 30$

$\implies x = 7.5$

2. E

The equation of the line is $y = -x$, and the shaded region is represented by the inequality $y < -x$.

Choice (A) : $(6, -5)$ $-5 < -6$. Not true.
Choice (B) : $(5, -4)$ $-4 < -5$. Not true.
Choice (C) : $(4, -3)$ $-3 < -4$. Not true.
Choice (D) : $(3, -2)$ $-2 < -3$. Not true.
Choice (E) : $(2, -3)$ $-3 < -2$. True.

3. A

$$\text{slope} = \frac{t-2}{4-s} = -\frac{1}{2} \implies 2(t-2) = -1(4-s)$$

$\implies 2t - 4 = -4 + s \implies 2t = s \implies \frac{s}{t} = \frac{2}{1}$

4. E

$y = mx + b$	Slope-intercept form of a line
$y = 2x + b$	Slope is 2.
$1 = 2(-3) + b$	Substitution ($x = -3$, $y = 1$)
$b = 7$	Solve for b.
$y = 2x + 7$	Substitution

5. B

Solve the given equation for y.
$6x - 2y = 12 \implies y = 3x - 6$

(A) $y = 3x - 1$ is parallel to $y = 3x - 6$.

(B) Two lines are perpendicular if their slopes, m_1 and m_2, are negative reciprocals of each other, that is, $m_1 \cdot m_2 = -1$. $y = \frac{1}{3}x + 1$ and $y = 3x - 6$ are not perpendicular to each other since $3 \cdot \frac{1}{3} = 1$, not -1.

(C) The point $(1, -3)$ lies on the line, since when $x = 1$, $y = -3$. $\implies -3 = 3(1) - 6$

(D) Let $y = 0$, then $0 = 3x - 6 \implies x = 2$

$\implies$ The x-intercept is 2.

(E) Let $x = 0$, then $y = 3(0) - 6 \implies y = -6$

$\implies$ The y-intercept is -6.

6. D

Slope of $\overline{PQ} = \frac{3-1}{-2-4} = \frac{2}{-6} = -\frac{1}{3}$

Since R is on the same line, slope of $\overline{QR}$ should be the same as the slope of $\overline{PQ}$.

Slope of $\overline{QR} = \frac{1-r}{4-25} = \frac{1-r}{-21} = -\frac{1}{3}$

$3(1-r) = -1 \cdot (-21) \implies 3 - 3r = 21$

$\implies r = -6$

7. A

Let the coordinates of $P(2,1) = (x_1, y_1)$ and let the coordinates given in each answer choice be (x_2, y_2).

Choice (A) : (1, –2) slope $= \dfrac{-2-1}{1-2} = \dfrac{-3}{-1} = 3$

Choice (A) is correct.

Choice (B) : (5, 2) slope $= \dfrac{2-1}{5-2} = \dfrac{1}{3} = \dfrac{1}{3}$

Choice (C) : (4, 6) slope $= \dfrac{6-1}{4-2} = \dfrac{5}{2}$

Choice (D) : (–1, 0) slope $= \dfrac{0-1}{-1-2} = \dfrac{-1}{-3} = \dfrac{1}{3}$

Choice (E) : (3, 3) slope $= \dfrac{3-1}{3-2} = \dfrac{2}{1} = 2$

8. C

Point P (2,1) moves up 1 unit $\Rightarrow$ (2,2)
Point (2,2) is reflected over the y-axis $\Rightarrow$
Q (–2, 2)

The slope of line $PQ = \dfrac{2-1}{-2-2} = \dfrac{1}{-4}$.

9. C

If a line is perpendicular to the y-axis, it is a horizontal line.
If a horizontal line passes through the point (3, –2) the equation of the line is $y = -2$.

10. A

The opposite sides of a parallelogram are parallel.
Thus, slope of $\overline{PQ}$ = slope of $\overline{SR}$.

slope of $\overline{PQ} = \dfrac{4-0}{0-(-2)} = 2$

Choice (A) : If $R = (6, 4)$,

slope of $\overline{SR} = \dfrac{4-0}{6-4} = \dfrac{4}{2} = 2$

If you try the other answer choices, the slope will not be equal to 2.

11. E

Since the coordinate of R is (6, 4), the midpoint of PR is $\left(\dfrac{6+(-2)}{2}, \dfrac{4+0}{2} \right) = (2,2)$.

12. B

Plug the coordinates for each answer choice into the given equation, which is $(x-6)^2 + y^2 = 25$.

Choice (A) : $(2-6)^2 + 3^2 = 25$ True.
$\qquad\qquad (9-6)^2 + 3^2 = 25$ Not true.

Choice (B) : $(2-6)^2 + 3^2 = 25$ True.
$\qquad\qquad (10-6)^2 + 3^2 = 25$ True.

If you try the rest of the answer choices, none of them will make both equations true.

13. B

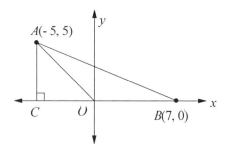

Draw a segment $\overline{AC}$ that is perpendicular to the x-axis, then $AC = 5$, $OC = 5$ and $BC = 12$.
$AO^2 = AC^2 + OC^2$ (Pythagorean theorem)
$\qquad = 5^2 + 5^2 = 50$
$\Rightarrow AO = 5\sqrt{2}$
$AB^2 = AC^2 + BC^2 = 5^2 + 12^2 = 169$
$\Rightarrow AB = 13$

Perimeter of triangle AOB
$= AB + AO + BO$
$= 13 + 5\sqrt{2} + 7 = 20 + 5\sqrt{2}$

14. C

Since the slope of the line $y = 2x$ is 2, the slope of the perpendicular line must be $-\dfrac{1}{2}$.

15. A

Let (x, y) be the coordinates of Q.

$(-3, 2) = \left(\dfrac{2+x}{2}, \dfrac{-3+y}{2} \right)$

$-3 = \dfrac{2+x}{2}$ and $2 = \dfrac{-3+y}{2}$ $\Rightarrow$ $x = -8$ and $y = 7$

The coordinates of Q are $(-8, 7)$.

16. D

$AB = \sqrt{6^2 + 2^2} = \sqrt{40}$
$AD = \sqrt{6^2 + 2^2} = \sqrt{40}$

Area of square $ABCD$
$= AB \cdot AD = \sqrt{40} \cdot \sqrt{40} = 40$

17. C

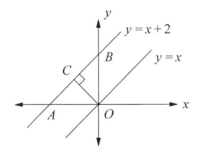

Draw a segment $\overline{OC}$ from the origin that is perpendicular to the line $y = x + 2$. This is the shortest distance between the lines $y = x$ and $y = x + 2$.
Since the x-intercept of the line $y = x + 2$ is -2 and the y-intercept of the same line is 2, triangle AOB is a $45°$-$45°$-$90°$ triangle.
$\Rightarrow$ triangle AOC is also a $45°$-$45°$-$90°$ triangle.
$\Rightarrow \dfrac{AO}{CO} = \dfrac{\sqrt{2}}{1}$ $\Rightarrow$ $\dfrac{2}{CO} = \dfrac{\sqrt{2}}{1}$ $\Rightarrow CO = \sqrt{2}$

Grid-In Questions

1. 12

Since $\overline{CD}$ and $\overline{BC}$ are radii of the semicircle, $CD = BC = 6$.
Therefore, the y-coordinate of D is 6. Also, the x-coordinate of D is 6.
$x + y = 6 + 6 = 12$

2. 9

Draw a triangle on a coordinate plane.
$\overline{AB}$ and $\overline{BC}$ are perpendicular.

Area of triangle ABC
$= \dfrac{1}{2} \cdot \text{base} \cdot \text{height}$ $= \dfrac{1}{2} \cdot AB \cdot BC$
$= \dfrac{1}{2}(6)(3) = 9$

3. 12

The coordinates of B are $(4,4)$. $\Rightarrow$ $OC = BC = 4$
Area of square $OABC = 4 \cdot 4 = 16$

The coordinates of D are $(k, 0)$. $\Rightarrow$ $OD = k$
$CD = OD - OC = k - 4$
Area of triangle BCD
$= \dfrac{1}{2} \cdot CD \cdot BC = \dfrac{1}{2}(k - 4)(4) = 2(k - 4)$

Area of square $OABC$ = Area of triangle BCD
$\Rightarrow$ $16 = 2(k - 4)$ $\Rightarrow$ $8 = k - 4$ $\Rightarrow$ $k = 12$

4. 10

The midpoint of $A(-1, 1)$ and $B(s, t)$ is $(2, 3)$.
$\Rightarrow$ $(2, 3) = \left(\dfrac{-1+s}{2}, \dfrac{1+t}{2} \right)$
$\Rightarrow$ $2 = \dfrac{-1+s}{2}$ and $3 = \dfrac{1+t}{2}$
$\Rightarrow$ $s = 5$, $t = 5$ $\Rightarrow$ $s + t = 5 + 5 = 10$

5. 2

slope of line $\ell = \dfrac{\text{change in } y}{\text{change in } x} = \dfrac{a}{2} = 2$

$\Rightarrow \ a = 4$

slope of line $m = \dfrac{\text{change in } y}{\text{change in } x} = \dfrac{b}{4} = \dfrac{1}{2}$

$\Rightarrow \ b = 2$

$a - b = 4 - 2 = 2$

6. 12

Area of the shaded region
= Area of triangle OBD − Area of triangle OAC

$= \dfrac{1}{2} \cdot 6 \cdot 5 - \dfrac{1}{2} \cdot 2 \cdot 3 = 15 - 3 = 12$

7. $\dfrac{3}{2}$

x-intercept of the line is $-4 \ \Rightarrow \ (-4, 0)$

y-intercept of the line is $6 \ \Rightarrow \ (0, 6)$

$\text{slope} = \dfrac{y_2 - y_1}{x_2 - x_1} = \dfrac{6 - 0}{0 - (-4)} = \dfrac{6}{4} = \dfrac{3}{2}$

8. 0

On the x-axis, the y-coordinate is 0. $\Rightarrow \ b = 0$
On the y-axis, the x-coordinate is 0. $\Rightarrow \ c = 0$
$b + c = 0 + 0 = 0$

9. 4

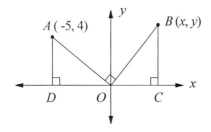

Draw segments $\overline{AD}$ and $\overline{BC}$ that are perpendicular to the x-axis.

$\angle ADO \cong \angle OCB$ (all right angles are congruent)
$\angle AOD \cong \angle OBC$ (Since $\angle AOB$ is a right angle, $\angle AOD$ and $\angle BOC$ are complementary. In the right triangle OBC, $\angle OBC$ and $\angle BOC$ are complementary.)
$\overline{AO} \cong \overline{OB}$

Therefore $\triangle AOD \cong \triangle OBC$ by AAS.
$AD = OC$ (by cpctc) $\ \Rightarrow \ OC = 4$
$\ \Rightarrow \ x = 4$

Another method for solving the problem:

The clockwise rotation about the origin through a $90°$ angle maps each point $P(a, b)$ to the point $P'(b, -a)$.

$A(-5, 4) \to A'(4, 5) = (x, y)$
$\ \Rightarrow \ x = 4$

10. 8

Use the distance formula.
$d = \sqrt{(x_2 - x_1)^2 + (y_2 - y_1)^2}$
$OB = \sqrt{(5 - 0)^2 + (3 - 0)^2} = \sqrt{25 + 9} = \sqrt{34}$
$AB = \sqrt{(2 - 5)^2 + (y - 3)^2} = \sqrt{9 + (y - 3)^2}$
$AB = OB \Rightarrow \sqrt{9 + (y - 3)^2} = \sqrt{34}$
$\Rightarrow 9 + (y - 3)^2 = 34 \ \Rightarrow \ (y - 3)^2 = 25$
$\Rightarrow y - 3 = \pm \sqrt{25} = \pm 5 \ \Rightarrow \ y = \pm 5 + 3$
$\Rightarrow y = 8 \ \text{or} \ y = -2$

However point A is in the first quadrant, so $y = 8$.

11. 17

Area of triangle OAB
$= \dfrac{1}{2} OB \cdot AB = \dfrac{1}{2} \sqrt{34} \cdot \sqrt{34} = \dfrac{1}{2} \cdot 34 = 17$

13. Lines and Angles

Key Terms / Illustrations

Examples

---

1. Segment Addition Postulate

If Q is between P and R, then $PQ + QR = PR$.

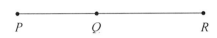

2. Definition of Midpoint

If M is the midpoint of $\overline{PQ}$, then

$$PM = MQ = \frac{1}{2}PQ.$$

3. A **segment bisector** is a line or a segment that intersects a segment at its midpoint.

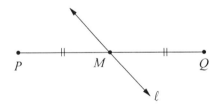

Line ℓ is a segment bisector.

4. Angle Addition Postulate

If C is in the interior of $\angle AOB$, then
$m\angle AOB = m\angle AOC + m\angle COB$

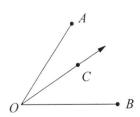

Example 1 □   **Segment addition postulate**

On the segment PS above, $PR = 12$, $QS = 16$, and $QR = \frac{1}{3}PS$. What is the length of PS?

Solution □

Let $QR = x$, then $PS = 3x$.

$PQ + QR = PR$	Segment addition postulate
$PQ + x = 12$	Substitution
$PQ = 12 - x$	Solve for PQ.
$QR + RS = QS$	Segment addition postulate
$x + RS = 16$	Substitution
$RS = 16 - x$	Solve for RS.
$PQ + QR + RS = PS$	Segment addition postulate
$(12 - x) + x + (16 - x)$	Substitution
$= 3x$	
$28 - x = 3x$	Simplify.
$x = 7$	Solve for x.
$PS = 3x = 3(7) = 21$	Answer

5. An **angle bisector** divides an angle into two
   congruent angles.

   If $\overrightarrow{OC}$ is the angle bisector of $\angle AOB$, then

   $m\angle AOC = m\angle COB = \dfrac{1}{2}m\angle AOB$

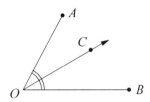

6. **Vertical angles** are congruent.

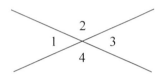

   $\angle 1$ and $\angle 3$ are vertical angles. $m\angle 1 = m\angle 3$
   $\angle 2$ and $\angle 4$ are vertical angles. $m\angle 2 = m\angle 4$

7. All **right angles** are congruent.

8. A **straight angle** measures 180°.

9. Two angles whose measures have a sum of 180 are
   called **supplementary angles**.

10. Two angles whose measures have a sum of 90 are
    called **complementary angles**.

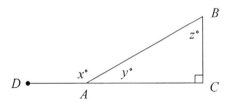

    In the figure above, x and y are **supplementary**
    and y and z are **complementary**.

Example 2 □   **Midpoint**

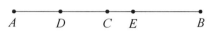

On the segment AB above, point C is the midpoint
of $\overline{AB}$, point D is the midpoint of $\overline{AC}$, and point
E is the midpoint of $\overline{BD}$. If the length of segment
DE is 9, what is the length of segment CE?

Solution □

   Let $AD = x$, then $AC = 2x$, and $AB = 4x$.

$DB = 2DE = 18$	Definition of midpoint.
$AD + DB = AB$	Segment addition postulate
$x + 18 = 4x$	Substitution
$x = 6$	Solve for x.

$AD = DC = 6$	D is the midpoint of AC.
$DC + CE = DE$	Segment addition postulate
$6 + CE = 9$	Substitution
$CE = 3$	Answer

Example 3 □   **Finding the measures of angles**

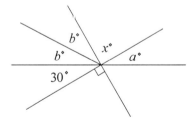

In the figure above, what is the value of $a + b$?

Solution □

$x = 90$	Vertical angles are congruent.
$a = 30$	Vertical angles are congruent.
$b + b + x + a = 180$	A straight angle measures 180.
$2b + 90 + 30 = 180$	Substitution
$b = 30$	Solve for b.
$a + b = 30 + 30$	
$= 60$	Answer

11. Parallel Lines and Transversals

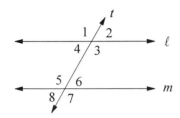

Two parallel lines ℓ and m are cut by a transversal t.

If two parallel lines are cut by a transversal, then

1) each pair of **corresponding angles** are equal in measure.

$m\angle 1 = m\angle 5$, $m\angle 2 = m\angle 6$,
$m\angle 3 = m\angle 7$, $m\angle 4 = m\angle 8$,

2) each pair of **alternate interior angles** are equal in measure.

$m\angle 3 = m\angle 5$, $m\angle 4 = m\angle 6$

3) each pair of **alternate exterior angles** are equal in measure.

$m\angle 1 = m\angle 7$, $m\angle 2 = m\angle 8$

4) each pair of **consecutive interior (same-side interior) angles** are supplementary.

$m\angle 3 + m\angle 6 = 180°$, $m\angle 4 + m\angle 5 = 180°$

Example 4 □ **Supplementary angles**

The measure of an angle is 15 more than twice its supplement. Find the measure of the two angles.

Solution □

Let x = measure of an angle.
Then $180 - x$ = its supplementary angle.

The measure of an angle	is	15 more than	twice its supplement
x	$=$	$15 +$	$2(180 - x)$

$$x = 15 + 360 - 2x$$
$$x = 125$$

$$180 - x = 180 - 125$$
$$= 55$$

The measures of the two angles are
125° and 55°.   Answer

Example 5 □ **Parallel lines and transversals**

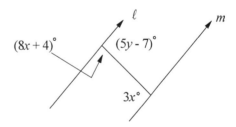

In the figure above, $\ell \| m$. Find the values of x and y.

Solution □

$3x + (8x + 4) = 180$	Consecutive interior angles are supplementary.
$11x + 4 = 180$	Simplify.
$x = 16$	Answer
$3x = 5y - 7$	Alternate interior angles are equal in measure.
$3(16) = 5y - 7$	Substitution
$y = 11$	Answer

12. **Perpendicular Lines** intersect to form four right angles.

☑ Any point on the **perpendicular bisector** of a segment is equidistant from the endpoints of the segment.

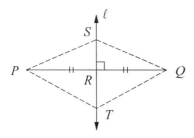

In the figure above, $PS = QS$ and $PT = QT$.

13. **A Line Perpendicular to One of Two Parallel Lines**

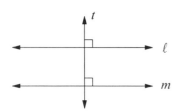

Lines ℓ and m are parallel lines.

In a plane, if a line is perpendicular to one of two parallel lines, then it is also perpendicular to the second line.

Example 6 □ **A line perpendicular to two parallel lines**

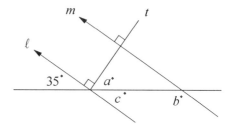

In the figure above, $\ell \parallel m$. What is the value of $a + b$?

Solution □

$m\angle c = 35$ — Vertical angles are $\cong$.
$m\angle a + m\angle c = 90$ — $\angle a$ and $\angle c$ are complementary.
$m\angle a + 35 = 90$ — Substitution
$m\angle a = 55$

$m\angle b + m\angle c = 180$ — Consecutive interior angles are supplementary.
$m\angle b + 35 = 180$ — Substitution
$m\angle b = 145$

$m\angle a + m\angle b = 55 + 145$ — Substitution
$= 200$ — Answer

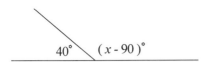

1. In the figure above, $x =$

(A) 50   (B) 70   (C) 130

(D) 170   (E) 230

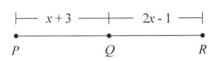

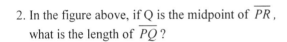

2. In the figure above, if Q is the midpoint of $\overline{PR}$, what is the length of $\overline{PQ}$?

(A) 4   (B) 7   (C) 9

(D) 11   (E) 14

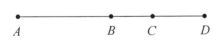

3. In the figure above, if $AC = 17$, $BD = 12$, and B is the midpoint of $\overline{AD}$, what is the length of $\overline{CD}$?

(A) 4   (B) 7   (C) 9

(D) 11   (E) 14

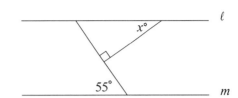

4. In the figure above, lines ℓ and m are parallel. What is the value of x?

(A) 25   (B) 30   (C) 35

(D) 40   (E) 45

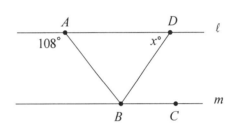

5. In the figure above, lines ℓ and m are parallel and $\overline{BD}$ bisects $\angle ABC$. What is the value of x?

(A) 72   (B) 68   (C) 62

(D) 54   (E) 42

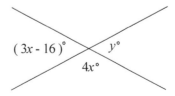

6. In the figure above, $y =$

(A) 68   (B) 60   (C) 54

(D) 48   (E) 42

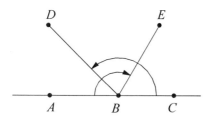

7. In the figure above, $m\angle ABE = 120°$ and $m\angle CBD = 135°$. What is the measure of $\angle DBE$?

(A) 40   (B) 50   (C) 65

(D) 75   (E) 80

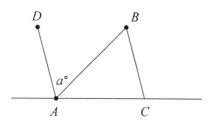

8. In the figure above, $\overline{DA} \parallel \overline{BC}$ and $\overline{AB}$ bisects $\angle DAC$. What is the measure of $\angle BCA$ in terms of a?

(A) $180 - a$

(B) $2a - 180$

(C) $180 - 2a$

(D) $2a - 90$

(E) $90 - a$

9. The measure of the supplement of an angle is 50 more than twice the measure of the complement of the angle. Which of the following equations can be used to find the measure of the angle?

(A) $90 - x = (180 - x) + 50$

(B) $180 - x = 2(90 - x) + 50$

(C) $180 - x = 2(x - 90) + 50$

(D) $180 - x = 2(50 + x)$

(E) $180 - x = 2x + 50$

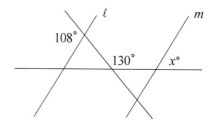

10. In the figure above, lines ℓ and m are parallel. What is the value of x?

(A) 36   (B) 46   (C) 58

(D) 61   (E) 72

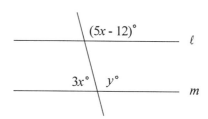

11. In the figure above, $\ell \parallel m$. What is the value of $x + y$?

(A) 105   (B) 112   (C) 132

(D) 140   (E) 155

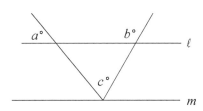

12. In the figure above, $\ell \parallel m$. If $a = 50°$ and $b = 120°$, what is the value of c?

(A) 40   (B) 50   (C) 60

(D) 70   (E) 80

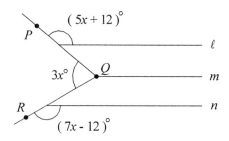

14. In the figure above, $\ell \parallel m \parallel n$. What is the measure of $\angle PQR$?

(A) 72   (B) 60   (C) 48

(D) 36   (E) 24

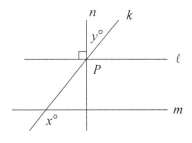

13. In the figure above, $\ell \parallel m$ and $\ell \perp n$. Lines k, ℓ, and n intersect at point P. Which of the following is true?

(A) $x - y = 90$

(B) $180 - x = y$

(C) $x + y = 90$

(D) $x = 2y$

(E) $x + 2y = 180$

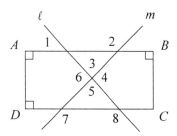

15. In the figure above, $ABCD$ is a rectangle, and two lines ℓ and m intersect as shown. Which of the following must be true?

 I. $m\angle 1 + m\angle 8 = 180$

 II. $m\angle 2 = m\angle 7$

 III. $m\angle 6 = m\angle 8$

 IV. $m\angle 4 + m\angle 6 = 180$

(A) I only

(B) I and II only

(C) II and III only

(D) I, II, and III only

(E) I, II, III, and IV

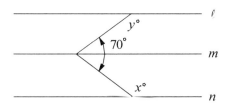

1. In the figure above, if lines ℓ, m, and n are parallel, what is the value of $x + y$?

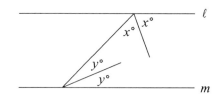

4. In the figure above, lines ℓ and m are parallel. What is the value of $x + y$?

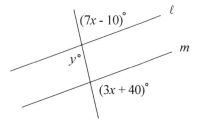

2. In the figure above, if lines ℓ and m are parallel, what is the value of y?

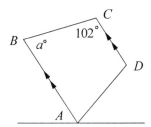

3. In the figure above, if lines $\overline{AB}$ and $\overline{CD}$ are parallel, what is the value of a?

```
•        •        •              •
A        B        C              D
```

Note : Figure not drawn to scale.

5. In the figure above, $AD = 15$, $AB = \dfrac{3}{2}BC$, and $BC = \dfrac{2}{5}CD$. What is the length of $\overline{AC}$?

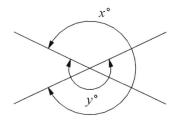

6. In the figure above, what is the value of $x + y$?

Answer Key

<u>Multiple Choice Questions</u>

1. E	2. B	3. B	4. C	5. D
6. A	7. D	8. C	9. B	10. C
11. C	12. D	13. A	14. A	15. B

<u>Grid-In Questions</u>

1. 290	2. 95	3. 78	4. 90	5. 7.5
6. 540				

Answers and Explanations

<u>Multiple Choice Questions</u>

1. E

$$40 + (x - 90) = 180 \implies x - 50 = 180$$
$$\implies x = 230$$

2. B

Q is the midpoint of $\overline{PR} \implies x + 3 = 2x - 1$
$$\implies x = 4$$
$$\implies PQ = x + 3 = 4 + 3 = 7$$

3. B

Given $BD = 12$ and B is the midpoint of $\overline{AD}$.
$$\implies AB = BD = 12$$
$$AC = AB + BC = 12 + BC = 17 \implies BC = 5$$

$$BD = BC + CD \implies 12 = 5 + CD$$
$$\implies CD = 7$$

4. C

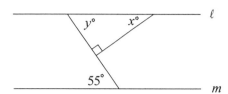

$y = 55°$ (If 2 lines are ‖ then the alternate interior
                angles are ≅ .)
$x + y = 90$ (The acute angles of a right triangle are
                complementary.)
$\implies x + 55 = 90 \implies x = 35$

5. D

$m\angle ABC = 108$ (If 2 lines are ‖ then the alternate
                interior angles are ≅ .)

$\overline{BD}$ bisects $\angle ABC \implies m\angle DBC = 54$
$\implies x = 54$ (If 2 lines are ‖ then the alternate interior
                angles are ≅ .)

6. A

$(3x - 16) + 4x = 180$ (The measure of a straight angle
                equals 180.)
$\implies 7x - 16 = 180 \implies 7x = 196$
$\implies x = 28$
$3x - 16 = y$ (Vertical angles are congruent.)
$3(28) - 16 = y \implies y = 68$

7. D

Let $x = m\angle DBE$.
$m\angle ABE = m\angle ABD + x = 120°$
$\implies m\angle ABD = 120 - x$

$m\angle ABD + m\angle CBD = 180$
(The measure of a straight angle equals 180.)

$(120 - x) + 135 = 180 \implies 255 - x = 180$
$\implies x = 75$

8. C

Since $\overline{AB}$ bisects $\angle DAC$, $m\angle BAC = a$.
$m\angle DAB = m\angle ABC$ (If 2 lines are ∥ then the alternate
interior angles are ≅.)
$\Rightarrow m\angle ABC = a$

$a + a + m\angle BCA = 180$ (The sum of the angle measures
of a triangle is 180.)
$\Rightarrow m\angle BCA = 180 - 2a$

9. B

Let the measure of an angle $= x$, then $(180 - x)$
is the measure of the supplement of the angle, and
$(90 - x)$ is the measure of the complement of the
angle.

$$\underbrace{180 - x}_{\substack{\text{The measure of the} \\ \text{supplement of the angle}}} = \underbrace{2(90 - x)}_{\substack{\text{twice the measure of the} \\ \text{complement of the angle.}}} \underbrace{+ \; 50}_{\substack{\text{50 more than}}}$$

10. C

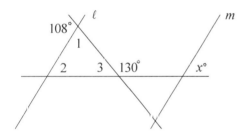

$m\angle 1 = 180 - 108 = 72$
$m\angle 2 = x$ (If 2 lines are ∥ then the corresponding
angles are ≅.)
$m\angle 3 = 180 - 130 = 50$

$m\angle 1 + m\angle 2 + m\angle 3 = 180$
$72 + x + 50 = 180 \Rightarrow x = 58$

11. C

$3x + y = 180$ (The measure of a straight angle
equals 180.)
$y = 5x - 12$ (Corresponding angles are ≅.)

$3x + (5x - 12) = 180$ (Substitution)
$\Rightarrow 8x - 12 = 180 \Rightarrow 8x = 192$
$\Rightarrow x = 24$
$y = 5x - 12 = 5(24) - 12 = 108$
$x + y = 24 + 108 = 132$

12. D

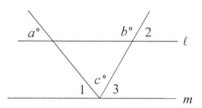

Given $a = 50°$, $b = 120°$.
$a = m\angle 1$ (Corresponding angles are ≅.)
$\Rightarrow m\angle 1 = 50$
$b = 120° \Rightarrow m\angle 2 = 60$
$m\angle 2 = m\angle 3$ (Corresponding angles are ≅.)
$\Rightarrow m\angle 3 = 60$

$m\angle 1 + c + m\angle 2 = 180$
$\Rightarrow 50 + c + 60 = 180 \Rightarrow c = 70$

13. A

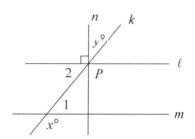

$m\angle 1 + x = 180 \Rightarrow m\angle 1 = 180 - x$
$m\angle 1 = m\angle 2$ (Alternate interior angles are ≅.)

$\Rightarrow m\angle 2 = 180 - x$

$m\angle 2 + 90 + y = 180 \Rightarrow (180 - x) + 90 + y = 180$
$\Rightarrow 270 - x + y = 180$
$\Rightarrow x - y = 90$

14. A

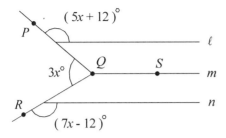

Let S be a point on line m.
$m\angle PQS = 5x + 12$ (Corresponding angles are $\cong$.)
$m\angle RQS = 7x - 12$ (Corresponding angles are $\cong$.)

$\Rightarrow \ 3x + m\angle PQS + m\angle RQS = 360$
$\Rightarrow \ 3x + (5x+12) + (7x-12) = 360$
$\Rightarrow \ 15x = 360 \ \Rightarrow \ x = 24$

$m\angle PQR = 3x = 3 \cdot 24 = 72$

15. B

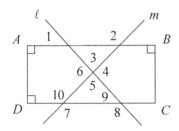

 I. True.

   $m\angle 1 = m\angle 9$ and $m\angle 9 + m\angle 8 = 180$

   By substitution, $m\angle 1 + m\angle 8 = 180$

 II. True.

   $m\angle 2 = m\angle 10$ and $m\angle 7 = m\angle 10$

   By substitution, $m\angle 2 = m\angle 7$

III. Not true.

   Since $\overline{DC}$ is not parallel to ℓ, $m\angle 6 \ne m\angle 8$.

IV. Not true.

   Vertical angles are congruent. But we don't have information about the measure of $\angle 6$ or $\angle 4$, so we cannot conclude that the sum of the vertical angle measures is 180.

<u>Grid-In Questions</u>

1. 290

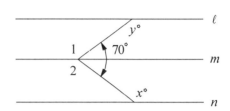

$m\angle 1 = y$ and $m\angle 2 = x$
(If 2 lines are || then the alt. int. $\angle$ are $\cong$.)
$m\angle 1 + m\angle 2 + 70 = 360$
$\Rightarrow \ y + x + 70 = 360$
$\Rightarrow \ y + x = 290$

2. 95

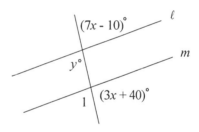

$y = 7x - 10$ (Vertical angles are congruent.)
$m\angle 1 = y$ (Corresponding angles are $\cong$.)
$m\angle 1 + (3x+40) = 180 \ \Rightarrow \ y + (3x+40) = 180$

$(7x-10) + (3x+40) = 180$ (Make a substitution:
$\qquad\qquad\qquad\qquad\qquad y = 7x-10$)
$\Rightarrow \ 10x + 30 = 180 \ \Rightarrow \ 10x = 150$
$\Rightarrow \ x = 15$
$y = 7x - 10 = 7(15) - 10 = 95$

3. 78

If 2 lines are ||, then the same-side (consecutive) interior angles are supplementary.

$a + 102 = 180 \ \Rightarrow \ a = 78$

4. 90

$2x + 2y = 180$ (If 2 lines are ∥, then the same side
interior angles are supplementary.)

$2(x + y) = 180 \implies x + y = 90$

5. 7.5

Let the length of $\overline{CD} = x$.

$BC = \dfrac{2}{5}CD = \dfrac{2}{5}x$

$AB = \dfrac{3}{2}BC = \dfrac{3}{2}(\dfrac{2}{5}x) = \dfrac{3}{5}x$

$AB + BC + CD = AD$

$\implies \dfrac{3}{5}x + \dfrac{2}{5}x + x = 15 \implies 2x = 15$

$x = 7.5$

$AC = AB + BC = \dfrac{3}{5}x + \dfrac{2}{5}x = x = 7.5$

6. 540

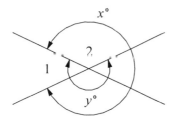

$m\angle 1 + x = 360$
$m\angle 2 + y = 360$

By adding these two equations, we have
$m\angle 1 + m\angle 2 + x + y = 720$

$m\angle 1 + m\angle 2 = 180$ (The measure of a straight angle
equals 180.)

$180 + x + y = 720$ (180 is substituted for $m\angle 1 + m\angle 2$.)

$\implies x + y = 540$

14. Triangles

Key Terms / Illustrations   Examples

---

1. Angle Sum Theorem

The angle sum in a triangle is $180°$.

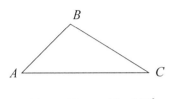

$$m\angle A + m\angle B + m\angle C = 180^0$$

☑ The acute angles of a right triangle are complementary.

2. Exterior Angle Theorem

The measure of an exterior angle of a triangle is equal to the sum of the measures of the two remote interior angles.

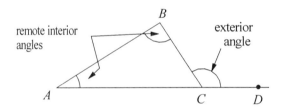

$$m\angle BCD = m\angle A + m\angle B$$

☑ The measure of an exterior angle is greater than the the measure of either of its corresponding remote interior angles.

$$m\angle BCD > m\angle A, \quad m\angle BCD > m\angle B$$

3. Isosceles Triangle Theorem

If two sides of a triangle are congruent, then the angles opposite those sides are congruent.

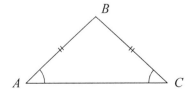

If $AB = BC$ then $m\angle C = m\angle A$.
The converse is also true.

Example 1 ☐ Angle sum theorem

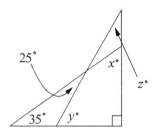

In the figure above, find the value of x, y, and z.

Solution ☐

$x + 35 = 90$	The acute angles of a right triangle are complementary.
$x = 55$	Answer
$y = 35 + 25$	Exterior angle theorem
$= 60$	Answer
$y + z = 90$	The acute angles of a right triangle are complementary.
$60 + z = 90$	Make a substitution for y.
$z = 30$	Answer

Example 2 ☐ Isosceles triangle, exterior angle

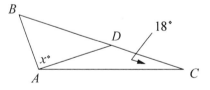

In $\triangle ABC$ above, if $AB = AD = DC$ then $x =$

Solution ☐

$m\angle DAC = m\angle C = 18$	Isosceles Triangle Theorem
$m\angle BDA = m\angle DAC + m\angle C$	Exterior Angle
$= 18 + 18 = 36$	Theorem
$m\angle B = m\angle BDA = 36$	Isosceles Triangle Theorem
$m\angle B + m\angle BDA + x = 180$	Angle Sum Theorem
$36 + 36 + x = 180$	Substitution
$x = 108$	Answer

4. Pythagorean Theorem

In a right triangle, the sum of the squares of the lengths of the legs equals the square of the length of the hypotenuse.

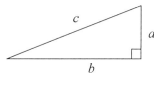

$$a^2 + b^2 = c^2$$

☑ **A Pythagorean triple** is a group of three whole numbers that satisfy the equation $a^2 + b^2 = c^2$. Integers such as 3, 4, 5 $(3^2 + 4^2 = 5^2)$ and 5, 12, 13 $(5^2 + 12^2 = 13^2)$ are Pythagorean triples.

5. Special Right Triangles

1) In a **45°- 45°- 90° triangle**, the hypotenuse is $\sqrt{2}$ times as long as a leg.

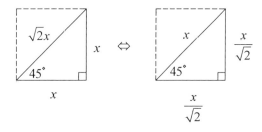

2) In a **30°- 60°- 90° triangle,** the hypotenuse is twice as long as the shorter leg, and the longer leg is $\sqrt{3}$ times as long as the shorter leg.

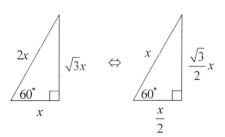

Example 3 □ Pythagorean theorem

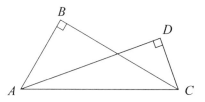

In the figure above, if $AB = 5$, $BC = 8$, and $AD = 9$, what is the length of CD?

Solution □

$$\begin{aligned}
AB^2 + BC^2 &= AC^2 && \text{Pythagorean Theorem}\\
AD^2 + CD^2 &= AC^2 && \text{Pythagorean Theorem}\\
AB^2 + BC^2 &= AD^2 + CD^2 && \text{Make substitutions.}\\
5^2 + 8^2 &= 9^2 + CD^2 && \text{Make substitutions.}\\
89 &= 81 + CD^2\\
CD &= \sqrt{8} = \sqrt{4}\cdot\sqrt{2} = 2\sqrt{2} && \text{Answer}
\end{aligned}$$

Example 4 □ Special right triangles

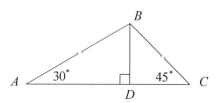

In $\triangle ABC$ above $BD = 3$. Find the length of AB, AD, CD, and BC.

Solution □

$$\begin{aligned}
AB &= 2(BD) = 2(3) = 6\\
AD &= \sqrt{3}(BD) = \sqrt{3}(3) = 3\sqrt{3}
\end{aligned}$$

$$\begin{aligned}
BD &= CD = 3\\
BC &= \sqrt{2}(BD) = \sqrt{2}(3) = 3\sqrt{2} && \text{Answer}
\end{aligned}$$

6. Area of a Triangle

The area of a triangle equals half the product of a base and the height to that base.

$$\text{Area of a triangle} = \frac{1}{2}b \cdot h$$

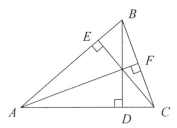

Area of $\triangle ABC$

$$= \frac{1}{2}AC \cdot BD = \frac{1}{2}BC \cdot AF = \frac{1}{2}AB \cdot CE$$

☑ *If two sides of a triangle **r** and **s** are given, the maximum possible area of the triangle is $\frac{1}{2}rs$.*

$$0 < \text{Area of } \triangle \text{ with two sides } r \text{ and } s \le \frac{1}{2}r \cdot s$$

7. Angle-Angle Similarity (AA Similarity)

If two angles of one triangle are congruent to two angles of another triangle, then the two triangles are similar.

☑ If two triangles are similar, their corresponding angles are congruent and their corresponding sides are in proportion.

☑ If two triangles are similar, their perimeters are proportional to the measures of the corresponding sides.

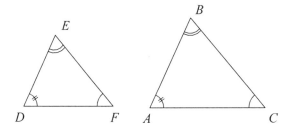

In the figure above, if $\angle A \cong \angle D$ and $\angle B \cong \angle E$ then it follows that $\angle C \cong \angle F$. Therefore $\triangle ABC \sim \triangle DBE$, and $\dfrac{AB}{DE} = \dfrac{BC}{EF} = \dfrac{AC}{DF}$.

Example 5 □   **Area of a triangle**

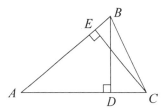

In the figure above if $AC = 6$, $BD = 4$, and $AB = 8$, what is the length of CE?

Solution □

$$\text{Area of triangle } ABC = \frac{1}{2}AC \cdot BD = \frac{1}{2}AB \cdot CE$$

$$\frac{1}{2}(6)(4) = \frac{1}{2}(8)(CE)$$

$$CE = 3 \qquad \text{Answer}$$

Example 6 □   **Similar triangles**

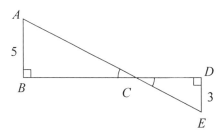

In the figure above $AB = 5$, $DE = 3$, and $BD = 12$. Find the length of BC.

Solution □

The two triangles are similar, since $m\angle B = m\angle D$ and $m\angle ACB = m\angle ECD$. Therefore the ratios of their corresponding sides are proportional.

Let $BC = x$, then $CD = 12 - x$.

$$\frac{AB}{ED} = \frac{BC}{DC} \Rightarrow \frac{5}{3} = \frac{x}{12 - x}$$

$$\Rightarrow 5(12 - x) = 3x$$
$$\Rightarrow x = 7.5 \qquad \text{Answer}$$

8. Triangle Proportionality

If a line parallel to one side of a triangle intersects the other two sides, then it divides those sides proportionally.

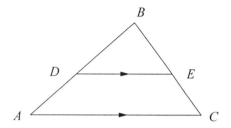

In the triangle above, $AC \parallel DE$.

$$\frac{BD}{DA} = \frac{BE}{EC}, \ \frac{DA}{BA} = \frac{EC}{BC},$$

$$\frac{BD}{DE} = \frac{BA}{AC}, \text{ and } \frac{BE}{DE} = \frac{BC}{AC}$$

☑ A segment whose endpoints are the midpoints of two sides of a triangle is parallel to the third side of the triangle, and the length of the segment is one-half the length of the third side.

9. Similarity in Right Triangles

If an altitude is drawn to the hypotenuse of a right triangle, then the two triangles formed are similar to the original triangle and to each other.

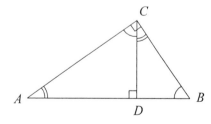

$\Delta CBD \sim \Delta ACD \sim \Delta ABC$

$\angle BCD \cong \ \angle A \ \cong \angle A$

$\angle B \ \ \ \cong \angle ACD \cong \angle B$

$\angle CDB \cong \angle ADC \cong \angle ACB$

Example 7 □   Triangle proportionality

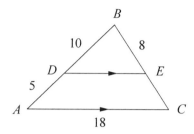

In the figure above $DE \parallel AC$. Find DE and EC.

Solution □

$$\frac{BD}{DA} = \frac{BE}{EC} \ \Rightarrow \ \frac{10}{5} = \frac{8}{EC}$$

$$\frac{BD}{DE} = \frac{BA}{AC} \ \Rightarrow \ \frac{10}{DE} = \frac{10+5}{18}$$

$EC = 4$, $DE = 12$ Answer

Example 8 □   Similarity in right triangles

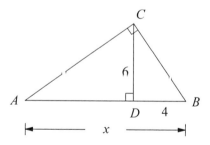

In the figure above, find the value of x.

Solution □

$$\frac{AD}{CD} = \frac{CD}{BD} \qquad \Delta ADC \sim \Delta CDB$$

$$\frac{x-4}{6} = \frac{6}{4} \qquad\qquad \text{Substitution}$$

$$4(x-4) = 6 \cdot 6 \qquad\quad \text{Cross product}$$

$$x = 13 \qquad\qquad\qquad \text{Answer}$$

10. Ratios of Areas of Triangles

(1) If two triangles are similar with corresponding sides in the ratio of $a:b$, then the ratio of their areas equals $a^2:b^2$.

(2) If two triangles have equal heights, then the ratio of their areas equals the ratio of their bases.

(3) If two triangles have equal bases, then the ratio of their areas equals the ratio of their heights.

11. Inequality for Sides and Angles of a Triangle

If one side of a triangle is longer than another side, then the angle opposite the longer side has a greater measure than the angle opposite the shorter side.

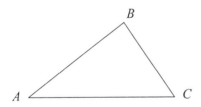

If $AB > BC$ then $m\angle C > m\angle A$

The converse is also true.
If $m\angle C > m\angle A$ then $AB > BC$

12. Triangle Inequality

The length of one side of a triangle is greater than the positive difference of the lengths of the two other sides, and is less than the sum of the lengths of the two other sides.

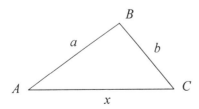

In the $\triangle ABC$ above if $a > b$, then the length of the third side x of the triangle is

$$a - b < x < a + b$$

Example 9 □   **Ratio of the areas of similar triangles**

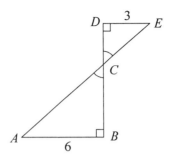

In the figure above $AB = 6$ and $DE = 3$. Find the ratio of the area of $\triangle ABC$ to the area of $\triangle CDE$.

Solution □

The two triangles are similar, since $m\angle B = m\angle D$, and $m\angle ACB = m\angle ECD$. Therefore the ratio of the areas of the two triangles is equal to the ratio of the squares of their corresponding sides.

$$\frac{\text{area of } \triangle ABC}{\text{area of } \triangle EDC} = \frac{6^2}{3^2} = \frac{4}{1} \quad \text{Answer}$$

Example 10 □   **Ratio of the areas of two triangles with equal heights**

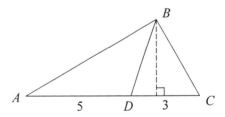

In the figure above $AD = 5$ and $DC = 3$. Find the ratio of the area of $\triangle ABD$ to the area of $\triangle CBD$.

Solution □

The two triangles have the same height, so the ratio of the areas of the two triangles is equal to the ratio of their bases.

$$\frac{\text{area of } \triangle ABD}{\text{area of } \triangle CBD} = \frac{5}{3} \quad \text{Answer}$$

13. **Pythagorean Inequality**

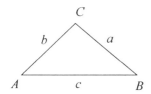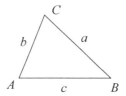

If $c^2 > a^2 + b^2$, then $\angle C$ is an obtuse angle.

If $c^2 < a^2 + b^2$, then $\angle C$ is an acute angle.

The converse is also true.

If $\angle C$ is an obtuse angle, then $c^2 > a^2 + b^2$.

If $\angle C$ is an acute angle, then $c^2 < a^2 + b^2$.

14. **Trigonometric Ratio**

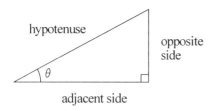

$$\sin \theta = \frac{\text{opposite}}{\text{hypotenuse}} \qquad \cos \theta = \frac{\text{adjacent}}{\text{hypotenuse}}$$

$$\tan \theta = \frac{\text{opposite}}{\text{adjacent}}$$

Trigonometric ratios are related to the acute angles of a right triangle, *not* to the right angle.

15. **Definition of Congruent Triangles**

Two triangles are congruent if and only if their corresponding parts are congruent.

☑ The abbreviation **cpctc** means "corresponding parts of congruent triangles are congruent."

Example 11 □   **Inequalities of a triangle**

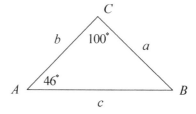

Which of the following is true about $\triangle ABC$ above?

  I. $c^2 > a^2 + b^2$
 II. $c > a + b$
III. $a > b$

(A) I only

(B) II only

(C) III only

(D) I and III only

(E) I, II, and III

Solution □

$m\angle C > 90 \;\Rightarrow\; c^2 > a^2 + b^2$

Triangle inequality $\;\Rightarrow\; c < a + b$

$m\angle A > m\angle B \;\Rightarrow\; a > b$

Choice (D) is correct.

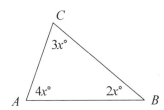

1. In the triangle above, what is the measure of ∠B ?

(A) 20   (B) 30   (C) 40

(D) 60   (E) 80

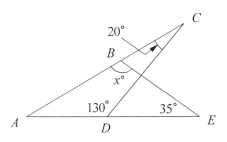

2. In the figure above, what is the value of x?

(A) 115   (B) 120   (C) 125

(D) 130   (E) 135

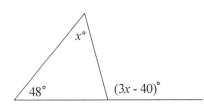

3. In the figure above, what is the value of x?

(A) 40   (B) 44   (C) 48

(D) 56   (E) 64

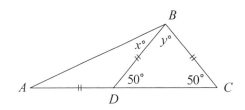

4. In the triangle above, what is the value of $x + y$?

(A) 65   (B) 70   (C) 80

(D) 95   (E) 105

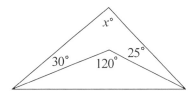

5. In the triangle above, what is the value of x?

(A) 60   (B) 65   (C) 70

(D) 75   (E) 80

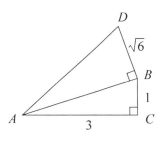

6. In the figure above, $\overline{AC} \perp \overline{BC}$ and $\overline{AB} \perp \overline{DB}$. What is the length of $\overline{AD}$?

(A) 4   (B) $2\sqrt{5}$ (C) 5

(D) $\sqrt{26}$ (E) 6

7. In triangle PQR, $PQ = QR$ and the measure of angle PQR is three times the measure of angle QPR. If $\overline{PS}$ and $\overline{QS}$ are angle bisectors of angle QPR and angle PQR, respectively, what is the degree measure of angle PSQ?

(A) 58　　　　(B) 64　　　　(C) 72

(D) 86　　　　(E) 108

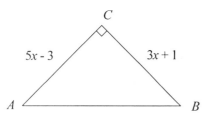

8. In the figure above, $\overline{AC} \perp \overline{BC}$ and $AC = BC$. What is the length of $\overline{AB}$?

(A) 2　　　　(B) 4　　　　(C) 7

(D) $7\sqrt{2}$　　　　(E) $8\sqrt{2}$

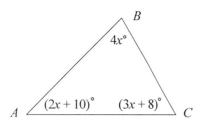

9. In $\triangle ABC$ above, which of the following must be true?

(A) $AC > AB > BC$

(B) $AB > BC > AC$

(C) $BC > AB > AC$

(D) $AB > AC > BC$

(E) It cannot be determined from the information given.

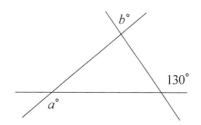

10. In the figure above, $a - b =$

(A) 40　　　　(B) 50　　　　(C) 60

(D) 70　　　　(E) 80

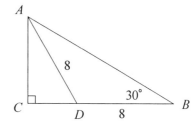

11. In the figure above, if $AD = BD = 8$, then $BC =$

(A) 10　　　　(B) 12　　　　(C) $8 + 4\sqrt{2}$

(D) 15　　　　(E) $8 + 4\sqrt{3}$

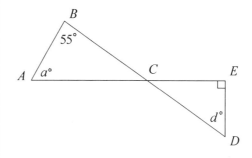

12. In the figure above, $\overline{AE} \perp \overline{DE}$. What is the value of $a - d$?

(A) 25　　　　(B) 30　　　　(C) 35

(D) 40　　　　(E) 45

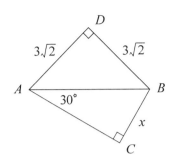

13. In the figure above, what is the value of x?

(A) 3   (B) $3\sqrt{3}$ (C) $\sqrt{6}$

(D) $2\sqrt{6}$ (E) 6

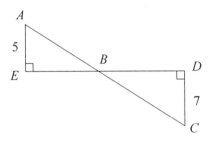

14. In the figure above, if $AE = 5$, $CD = 7$, and $DE = 16$, what is the length of AC?

(A) 12   (B) $10\sqrt{3}$ (C) 20

(D) $12\sqrt{2}$ (E) 24

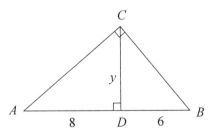

15. In the figure above, $\overline{AC} \perp \overline{BC}$, and $\overline{AB} \perp \overline{CD}$. What is the value of y?

(A) 4   (B) $4\sqrt{3}$ (C) 5

(D) 7   (E) $5\sqrt{2}$

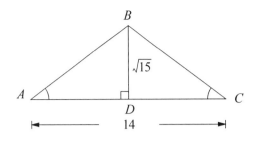

16. In the figure above, $\angle A \cong \angle C$ and $\overline{BD} \perp \overline{AC}$. What is the length of $\overline{AB}$?

(A) 7

(B) 8

(C) 9

(D) $5\sqrt{3}$

(E) 10

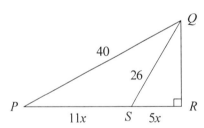

17. In the figure above, what is the length of $\overline{QR}$?

(A) 16

(B) 18

(C) 20

(D) 22

(E) 24

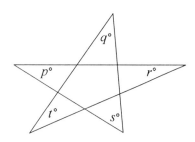

18. In the figure above, if $p = 35, q = 30, s = 40$, and $t = 25$, what is the value of r?

    (A) 30
    (B) 35
    (C) 40
    (D) 45
    (E) 50

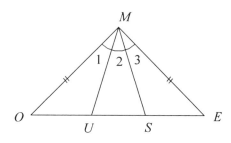

20. In the figure above, $\overline{MO} \cong \overline{ME}$ and $\angle 1 \cong \angle 2 \cong \angle 3$. Which of the following must be true?

    I. $\overline{OU} \cong \overline{US} \cong \overline{SE}$
    II. $\overline{MU} \cong \overline{MS}$
    III. $m\angle O \cong m\angle E$

    (A) None
    (B) I only
    (C) II only
    (D) II and III only
    (E) I, II, and III

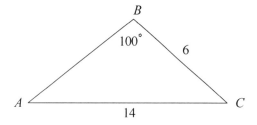

19. Which of the following must be true of $\triangle ABC$ above?

    (A) The perimeter of $\triangle ABC$ is less than 28.
    (B) $AB < BC$
    (C) $AB < 8$
    (D) The area of $\triangle ABC$ is less than 42.
    (E) $AB^2 + 6^2 > 14^2$

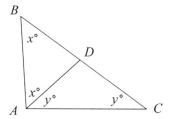

21. In $\triangle ABC$ above, which of the following must be true ?

    I. $\overline{AB} \perp \overline{AC}$
    II. $\overline{AD} \perp \overline{BC}$
    III. $\overline{BD} \cong \overline{CD}$

    (A) None
    (B) I only
    (C) II only
    (D) I and III only
    (E) I, II, and III

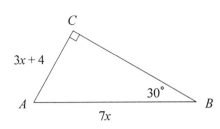

1. In $\triangle ABC$ above, what is the length of $\overline{AB}$?

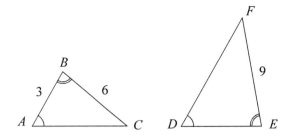

4. In the figure above, $\angle A \cong \angle D$ and $\angle B \cong \angle E$. If the perimeter of $\triangle ABC$ is 16, what is the perimeter of $\triangle DEF$?

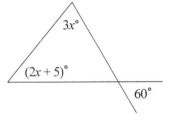

2. In the figure above, $x =$

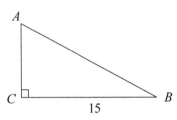

5. If the area of right triangle ABC is 60, what is the perimeter of $\triangle ABC$?

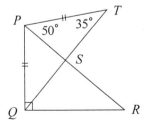

3. In the figure above, $\overline{PQ} \perp \overline{QR}$, $\overline{PQ} \cong \overline{PT}$. What is the measure of $\angle R$?

6. The measures of three sides of a triangle are 4, 10, and $(3x+1)$. If x is an integer, what is one possible value of x?

Questions 7 – 8 refer to the following figure.

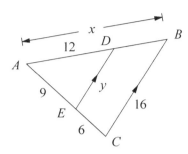

7. In the figure above, $\overline{DE} \parallel \overline{BC}$. What is the value of $x + y$?

8. In the figure above, what is the ratio of the area of $\triangle ADE$ to the area of $\triangle ABC$?

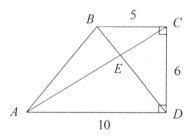

9. In the figure above, what is the area of $\triangle CED$?

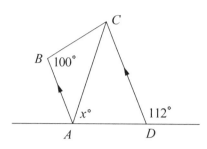

10. In the figure above, if $AB = BC$ and $\overline{AB} \parallel \overline{DC}$, what is the value of x?

11. In $\triangle PQR$ $PQ = 13$, $QR = 15$, and $PR = 14$. If the length of the altitude to the base $\overline{PR}$ is 12, what is the length of the altitude to the base $\overline{QR}$?

Answer Key

<u>Multiple Choice Questions</u>

1. C	2. A	3. B	4. E	5. B
6. A	7. E	8. D	9. A	10. B
11. B	12. C	13. A	14. C	15. B
16. B	17. E	18. E	19. D	20. D
21. D				

<u>Grid-In Questions</u>

1. 56	2. 23	3. 30	4. 24	5. 40
6. 2,3 or 4	7. 29.6	8. 0.36	9. 10	10. 72
11. 11.2				

Answers and Explanations

<u>Multiple Choice Questions</u>

1. C

The angle sum of a triangle is $180°$.

$2x + 3x + 4x = 180 \implies 9x = 180$
$\implies x = 20$

$m\angle B = 2x = 2 \cdot 20 = 40$

2. A

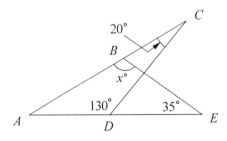

$m\angle A + m\angle C + m\angle ADC = 180$

(The angle sum of a triangle is $180°$.)
$m\angle A + 20 + 130 = 180 \implies m\angle A = 30$

$m\angle A + m\angle ABE + m\angle E = 180$
$30 + x + 35 = 180 \implies x = 115$

3. B

$3x - 40 = 48 + x$ (Exterior Angle Theorem)
$2x = 88 \implies x = 44$

4. E

$y + 50 + 50 = 180 \implies y = 80$
$\triangle ABD$ is an isosceles triangle, where $AD = BD$
$\implies m\angle A = x$
$x + x = 50$ (Exterior Angle Theorem)
$\implies x = 25$

$x + y = 25 + 80 = 105$

5. B

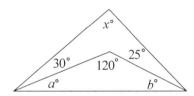

The angle sum of a triangle is $180°$.
$a + b + 120 = 180 \implies a + b = 60$
$x + (30 + a) + (25 + b) = 180$
$\implies x + a + b + 55 = 180 \implies x + a + b = 125$
$\implies x + 60 = 125$ ($a + b = 60$)
$\implies x = 65$

6. A

$AB^2 = AC^2 + BC^2$ (Pythagorean Theorem)
$AB^2 = 3^2 + 1^2 = 9 + 1 = 10$

$AD^2 = AB^2 + BD^2$ (Pythagorean Theorem)
$AD^2 = 10 + (\sqrt{6})^2 = 10 + 6 = 16$
$\implies AD = \sqrt{16} = 4$

7. E

Draw triangle PQR and segments $\overline{PS}$ and $\overline{QS}$.

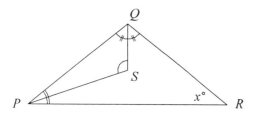

Let the measure of $\angle QPR = \angle QRP = x$, then
$m\angle PQR = 3x$.
$x + x + 3x = 180 \implies 5x = 180 \implies x = 36$
$\implies m\angle PQR = 3x = 108$ and $m\angle QPR = x = 36$

$m\angle QPS = \dfrac{1}{2}m\angle QPR = \dfrac{1}{2}(36) = 18$

$m\angle PQS = \dfrac{1}{2}m\angle PQR = \dfrac{1}{2}(108) = 54$

$m\angle PQS + m\angle QPS + m\angle PSQ = 180$
$54 + 18 + m\angle PSQ = 180$
$\implies m\angle PSQ = 108$

8. D

$AC = BC \implies 5x - 3 = 3x + 1 \implies 2x = 4$
$\implies x = 2$
$\implies AC = BC = 7$
$\implies AB = 7\sqrt{2}$ (In a 45°- 45°- 90° triangle, the
  hypotenuse is $\sqrt{2}$ times as long as a leg.)

9. A

$(2x + 10) + 4x + (3x + 8) = 180$
$\implies 9x + 18 = 180 \implies 9x = 162$
$\implies x = 18$
$m\angle A = 2x + 10 = 2 \cdot 18 + 10 = 46$
$m\angle B = 4x = 4 \cdot 18 = 72$
$m\angle C = 3x + 8 = 3 \cdot 18 + 8 = 62$

Therefore $m\angle A < m\angle C < m\angle B$
$\implies BC < AB < AC$

10. B

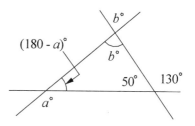

The angle sum of a triangle is $180°$.
$(180 - a) + b + 50 = 180$
$\implies -a + b = -50$
$\implies a - b = 50$

11. B

$AD = BD \implies m\angle DAB = m\angle B = 30$
$\implies m\angle ADC = 60$ (Exterior Angle Theorem)
$\implies \triangle ADC$ is a 30°-60°- 90° triangle.
$\implies CD = 4$ (In a 30°-60°- 90° triangle, the hypotenuse
  is twice as long as the shorter leg.)

Therefore $BC = BD + CD = 8 + 4 = 12$

12. C

In $\triangle ABC$ $a + 55 + m\angle ACB = 180$.
In $\triangle CED$ $d + 90 + m\angle ECD = 180$.
$m\angle ACB = m\angle ECD$ (Vertical angles are $\cong$.)

Therefore $a + 55 = d + 90$
$\implies a - d = 35$

13. A

$\triangle ABD$ is a 45°- 45°- 90° triangle.
$\implies AB = \sqrt{2}(AD) = \sqrt{2}(3\sqrt{2}) = 6$

$\triangle ABC$ is a 30°-60°- 90° triangle.
$\implies AB = 2BC \implies 6 = 2x \implies x = 3$

14. C

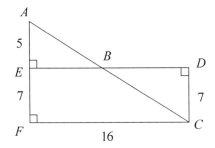

Draw an auxiliary segment, $\overline{CF}$, which is parallel and congruent to $\overline{DE}$. Extend $\overline{AE}$ to point F.

Then $DC = EF = 7$ and $DE = CF = 16$.
$AF = AE + EF = 5 + 7 = 12$
$AC^2 = AF^2 + CF^2$ (Pythagorean Theorem)
$\Rightarrow \ AC^2 = 12^2 + 16^2 = 400$
$\Rightarrow \ AC = 20$

15. B

If the altitude is drawn to the hypotenuse of a right triangle, then $\triangle ABC \sim \triangle ACD \sim \triangle CBD$.

$\triangle ACD \sim \triangle CBD \ \Rightarrow \ \dfrac{8}{y} = \dfrac{y}{6}$

$\Rightarrow \ y^2 = 6 \cdot 8 = 48$

$\Rightarrow \ y = \sqrt{48} = \sqrt{16} \cdot \sqrt{3} = 4\sqrt{3}$

16. B

$\angle A \cong \angle C \ \Rightarrow \ AB = BC$
$\triangle ABD \cong \triangle CBD \ \Rightarrow \ AD = CD = 7$

$AB^2 = AD^2 + BD^2$ (Pythagorean Theorem)
$AB^2 = 7^2 + (\sqrt{15})^2 = 49 + 15 = 64$
$\Rightarrow \ AB = 8$

17. E

Let $QR = y$.
$PQ^2 = PR^2 + QR^2$ (Pythagorean Theorem)
$40^2 = (16x)^2 + y^2$
$1600 = 256x^2 + y^2$
$QS^2 = SR^2 + QR^2$ (Pythagorean Theorem)
$26^2 = (5x)^2 + y^2$
$676 = 25x^2 + y^2$

Subtract the second equation from the first.
$$1600 = 256x^2 + y^2$$
$$- \ \underline{\ 676 = 25x^2 + y^2}$$
$$924 = 231x^2 \quad \Rightarrow x^2 = 4$$

Substitute $x^2 = 4$ into the second equation.

$676 = 25(4) + y^2 \ \Rightarrow \ y^2 = 676 - 25(4) = 576$
$\Rightarrow \ y = 24$

18. E

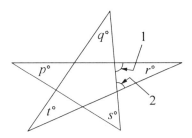

$m\angle 1 = p + s$ (Exterior Angle Theorem)
$m\angle 2 = q + t$ (Exterior Angle Theorem)
$m\angle 1 + m\angle 2 + r = 180$ (Angle Sum Theorem)
$(p + s) + (q + t) + r = 180$ (Substitution)
$(35 + 40) + (30 + 25) + r = 180$ (Substitution)
$\Rightarrow \ r = 50$

19. D

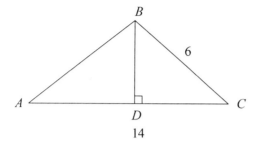

Draw $\overline{BD}$, which is perpendicular to $\overline{AC}$.
Then $BD < BC$, since the hypotenuse is the longest side in a right triangle.

Area of $\triangle ABC = \dfrac{1}{2} AC \cdot BD < \dfrac{1}{2} AC \cdot BC$

Therefore area of $\triangle ABC < \dfrac{1}{2}(14)(6) = 42$.

Choice (D) is correct.

By the triangle inequality theorem
$14 - 6 < AB < 14 + 6$, or $8 < AB < 20$.

But $\overline{AC}$ is the longest side of $\triangle ABC$, since $\angle B$ is the largest angle of $\triangle ABC$.
So $AB < AC = 14$.
Therefore $8 < AB < 14$.
(Discard answer choices B and C.)

Perimeter of $\triangle ABC = 14 + 6 + AB = 20 + AB$
Since $8 < AB < 14$, $20 + 8 < 20 + AB < 20 + 14$,
or $28 < 20 + AB < 34$. Therefore
$28 < $ Perimeter of $\triangle ABC < 34$
(Discard answer choice A.)

Since $\angle ABC$ is an obtuse angle, by the Pythagorean inequality $AB^2 + 6^2 < 14^2$.
(Discard answer choice E.)

20. D

In $\triangle OME$, $\overline{MO} \cong \overline{ME}$. Therefore by the Isosceles Triangle Theorem $\angle O \cong \angle E$.
Roman numeral III is true.

$\triangle MOU \cong \triangle MES$ by ASA.
($\angle O \cong \angle E$, $\overline{MO} \cong \overline{ME}$, $\angle 1 \cong \angle 3$)

Therefore, $\overline{MU} \cong \overline{MS}$ by cpctc.
Roman numeral II is true.

In $\triangle OMS$, $\overline{MU}$ is an angle bisector and an angle bisector does not always bisect the opposite side of the bisected angle, so $\overline{OU} \not\cong \overline{US}$.
Roman numeral I is false.

21. D

$x + x + y + y = 180$ (Angle Sum Theorem)
$\Rightarrow 2(x + y) = 180 \Rightarrow x + y = 90$
$\Rightarrow m\angle BAC = 90 \Rightarrow \overline{AB} \perp \overline{AC}$
Roman numeral I is true.

$m\angle ADC = 2x$ (Exterior Angle Theorem)

Since we do not know the value of x, we cannot conclude that $\angle ADC$ is a right angle.
Roman numeral II is false.

$\left.\begin{array}{l} \text{In } \triangle ABD, \ \overline{BD} \cong \overline{AD} \\ \text{In } \triangle ACD, \ \overline{CD} \cong \overline{AD} \end{array}\right\} \Rightarrow \overline{BD} \cong \overline{CD}$
Roman numeral III is true.

Grid-In Questions

1. 56

$\triangle ABC$ is a 30°-60°- 90° triangle.
$\Rightarrow \ AB = 2AC \ \Rightarrow \ 7x = 2(3x+4)$
$\Rightarrow \ 7x = 6x+8 \ \Rightarrow \ x = 8$

$AB = 7x = 7 \cdot 8 = 56$

2. 23

Since vertical angles are congruent, the third angle of the triangle is also 60°.

$3x + (2x+5) + 60 = 180 \ \Rightarrow \ 5x + 65 = 180$
$\Rightarrow \ 5x = 115 \ \Rightarrow \ x = 23$

3. 30

$\overline{PQ} \perp \overline{QR} \ \Rightarrow \ m\angle PQR = 90$
$\overline{PQ} \cong \overline{PT} \ \Rightarrow \ m\angle PQT = 35$
$m\angle SQR = m\angle PQR - m\angle PQT$
$\Rightarrow \ m\angle SQR = 90 - 35 = 55$

In $\triangle PST$, $m\angle PST + 35 + 50 = 180$
$\Rightarrow \ m\angle PST = 95 \ \Rightarrow \ m\angle RSQ = 95$

In $\triangle RSQ$, $m\angle RSQ + m\angle SQR + m\angle R = 180$
$\Rightarrow \ 95 + 55 + m\angle R = 180$
$\Rightarrow \ m\angle R = 30$

4. 24

$\triangle ABC \sim \triangle DEF$ by AA similarity.

If two triangles are similar, then the perimeters are proportional to the measures of corresponding sides.

$\Rightarrow \ \dfrac{BC}{EF} = \dfrac{\text{Perimeter of } \triangle ABC}{\text{Perimeter of } \triangle DEF}$

$\Rightarrow \ \dfrac{6}{9} = \dfrac{16}{\text{Perimeter of } \triangle DEF}$

$\Rightarrow \ \text{Perimeter of } \triangle DEF = \dfrac{16 \cdot 9}{6} = 24$

5. 40

Area of $\triangle ABC = \dfrac{1}{2} BC \cdot AC = \dfrac{1}{2}(15)AC = 60$
$\Rightarrow \ AC = 8$
$AB^2 = BC^2 + AC^2$ (Pythagorean Theorem)
$AB^2 = 15^2 + 8^2 = 225 + 64 = 289$
$\Rightarrow \ AB = \sqrt{289} = 17$

Perimeter of $\triangle ABC = 17 + 15 + 8 = 40$

6. 2, 3, or 4

By the triangle inequality theorem,
$10 - 4 < 3x + 1 < 10 + 4$
$\Rightarrow \ 6 < 3x + 1 < 14 \ \Rightarrow \ 5 < 3x < 13$
$\Rightarrow \ \dfrac{5}{3} < x < \dfrac{13}{3}$, and x is an integer.

Therefore possible values of x are 2, 3, and 4.

7. 29.6

$\dfrac{AE}{ED} = \dfrac{AC}{CB} \ \Rightarrow \ \dfrac{9}{y} = \dfrac{15}{16} \ \Rightarrow \ 15y = 9 \cdot 16$
$\Rightarrow \ y = 9.6$

$\dfrac{AD}{AE} = \dfrac{AB}{AC} \ \Rightarrow \ \dfrac{12}{9} = \dfrac{x}{15} \ \Rightarrow \ 9x = 12 \cdot 15$
$\Rightarrow \ x = 20$

$x + y = 20 + 9.6 = 29.6$

8. $\dfrac{9}{25}$ or 0.36

$\triangle ADE \sim \triangle ABC$ by AA similarity.
If two triangles are similar with corresponding sides in the ratio of $\dfrac{a}{b}$, then the ratio of their areas equals $\dfrac{a^2}{b^2}$.

$\dfrac{\text{Area of } \triangle ADE}{\text{Area of } \triangle ABC} = \dfrac{9^2}{15^2} = \dfrac{81}{225} = \dfrac{9}{25}$

9. 10

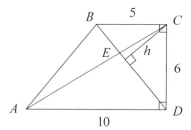

11 11.2

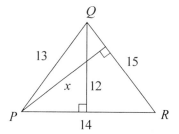

In the figure above, $\angle CBE \cong \angle ADE$ (Alternate Interior Angle Theorem) and $\angle BEC \cong \angle DEA$ (Vertical angles are $\cong$). Therefore $\triangle AED \sim \triangle CEB$ by AA similarity.

The corresponding sides are in the ratio of $\dfrac{5}{10}$, or $\dfrac{1}{2}$.

$$\Rightarrow \frac{BC}{AD} = \frac{BE}{DE} = \frac{1}{2}$$

In the figure above, $\triangle CEB$ and $\triangle CED$ have equal heights. Therefore the ratio of their areas is equal to the ratio of their base lengths.

$$\frac{\text{Area of } \triangle CEB}{\text{Area of } \triangle CED} = \frac{BE}{ED} = \frac{1}{2}$$

Area of $\triangle BCD = \dfrac{1}{2} \cdot 5 \cdot 6 = 15$

$\Rightarrow$ Area of $\triangle CEB = \dfrac{1}{3}$ the area of $\triangle BCD = 5$

$\Rightarrow$ Area of $\triangle CED = \dfrac{2}{3}$ the area of $\triangle BCD = 10$

Let x = the length of the altitude to the base $\overline{QR}$.

Area of $\triangle PQR = \dfrac{1}{2} \cdot \text{base} \cdot \text{height}$

$$= \frac{1}{2} \cdot \underbrace{14}_{\overline{PR} \text{ is the base}} \cdot \underbrace{12}_{\text{altitude to the base}} = 84$$

Area of $\triangle PQR = \dfrac{1}{2} \cdot \text{base} \cdot \text{height}$

$$= \frac{1}{2} \cdot \underbrace{15}_{\overline{QR} \text{ is the base}} \cdot \underbrace{x}_{\text{altitude to the base}} = \underbrace{84}_{\text{area of the same triangle}}$$

$\Rightarrow 7.5x = 84 \Rightarrow x = 11.2$

10. 72

$\overline{AB} = \overline{BC} \Rightarrow m\angle BAC = m\angle BCA = 40$
$\overline{AB} \parallel \overline{DC} \Rightarrow m\angle BAD = 112$
$m\angle BAD = m\angle BAC + x$
$\Rightarrow 112 = 40 + x \Rightarrow x = 72$

15. Quadrilaterals and Other Polygons

Key Terms / Illustrations

Examples

1. A **parallelogram** is a quadrilateral in which the opposite sides are parallel to each other.

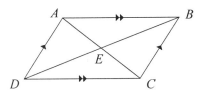

In $\square ABCD$ above, $\overline{AB} \parallel \overline{CD}$, $\overline{AD} \parallel \overline{BC}$.

☑ **Properties of a Parallelogram**

1) Opposite sides are congruent.

2) Opposite angles are congruent.

3) Consecutive angles are supplementary.

4) The diagonals bisect each other.

Area of a Parallelogram $= \text{base} \times \text{height}$

2. A **rhombus** is a parallelogram with four sides of equal measure.

☑ The diagonals of rhombus are perpendicular to each other, and each diagonal of a rhombus bisects a pair of opposite angles.

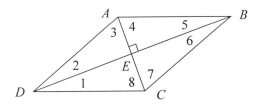

In rhombus $ABCD$ above, $AB = BC = CD = DA$, $\overline{AC} \perp \overline{BD}$, $m\angle 1 = m\angle 2 = m\angle 5 = m\angle 6$, and $m\angle 3 = m\angle 4 = m\angle 7 = m\angle 8$.

Therefore $\triangle ABE \cong \triangle CBE \cong \triangle CDE \cong \triangle ADE$.

Example 1 **ABCD is a parallelogram.**

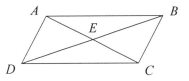

In $\square ABCD$ above, $AE = 2x - 3$, $AC = 18$, $m\angle ABD = 28°$, and $m\angle ADB = 46°$.
Find the value of x, $m\angle DAB$, and $m\angle ABC$.

Solution $\square$

$AC = 2AE$	Diagonals of $\square$ bisect each other.
$18 = 2(2x - 3)$	Substitution
$x = 6$	Answer
$m\angle CBD = m\angle ADB$	Alternate interior angles are $\cong$.
$m\angle CBD = 46$	Substitution
$m\angle ABC = m\angle ABD$ $+ m\angle CBD$	Angle addition postulate
$= 28 + 46$	Substitution
$= 74$	Answer
$m\angle DAB + m\angle ABC = 180$	Consecutive angles of $\square$ are complementary.
$m\angle DAB + 74 = 180$	
$m\angle DAB = 106$	Answer

3. A **rectangle** is a quadrilateral with four right angles.

☑ The diagonals of a rectangle are congruent and bisect each other.

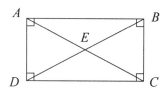

In the rectangle above, $AD = BC$, $AB = CD$, and $AE = DE = BE = CE$.

Area of $\triangle ABE =$ Area of $\triangle BCE =$ Area of $\triangle CDE =$ Area of $\triangle ADE$

Perimeter of a Rectangle $= 2\ell + 2w$
Area of a Rectangle $= \ell \times w$

4. **The Perimeter and Area of a Rectangle**

If the perimeter of a rectangle is known, the maximum area occurs when the length and width are equal in measure. This shape is a square.

Illustration :

The following rectangles have a perimeter of 16 units.

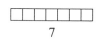 1 $P = 16$ Area = 7
7

 2    $P = 16$ Area = 12
6

 3    $P = 16$ Area = 15
5

 4    $P = 16$ Area = 16
4

Example 2 □ **ABCD is a rhombus.**

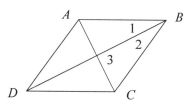

In rhombus $ABCD$ above, $m\angle 1 = 2x + 14$ and $m\angle 3 = x^2 - 31$. Find $m\angle 2$.

Solution □

Since the diagonals of a rhombus are perpendicular, $\angle 3$ is a right angle.
$m\angle 3 = 90$
$x^2 - 31 = 90 \Rightarrow x^2 = 121 \Rightarrow x = 11$

The diagonal of a rhombus bisects a pair of opposite angles. So, $\overline{DB}$ bisects $\angle ABC$ and $m\angle 1 = m\angle 2$.
$m\angle 1 = 2x + 14 = 2(11) + 14 = 36$
Thus, $m\angle 1 = m\angle 2 = 36$ Answer

Example 3 □ **The Area of a Rectangle**

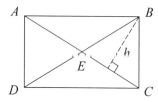

In the rectangle $ABCD$ above, if the area of $\triangle ABE$ is 12, what is the area of $\triangle BCE$?

Solution □

The diagonals of a rectangle bisect each other. So $AE = CE$. The area of $\triangle ABE = \frac{1}{2}AE \cdot h$ and

the area of $\triangle BCE = \frac{1}{2}CE \cdot h$.

Since $AE = CE$, the area of $\triangle ABE$ is equal to the area of $\triangle BCE$.

Therefore the area of $\triangle BCE = 12$.   Answer

5. Ratio of Areas and Ratio of Perimeters of Similar Polygons

If two polygons are similar with corresponding sides in the ratio of $a:b$, then

1) the ratio of their perimeters is $a:b$
2) the ratio of their areas is $a^2:b^2$

6. A **trapezoid** is a quadrilateral with exactly one pair of parallel sides.

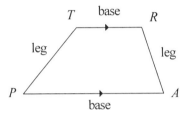

☑ The **median** of a trapezoid is parallel to the bases, and its measure is one-half the sum of the measures of the bases.

☑ If the legs of a trapezoid are congruent, then the trapezoid is an **isosceles trapezoid**.

☑ Both pairs of base angles of an isosceles trapezoid are congruent.

☑ The diagonals of an isosceles trapezoid are congruent.

$$\textbf{Area of a Trapezoid} = \frac{1}{2}h(b_1 + b_2)$$

7. A **regular polygon** is a convex polygon with all sides congruent and all angles congruent.

8. Interior Angle Sum Theorem

The sum of measures of the interior angles of an n-sided polygon is $180(n-2)$.

☑ The measure of each angle of a regular n-sided polygon is $\dfrac{180(n-2)}{n}$.

Example 4 □ Ratio of areas and ratio of perimeters of similar polygons

Quadrilateral $ABCD$ with sides measuring 4, 5, 6, and 9 has an area of 30. If the longest side of the similar quadrilateral $PQRS$ measures 27, find the perimeter and the area of quadrilateral $PQRS$.

Solution □

$$\frac{\text{length of longest side of } ABCD}{\text{length of longest side of } PQRS} = \frac{9}{27} = \frac{1}{3}$$

$$\frac{\text{perimeter of } ABCD}{\text{perimeter of } PQRS} = \frac{4+5+6+9}{\text{perimeter of } PQRS} = \frac{1}{3}$$

$\Rightarrow$ perimeter of $PQRS = 72$ Answer

The ratio of the areas of two similar polygons equals the square of the ratio of their corresponding side lengths.

$$\frac{\text{area of } ABCD}{\text{area of } PQRS} = \frac{30}{\text{area of } ABCD} = \frac{1^2}{3^2} = \frac{1}{9}$$

area of $PQRS = 270$ Answer

Example 5 □ Finding the area of an isosceles trapezoid

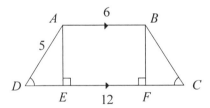

What is the area of the isosceles trapezoid above if $AB = 6$, $DC = 12$ and $AD = 5$?

Solution □

In the isosceles trapezoid $ABCD$, $DE = CF = 3$

In triangle ADE
$AD^2 = AE^2 + DE^2$ Pythagorean Theorem
$5^2 = 3^2 + AE^2 \Rightarrow AE = 4$

Area of isosceles trapezoid $ABCD$

$$= \frac{1}{2} \cdot 4(12 + 6) = 36 \text{ square units}$$ Answer

9. The area of a region is the sum of the areas of all its non-overlapping parts.

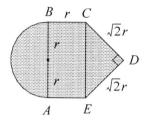

The area of the shaded region
= area of semicircle + area of rectangle $ABCE$
  + area of triangle CDE

$$= \frac{1}{2}\pi r^2 + 2r \cdot r + \frac{1}{2}(\sqrt{2}r)(\sqrt{2}r)$$

$$= \frac{1}{2}\pi r^2 + 3r^2$$

Example 6 □   **Finding the area of a shaded region**

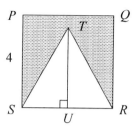

In the figure above, $PQRS$ is a square and STR is an equilateral triangle. If $PS = 4$, what is the area of the shaded region?.

Solution □

Area of square $PQRS = 4 \times 4 = 16$

$\triangle STU$ is a $30°$-$60°$-$90°$ triangle with
$$SU = \frac{1}{2}SR = \frac{1}{2}(4) = 2 .$$
$$TU = (SU)\sqrt{3} = 2\sqrt{3}$$

Area of $\triangle STR = \frac{1}{2}(4)(2\sqrt{3}) = 4\sqrt{3}$

Area of shaded region
= Area of square $PQRS$ − Area of $\triangle STR$
$= 16 - 4\sqrt{3}$ Answer

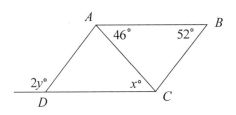

1. In parallelogram *ABCD* above, what is the value of $x + y$?

(A) 98   (B) 110   (C) 122

(D) 134   (E) 174

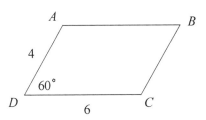

2. What is the area of parallelogram *ABCD* above?

(A) 12   (B) $12\sqrt{2}$ (C) 18

(D) $12\sqrt{3}$ (E) 24

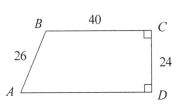

3. What is the area of the trapezoid above?

(A) 960
(B) 1020
(C) 1080
(D) 1170
(E) It cannot be determined from the information given.

4. The length of a rectangle is 4 inches more than its width. When each side of the rectangle is decreased by 2 inches, the area is decreased by 24 square inches. What is the area, in square inches, of the original rectangle?

(A) 45   (B) 60   (C) 77

(D) 96   (E) 117

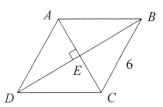

5. In rhombus *ABCD* above, if $m\angle ABC = 60°$ and $BC = 6$, what is the area of $\triangle ADE$?

(A) $4\sqrt{2}$ (B) $4.5\sqrt{3}$ (C) 9

(D) $6\sqrt{2}$ (E) $6\sqrt{3}$

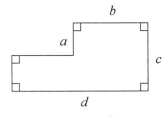

6. Which of the following is equal to the perimeter of the figure above?

(A) $2(c+d)$
(B) $2a+b+c+d$
(C) $a+2b+c+d$
(D) $2(c+d)-(a+b)$
(E) It cannot be determined from the information given.

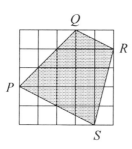

7. In the figure above, if the grid consists of unit squares, what is the area of quadrilateral $PQRS$?

   (A) 12.5

   (B) 13

   (C) 13.5

   (D) 14

   (E) 14.5

8. If the perimeter of a rectangle is $\frac{5}{3}x$ and its width is $\frac{1}{3}x$, which of the following is the area of the rectangle?

   (A) $\frac{1}{6}x^2$ (B) $\frac{1}{3}x^2$ (C) $\frac{1}{2}x^2$

   (D) $\frac{2}{3}x^2$ (E) $\frac{5}{6}x^2$

9. In parallelogram $ABCD$, point E is the midpoint of side AD. If the area of quadrilateral $BCDE$ is 1.5, what is the area of parallelogram $ABCD$?

   (A) 2

   (B) 2.1

   (C) 2.4

   (D) 2.7

   (E) 3

10. A regular hexagon with sides of length x, a square with sides of length s, and an equilateral triangle with sides of length t, have equal areas. Which of the following must be true?

   (A) $x > s > t$

   (B) $t > s > x$

   (C) $t > x > s$

   (D) $x > t > s$

   (E) It cannot be determined from the information given.

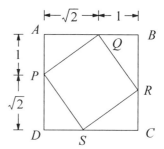

11. In the figure above, if s represents the area of square $ABCD$ and q represents the area of square $PQRS$, what is the value of $s - q$?

   (A) 1   (B) $\sqrt{2}$ (C) $2\sqrt{2} - 1$

   (D) $2\sqrt{2}$ (E) 3

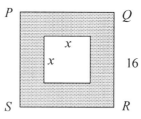

12. In the figure above, the ratio of the area of square $PQRS$ to the area of the shaded region is $\frac{4}{3}$. What is the value of x?

   (A) 5   (B) 6   (C) 7

   (D) 8   (E) 9

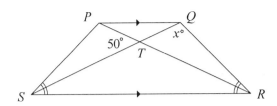

13. In the isosceles trapezoid above, if $m\angle PTS = 50°$ and $m\angle PSR = m\angle QRS = 47°$, then $x =$

(A) 83

(B) 92

(C) 97

(D) 108

(E) 112

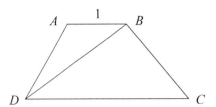

15. In the trapezoid shown above, the area of $\triangle ABD$ is $\dfrac{1}{4}$ the area of trapezoid $ABCD$. If $AB = 1$, what is the length of $\overline{CD}$?

(A) 1.5

(B) 2

(C) 2.5

(D) 3

(E) 4

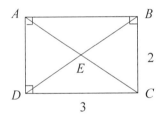

14. In the rectangle shown above, what is the area of $\triangle ADE$?

(A) 1

(B) 1.2

(C) 1.5

(D) 1.75

(E) 1.8

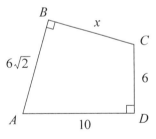

16. In the figure above, $x =$

(A) $6\sqrt{2}$

(B) 8

(C) $8\sqrt{2}$

(D) 9

(E) $9\sqrt{2}$

1. In parallelogram *ABCD*, if $AB = 2x + 3$, $BC = 5x - 2$, and $CD = 3x$, what is the perimeter of parallelogram *ABCD*?

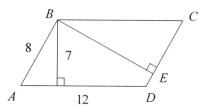

4. In the parallelogram above, $BE =$

2. The length of each side of square *S* is increased by 50 percent to make square *Q*. By what percent is the area of square *Q* greater than the area of square *S*?

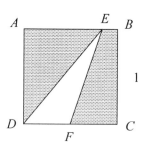

5. In the figure above, *ABCD* is a square. If *F* is midpoint of $\overline{CD}$, what is the area of the shaded region?

3. In the figure above, $x =$

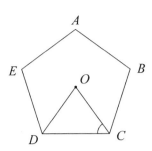

6. In the figure above, *O* is the center of regular pentagon *ABCDE*. What is the measure of ∠*OCD* ?

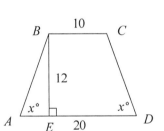

7. What is the perimeter of trapezoid *ABCD* above?

8. If the diagonal of square *S* is 1 and the diagonal of square *Q* is $\sqrt{2}$, what is the ratio of the area of square *S* to the area of square *Q*?

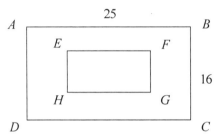

Note: Figure not drawn to scale.

9. In the figure above, rectangle *ABCD* and rectangle *EFGH* are similar, and the area of rectangle *EFGH* is 25% of the area of rectangle *ABCD*. If *AB* = 25 and *BC* = 16 , what is the perimeter of *EFGH*?

Answer Key

<u>Multiple Choice Questions</u>

1. B   2. D   3. C   4. A   5. B

6. A   7. C   8. A   9. A   10. B

11. D   12. D   13. D   14. C   15. D

16. B

<u>Grid-In Questions</u>

1. 44   2. 125   3. 45   4. 10.5   5. $\dfrac{3}{4}$

6. 54   7. 56   8. $\dfrac{1}{2}$ 9. 41

Answers and Explanations

<u>Multiple Choice Questions</u>

1. B

Since $ABCD$ is a parallelogram, $\overline{AB} \parallel \overline{CD}$.
$\Rightarrow x = 46$ (Alternate Interior Angle Theorem)

$m\angle ADC + 2y = 180$
$\Rightarrow m\angle ADC = 180 - 2y$
$m\angle ADC = m\angle ABC$ (Opposite angles of a $\square$ are $\cong$.)

Therefore $180 - 2y = 52 \Rightarrow y = 64$
$x + y = 46 + 64 = 110$

2. D

Draw $\overline{AE}$, which is $\perp$ to $\overline{DC}$.
Then $DE = 2$ and $AE = 2\sqrt{3}$ by the
$30° \text{-} 60° \text{-} 90°$ triangle theorem.

Area of parallelogram $ABCD$
$= \text{base} \cdot \text{height} = 6 \cdot 2\sqrt{3} = 12\sqrt{3}$

3. C

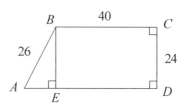

Draw a segment $\overline{BE}$ that is perpendicular to $\overline{AD}$.
Then $BE = CD = 24$, and $ED = BC = 40$.

$AB^2 = AE^2 + BE^2$ (Pythagorean Theorem)
$\Rightarrow 26^2 = AE^2 + 24^2$ (Substitution)
$\Rightarrow AE^2 = 676 - 576 = 100 \Rightarrow AE = 10$

$AD = AE + ED = 10 + 40 = 50$

Area of Trapezoid $ABCD$
$= \dfrac{1}{2}(b_1 + b_2) \cdot h = \dfrac{1}{2}(50 + 40) \cdot 24 = 1080$

4. A

Let $x = $ the width of the original rectangle,
then $x + 4 = $ the length of the original rectangle.

$x - 2 = $ the width of the new rectangle, and
$x + 2 = $ the length of the new rectangle.

$$\overbrace{(x-2)(x+2)}^{\text{Area of new rectangle}} = \overbrace{x \cdot (x+4)}^{\text{Area of original rectangle}} - \overbrace{24}^{\text{decreased by 24}}$$
$\Rightarrow x^2 - 4 = x^2 + 4x - 24 \Rightarrow 4x = 20$
$\Rightarrow x = 5$

Area of the original rectangle
$= x(x + 4) = 5(5 + 4) = 45$

5. B

$m\angle ABC = 60° \Rightarrow m\angle ADC = 60°$
$\Rightarrow m\angle ADE = 30° \Rightarrow m\angle DAE = 60°$
Therefore $\triangle ADE$ is a $30° \text{-} 60° \text{-} 90°$.

$BC = AD = 6$
$AE = \dfrac{1}{2} AD = 3$, $DE = AE \cdot \sqrt{3} = 3\sqrt{3}$

Area of $\triangle ADE = \dfrac{1}{2} \cdot AE \cdot DE = \dfrac{1}{2} \cdot 3 \cdot 3\sqrt{3} = 4.5\sqrt{3}$

6. A

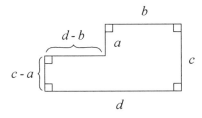

Perimeter of the figure
$= a + b + c + d + (c - a) + (d - b)$
$= 2c + 2d = 2(c + d)$

7. C

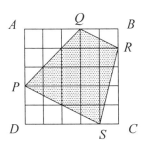

The area of quadrilateral $PQRS$
= area of square $ABCD$ − (area of $\triangle APQ$ +
area of $\triangle BQR$ + area of $\triangle CRS$ + area of $\triangle DPS$)

$= 25 - \dfrac{1}{2}(3 \cdot 3 + 2 \cdot 1 + 1 \cdot 4 + 4 \cdot 2)$

$= 25 - 11.5 = 13.5$

8. A

The perimeter of the rectangle $= 2\ell + 2w$

$\dfrac{5}{3}x = 2\ell + 2 \cdot \dfrac{1}{3}x \ \Rightarrow \ 2\ell = x \ \Rightarrow \ \ell = \dfrac{1}{2}x$

The area of the rectangle $= \ell \times w = \dfrac{1}{2}x \cdot \dfrac{1}{3}x = \dfrac{1}{6}x^2$

9. A

Draw parallelogram $ABCD$. Let point F be the midpoint of side BC. Draw EF.

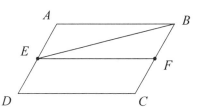

Let x = the area of quadrilateral $ABCD$,

then $\dfrac{1}{2}x$ = the area of quadrilateral $CDEF$ and

$\dfrac{1}{4}x$ = the area of triangle BEF.

The area of quadrilateral $BCDE = \dfrac{1}{2}x + \dfrac{1}{4}x = \dfrac{3}{4}x$.

$\dfrac{3}{4}x = 1.5 \ \Rightarrow \ x = 2$

10. B

If the regular polygons have equal areas, then the regular polygon with the least number of sides has the longest sides.
$\Rightarrow \ t > s > x$

11. D

In the figure shown, $AP = BQ = CR = DS = 1$
$PS^2 = PD^2 + DS^2$
$\Rightarrow \ PS^2 = (\sqrt{2})^2 + (1)^2 = 2 + 1 = 3$
$\Rightarrow$ The area of square $PQRS = PS^2 = 3$
$\Rightarrow \ q = 3$

The area of square $ABCD$
$= (\sqrt{2} + 1)(\sqrt{2} + 1) = 2 + \sqrt{2} + \sqrt{2} + 1 = 3 + 2\sqrt{2}$
$\Rightarrow \ s = 3 + 2\sqrt{2}$

$s - q = (3 + 2\sqrt{2}) - 3 = 2\sqrt{2}$

12. D

The area of square $PQRS = 16^2 = 256$

The area of the shaded region $= 16^2 - x^2 = 256 - x^2$

$$\frac{\text{the area of square } PQRS}{\text{the area of the shaded region}} = \frac{4}{3}$$

$$\Rightarrow \frac{256}{256 - x^2} = \frac{4}{3} \Rightarrow 4(256 - x^2) = 256 \cdot 3$$

$$\Rightarrow 1024 - 4x^2 = 768 \Rightarrow 4x^2 = 256$$
$$\Rightarrow x^2 = 64 \Rightarrow x = 8$$

13. D

$$m\angle PTS = 50° \Rightarrow m\angle STR = 130°$$
$$\Rightarrow m\angle QSR = m\angle PRS = 25°$$

In $\triangle QRS$ $m\angle SQR + m\angle QRS + m\angle QSR = 180°$.
$$\Rightarrow x + 47 + 25 = 180 \Rightarrow x = 108$$

14. C

The diagonals of a rectangle are $\cong$ and bisect each other. $\Rightarrow AE = BE = CE = DE$

$$\Rightarrow \left\{ \begin{array}{l} \text{area of } \triangle ABE = \text{area of } \triangle BCE \\ = \text{area of } \triangle CDE = \text{area of } \triangle DEA \end{array} \right\}$$

$$\Rightarrow \text{Area of } \triangle ADE = \frac{1}{4} \cdot \text{Area of rectangle } ABCD$$

$$= \frac{1}{4}(3 \times 2) = 1.5$$

15. D

Since $ABCD$ is a trapezoid $\overline{AB} \parallel \overline{CD}$.
$\Rightarrow$ The height of $\triangle ABD$ and the height of $\triangle BCD$
are congruent.

Let the area of trapezoid $ABCD$ be 4. Then the area of $\triangle ABD$ is 1, since the area of $\triangle ABD$ is $\frac{1}{4}$ of the area of the trapezoid.

Area of $\triangle BCD$ = Area of $ABCD$ − Area of $\triangle ABD$
$$= 4 - 1 = 3$$

If two triangles have equal heights, then the ratio of their areas equals the ratio of their base lengths.

$$\Rightarrow \frac{AB}{CD} = \frac{1}{3} \Rightarrow CD = 3$$

16. B

Draw segment $\overline{AC}$.

$AC^2 = (6\sqrt{2})^2 + x^2$ (Pythagorean Theorem)
$AC^2 = 6^2 + 10^2$ (Pythagorean Theorem)

$(6\sqrt{2})^2 + x^2 = 6^2 + 10^2$ (Substitution)
$72 + x^2 = 36 + 100 \Rightarrow x^2 = 64$
$\Rightarrow x = 8$

Grid-In Questions

1. 44

$AB = CD$ (Opposite sides of a $\square$ are $\cong$.)
$\Rightarrow 2x + 3 = 3x \Rightarrow x = 3$
$\Rightarrow AB = CD = 9$ and $BC = AD = 13$

Perimeter of $ABCD = 9 + 9 + 13 + 13 = 44$

2. 125

Let $x =$ the length of each side of square S, then $1.5x =$ the length of each side of square Q.

The area of square $S = x^2$
The area of square $Q = (1.5x)(1.5x) = 2.25x^2$

The area of square Q	is	the area of square S	125% more than the area of square S
$2.25x^2$	$=$	x^2	$+$ $\quad 1.25x^2$

3. 45

The sum of the measures of the interior angles of an n-sided polygon $= 180(n-2)$.

$2x + 3x + 3x + 2x + 3x + 3x = 180(6-2)$
$\Rightarrow 16x = 720 \Rightarrow x = 45$

4. 10.5

In the parallelogram shown, $AB = CD = 8$.
Area of parallelogram $ABCD$
$= \text{base} \cdot \text{height} = 12 \cdot 7$
$= \text{base} \cdot \text{height} = CD \cdot BE$
$\Rightarrow 12 \cdot 7 = 8 \cdot BE \Rightarrow BE = \dfrac{12 \cdot 7}{8} = 10.5$

5. $\dfrac{3}{4}$

Area of square $ABCD = 1$
Area of $\Delta DEF = \dfrac{1}{2} \cdot DF \cdot 1 = \dfrac{1}{2} \cdot \dfrac{1}{2} \cdot 1 = \dfrac{1}{4}$

The area of the shaded region
$= \text{Area of square } ABCD - \text{Area of } \Delta DEF$
$= 1 - \dfrac{1}{4} = \dfrac{3}{4}$

6. 54

$ABCDE$ is a regular pentagon.
$\Rightarrow m\angle COD = 360 \div 5 = 72$ and $OD = OC$
$\Rightarrow m\angle OCD = \dfrac{1}{2}(180 - 72) = \dfrac{1}{2}(108) = 54$

7. 56

From C draw $\overline{CF}$, which is perpendicular to $\overline{AD}$.
Then $AE = DF = 5$, since trapezoid $ABCD$ is an isosceles trapezoid.

$AB^2 = 5^2 + 12^2$ (Pythagorean Theorem)
$AB^2 = 25 + 144 = 169$
$\Rightarrow AB = \sqrt{169} = 13$

The perimeter of trapezoid $ABCD$
$= 13 + 10 + 13 + 20 = 56$

8. $\dfrac{1}{2}$

The ratio of the areas of two similar polygons equals the square of the ratio of their corresponding sides.

$\dfrac{\text{area of square } S}{\text{area of square } Q} = \dfrac{1^2}{(\sqrt{2})^2} = \dfrac{1}{2}$

9. 41

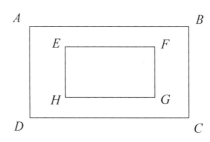

Rectangle $ABCD$ and rectangle $EFGH$ are similar,
and $\dfrac{\text{area of } ABCD}{\text{area of } EFGH} = \dfrac{100}{25} = \dfrac{4}{1} = \dfrac{2^2}{1^2}$.

Since the ratio of the areas of two similar polygons equals the square of the ratio of their corresponding sides, $\dfrac{AB}{EF} = \dfrac{2}{1}$, and $\dfrac{BC}{FG} = \dfrac{2}{1}$.

Given: $AB = 25$ and $BC = 16$.

$\dfrac{25}{EF} = \dfrac{2}{1} \Rightarrow EF = 12.5$
$\dfrac{16}{FG} = \dfrac{2}{1} \Rightarrow FG = 8$

Perimeter of $EFGH = 2(12.5) + 2(8) = 41$

16. Circles

1. **In a circle, all radii are equal in measure**.

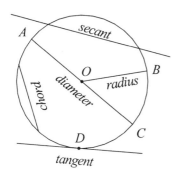

In $\odot O$, $\overarc{AB}$ is a **minor arc** and $\overarc{ADB}$ is a **major arc**. $\overarc{ADC}$ and $\overarc{ABC}$ are **semicircles**.

2. **Circumference of a Circle**

$C = 2\pi r$ (r is the radius of the circle)
$ = \pi d$ (d is the diameter of the circle)

3. **The distance traveled by a wheel**
$= 2\pi r \times$ number of revolutions

4. **Length of an Arc**

If the degree measure of a central angle is x, and the length of a radius of the circle is r, then the length ℓ of the arc $\overarc{AB}$ is

$\ell = 2\pi r \cdot \dfrac{x}{360}$

or

$\dfrac{\ell}{2\pi r} = \dfrac{x}{360}$

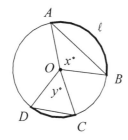

☑ In a circle, the lengths of the arcs are proportional to the measures of the corresponding central angles. But the lengths of chords are not proportional to the measures of the corresponding central angles.

$$\frac{\overarc{AB}}{\overarc{CD}} = \frac{x}{y}, \quad \frac{AB}{CD} \ne \frac{x}{y}$$

Example 1 □   **An isosceles triangle is formed by two radii and a chord of a circle.**

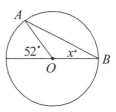

In the circle with center O above, $\overline{AO}$ and $\overline{BO}$ are radii of the circle. Find the value of x.

Solution □

$\overline{AO} \cong \overline{BO}$	In a circle all radii are $\cong$.
$m\angle OAB = m\angle OBA$	Isosceles Triangle Theorem
$m\angle OAB = x$	Substitution
$m\angle OAB + m\angle OBA = 52$	Exterior Angle Theorem
$x + x = 52$	Substitution
$2x = 52$	Simplify.
$x = 26$	Answer

Example 2 □   **The distance traveled by a wheel**

The radius of each wheel of a bicycle is $1\dfrac{1}{12}$ feet.

If the wheels are turning at the rate of 264 revolutions per minute, how many miles will the wheels travel in one hour? (1 mile = 5280 ft)

Solution □

The distance the wheel travels in 1 minute
    $= 2\pi r \times$ number of revolutions per minute

    $= 2\pi(1\dfrac{1}{12}\,\text{ft})(264)$ revolutions per minute

    $= 572\pi$ ft

Total distance the wheel travels in 1 hour
    $= 572\pi$ ft per minute $\times 60$ minutes
    $= 34320\pi$ ft $= (34320\pi \div 5280)$ miles
    $= 6.5\pi$ miles   Answer

5. Area of a Circle

$$A = \pi r^2$$

6. Area of a Sector

A **sector** of a circle is the region bounded by two radii of the circle and the arc determined by the the two radii.

Area of sector $= \pi r^2 \cdot \dfrac{x}{360}$

or

$\dfrac{\text{Area of sector}}{\pi r^2} = \dfrac{x}{360}$

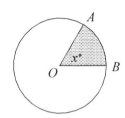

where x is the central angle measure.

7. In a circle, congruent chords have congruent arcs.

If $\quad AB = CD$

then $\overarc{AB} \cong \overarc{CD}$.

The converse is also true.

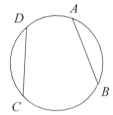

8. In a circle, congruent chords are equidistant from the center.

If $\quad AB = CD$

then $OP = OQ$.

The converse is also true.

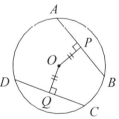

9. In a circle, if a diameter is perpendicular to a chord, then it bisects the chord.

$\overline{CD}$ is a diameter and

$\overline{AB}$ is a chord.

If $\overline{CD} \perp \overline{AB}$

then $AE = BE$.

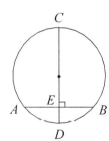

Example 3 □ Finding the length of an arc

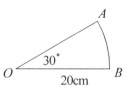

In the figure above, $\overarc{AB}$ is the arc of a circle with radius 20 centimeters. Find the length of arc AB.

Solution □

$$\ell = \frac{x}{360} \cdot 2\pi r = \frac{30}{360} \cdot 2\pi \cdot 20$$

$$= \frac{10}{3}\pi \text{ centimeters} \quad \text{Answer}$$

....

Example 4 □ Finding the area of a shaded region

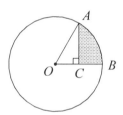

In the circle with center O above, the radius of the circle is 8 inches and BC is 4 inches. Find the area of shaded region.

Solution □

$OA = OB = 8$ (radius of the circle is 8)
$OC = OB - BC = 8 - 4 = 4$

In $\triangle AOC$, $\dfrac{\text{hypotenuse}}{\text{shortest side}} = \dfrac{AO}{CO} = \dfrac{8}{4} = \dfrac{2}{1} \Rightarrow$

$\triangle AOC$ is a $30°$-$60°$-$90°$ triangle $\Rightarrow$
$m\angle AOC = 60$ and $AC = 4\sqrt{3}$

Area of shaded region
$\quad = $ Area of sector AOB $-$ Area of $\triangle AOC$

$$= \frac{60}{360}\pi(8)^2 - \frac{1}{2}(4)(4\sqrt{3})$$

$$= \frac{32}{3}\pi - 8\sqrt{3} \approx 19.7 \text{ in}^2 \quad \text{Answer}$$

10. **The measure of an inscribed angle is equal to one-half the measure of its intercepted arc.**

If $\angle ABC$ is inscribed in $\odot O$, then

$$m\angle ABC = \frac{1}{2}\,m\widehat{AC}$$

$$m\angle ABC = \frac{1}{2}\,m\angle AOC$$

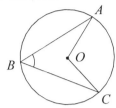

11. **An angle inscribed in a semicircle is a right angle.**

If $\overline{AB}$ is a diameter of circle O, then

$$m\angle ACB = 90°$$

$$m\angle ADB = 90°$$

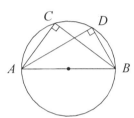

☑ If a rectangle is inscribed in a circle, then the diagonal of the rectangle is the diameter of the circle.

ABCD is a rectangle.
BD is a diagonal of
the rectangle.
BD is also a diameter
of the circumscribed
circle.

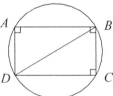

12. **If a line is tangent to a circle, then it is perpendicular to the radius drawn to the point of tangency.**

   Tangents to a circle from the same exterior point are congruent.

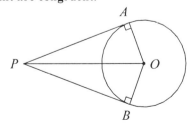

If $\overline{PA}$ and $\overline{PB}$ are tangents to $\odot O$, then
$PA = PB$, $\overline{PA} \perp \overline{OA}$, and $\overline{PB} \perp \overline{OB}$.

Example 5 □ **Finding the measure of an inscribed angle and an arc**

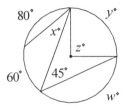

Find the values of *w, x, y,* and *z*.

Solution □

$$x = \frac{1}{2}\cdot 60 = 30$$

$$\frac{1}{2}y = 45\,,\ \ y = 90$$

$$z = y = 90$$

$$w = 360 - (60 + 80 + 90) = 130 \qquad \text{Answer}$$

. . . .

Example 6 □ **An angle inscribed in a semicircle**

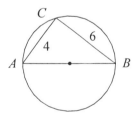

In the circle above, *AB* is a diameter. If *AC* is 4 and *BC* is 6, what is the area of the circle?

Solution □

$$m\angle ACB = 90°$$ — An angle inscribed in a semicircle is a right angle.

$$AB^2 = AC^2 + BC^2$$ — Pythagorean Theorem

$$AB^2 = 4^2 + 6^2$$ — Substitution

$$AB^2 = 52$$

$$AB = \sqrt{52} = \sqrt{4}\cdot\sqrt{13} = 2\sqrt{13}$$

$$\Rightarrow\ r = \sqrt{13}$$

Area of circle = $\pi(\sqrt{13})^2$

$$= 13\pi \qquad \text{Answer}$$

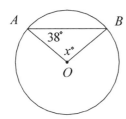

1. In circle O above, what is the value of x?

   (A) 76

   (B) 86

   (C) 92

   (D) 104

   (E) 116

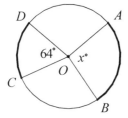

2. In circle O above, the ratio of the length of arc AB to the length of arc CD is 3 to 2. What is the value of x?

   (A) 80

   (B) 90

   (C) 96

   (D) 100

   (E) 108

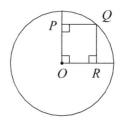

3. In circle O above, Q is a point on the circle. In rectangle $OPQR$, if $OP = 6$ and $PQ = 4$, what is the area of the circle?

   (A) $2\sqrt{13}\pi$ (B) $4\sqrt{13}\pi$ (C) 25π

   (D) 36π (E) 52π

4. If an arc with a length of 3π is $\dfrac{3}{4}$ of the circumference of the circle, what is the shortest distance between the endpoints of the arc?

   (A) 2   (B) $2\sqrt{2}$ (C) $3\sqrt{2}$

   (D) 4   (E) $3\sqrt{3}$

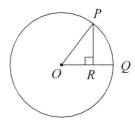

5. In circle O above, if the area of the circle is 9π and $PR = \sqrt{5}$, what is the length of QR?

   (A) 1   (B) $\sqrt{2}$ (C) $\sqrt{3}$

   (D) 2   (E) 4

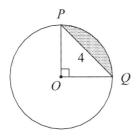

6. In circle O above, if $PQ = 4$, what is the area of the shaded region?

(A) $2\pi + 2$

(B) $2\pi - 2$

(C) $4\pi - 2$

(D) $4\pi - 4$

(E) $2\pi - 4$

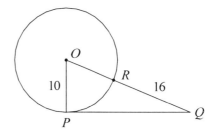

8. In the figure above, $\overline{PQ}$ is tangent to circle O. If the radius of circle O is 10 and $QR = 16$, what is the length of $\overline{PQ}$?

(A) 16

(B) 20

(C) 24

(D) 26

(E) 28

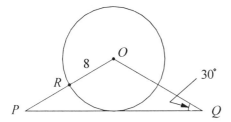

7. In the figure above, $OP = OQ$ and $\overline{PQ}$ is tangent to circle O. If the radius of circle O is 8, what is the length of $\overline{PR}$?

(A) 6

(B) 8

(C) 16

(D) $10(\sqrt{2} - 1)$

(E) $10(\sqrt{3} - 1)$

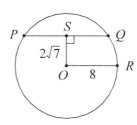

9. In the figure above, $PQ =$

(A) 4

(B) 6

(C) 8

(D) 10

(E) 12

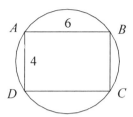

10. If a rectangle is inscribed in a circle as shown above, then the area of the circle is

   (A) 10π (B) $2\sqrt{13}\pi$ (C) 13π

   (D) 26π (E) 52π

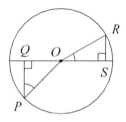

11. In circle O above, $m\angle OPQ = 45°$, $m\angle ROS = 30°$, $PQ = x$, and $RS = y$. If $2x^2 + 4y^2 = 50$, what is the area of circle O?

   (A) 5π (B) 8π (C) 10π

   (D) 25π (E) 50π

12. A wheel with a radius of 2.2 feet is rotating at 500 revolutions per minute. If a point P is on the wheel's circumference, how many miles will point P travel in one hour? (1 mile = 5,280 feet)

   (A) 6.25π (B) 12.5π (C) 25π

   (D) 37.5π (E) 60π

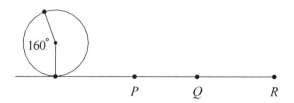

13. A wheel, shown above, rolls along the floor. The points P, Q, and R are the marks left on the line when the two points on the circle touch the floor. If $PQ = 10$ and $PQ < QR$, what is the length of QR?

   (A) 11

   (B) 11.5

   (C) 12

   (D) 12.5

   (E) 13

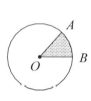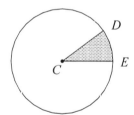

14. In the figure above, the radius of circle C is twice the radius of circle O, and $m\angle AOB = 48°$. If the area of the shaded region in circle C is three times the area of the shaded region in circle O, what is the measure of $\angle DCE$?

   (A) 20

   (B) 28

   (C) 32

   (D) 36

   (E) 40

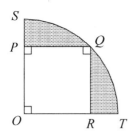

15. In the figure above, the length of arc *ST* is 2π and *OPQR* is a square. What is the sum of the areas of the shaded regions?

    (A) $2(\pi-1)$

    (B) $2(\pi-2)$

    (C) $4(\pi-1)$

    (D) $4(\pi-2)$

    (E) $4(\pi-\sqrt{2})$

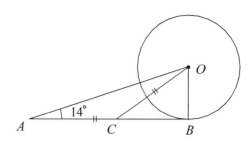

17. In the figure above, $\overline{AB}$ is tangent to circle *O*. If $OC = AC$ and $m\angle OAC = 14°$, what is the measure of $\angle COB$?

    (A) 48

    (B) 56

    (C) 62

    (D) 68

    (E) 76

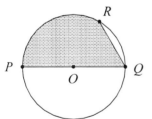

16. In circle *O* above, the length of diameter *PQ* is 6 and $m\angle PQR = 60°$. What is the perimeter of the shaded region?

    (A) $\pi+6$

    (B) $2\pi+9$

    (C) $3\pi+9$

    (D) $3\pi+10$

    (E) $3\pi+12$

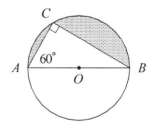

18. In circle *O* above, the diameter of the circle is 8. Of the following, which is the best approximation of the area of the shaded region?

    (A) 9

    (B) 10

    (C) 11

    (D) 12

    (E) 13

1. A square is inscribed in a circle of radius 5. What is the area of the square?

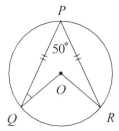

2. In the figure above, if $PQ = PR$, what is the measure of $\angle PQO$?

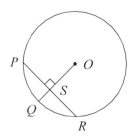

3. In the circle above, if the radius is 10 and $PR = 16$, what is the length of $\overline{QS}$?

4. If the diameter of a circle increases by 10 percent, by what percent will the area of the circle increase?

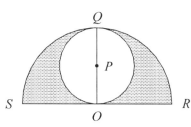

5. In the figure above, $\overline{OQ}$ is the diameter of circle P and $\overline{SR}$ is the diameter of the semicircle. What is the ratio of the area of the shaded region to the area of circle P?

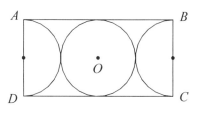

6. In the figure above, the radius of circle O and the radius of the two semicircles is $\sqrt{3}$. What is the area of rectangle $ABCD$?

Answer Key

<u>Multiple Choice Questions</u>

1. D	2. C	3. E	4. B	5. A
6. E	7. B	8. C	9. E	10. C
11. D	12. C	13. D	14. D	15. D
16. B	17. C	18. C		

<u>Grid-In Questions</u>

1. 50	2. 25	3. 4	4. 21	5. 1
6. 24				

Answers and Explanations

<u>Multiple Choice Questions</u>

1. D

$OA = OB$ (In a circle all radii are $\cong$.)
$\Rightarrow m\angle OAB = m\angle OBA = 38$

$\Rightarrow x + 38 + 38 = 180 \Rightarrow x = 104$

2. C

$\dfrac{\text{length of arc } AB}{\text{length of arc } CD} = \dfrac{x}{64} = \dfrac{3}{2}$
$\Rightarrow 2x = 64 \cdot 3 \Rightarrow x = 96$

3. E

$OQ^2 = OP^2 + PQ^2$ (Pythagorean Theorem)
$OQ^2 = 6^2 + 4^2 = 36 + 16 = 52$
$\Rightarrow r^2 = 52$ ($\overline{OQ}$ is the radius of circle O)
Area of circle $= \pi r^2 = \pi \cdot 52$

4. B

Draw a circle O.

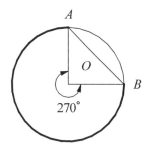

$\dfrac{3}{4}$ of the circumference of the circle covers a central

angle of $270°$.

$\dfrac{3\pi}{\text{circumference}} = \dfrac{270}{360} \Rightarrow \text{circumference} = 4\pi$

$\Rightarrow \text{radius} = 2$

AB is the shortest distance between the endpoints of
the arc AB.
ΔAOB is a $45°$ - $45°$ - $90°$ triangle.
$\Rightarrow AB = 2\sqrt{2}$

5. A

The area of the circle is 9π .
$\Rightarrow r = 3 \Rightarrow OP = OQ = 3$

$OP^2 = PR^2 + OR^2$ (Pythagorean Theorem)
$3^2 = (\sqrt{5})^2 + OR^2 \Rightarrow OR^2 = 4$
$\Rightarrow OR = 2$
$QR = OQ - OR = 3 - 2 = 1$

6. E

$PQ = 4 \Rightarrow OP = OQ = 2\sqrt{2}$

The area of the shaded region
= area of sector PQO – area of ΔPQO

$= \dfrac{1}{4}\pi(2\sqrt{2})^2 - \dfrac{1}{2}(2\sqrt{2})(2\sqrt{2})$

$= 2\pi - 4$

7. B

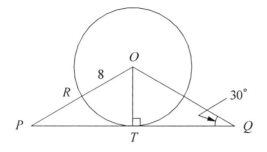

Let T be a point of tangency, then $\overline{OT} \perp \overline{PQ}$. (If a line is tangent to a circle, then it is $\perp$ to the radius drawn to the point of tangency.)

ΔPOT is a $30° - 60° - 90°$ triangle and $OT = 8$.
$\Rightarrow\ OP = 16$

$PR = OP - OR = 16 - 8 = 8$

8. C

The radius of circle O is 10. $\Rightarrow\ OR = 10$
$\overline{PQ}$ is tangent to circle O. $\Rightarrow\ \overline{OP} \perp \overline{PQ}$

$OQ = QR + OR = 16 + 10 = 26$
$OQ^2 = OP^2 + PQ^2$ (Pythagorean Theorem)
$26^2 = 10^2 + PQ^2\ \Rightarrow\ PQ^2 = 576$
$\Rightarrow\ PQ = 24$

9. E

$OQ = 8$ ($\overline{OQ}$ is a radius.)
$OQ^2 = OS^2 + SQ^2$ (Pythagorean Theorem)
$8^2 = (2\sqrt{7})^2 + SQ^2$
$\Rightarrow\ SQ^2 = 8^2 - (2\sqrt{7})^2 = 64 - 28 = 36$
$\Rightarrow\ SQ = 6$

$PQ = 2SQ = 2 \cdot 6 = 12$

10. C

If a rectangle is inscribed in a circle, the diagonal of the rectangle is the diameter of the circle.

$BD^2 = AD^2 + AB^2$ (Pythagorean Theorem)
$BD^2 = 4^2 + 6^2 = 16 + 36 = 52$
$\Rightarrow\ BD = \sqrt{52} = \sqrt{4 \cdot 13} = 2\sqrt{13}$
$\Rightarrow\ \text{radius} = \sqrt{13}$

The area of the circle $= \pi r^2 = \pi(\sqrt{13})^2 = 13\pi$

11. D

$m\angle OPQ = 45°\ \Rightarrow\ m\angle POQ = 45°$
$\Rightarrow\ \Delta POQ$ is a $45° - 45° - 90°$
$OP = \sqrt{2} \cdot OQ = \sqrt{2}x$

$m\angle ROS = 30°\ \Rightarrow\ \Delta ROS$ is a $30° - 60° - 90°$
triangle $\Rightarrow\ OR = 2RS = 2y$

Let the radius of circle O be r.
Then $OP = OR = r$.
$OP^2 + OR^2 = r^2 + r^2 = 2r^2$
$(\sqrt{2}x)^2 + (2y)^2 = 2r^2$ (Substitution)
$2x^2 + 4y^2 = 2r^2$ (Simplify)

$2x^2 + 4y^2 = 50$ (Given equation)

Therefore $2r^2 = 50\ \Rightarrow\ r^2 = 25$.

Area of circle $O = \pi r^2 = \pi(25) = 25\pi$.

12. C

500 revolutions per minute $= 500 \times 60$ revolutions per hour

The distance traveled by a wheel in one hour
$= 2\pi r \times \text{number of revolutions}$
$= 2\pi(2.2\text{ft}) \times 30,000 = 132,000\pi$ ft
$= (132,000\pi \text{ ft}) \times \dfrac{1}{5,280}$
$= 25\pi$ miles

13. D

$$PQ = \frac{160}{360} \times 2\pi r = \frac{8}{9}\pi r \implies 10 = \frac{8}{9}\pi r$$

$$\implies r = 10 \cdot \frac{9}{8\pi} = \frac{45}{4\pi}$$

$$\implies QR = \frac{(360-160)}{360} \times 2\pi r = \frac{200}{360} \times 2\pi(\frac{45}{4\pi})$$
$$= 12.5$$

14. D

Let the radius of circle $O = 1$, and the radius of circle $C = 2$.

The area of sector AOB
$$= \pi r^2 \times \frac{m\angle AOB}{360} = \pi(1)^2 \times \frac{48}{360} = \frac{2\pi}{15}$$

The area of sector DCE
$$= \pi r^2 \times \frac{m\angle DCE}{360} = \pi(2)^2 \times \frac{m\angle DCE}{360}$$
$$= \frac{\pi}{90} \times m\angle DCE$$

The area of sector DCE is 3 times the area of sector AOB. $\implies \frac{\pi}{90} \times m\angle DCE = 3 \cdot \frac{2\pi}{15}$

$$\implies m\angle DCE = 3 \cdot \frac{2\pi}{15} \cdot \frac{90}{\pi} = 36$$

15. D

The length of arc ST is 2π.
$\implies$ circumference of the circle $= 8\pi$
$\implies$ radius of the circle $= 4$

In square $OPQR$, $OQ = 4$. ($\overline{OQ}$ is a radius.)
$\implies OR = QR = 2\sqrt{2}$
The area of square $OPQR$
$$= OR \cdot QR = (2\sqrt{2})(2\sqrt{2}) = 8$$

The area of sector STO
$$= \pi r^2 \times \frac{90}{360} = \pi(4)^2 \times \frac{90}{360} = 4\pi$$

The sum of the areas of the shaded regions
= area of sector STO − area of square $OPQR$
$= 4\pi - 8 = 4(\pi - 2)$

16. B

Draw a radius $\overline{OR}$. Since $OR = OQ$,
$m\angle ORQ = m\angle PQR = 60$
$\implies m\angle QOR = 60°$ and $m\angle POR = 120°$
$OR = OQ = RQ = 3$

Length of the arc PR
$$= 2\pi r \cdot \frac{m\angle POR}{360} = 2\pi(3) \cdot \frac{120}{360} = 2\pi$$

Perimeter of the shaded region
= length of arc $PR + RQ + PQ$
$= 2\pi + 3 + 6 = 2\pi + 9$

17. C

$\overline{AB}$ is tangent to circle $O \implies \overline{OB} \perp \overline{AB}$
$\implies m\angle OBC = 90$

$OC = AC \implies m\angle OAC = m\angle AOC = 14$
$\implies m\angle OCB = 14 + 14 = 28$ (Exterior Angle Theorem)

$m\angle OCB + m\angle COB + m\angle OBC = 180$
$28 + m\angle COB + 90 = 180$
$\implies m\angle COB = 62$

18. C

In the figure shown, $\triangle ABC$ is a $30°$-$60°$-$90°$ triangle.

$AB = 8 \implies AC = 4$ and $BC = 4\sqrt{3}$
Area of $\triangle ABC = \frac{1}{2} \cdot AC \cdot BC = \frac{1}{2} \cdot 4 \cdot 4\sqrt{3} = 8\sqrt{3}$

Area of semicircle $= \frac{1}{2}\pi(4)^2 = 8\pi$

Area the shaded region
= Area of semicircle − Area of $\triangle ABC$
$= 8\pi - 8\sqrt{3} \approx 25.1 - 13.9 = 11.2$

Grid-In Questions

1. 50

If a square is inscribed in a circle, then the diagonal of the square is the diameter of the circle.

diameter of the circle $= 10$
$\Rightarrow$ diagonal of the square $= 10$
$\Rightarrow$ edge of square

$$= 10 \cdot \frac{1}{\sqrt{2}} = \frac{10 \cdot \sqrt{2}}{\sqrt{2} \cdot \sqrt{2}} = \frac{10 \cdot \sqrt{2}}{2} = 5\sqrt{2}$$

Area of the square $= (5\sqrt{2})^2 = 25 \cdot 2 = 50$

2. 25

Draw $\overline{PO}$, then $PO = QO = RO$.
$PQ = QR$ (Given)

$\Delta POQ \cong \Delta POR$ by SSS.

Therefore $m\angle QPO = m\angle RPO = 25$ (by cpctc)
$m\angle PQO = m\angle QPO = 25$, since $PQ = QR$.

3. 4

The radius of the circle is 10.
$\Rightarrow OP = OR = OQ = 10$

$PR = 16 \Rightarrow PS = RS = 8$

$OP^2 = OS^2 + PS^2$ (Pythagorean Theorem)
$10^2 = OS^2 + 8^2$
$\Rightarrow OS^2 = 36$
$\Rightarrow OS = 6$

$QS = OQ - OS = 10 - 6 = 4$

4. 21

If the diameter of the circle increases by 10 percent, then the radius of the circle increases by 10 percent.

Let $r =$ the radius of the original circle,
then $1.1r =$ the radius of the new circle.

Area of the original circle $= \pi r^2$
Area of the new circle $= \pi(1.1r)^2 = 1.21r^2$

$$\underbrace{1.21r^2}_{\substack{\text{Area of the} \\ \text{new circle}}} = \underbrace{r^2}_{\substack{\text{Area of the} \\ \text{original circle}}} \qquad \underbrace{+0.21r^2}_{\substack{\text{increased by 21\% of} \\ \text{the area of original circle}}}$$

The area of the circle increased by 21 percent.

5. 1

Let $OQ = OR = 2$.
Then the area of circle $P = \pi(1)^2 = \pi$.
Area of the semicircle $= \frac{1}{2}\pi(2)^2 = 2\pi$.
The area of the shaded region
$=$ Area of semicircle $-$ Area of circle P
$= 2\pi - \pi = \pi$

$$\frac{\text{area of shaded region}}{\text{area of circle } P} = \frac{\pi}{\pi} = 1$$

6. 24

$AB = \sqrt{3} + 2\sqrt{3} + \sqrt{3} = 4\sqrt{3}$
$AD = 2\sqrt{3}$

The area of rectangle $ABCD$
$= AB \cdot AD = 4\sqrt{3} \cdot 2\sqrt{3} = 24$

17. Solids

Key Terms / Illustrations   Examples

1. A **cube** is a prism in which all the faces are squares.

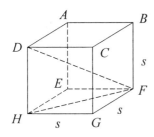

$$\text{Volume} = s^3$$
$$\text{Total Surface Area} = 6s^2$$
$$\text{Length of Diagonal } \overline{DF} = \sqrt{s^2 + s^2 + s^2}$$
$$= \sqrt{3}\,s$$

2. Rectangular Prism

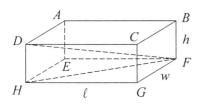

$$\text{Volume} = \text{Base area} \times \text{Height}$$
$$= \ell \cdot w \cdot h$$
$$\text{Total Surface Area} = 2\ell w + 2wh + 2\ell h$$
$$\text{Length of a Diagonal} = \sqrt{\ell^2 + w^2 + h^2}$$

3. Triangular Prism

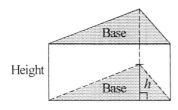

$$\text{Volume} = \text{Area of Base} \times \text{Height}$$
$$= \frac{1}{2} b \cdot h \times \text{height of prism}$$
$$\text{Total Surface Area}$$
$$= \text{Perimeter of Base} \times \text{Height}$$
$$+ 2 \cdot \text{base area}$$

Example 1 □ Cube

The total surface area of a cube is 96 in^2. What is the volume of the cube?

Solution □

$$6s^2 = 96 \qquad \text{Surface area of cube} = 6s^2$$
$$s^2 = 16 \implies s = 4$$
$$\text{Volume} = s^3$$
$$= 4^3 = 64 \text{ in}^3 \qquad \text{Answer}$$

....

Example 2 □ Rectangular prism

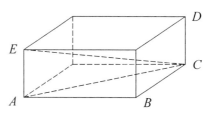

The figure above is a rectangular solid with $AB = 12$, $BC = 9$, and $CD = 8$. Find
(1) the total surface area of the prism
(2) the area of $\triangle ACE$
(3) the length of the diagonal $\overline{CE}$

Solution □

(1) Total surface area $= 2\ell w + 2wh + 2\ell h$
$$= 2 \cdot 12 \cdot 9 + 2 \cdot 9 \cdot 8 + 2 \cdot 12 \cdot 8$$
$$= 552 \qquad \text{Answer}$$

(2) $AC^2 = AB^2 + BC^2 \qquad$ Pythagorean Theorem
$$= 12^2 + 9^2$$
$$= 225 \implies AC = 15$$
$$\text{Area of } \triangle ACE = \frac{1}{2} \cdot AC \cdot AE$$
$$= \frac{1}{2} \cdot 15 \cdot 8 = 60 \qquad \text{Answer}$$

(3) $CE = \sqrt{\ell^2 + w^2 + h^2}$
$$= \sqrt{12^2 + 9^2 + 8^2} = 17 \text{ Answer}$$

4. **Cylinder**

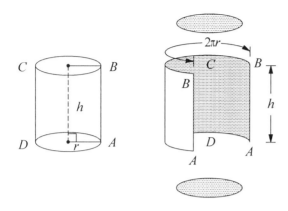

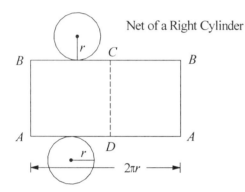

Net of a Right Cylinder

$$\text{Volume} = \text{Base Area} \times \text{Height}$$
$$= \pi r^2 h$$

$$\text{Total Surface Area} = 2\pi rh + 2\pi r^2$$

5. **Circular Cone**

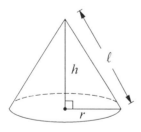

$$\text{Volume} = \frac{1}{3}\pi r^2 h$$

$$\text{Total Surface Area} = \pi r^2 + \pi r\ell$$

Example 3 □ **Triangular prism**

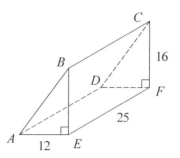

In the triangular prism shown above, find
(1) the volume of the prism
(2) the area of the rectangle $ABCD$

Solution □

(1) Volume = area of base × height
$$= \frac{1}{2}(12 \cdot 16) \cdot 25 = 2400 \qquad \text{Answer}$$

(2) $\qquad AB^2 = AE^2 + BE^2$
$$= 12^2 + 16^2 = 400 \implies AB = 20$$

Area of the rectangle $ABCD$
$$= 20 \times 25 = 500 \qquad \text{Answer}$$

Example 4 □ **Cylinder**

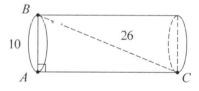

In the cylinder shown above, the diameter of the base, the diagonal, and the height of the cylinder AC form a right triangle. Find the volume of the cylinder.

Solution □
$$26^2 = AC^2 + 10^2 \qquad \text{Pythagorean Theorem}$$
$$676 = AC^2 + 100$$
$$AC^2 = 576 \implies AC = 24$$
$$\text{Volume} = \pi r^2 h \qquad \text{Volume of Cylinder}$$
$$= \pi(5)^2 \cdot 24 \qquad \text{Radius is 5.}$$
$$= 600\pi \qquad \text{Answer}$$

6. Pyramid

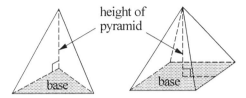

height of pyramid

base   base

Volume of a Pyramid $= \frac{1}{3}Bh$, where B is the area

of the base and h is the height of the pyramid.

7. Sphere

Volume $= \frac{4}{3}\pi r^3$

Surface Area $= 4\pi r^2$

A plane can intersect a sphere at a point or in a circle.
When a plane intersects a sphere so that it contains the center of the sphere, the intersection is called a **great circle**.

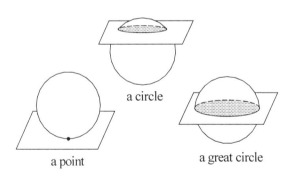

a circle

a point   a great circle

8. Ratios of Surface Areas and Volumes of Solids

If two solids are similar with corresponding sides in the ratio of $a : b$, then their surface areas have a ratio of $a^2 : b^2$, and their volumes have a ratio of $a^3 : b^3$.

Example 5 □   **A plane intersects a sphere in a circle**

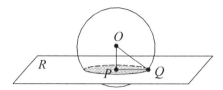

In the figure above, O is the center of the sphere, and plane R intersects the sphere in circle P.
If the volume of the sphere is 288π and $OP = 4$, what is the area of circle P?

Solution □

Volume of sphere $= \frac{4}{3}\pi r^3 = 288\pi$

$\Rightarrow r^3 = 288 \times \frac{3}{4} = 216$

$\Rightarrow r = 6 \Rightarrow OQ = 6$

$OQ^2 = OP^2 + PQ^2 \Rightarrow 6^2 = 4^2 + PQ^2$

$\Rightarrow PQ^2 = 20$

Area of circle $P = \pi(PQ^2) = 20\pi$ Answer

Questions 1 – 2 refer to the following figure.

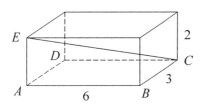

1. In the rectangular solid shown above, what is the length of $\overline{CE}$?

(A) $3\sqrt{5}$

(B) 7

(C) $4\sqrt{3}$

(D) 9

(E) $4\sqrt{5}$

2. In the rectangular solid shown above, what is the total surface area of the prism?

(A) 36   (B) 48   (C) 64

(D) 72   (E) 84

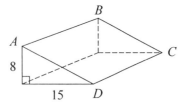

3. In the figure above, the volume of the triangular prism is 900. What is the area of rectangle $ABCD$?

(A) 255   (B) 320   (C) 380

(D) 445   (E) 510

Questions 4 – 5 refer to the following figure.

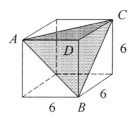

4. The cube shown above has an edge length of 6. What is the perimeter of $\triangle ABC$?

(A) $12\sqrt{2}$

(B) 18

(C) $18\sqrt{2}$

(D) $12\sqrt{3}$

(E) 36

5. In the cube shown above, A, B, and C are the vertices of the base of the pyramid with vertex D. What is the volume of the pyramid?

(A) 36   (B) $18\sqrt{2}$ (C) $24\sqrt{2}$

(D) 72   (E) 108

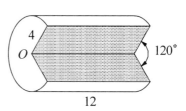

6. What is the volume of the partial right cylinder shown above?

(A) 64π (B) 72π (C) 80π

(D) 96π (E) 128π

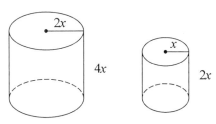

Note: Figure not drawn to scale.

7. In the figure above, if the volume of the larger cylinder is 128π, what is the volume of the smaller cylinder?

(A) 8π (B) 16π (C) 20π

(D) 24π (E) 32π

8. A cone has radius 6 and height 30. If a cylinder with height 10 has the same volume as the cone, what is the radius of the cylinder?

(A) 4   (B) 6   (C) 8

(D) 9   (E) 12

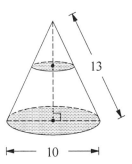

9. In the circular cone shown above, a plane parallel to the base of the cone divides the cone into two pieces. If the diameter of the base of the smaller cone is 4, what is the height of the smaller cone?

(A) 3   (B) 3.6   (C) 4

(D) 4.8   (E) 5.6

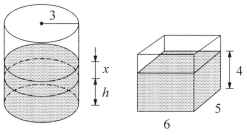

Note: Figure not drawn to scale.

10. In the figure shown above, if all the water in the rectangular-shaped container is poured into the cylindrical-shaped container, the water level rises from h inches to $(h + x)$ inches. Which of the following is the best approximation of the value of x?

(A) 2   (B) 2.5   (C) 3

(D) 3.5   (E) 4.2

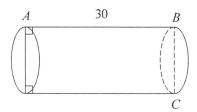

11. In the cylindrical tube shown above, the height of the tube is 30 and the circumference of the circular base is 32. If the tube is cut along $\overline{AB}$ and laid out flat to make a rectangle, what is the length of $\overline{AC}$ to the nearest whole number?

(A) 24   (B) 30   (C) 34

(D) 38   (E) 44

1. If the volume of a cube is 1000 cubic inches, what is the total surface area, in square inches, of the cube?

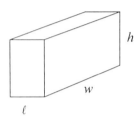

2. In the figure above, the areas of two of the faces are 12 and 20. If each of the dimensions ℓ, w, and h is an even integer, what is the volume of the rectangular prism?

3. A solid wood cube with a total surface area of 1350 square inches is cut into smaller wood cubes, each with a total surface area of 150 square inches. How many of these smaller cubes are cut from the original cube?

4. What is the volume of the smallest rectangular prism that can hold 3 identical spheres of radius 3?

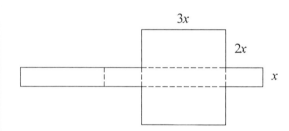

5. If the figure shown above is folded into a rectangular prism, the volume of the prism will be 384 cm^3. What is the total surface area of the prism in square centimeters?

6. If two cubes each with edge of length 3 are glued together to form a rectangular solid, what is the surface area of the rectangular solid?

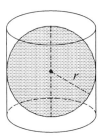

7. In the figure above, a sphere is inscribed in a cylinder, so that the diameter of the sphere is the same as the diameter of the cylinder and the height of the cylinder. What is the value

of $\dfrac{\text{volume of cylinder}}{\text{volume of sphere}}$?

Answer Key

Multiple Choice Questions

1. B	2. D	3. A	4. C	5. A
6. E	7. B	8. B	9. D	10. E
11. C				

Grid-In Questions

1. 600	2. 120	3. 27	4. 648	5. 352
6. 90	7. 1.5			

Answers and Explanations

Multiple Choice Questions

1. B

Length of the diagonal $= \sqrt{\ell^2 + w^2 + h^2}$
$= \sqrt{6^2 + 3^2 + 2^2} = \sqrt{36 + 9 + 4} = \sqrt{49} = 7$

2. D

Total surface area
$= 2\ell w + 2wh + 2\ell h = 2(6 \cdot 3 + 3 \cdot 2 + 6 \cdot 2) = 72$

3. A

Volume of a triangular prism
$=$ area of base $\times$ height
$= (\frac{1}{2} \cdot 8 \cdot 15)(CD) = 900 \implies CD = 15$

$AD^2 = 8^2 + 15^2$ (Pythagorean Theorem)
$AD^2 = 8^2 + 15^2 = 64 + 225 = 289$
$\implies AD = 17$

Area of rectangle $ABCD = AD \cdot CD = 17 \cdot 15 = 255$

4. C

Each face of a cube is a square, and $\overline{AB}$, $\overline{BC}$, and $\overline{AC}$ are diagonals of the faces.

$AB = BC = AC = 6\sqrt{2}$
Perimeter of $\triangle ABC$
$= AB + BC + AC = 6\sqrt{2} + 6\sqrt{2} + 6\sqrt{2} = 18\sqrt{2}$

5. A

We can use $\triangle ABD$ as a base of the pyramid, and $\overline{CD}$ as the altitude to the base.

Volume of the pyramid
$= \frac{1}{3} \cdot B \cdot h = \frac{1}{3}(\frac{1}{2} \cdot 6 \cdot 6) \cdot 6 = 36$

6. E

Volume of the partial right cylinder
$= \pi r^2 h - \pi r^2 h \times \frac{120}{360}$
$= \pi(4)^2(12) - \pi(4)^2(12) \times \frac{120}{360}$
$= 192\pi - 64\pi = 128\pi$

7. B

Volume of the larger cylinder
$= \pi(2x)^2(4x) = 128\pi \implies 16\pi x^3 = 128\pi$
$\implies x^3 = 8$
Volume of the smaller cylinder
$= \pi(x)^2(2x) = 2x^3\pi = 2(8)\pi = 16\pi$

8. B

Given: Volume of a cone with radius 6 and height 30
$=$ Volume of a cylinder with height 10.

Let $r =$ the radius of the cylinder.

$\frac{1}{3}\pi(6)^2 \cdot 30 = \pi r^2 \cdot 10 \implies 360\pi = 10\pi r^2$
$\implies r = 6$

9. D

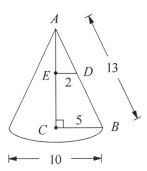

In the figure above, $\overline{DE}$ is the radius of the base of the smaller cone.

$BC = \frac{1}{2} \cdot 10 = 5$ and $DE = \frac{1}{2} \cdot 4 = 2$

$AB^2 = BC^2 + AC^2$ (Pythagorean Theorem)

$13^2 = 5^2 + AC^2 \Rightarrow AC = 12$

By AA similarity, $\triangle ABC \sim \triangle ADE$.

$\Rightarrow \frac{AC}{BC} = \frac{AE}{DE} \Rightarrow \frac{12}{5} = \frac{AE}{2}$

$\Rightarrow AE = \frac{24}{5} = 4.8$

10. E

Given: Volume of water in the rectangular-shaped Container = Volume of water in the cylinder whose radius is 3 and height is x.

$\Rightarrow 6 \cdot 5 \cdot 4 = \pi(3)^2 x \Rightarrow 120 = 9\pi x$

$\Rightarrow x = \frac{120}{9\pi} \approx 4.2$

11. C

Cut along $\overline{AB}$ and make it flat to form a rectangle.

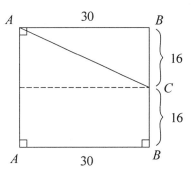

In the rectangle above, C is the midpoint of $\overline{BB}$ and the length of $\overline{BB}$ is 32.

$BC = \frac{1}{2} BB = \frac{1}{2} \cdot 32 = 16$

$AC^2 = AB^2 + BC^2$ (Pythagorean Theorem)

$AC^2 = 30^2 + 16^2 = 900 + 256 = 1156$

$\Rightarrow AC = 34$

Grid-In Questions

1. 600

Volume of the cube $= s^3 = 1000$

$\Rightarrow s = 10$

Total surface area $= 6s^2 = 6 \cdot (10)^2 = 600$

2. 120

The areas of two of the faces are 12 and 20, and each of the dimensions ℓ, w, and h is an even integer.

$\Rightarrow \left. \begin{array}{l} 12 = 2 \cdot 6 \\ 20 = 2 \cdot 10 \end{array} \right\} \Rightarrow \ell \cdot h = 2 \cdot 6 \text{ and } \ell \cdot w = 2 \cdot 10$

($12 = 3 \cdot 4$ and $20 = 4 \cdot 5$ is not possible, since ℓ, w, and h are all even integers.)

Volume of the rectangular prism

$= \ell \cdot w \cdot h = 2 \cdot 10 \cdot 6 = 120$

3. 27

Total surface area of the cube $= 6s^2 = 1350$
$\Rightarrow s^2 = 225 \Rightarrow s = 15$

Volume of the cube $= s^3 = (15)^3 = 3375$

Total surface area of the smaller cube $= 150$
$\Rightarrow 6s^2 = 150 \Rightarrow s^2 = 25 \Rightarrow s = 5$

Volume of the smaller cube $= s^3 = (5)^3 = 125$

The number of smaller cubes that can be cut from the original cube $= 3375 \div 125 = 27$

4. 648

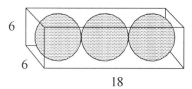

The figure above shows the smallest rectangular prism that can hold 3 identical spheres of radius 3.

Volume of the rectangular prism
$= 6 \cdot 6 \cdot 18 = 648$

5. 352

When the net shown is folded into a rectangular prism, the volume will be
$x \cdot 2x \cdot 3x = 6x^3$.

$6x^3 = 384 \Rightarrow x^3 = 64 \Rightarrow x = 4$

Therefore, the dimensions of the prism are 4, 8, and 12.

Total surface area of the prism
$= 2\ell \cdot w + 2w \cdot h + 2\ell \cdot h$
$= 2(4 \cdot 8 + 8 \cdot 12 + 4 \cdot 12) = 352$

6. 90

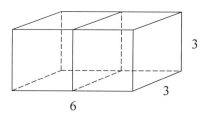

The figure above shows the rectangular solid made from the two cubes glued together.

$\ell = 6, \ w = 3, \text{ and } h = 3$.

Total surface area
$= 2\ell w + 2wh + 2\ell h = 2(6 \cdot 3 + 3 \cdot 3 + 6 \cdot 3) = 90$

7. 1.5

Volume of sphere $= \dfrac{4}{3}\pi r^3$

Radius of the cylinder $= r$
Height of the cylinder $= 2r$
Volume of cylinder
$= \pi \cdot (\text{radius})^2 \cdot \text{height} = \pi(r)^2(2r) = 2\pi r^3$

$\dfrac{\text{volume of cylinder}}{\text{volume of sphere}} = \dfrac{2\pi r^3}{\frac{4}{3}\pi r^3} = \dfrac{2 \cdot 3}{4} = 1.5$

III. Other Topics

18. Data Interpretation, Scatter Plots, and Matrices

Key Terms / Illustrations   Examples

1. Bar Graphs

A bar graph has two axes. One axis is labeled with a numerical scale and the other is labeled with the categories.
The height of each bar shows its value.

2. Line Graphs

A line graph shows the values and direction of change for certain data over a period of time.
The values are represented by points. These points are connected by line segments.

3. Circle Graphs (Pie Charts)

A circle graph is used to represent data expressed as part of a whole.
The entire circle represents the whole, or 100%, of the data.
Each section is labeled with a category name, accompanied by the corresponding percentage.

4. Scatter Plots

A scatter plot is a coordinate graph containing points that represent real-life data.

Usually, there is no single line that passes through all the data points, but we can find a line that best fits the data. This is called the **line of best fit**.

☑ On the SAT, students are expected to identify the general characteristics of the line of best fit for a given scatter plot. Students might determine the slope of the line of best fit, but would not be expected to use formal methods of finding the equation of the line of best fit.

☑ Approximating the **slope of the line of best fit.**

1. Sketch the line that appears to most closely follow the pattern given by the points.
2. Locate two points on the line and approximate the x-coordinate and y-coordinate of each point. Use these two points or the original data points to calculate the slope of the line. Use the slope formula:

$$\text{slope} = \frac{y_2 - y_1}{x_2 - x_1}$$

Example 1 □ **Scatter plots**

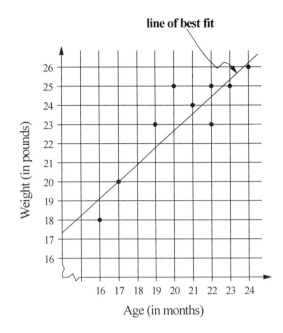

A group of nine male children was weighed, and the individual ages and weights were plotted as shown above. (The weights are rounded to the nearest whole number.)

1. What is the average weight of the 9 children?
2. What is the median weight of the 9 children?
3. What is the mode of the weights?
4. Find the slope of the line of best fit.
5. Use the slope of the line to approximate the weight of a 30-month-old boy.

Solution □

1. Average
$$= \frac{18 + 20 + 23 + 25 + 24 + 23 + 25 + 25 + 26}{9}$$
≈ 23.2 Answer

2. Arrange the weights of the 9 children in increasing order.

18, 20, 23, 23, 24, 25, 25, 25, 26

The median is 24.   Answer

3. The mode is 25.   Answer

5. Determining the Correlation of x and y

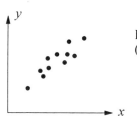

Positive Correlation
(Slope of the line of
best fit is positive.)

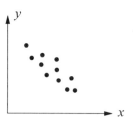

Negative Correlation
(Slope of the line of
best fit is negative.)

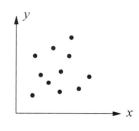

No Correlation
(A line of best fit
cannot be determined.)

6. Matrices

A **matrix** is a rectangular array of real numbers.

The **rows** of a matrix run horizontally, and the **columns** run vertically.

Each number in a matrix is called an **element**.

A matrix with m rows and n columns has **dimensions** $m \times n$.

Illustration

$$\begin{bmatrix} 2 & -1 & 3 \\ 1 & 0 & 7 \end{bmatrix} \Leftarrow 2 \text{ rows}$$

⇑
3 columns

The dimensions of the matrix above are 2×3.

The element in row 2, column 3 is 7.

4. Choose the two points that are closest to the line of best fit: (17,20) and (24,26). The slope of the line passing through these points is

$$m = \frac{y_2 - y_1}{x_2 - x_1} = \frac{26 - 20}{24 - 17} = \frac{6}{7} \qquad \text{Answer}$$

5. Let $y =$ the weight of a 30-month-old boy. The slope of the line passing through the points (17,20) and (30, y) should approximate $6/7$.

$$m = \frac{y - 20}{30 - 17} = \frac{6}{7} \implies y \approx 31 \qquad \text{Answer}$$

Example 2 ◻ **Finding score totals using matrix multiplication**

In a district-wide track meet, first-, second-, and third-place finishes were recorded for each of three participating schools.

	Reseda	West Hills	Oak Park
1 st place	5	8	10
2 nd place	12	6	9
3 rd place	8	8	4

Use matrix multiplication to find the final scores of each school, if 10 points are awarded for a first-place finish, 5 for second, and 3 for third.

Solution ◻

Total score for Reseda

$$= \begin{bmatrix} 10 & 5 & 3 \end{bmatrix} \cdot \begin{bmatrix} 5 \\ 12 \\ 8 \end{bmatrix} = 10 \cdot 5 + 5 \cdot 12 + 3 \cdot 8 = 134$$

Total score for West Hills

$$= \begin{bmatrix} 10 & 5 & 3 \end{bmatrix} \cdot \begin{bmatrix} 8 \\ 6 \\ 8 \end{bmatrix} = 10 \cdot 8 + 5 \cdot 6 + 3 \cdot 8 = 134$$

Total score for Oak Park

$$= \begin{bmatrix} 10 & 5 & 3 \end{bmatrix} \cdot \begin{bmatrix} 10 \\ 9 \\ 4 \end{bmatrix} = 10 \cdot 10 + 5 \cdot 9 + 3 \cdot 4 = 157$$

7. Multiplying Matrices

The product of the two matrices is found by multiplying rows and columns.

If $R = \begin{bmatrix} r_1 & r_2 & r_3 \end{bmatrix}$ and $C = \begin{bmatrix} c_1 \\ c_2 \\ c_3 \end{bmatrix}$, then by the product of R and C we mean the number $r_1 c_1 + r_2 c_2 + r_3 c_3$.

8. Arranging Data in a Matrix

A matrix is used to organize and display data that falls into several categories.

Illustration

A sporting goods store sells three different brands of running shoes. The profit from a sale of Brand A shoes is $12, the profit from a sale of Brand B shoes is $15, and the profit from a sale of Brand C shoes is $20. This information is organized into a matrix below.

$$\text{Profit(\$)} = \begin{array}{ccc} \text{Brand } A & \text{Brand } B & \text{Brand } C \\ \begin{bmatrix} 12 & 15 & 20 \end{bmatrix} \end{array}$$

In November, sales of Brand A, Brand B, and Brand C shoes numbered 70, 55, and 40 pairs, respectively. In December, sales were 150, 120, and 90. This information is organized into a matrix, shown below.

$$\begin{array}{c} \text{Number of Pairs Sold} \\ \begin{array}{cc} \text{Nov} & \text{Dec} \end{array} \\ \begin{array}{c} \text{Brand } A \\ \text{Brand } B \\ \text{Brand } C \end{array} \begin{bmatrix} 70 & 150 \\ 55 & 120 \\ 40 & 90 \end{bmatrix} \end{array}$$

Total profits for the month of November can be found by multiplying the profit matrix with the sales matrix.

$$\begin{bmatrix} 12 & 15 & 20 \end{bmatrix} \cdot \begin{bmatrix} 70 \\ 55 \\ 40 \end{bmatrix}$$

$$= 12 \cdot 70 + 15 \cdot 55 + 20 \cdot 40 = 2,465$$

Example 5 □ **Finding the total income earned from sportswear sales**

The table below shows the numbers of T-shirts, shorts, and sweatshirts ordered at a sports club, and the price of regular and extra large sizes for each item.

$$\begin{array}{c} \text{Sportswear Prices} \\ \begin{array}{cc} \text{Regular} & \text{Extra Large} \end{array} \\ \begin{array}{c} \text{T-shirts} \\ \text{Shorts} \\ \text{Sweatshirts} \end{array} \begin{bmatrix} \$10 & \$12 \\ \$14 & \$16 \\ \$20 & \$24 \end{bmatrix} \end{array}$$

$$\begin{array}{c} \text{Number of Items Ordered} \\ \begin{array}{ccc} \text{T-shirts} & \text{Shorts} & \text{Sweatshirts} \end{array} \\ \begin{array}{c} \text{Regular} \\ \text{Extra large} \end{array} \begin{bmatrix} 80 & 120 & 180 \\ 70 & 110 & 160 \end{bmatrix} \end{array}$$

a) Find the total income earned from T-shirts ordered in both regular and extra large sizes.

b) Find the total income earned from all sportswear ordered in regular sizes.

Solution □

a) The total income earned from T-shirts ordered in both sizes

$$\begin{bmatrix} 10 & 12 \end{bmatrix} \cdot \begin{bmatrix} 80 \\ 70 \end{bmatrix} = 10 \cdot 80 + 12 \cdot 70$$

$$= 1,640 \qquad\qquad \text{Answer}$$

b) The total income earned from all items ordered in regular sizes

$$\begin{bmatrix} 80 & 120 & 180 \end{bmatrix} \cdot \begin{bmatrix} 10 \\ 14 \\ 20 \end{bmatrix}$$

$$= 80 \cdot 10 + 120 \cdot 14 + 180 \cdot 20$$
$$= 6,080 \qquad\qquad \text{Answer}$$

Questions 1-3 refer to the following line graph.

Enrollment for College *R*

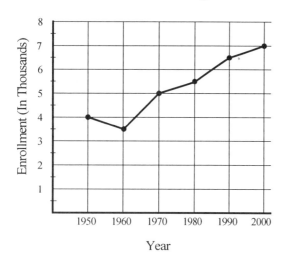

1. According to the graph above, College *R* showed the greatest change in enrollment in which decade?

   (A) 1950 to 1960

   (B) 1960 to 1970

   (C) 1970 to 1980

   (D) 1980 to 1990

   (E) 1990 to 2000

2. According to the graph above, what is the average increase in enrollment <u>per decade</u>, between 1950 and 2000?

   (A) 500

   (B) 600

   (C) 750

   (D) 875

   (E) 950

3. If enrollment increases by approximately the same percentage between 2000 and 2010 as it decreased between 1950 and 1960, what is the expected enrollment in 2010?

   (A) 7,250

   (B) 7,540

   (C) 7,650

   (D) 7,875

   (E) 8,150

Number of Hours Worked by the 20 Salespersons in Company G

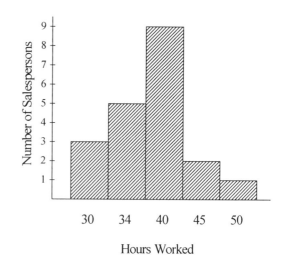

4. According to the bar graph above, what is the average number of hours worked by the 20 salespersons in Company G?

   (A) 36

   (B) 37

   (C) 38

   (D) 39

   (E) 40

Questions 5-6 refer to the following circle graph.

Annual Budget for a Student
at a Four-Year College

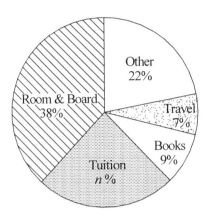

5. In the circle graph above, what is the measure of the central angle of the sector representing travel?

(A) 7

(B) 12.6

(C) 14

(D) 25.2

(E) 28

6. In the circle graph above, if $1,155.00 was spent on travel, how much was tuition?

(A) $2,400

(B) $3,960

(C) $4,150

(D) $4,760

(E) It cannot be determined from the information given.

Total earnings (in 1995 dollars) of the commercial banks in country X in 1965.

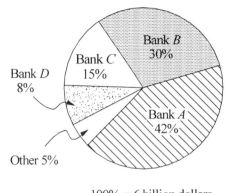

100% = 6 billion dollars

Total earnings (in 1995 dollars) of the commercial banks in country X in 1995.

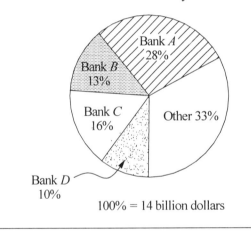

100% = 14 billion dollars

7. According to the graphs above, which commercial bank had actual earnings (in 1995 dollars) that were nearly equal in 1965 and 1995?

(A) Bank A

(B) Bank B

(C) Bank C

(D) Bank D

(E) It cannot be determined from the information given.

Questions 8-9 refer to the following graph.

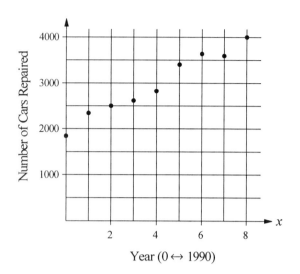

Year (0 ↔ 1990)

8. The number of cars repaired at Jay's Motor between 1990 and 1998 is plotted in the scatter plot shown above. In the graph, x represents the year, with $x = 0$ corresponding to 1990, and y represents the number of cars repaired each year. Which of the following is the best approximation of the slope of the line of best fit?

(A) 100

(B) 250

(C) 500

(D) 750

(E) 1,000

9. What is the best approximation of the number of cars that will be repaired in the year 2010?

(A) 7,000

(B) 8,000

(C) 9,000

(D) 10,000

(E) 11,000

Questions 10-11 refer to the following tables.

The tables below show the numbers of different types of clock radios manufactured each day by a certain company, and the profits earned each day from the radios.

Number of Clock Radios Manufactured

Clock Radios	Model A	Model B	Model C
with CD Player	150	200	300
with Cassette Player	200	350	500

Profits from Clock Radios

Clock Radios	with CD Player	with Cassette Player
Model A	$10	$5
Model B	$14	$6
Model C	$18	$8

10. What are the total profits earned in one day from model B clock radios?

(A) $2,500

(B) $3,300

(C) $3,750

(D) $4,300

(E) $4,900

11. What are the total profits earned in one day from clock radios with a CD player?

(A) $4,350

(B) $7,100

(C) $9,700

(D) $12,800

(E) $15,900

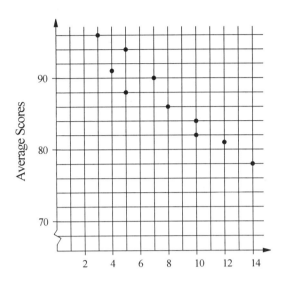

Avg. Practice Time Per Week (in hours)

12. The scatter plot above shows the average scores of 10 golfers and their average weekly practice times. Which of the following is true of the data shown above?

   I. If the slope of the line of best fit (not shown) is m, then $1 \le m \le 2$.

   II. There is no mode of the average scores.

   III. The median score is 88.

   (A) I only

   (B) II only

   (C) III only

   (D) I and II only

   (E) II and III only

Price of Candies (in different sizes)	$1	$2	$5	$10
Number of Candies Sold	120	75	58	25

13. The table above shows the amount of money collected from a church youth group's candy sales. If the goal was to collect $1,200 from the sales, what percent of the goal was reached?

   (A) 48%

   (B) 56%

   (C) 62.5%

   (D) 67.5%

   (E) 72%

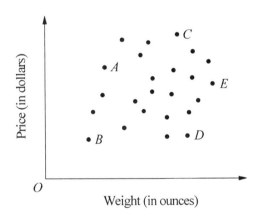

14. The scatter plot above shows the prices and weights of various boxed products. Of the five labeled points, which of the following has the best unit price?

   (A) A

   (B) B

   (C) C

   (D) D

   (E) E

Questions 1-2 refer to the following tables.

The tables below show the ticket prices and the number of tickets sold at a tennis tournament.

Prices of Tickets

	Grand	Box	Prime
Friday	$10	$15	$25
Saturday	$15	$25	$40

Number of Tickets Sold

	Friday	Saturday
Grand	352	495
Box	163	228
Prime	84	125

1. What is the total income from Friday's ticket sales?

2. What is the total income from Prime seat tickets?

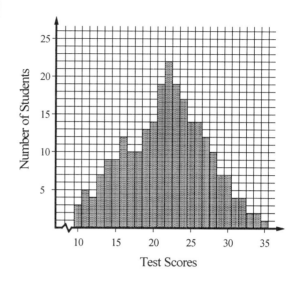

3. The graph above shows students' scores on a 40-item test, in a certain academic competition where no one scored more than 35 points or less than 10 points. If 8% of the students scored 30 or more points, how many students scored 29 points or less?

Answer Key

Multiple Choice Questions

1. B   2. B   3. D   4. C   5. D

6. B   7. B   8. B   9. A   10. E

11. C   12. B   13. D   14. D

Grid-In Questions

1. 8065   2. 7100   3. 230

Answers and Explanations

Multiple Choice Questions

1. B

Year	Changes in enrollment
1950 - 1960	500 (decrease)
1960 - 1970	1,500 (increase)
1970 - 1980	500 (increase)
1980 - 1990	1,000 (increase)
1990 - 2000	500 (increase)

The greatest change in enrollment occurred between 1960 and 1970.

2. B

The total increase in enrollment between 1950 and 2000 is 3,000.

$3,000 \div 5 = 600$

3. D

Percentage decrease between 1950 and 1960
$= \dfrac{\text{amount decreased}}{\text{original amount}} = \dfrac{500}{4,000} = .125 \Rightarrow 12.5\%$

Expected percentage increase between 2000 and 2010
$= \dfrac{\text{expected increase}}{\text{original amount}} = \dfrac{x}{7,000}$

$\Rightarrow \dfrac{x}{7000} = .125 \Rightarrow x = 875$

$7,000 + 875 = 7,875$

4. C

3 people worked for 30 hours.
5 people worked for 34 hours.
9 people worked for 40 hours.
2 people worked for 45 hours.
1 people worked for 50 hours.

Average # of hours $= \dfrac{\text{Total \# of hours}}{\text{Total \# of people}}$
$= \dfrac{3\cdot30+5\cdot34+9\cdot40+2\cdot45+1\cdot50}{3+5+9+2+1}$
$= \dfrac{760}{20} = 38$

5. D

The measure of the central angle of the sector representing travel $= 360° \cdot 0.07 = 25.2°$.

6. B

Let x = the total annual budget.

$1,155.00 was spent on travel.
$\Rightarrow 0.07x = 1,155 \Rightarrow x = 16,500$

In a circle graph, the entire circle represents 100%.
$\Rightarrow 38+22+7+9+n = 100$
$\Rightarrow n = 24$

Cost of tuition $= 16,500 \times .24 = 3,960$

7. B

Actual earnings in 1965:

Bank $A = 6 \times .042 = 2.52$ billion
Bank $B = 6 \times 0.30 = 1.80$ billion
Bank $C = 6 \times 0.15 = 0.90$ billion
Bank $D = 6 \times 0.08 = 0.48$ billion
Other $= 6 \times 0.05 = 0.30$ billion

Actual earnings in 1995:

Bank $A = 14 \times 0.28 = 3.92$ billion
Bank $B = 14 \times 0.13 = 1.82$ billion
Bank $C = 14 \times 0.16 = 2.24$ billion
Bank $D = 14 \times 0.10 = 1.40$ billion
Other $= 14 \times 0.33 = 4.62$ billion

Therefore the actual earnings, in 1995 dollars, of Bank B were nearly the same in 1965 and 1995.

8. B

From the graph, you might choose the points $(2,2500)$ and $(8,4000)$ to find the slope of the line of best fit.

The slope of the line passing through these two points is
$$m = \frac{4,000 - 2,500}{8 - 2} = \frac{1,500}{6} = 250$$
If you choose the points $(0,1800)$ and $(7,3600)$,
$$m = \frac{3,600 - 1,800}{7 - 0} = \frac{1,800}{7} \approx 257$$

9. A

Let $y =$ the expected number of cars repaired in the year 2010.
$x = 20$ represents the year 2010.

The slope of the line passing through points $(2,2500)$ and $(20,y)$ should approximate 250.

$$m = \frac{y - 2,500}{20 - 2} = \frac{y - 2,500}{18} = 250$$
$$\Rightarrow \quad y - 2500 = 250 \cdot 18 \quad \Rightarrow \quad y = 7000$$

The correct answer is A.

10. E

The total profits earned in one day from model B clock radios are

$$\begin{bmatrix} 14 & 6 \end{bmatrix} \cdot \begin{bmatrix} 200 \\ 350 \end{bmatrix} = 14 \times 200 + 6 \times 350 = 4,900$$

11. C

The total profits earned in one day from clock radios with CD players are

$$\begin{bmatrix} 150 & 200 & 300 \end{bmatrix} \cdot \begin{bmatrix} 10 \\ 14 \\ 18 \end{bmatrix} = 150 \cdot 10 + 200 \cdot 14 + 300 \cdot 18$$
$$= 9,700$$

12. B

From the graph, you might choose the points $(3,96)$ and $(14,78)$ to find the slope of the line of best fit.

The slope of the line passing through these two points is
$$m = \frac{78 - 96}{14 - 3} = \frac{-18}{11} \approx -1.64$$

Since the slope is negative,
Roman numeral I is not true.

Let's put the average scores of the golfers in order.

96, 94, 91, 90, 88, 86, 84, 82, 81, 78

There is no mode, since each number appears only once.

Roman numeral II is true.

There are two middle values: 88(the 5th number) and 86(the 6th number). The median is the mean of these two values.

$$\text{Median} = \frac{88 + 86}{2} = 87$$

Roman numeral III is not true.

13. D

Total amount of money collected
$= 1 \times 120 + 2 \times 75 + 5 \times 58 + 10 \times 25 = 810$

$\dfrac{810}{1,200} = 0.675 \implies 67.5\%$

14. D

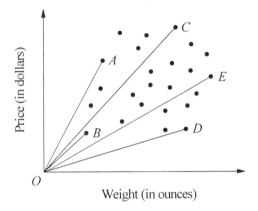

$\text{Unit Price} = \dfrac{\text{Price}}{\text{Number of Units}}$

For each of the points on the graph, the unit price corresponds to the slope of the line segment drawn from the origin to that point. Of the line segments $\overline{OA}$, $\overline{OB}$, $\overline{OC}$, $\overline{OD}$, and $\overline{OE}$, $\overline{OD}$ has the least slope.

Therefore product D is the one with the best unit price.

1. 8065

Total income from Friday's ticket sales
$= \begin{bmatrix} 10 & 15 & 25 \end{bmatrix} \cdot \begin{bmatrix} 352 \\ 163 \\ 84 \end{bmatrix}$

$= 10 \cdot 352 + 15 \cdot 163 + 25 \cdot 84$

$= 8,065$

2. 7100

Total income from Prime seat tickets
$= \begin{bmatrix} 84 & 125 \end{bmatrix} \cdot \begin{bmatrix} 25 \\ 40 \end{bmatrix} = 84 \cdot 25 + 125 \cdot 40$

$= 7,100$

3. 230

Let x = the total number of students who took the test.

The graph shows twenty students who scored 30 or more points.

$\implies 0.08x = 20 \implies x = 250$

The number of students who scored 29 or less
$= 250 - 20 = 230$

19. Number Sequences and Patterns

Key Terms / Illustrations

Examples

1. **Sequence**

   A sequence is a list of numbers with a specific order.

2. **Arithmetic Sequence**

   When the difference between successive terms is always the same, the sequence is called arithmetic.

   The nth Term of an Arithmetic Sequence
   is given by

   $$a_n = a_1 + (n-1)d \,,$$

   where a_n is the nth term, a_1 is the first term, and d is the common difference.

   The terms of an arithmetic sequence follow the pattern
   $$a_1, \ a_1 + d, \ a_1 + 2d, \ a_1 + 3d, \ \cdots$$

3. The **Sum of an Arithmetic Series**
   is given by

   $$S_n = \frac{n}{2}(a_1 + a_n) \,,$$

   where a_1 is the first term, a_n is the last term, and n is the number of terms.

4. **Geometric Sequence**

   When the ratio of successive terms is always the same, the sequence is called geometric.

   The nth Term of a Geometric Sequence
   is given by

   $$a_n = a_1 \cdot r^{n-1} \,,$$

   where a_n is the nth term, a_1 is the first term, and r is the common ratio.

   The terms of a geometric sequence follow the pattern
   $$a_1, \ a_1 \cdot r, \ a_1 \cdot r^2, \ a_1 \cdot r^3, \ \cdots$$

Example 1 □ **Using an arithmetic sequence to find multiples of a number**

How many multiples of 6 are between 100 and 1000?

Solution □

102, 108, 114, $\cdots$, 990, 996
↑   ↑
first multiple of 6   last multiple of 6

The list of numbers above are an arithmetic sequence with $a_1 = 102$, $a_n = 996$, and $d = 6$.

$$996 = 102 + (n-1)6$$
$$n = 150$$

Thus, there are 150 multiples of 6 between 100 and 1,000.   Answer

Example 2 □ **Geometric sequence**

In a sequence of numbers, each term after the first term is $\frac{1}{2}$ times the preceding term. If a and b are two terms in the sequence and there are 5 terms between a and b, what is the value of $\frac{a}{b}$?

Solution □

There are five terms between a and b.

$\cdots a, \square, \square, \square, \square, \square, b, \cdots$

The common ratio of the sequence is $\frac{1}{2}$.

$$\cdots a, \ \frac{1}{2}a, \ (\frac{1}{2})^2 a, \ (\frac{1}{2})^3 a, \ (\frac{1}{2})^4 a, \ (\frac{1}{2})^5 a, \ b \cdots$$

$$\Rightarrow \ b = (\frac{1}{2})^6 a \ \Rightarrow \ \frac{a}{b} = 2^6 = 64 \quad \text{Answer}$$

5. The **Sum of a Geometric Series**

is given by $S_n = \dfrac{a_1(1-r^n)}{1-r}$

where a_1 is the first term, r is the common ratio ($r \neq 1$), and n is the number of terms.

6. **Exponential Growth and Decay as Sequences**

Exponential growth and decay can be modeled by an exponential function $y_t = a \cdot b^t$ for every positive integer t.

Such a model can also be expressed as a geometric sequence $a_1 = ab$, $a_2 = ab^2$, $a_3 = ab^3$, ..., with a common ratio b.

The equation of an exponential sequence can be written in different ways.

1) **Compound Interest Formula**

$y_t = a \cdot (1+r)^t$, where

a = the initial amount of money invested,
t = the number of years elapsed since the money was invested, and
r = the annual interest rate (as a percentage).

2) **Population Doubling Time**

$y_t = a \times (2)^{t/n}$, where

a = the initial population count,
t = the number of years elapsed since a given starting point, and
n = the number of years required for the population to double.

3) **Half-life**

$y = a \times \left(\dfrac{1}{2}\right)^{t/n}$, where

a = the initial amount of a substance,
t = the number of years elapsed since a given starting point, and
n = the number of years required for the mass of substance to decay by half.

Example 3 □ **Exponential growth sequence**

A town has a population of 20,000 people that is increasing at the rate of 5% each year. Let y_t be the population at the end of the tth year. Show that $y_1, y_2, y_3, \ldots$ is a geometric sequence. What are the values of y_1 and the common ratio?

Solution □

$y_t = a \cdot (1+r)^t$
$\quad = 20,000(1+0.05)^t = 20,000(1.05)^t$

$y_1 = 20,000(1.05)$
$y_2 = 20,000(1.05)^2$
$y_3 = 20,000(1.05)^3$

The ratio of successive terms is 1.05, so this is by definition a geometric sequence with common ratio $r = 1.05$.   Answer

The first term $y_1 = 20,000(1.05)$
$\quad\quad\quad\quad = 21,000$ Answer

Example 4 □ **Exponential growth sequence**

A town has a population of 8,000 people. If the population doubles every six years, what is the town's population after twelve years and after fifteen years?

Solution □

$y = a \times (2)^{t/n}$
$y = 8,000 \times (2)^{t/6}$

After 12 years, $t = 12$.
$y = 8,000(2)^{12/6} = 8000(2)^2 = 32,000$ Answer

After 15 years, $t = 15$.
$y = 8,000(2)^{15/6} = 8000(2)^{2.5} \approx 45,255$ Answer

7. Recursive Formula

A recursive formula can be used to find the terms in a sequence. In a recursive formula, the first or the first few terms are given, and the nth term is defined in terms of the preceding terms of the sequence.

A block of six terms repeats if the first and the second terms of the sequence are given, and after the second term each term is obtained by subtracting from the previous term the term before that.
In this sequence, a recursive formula can be used to find the terms.

After the second term

$$a_n = a_{n-1} - a_{n-2}$$

$a_1 = a$	1st term
$a_2 = b$	2nd term

$a_3 = a_2 - a_1 = b - a$

$a_4 = a_3 - a_2 = (b - a) - b = -a$

$a_5 = a_4 - a_3 = -a - (b - a) = -b$

$a_6 = a_5 - a_4 = -b - (-a) = a - b$

$a_7 = a_6 - a_5 = (a - b) - (-b) = a$

$a_8 = a_7 - a_6 = a - (a - b) = b$

The terms of the sequence follow the pattern

$$\underbrace{a,\ b,\ b-a,\ -a,\ -b,\ -b+a,}_{\text{a block of 6 terms repeats}}\ a,\ b,\ \cdots$$

8. Fibonacci Sequence

$a_1 = 1$, $a_2 = 1$, $a_3 = a_2 + a_1$, $a_4 = a_3 + a_2$, $\cdots$, $a_n = a_{n-1} + a_{n-2}$

The terms of the sequence follow the pattern

$1, 1, 2, 3, 5, 8, 13, 21, 34, 55, 89, 144, \cdots$

☑ To solve sequence questions on the SAT, we usually need three more terms to find out the pattern of the given sequence.

Example 5 □ **Arithmetic sequence**

The fourth term of an arithmetic sequence is 16, and the seventh term is –5. What is the first term of the sequence?

Solution □

$a_n = a_1 + (n-1)d$	nth term of an arithmetic sequence
$a_4 = a_1 + (4-1)d$	$n = 4$, for the 4th term
$a_7 = a_1 + (7-1)d$	$n = 7$, for the 7th term

$\begin{array}{r} 16 = a_1 + 3d \\ (-)\ \underline{-5 = a_1 + 6d} \\ 21 = -3d \end{array}$ $\qquad a_4 = 16$ and $a_7 = -5$

$\Rightarrow\ d = -7$

$16 = a_1 + 3(-7)$ $\qquad$ Substitute –7 for d.

$a_1 = 37$ $\qquad$ Answer

Example 6 □ **A repeating sequence**

$$2, 3, 1, -2, -3, \cdots$$

The first five terms of a sequence are shown above. After the second term, each term is obtained by subtracting from the previous term the term before that. For example, the fourth term can be obtained by subtracting the second term from the third term. What is the 99th term of the sequence?

Solution □

A recursive formula can be used to find the next few terms.

$a_n = a_{n-1} - a_{n-2}$

$a_6 = a_5 - a_4 = -3 - (-2) = -1$

$a_7 = a_6 - a_5 = -1 - (-3) = 2$

$a_8 = a_7 - a_6 = 2 - (-1) = 3$

The terms of the sequence follow the pattern $2, 3, 1, -2, -3, -1, 2, 3 \cdots$, in which a block of 6 terms keeps repeating in this order. When 99 is divided by 6, the quotient is 16 and the remainder is 3. Therefore the 99th term is the same as the third term.

The 99th term is 1. $\qquad$ Answer

4, 8, 12, 16, …

1. In the sequence above, each term after the first is 4 more than the preceding term. Which of the following cannot be a term in the sequence?

(A) 246

(B) 264

(C) 288

(D) 324

(E) 380

$x - 7, 2, x + 3, …$

2. In the arithmetic sequence above, what is the value of x ?

(A) 2

(B) 3

(C) 4

(D) 5

(E) 6

$\dfrac{9}{4}, \dfrac{3}{2}, 1, …$

3. In the sequence above, each term after the first is equal to $\dfrac{2}{3}$ of the preceding term. Which of the following is the 7th term of the sequence?

(A) $\dfrac{8}{27}$ (B) $\dfrac{16}{81}$ (C) $\dfrac{32}{243}$

(D) $\dfrac{64}{729}$ (E) $\dfrac{128}{2187}$

4. If the fifth term of an arithmetic sequence is 2 and the ninth term is -10, what is the first term of the sequence?

(A) 6

(B) 8

(C) 10

(D) 12

(E) 14

$x + \dfrac{1}{3}, \ x, \ x - \dfrac{1}{4}, …$

5. In the geometric sequence above, what is the value of x ?

(A) 1   (B) $\dfrac{5}{12}$ (C) $\dfrac{1}{2}$

(D) $\dfrac{3}{4}$ (E) $\dfrac{4}{3}$

6. Barry drives pointed fence posts into the ground with a sledgehammer to build a fence across his backyard. On his first stroke, he drives each post 4 inches into the ground, and after the first stroke he can only drive the post 75% of the distance he did on the previous swing. If he wants to drive the post more than 12 inches into the ground, what is the minimum number of strokes he has to take?

(A) 4

(B) 5

(C) 6

(D) 7

(E) 8

7. The first term of a sequence of integers is 90. For each term after the first, if the preceding term is even, we multiply by $\frac{1}{2}$ to obtain the next term. If the preceding term is odd, we subtract one from that term then multiply by $\frac{1}{2}$ to obtain the next term. What is the sixth term of the sequence?

(A) 6

(B) 5

(C) 4

(D) 3

(E) 2

$$2, 3, 1, -2, -3, \ldots$$

10. The first five terms of a sequence are shown above. After the second term, each term in the sequence is the difference of the two terms that precede it. For example, the third term can be obtained by subtracting the first term from the second term. What is the sum of the first 20 terms of the sequence?

(A) 2

(B) 3

(C) 5

(D) 10

(E) 12

8. A certain radioactive substance has a half-life of 12 days. This means that every 12 days, half of the original amount of the substance is left. If a dish holds 128 milligrams of the radioactive substance, how many milligrams are left after 48 days?

(A) 2

(B) 4

(C) 8

(D) 16

(E) 32

11. A free-falling object falls 0.1 miles in the first minute, 0.3 miles in the second minute, and 0.5 miles in the third minute. If the object continues to fall at this rate, how many miles will it fall in 16 minutes?

(A) 12.8

(B) 17.0

(C) 21.2

(D) 25.6

(E) 28.0

9. The population of a certain town doubles every 24 years. If the population of the town was 8,000 in the year 2000, in what year will the population be 128,000?

(A) 2072

(B) 2096

(C) 2120

(D) 2144

(E) 2168

$$1, 3, 4, \ldots$$

12. The first three terms of a sequence are shown above. After the second term, each term in the sequence is obtained by adding the two terms that precede it. For example, $4 = 1 + 3$. Of the first 500 numbers in this sequence, how many are even?

(A) 166

(B) 167

(C) 168

(D) 333

(E) 334

13. A ball is dropped from a height of 64 ft. Each time it strikes the ground, the ball bounces up to $\frac{3}{4}$ of the previous height. What is the total distance, in feet, the ball has traveled when it hits the ground for the fourth time?

    (A) 175

    (B) 195.25

    (C) 232

    (D) 286

    (E) 326.5

15. The population of a certain town doubles every 25 years. If the population of the town was 51,200 in 1980, in what year was the population 6,400?

    (A) 1805

    (B) 1830

    (C) 1855

    (D) 1880

    (E) 1905

14. In the figure above, square $ABCD$ is quartered, and the upper left portion is shaded and the lower right portion is quartered again. At each succeeding step, the area shaded is $\frac{1}{4}$ of the area shaded in the previous step. The total area of the shaded regions is what fraction of the area of square $ABCD$?

    (A) $\frac{5}{16}$ (B) $\frac{21}{64}$ (C) $\frac{85}{256}$

    (D) $\frac{11}{32}$ (E) $\frac{3}{8}$

16. For all positive integers a and x, let $\langle a|x \rangle$ be defined as the sum of the integers from a to x, inclusive, where $a < x$. Which of the following equals $\langle 11|x \rangle - \langle 9|(x-2) \rangle$?

    (A) 0

    (B) $x - 19$

    (C) $x - 20$

    (D) $2x - 19$

    (E) $2x - 20$

$$0.\overline{23456} = 0.2345623456 \dots,$$

1. In the repeating decimal above, the digits 23456 repeat. Which digit is in the 999th place to the right of the decimal point?

2. The first term of a sequence is 5. Each term after the first is found by multiplying 0.1 to the previous term, then adding 5 to the result. What is the value of the fourth term, rounded to the nearest hundredth?

3. In the sequence of tile patterns above, the first three stages are shown. If the pattern continues, how many tiles will be in the sixth figure of this pattern?

$$a, b, c, d, e, f, g, \dots$$

4. In the geometric sequence above, each term after the first term is r times the preceding term. For example, $b = r \cdot a$, $c = r \cdot b$, and so on. If $\dfrac{g}{a}$ is 729, what is the value of $\dfrac{f}{b}$?

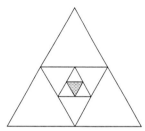

5. An equilateral triangle has sides that are 12 inches long. The midpoints of its sides are joined to form a smaller triangle. The midpoints of the smaller triangle are then joined to form another smaller triangle. After repeating this process 3 times, a small shaded triangle is formed. What is the perimeter of the shaded triangle?

6. A gumball machine contains gumballs of 8 different colors, which are dispensed in a regularly repeating cycle. The fourth gumball in the cycle is red and the sixth gumball in the cycle is yellow. If 100 gumballs are dispensed from the machine, how many are <u>not</u> either red or yellow?

7. The population of a small town doubles every 24 years. If the population of the town was 25,600 in the year 1988, what was the population in 1868?

Answer Key

<u>Multiple Choice Questions</u>

1. A   2. C   3. B   4. E   5. A

6. B   7. E   8. C   9. B   10. C

11. D   12. A   13. D   14. C   15. E

16. E

<u>Grid-In Questions</u>

1. 5   2. 5.56   3. 47   4. 81   5. 4.5

6. 59   7. 800

Answers and Explanations

<u>Multiple Choice Questions</u>

1. A

All the terms in the sequence are multiples of 4.

246 is the only number among the answer choices that is not a multiple of 4.

2. C

In an arithmetic sequence, the difference between successive terms is always the same.

$$\Rightarrow 2-(x-7) = (x+3)-2$$
$$\Rightarrow 9-x = x+1 \Rightarrow x = 4$$

3. B

The given sequence is a geometric sequence with $a_1 = \dfrac{9}{4}$, $r = \dfrac{2}{3}$.

$$a_7 = a_1 \cdot r^{n-1} = \frac{9}{4} \cdot \left(\frac{2}{3}\right)^{7-1} = \frac{9}{4} \cdot \left(\frac{2}{3}\right)^{6} = \frac{16}{81}$$

4. E

The nth term of an arithmetic sequence is $a_n = a_1 + (n-1)d$.

The fifth term of the arithmetic sequence is 2.
$$\Rightarrow a_5 = a_1 + (5-1)d = 2 \Rightarrow a_1 + 4d = 2$$

The ninth term of the arithmetic sequence is -10.
$$\Rightarrow a_9 = a_1 + (9-1)d = -10 \Rightarrow a_1 + 8d = -10$$

$$
\begin{array}{r}
a_1 + 8d = -10 \\
- \underline{\, a_1 + 4d = 2} \\
4d = -12
\end{array}
\qquad \Rightarrow d = -3
$$

Make the substitution into the first equation.
$$a_1 + 4(-3) = 2 \Rightarrow a_1 = 14$$

5. A

In a geometric sequence, the ratio of successive terms is always the same.

$$\Rightarrow \frac{x+\dfrac{1}{3}}{x} = \frac{x}{x-\dfrac{1}{4}}$$

$$\Rightarrow \left(x+\frac{1}{3}\right)\left(x-\frac{1}{4}\right) = x^2 \quad \text{(Cross multiplication)}$$

$$\Rightarrow x^2 - \frac{1}{4}x + \frac{1}{3}x - \frac{1}{12} = x^2$$

$$\Rightarrow \frac{1}{12}x - \frac{1}{12} = 0 \Rightarrow x = 1$$

6. B

The depth after each stroke is given by a geometric series in which $r = 0.75$ (75%) and $a_1 = 4$. Use the formula for the sum of a geometric series.

$$S_n = \frac{a_1(1-r^n)}{1-r} = \frac{4(1-(0.75)^n)}{1-0.75} > 12$$

$$\Rightarrow 1-(0.75)^n > 0.75 \Rightarrow (0.75)^n < 0.25$$

Use your calculator to find the smallest number such that $(0.75)^n < 0.25$. $\Rightarrow n = 5$

7. E

$$a_1 = 90 \qquad\qquad a_2 = \frac{1}{2} \cdot 90 = 45$$

$$a_3 = (45 - 1) \cdot \frac{1}{2} = 22 \qquad a_4 = \frac{1}{2} \cdot 22 = 11$$

$$a_5 = (11 - 1) \cdot \frac{1}{2} = 5 \qquad a_6 = (5 - 1) \cdot \frac{1}{2} = 2$$

8. C

Method I:

Make a chart.

initial amount	after 12 days	after 24 days	after 36 days	after 48 days
128	64	32	16	8

Method II:

Use the half-life equation.

$$y_t = a \times (\frac{1}{2})^{t/n} \Rightarrow$$

$$y_t = 128 \times (\frac{1}{2})^{48/12} = 128 \times (\frac{1}{2})^4 = 128 \times \frac{1}{16} = 8$$

9. B

Method I:

You can just keep multiplying by 2 until you get to a population of 128,000.

Year	Population
2000:	8,000
2024:	16,000
2048:	32,000
2072:	64,000
2096:	128,000

Method II:

Use the population doubling time equation.

$$y_t = a \times (2)^{t/n}$$
$$128,000 = 8,000(2)^{t/24}$$
Divide both sides by 8,000.
$$16 = (2)^{t/24} \Rightarrow 2^4 = (2)^{t/24}$$

$$\Rightarrow 4 = \frac{t}{24} \Rightarrow t = 96$$

10. C

$$a_6 = a_5 - a_4 = -3 - (-2) = -1$$
$$a_7 = a_6 - a_5 = -1 - (-3) = 2$$
$$a_8 = a_7 - a_6 = 2 - (-1) = 3$$

The terms of the sequence follow the pattern

$$\underbrace{2, 3, 1, -2, , -3, -1,}_{\text{every 6 terms are repeating}} 2, 3, \cdots$$

The sum of the first 6 terms of the sequence is
$2 + 3 + 1 + (-2) + (-3) + (-1) = 0$.
$\Rightarrow$ The sum of the first 18 terms of the sequence is also zero.

The sum of the first 20 terms of the sequence
$$= \underbrace{0}_{\substack{\text{the sum of the} \\ \text{first 18 terms}}} + \underbrace{2}_{\substack{\text{19th} \\ \text{term}}} + \underbrace{3}_{\substack{\text{20th} \\ \text{term}}} = 5$$

11. D

To find the total distance the object has fallen, add the first 16 terms of the sequence $0.1, 0.3, 0.5, \cdots$.

$$S_n = \frac{n}{2}\left[2a_1 + (n-1)d\right]$$

$$= \frac{16}{2}\left[2 \cdot (0.1) + (16 - 1) \cdot (0.2)\right]$$

$$= 8\left[0.2 + 15 \cdot (0.2)\right]$$

$$= 25.6$$

12. A

$$a_4 = a_3 + a_2 = 4 + 3 = 7$$
$$a_5 = a_4 + a_3 = 7 + 4 = 11$$
$$a_6 = a_5 + a_4 = 11 + 7 = 18$$
$$a_7 = a_6 + a_5 = 18 + 11 = 29$$

The terms of the sequence follow the pattern

$$\underset{\text{odd}}{1}, \underset{\text{odd}}{3}, \underset{\text{even}}{4}, \underset{\text{odd}}{7}, \underset{\text{odd}}{11}, \underset{\text{even}}{18}, \underset{\text{odd}}{29} \cdots$$

Of the first 498 numbers in this sequence,

$498 \times \dfrac{1}{3} = 166$ numbers are even. The 499th term

and 500th term are odd. Therefore there are 166 even terms.

13. D

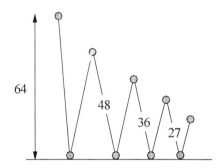

The ball has traveled 64 ft when it hits the ground for the first time.

The ball will bounce up to $64 \times \dfrac{3}{4} = 48$ ft after it

strikes the ground for the first time.

The ball will bounce up to $48 \times \dfrac{3}{4} = 36$ ft after it

strikes the ground for the second time.

The ball will bounce up to $36 \times \dfrac{3}{4} = 27$ ft after it

strikes the ground for the third time.

The total distance the ball has traveled when it hits the ground for the fourth time is
$64 + 2 \cdot 48 + 2 \cdot 36 + 2 \cdot 27 = 286$ ft.

14. C

Let x = the total area of square $ABCD$.
Then the area of the shaded region is

$$\frac{1}{4}x + \frac{1}{4} \cdot \frac{1}{4}x + \frac{1}{4} \cdot \frac{1}{4} \cdot \frac{1}{4}x + \frac{1}{4} \cdot \frac{1}{4} \cdot \frac{1}{4} \cdot \frac{1}{4}x$$

$$= \frac{1}{4}x + \frac{1}{16}x + \frac{1}{64}x + \frac{1}{256}x = \frac{64 + 16 + 4 + 1}{256}x$$

$$= \frac{85}{256}x$$

15. E

Method I:
You can just keep dividing by 2 until you get to a population of 6,400.

Year	Population
1980:	51,200
1955:	25,600
1930:	12,800
1905:	6,400

Method II:

Use the half-life equation. $y_t = a \times (\frac{1}{2})^{t/n}$

$$6,400 = 51,200(\frac{1}{2})^{t/25}$$

Divide both sides by 51,200.

$$\frac{1}{8} = (\frac{1}{2})^{t/24} \implies (\frac{1}{2})^3 = (\frac{1}{2})^{t/25}$$

$$\implies 3 = \frac{t}{25} \implies t = 75$$

$$1980 - 75 = 1905$$

16. E

$\langle a | x \rangle$ is defined as the sum of the integers from a to x, inclusive.

$$\langle 11 | x \rangle = 11 + 12 + \cdots + (x-3) + (x-2) + (x-1) + x$$
$$\langle 9 | (x-2) \rangle = 9 + 10 + 11 + \cdots + (x-3) + (x-2)$$

$$\langle 11 | x \rangle - \langle 9 | (x-2) \rangle$$
$$= [\cancel{11} + \cancel{12} + \cdots + \cancel{(x-3)} + \cancel{(x-2)} + (x-1) + x]$$
$$- [9 + 10 + \cancel{11} + \cdots + \cancel{(x-3)} + \cancel{(x-2)}]$$
$$= (x-1) + x - (9 + 10) = 2x - 20$$

Grid-In Questions

1. 5

5 digits are repeating.

$999 \div 5 = 199 \text{ R } 4 \Rightarrow$ The digit in the 999th place to the right of the decimal point is same as the 4th digit to the right of the decimal point, which is 5.

2. 5.56

The first term $= 5$.
The second term $= 0.1 \times 5 + 5 = 5.5$.
The third term $= 0.1 \times 5.5 + 5 = 5.55$.
The fourth term $= 0.1 \times 5.55 + 5 = 5.555$.

The value of the fourth term, rounded to the nearest hundredth, is 5.56.

3. 47

The first figure has 2 tiles.
The second figure has $2 + (5) = 7$ tiles.
The third figure has $(2+5)+7 = 14$ tiles.
The fourth figure has $(2+5+7)+9 = 23$ tiles.
The fifth figure has $(2+5+7+9)+11 = 34$ tiles.
The sixth figure has $(2+5+7+9+11)+13 = 47$ tiles.

4. 81

In the given geometric sequence, $g = a \cdot r^6$.

$\Rightarrow \dfrac{g}{a} = \dfrac{a \cdot r^6}{a} = r^6 \Rightarrow r^6 = 729$

$\Rightarrow r = (729)^{1/6} \Rightarrow r = 3$

$f = b \cdot r^4 = b \cdot 3^4 = 81b$

$\dfrac{f}{b} = \dfrac{81b}{b} = 81$

5. 4.5

The side length of the first triangle $= 12$.
The side length of the second triangle $= 6$.
The side length of the third triangle $= 3$.
The side length of the fourth triangle $= 1.5$.

The perimeter of the shaded triangle is $1.5 \times 3 = 4.5$.

6. 59

Since every fourth gumball is red there will be 25 ($100 \div 4 = 25$) red gumballs.

Since every sixth gumball is yellow there will be 16 ($100 \div 6 = 16 \text{ R } 4$) yellow gumballs.

The number of gumballs which are neither red nor yellow is $100 - (25+16) = 59$.

7. 800

Method I:

You can just keep dividing the population by 2 and subtracting 24 from the year.

Year	Population
1988:	25,600
1964:	12,800
1940:	6,400
1916:	3,200
1892:	1,600
1868:	800

Method II:

Use the half-life equation.
$y_t = a \times (\dfrac{1}{2})^{t/n}$,
where $a = 25,600$, $t = 1988 - 1868 = 120$ and $n = 24$.

$y_t = 25,600(\dfrac{1}{2})^{120/24} = 25,600(\dfrac{1}{2})^5$

$= 25,600(\dfrac{1}{32}) = 800$

20. Sets, Counting, and Probability

Key Terms / Illustrations   Examples

1. Sets

A **set** is a collection of distinct objects.

The objects of a set are called its **elements** or **members**.

2. Intersection and Union of Two Sets

Let A and B be any two sets. The **intersection** of A with B, written as $A \cap B$, is defined as the set consisting of those elements that are in **both A and B**. The **union** of A with B, written as $A \cup B$, is defined as the set consisting of those elements that belong to **either A or B, or both**.

3. Venn Diagram

A Venn Diagram represents sets as circles enclosed in a rectangle, which represents the universal set.

Illustration of a Venn Diagram

There are 120 students in the sophomore class.

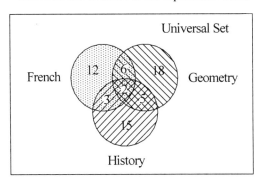

In the diagram above, out of all the sophomores

23 are taking French, $(12 + 6 + 2 + 3 = 23)$
31 are taking Geometry, $(18 + 6 + 2 + 5 = 31)$
25 are taking History, $(15 + 5 + 2 + 3 = 25)$
 8 are taking French and Geometry, $(6 + 2 = 8)$
 7 are taking Geometry and History, $(5 + 2 = 7)$
 5 are taking History and French, $(3 + 2 = 5)$
 2 are taking all three subjects, so that
61 are in French or Geometry or History.
       $(12 + 18 + 15 + 6 + 5 + 3 + 2 = 61)$
59 are not in any of these classes. $(120 - 61 = 59)$

Example 1 □   **Finding the intersection and union of two sets**

Let $A = \{2,3,5,7\}$ and $B = \{2,4,6,8,10\}$
Find : a) $A \cup B$ b) $A \cap B$

Solution □

a) $A \cup B = \{2,3,5,7\} \cup \{2,4,6,8,10\}$
$= \{2,3,4,5,6,7,8,10\}$

b) $A \cap B = \{2\}$

Example 2 □   **Using a Venn Diagram**

In a survey of a health club, 20 people play tennis and 28 people play golf. Of these, 8 people play both golf and tennis. How many people play only one of these sports?

Solution □

Draw a Venn Diagram :

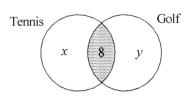

The overlapping region represents the people who play both tennis and golf.

Let $x =$ the # of people who play only tennis.
$x + 8 = 20 \implies x = 12$

Let $y =$ the # of people who play only golf.
$y + 8 = 28 \implies y = 20$

Therefore the number of people who play only one of these sports is
$x + y = 12 + 20 = 32$ Answer

4. A Table Categorized by Properties

The following chart shows 400 items in a music store categorized by type (tapes or CDs) and by price (sale or regular).

	Sale Price	Regular Price	Total
Tapes	60	180	240
CDs	40	120	160
Total	100	300	400

The **four categories** are
(1) sale-priced tapes,
(2) regular-priced tapes,
(3) sale-priced CDs, and
(4) regular-priced CDs.

5. Conditional Statements and Related Statements

"If-then" statements are called **conditional statements**.

Related "If-Then" Statements

Given statement :	If p, then q.
Contrapositive :	If not q, then not p.
Converse :	If q, then p.
Inverse :	If not p, then not q.

A statement and its contrapositive are logically equivalent.
A statement is *not* logically equivalent to its converse or to its inverse.

6. Negation

A denial of a statement is called a negation.

Statements		*Negations*
All p are q.	$\Leftrightarrow$	Some p are not q.
Some p are q.	$\Leftrightarrow$	No p is q.

Example 3 □ Using categorized tables

	Democrat	Republican	Total
Under 40	a	45	b
40 or over	50	c	160
Total	d	e	300

The table above shows a sample of 300 voters from a large city, categorized by age and voting preference. How many people under the age of 40 vote Democrat?

Solution □

$$b + 160 = 300 \implies b = 140$$
$$a + 45 = b \implies a + 45 = 140$$
$$\implies a = 95 \quad \text{Answer}$$

Example 4 □ Related "If-then" statements

Write the contrapositive and the converse of the following statements. Determine if the converse is true or false.

a) Vertical angles are congruent.

b) If x is an integer, then x is a real number.

Solution □

a) **Contrapositive** :
If two angles are not congruent, then the angles are not vertical angles.

Converse :
If two angles are congruent, then the angles are vertical angles.   (False.)

b) **Contrapositive** :
If x is not a real number, then x is not an integer.

Converse :
If x is a real number, then x is an integer. (False.)

7. The Counting Principle

If an event can occur in m different ways and another event can occur in n different ways, then there are $m \times n$ total ways that both events can occur.

The possible outcomes when two dice are tossed.

First die

	1	2	3	4	5	6
1	(1,1)	(2,1)	(3,1)	(4,1)	(5,1)	(6,1)
2	(1,2)	(2,2)	(3,2)	(4,2)	(5,2)	(6,2)
3	(1,3)	(2,3)	(3,3)	(4,3)	(5,3)	(6,3)
4	(1,4)	(2,4)	(3,4)	(4,4)	(5,4)	(6,4)
5	(1,5)	(2,5)	(3,5)	(4,5)	(5,5)	(6,5)
6	(1,6)	(2,6)	(3,6)	(4,6)	(5,6)	(6,6)

Second die

There are 36 different outcomes.

8. Tree Diagram

A tree diagram is a diagram for organizing information with a column of branches for each category.

The possible outcomes when two coins are tossed three times.

1st toss	2nd toss	3rd toss	Outcomes
heads	heads	heads	HHH
		tails	HHT
	tails	heads	HTH
		tails	HTT
tails	heads	heads	THH
		tails	THT
	tails	heads	TTH
		tails	TTT

There are 8 different outcomes.

Example 5 □   Counting

A die is rolled and a dime is tossed. How many different possible outcomes are there?

Solution □

Method 1 : Make a table.

There are 12 different outcomes.

Method 2 : Use the counting principle.

Roll a die   **Toss a penny**
6 different numbers   2 different sides

There are
$6 \times 2 = 12$ different outcomes.   Answer

Example 6 □   Counting

Rudi has a penny, a nickel, and a dime. If she selects one or more of her coins, how many different combinations are possible?

Solution □

Selecting one coin

{ penny }
{ nickel }   ← 3 different selections
{ dime }

Selecting two coins

{ penny and nickel }
{ penny and dime }   ← 3 different selections
{ nickel and dime }

Selecting three coins

{ penny, nickel, and dime }   ← 1 selection

There are $3 + 3 + 1 = 7$ combinations.   Answer

9. Factorial (!)

A factorial is the product of a whole number, n, and all the whole numbers less than n and greater than or equal to 1.

$$n! = n \cdot (n-1)(n-2) \; \cdots \; 3 \cdot 2 \cdot 1$$
$$6! = 6 \cdot 5 \cdot 4 \cdot 3 \cdot 2 \cdot 1 = 720$$

10. Permutation

When a group of objects or people is arranged in a certain order, the arrangement is called a permutation.

The number of permutations of n distinct objects taken r at a time is defined as follows:

$$_nP_r = \frac{n!}{(n-r)!}$$

11. Combination

When a group of objects or people is selected, and the order is not important, the selection is called a combination.

The number of combinations of n distinct objects taken r at a time is defined as follows:

$$_nC_r = \frac{n!}{r!\,(n-r)!}$$

☑ The basic difference between a permutation and a combination is that **order is considered** in a permutation and **order is *not* considered** in a combination.

Example 7 □ **Permutation**

In a row are 2 chairs. If there are 5 students, how many ways can the seats be filled?

Solution □

Method 1 : Use a diagram.

	1st chair	2nd chair
Number of choices	5	4

There are $5 \cdot 4$, or 20, possible seating arrangements.

Method 2 : Use $_nP_r$ (since order is considered).

$$_5P_2 = \frac{5!}{(5-2)!} = \frac{5 \cdot 4 \cdot 3 \cdot 2 \cdot 1}{3 \cdot 2 \cdot 1} = 20 \quad \text{Answer}$$

Example 8 □ **Combination**

How many different groups of 2 students can be formed from 5 students?

Solution □

Method 1 : Make a systematic list.

Represent the 5 students with letters $A, B, C, D,$ and E. The list of all possible combinations is

```
AB      BC      CD      DE
AC      BD      CE
AD      BE
AE
```

If one combination AB is taken, then BA is excluded because order is not considered in a combination.

There are 10 possible combinations.

Method 2 : Use $_nC_r$ (order is not considered).

$$_5C_2 = \frac{5!}{2!(5-2)!} = \frac{5!}{2!3!} = 10 \quad \text{Answer}$$

12. Probability

If an event can succeed in s ways and fail in f ways, then the probabilities of success $P(s)$ and of failure $P(f)$ are as follows:

$$P(s) = \frac{s}{s+f} \qquad P(f) = \frac{f}{s+f}$$

☑ If the outcome of one event *does not affect* the outcome of another event, then the events are called **independent events**.

☑ If the outcome of one event *does affect* the outcome of another event, then the events are called **dependent events**.

13. Area Probability

If a region S is in the interior of region T, and a point is chosen at random in region T, then the probability that the chosen point will be in region S is

$$\frac{\text{area of region } S}{\text{area of region } T}.$$

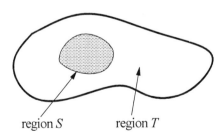

region S region T

Example 9 □ **Probability**

A bag contains 6 red marbles and 4 blue marbles. Two marbles are selected, one at a time.

a. Find the probability of selecting a red marble then a blue, if **the first marble is replaced** before the second one is drawn.

Solution □

Since the first marble is replaced, the selection of the second marble does not depend on the results of the first selection. The event is **independent**.

$$P(\text{red}) = \frac{6}{10} \quad \begin{array}{l} \leftarrow 6 \text{ red marbles} \\ \leftarrow 10 \text{ marbles total} \end{array}$$

$$P(\text{blue}) = \frac{4}{10} \quad \begin{array}{l} \leftarrow 4 \text{ blue marbles} \\ \leftarrow 10 \text{ marbles total} \end{array}$$

$$P(\text{red, then blue}) = \frac{6}{10} \cdot \frac{4}{10} = \frac{6}{25} \quad \text{Answer}$$

b. Find the probability of selecting a blue marble then another blue, if **the first marble is not replaced** before the second one is drawn.

Solution □

Since the first marble is **not** replaced, the selection of the second marble depends on the results of the first selection. The event is **dependent**.

$$P(\text{blue}) = \frac{4}{10} \quad \begin{array}{l} \leftarrow 4 \text{ blue marbles} \\ \leftarrow 10 \text{ marbles total} \end{array}$$

$$P(\text{blue}) = \frac{3}{9} \quad \begin{array}{l} \leftarrow 3 \text{ blue marbles are left} \\ \leftarrow 9 \text{ marbles are left total} \end{array}$$

$$P(\text{blue, then blue}) = \frac{4}{10} \cdot \frac{3}{9} = \frac{2}{15} \quad \text{Answer}$$

Soccer   Basketball

16   5   12

7   x   3

14

Volleyball

1. The diagram above shows the number of students who participated in a school sports team. If 24 students are on the basketball team, how many students are on the volleyball team?

  (A) 20   (B) 24   (C) 28

  (D) 30   (E) 32

2. In a group of students, 15 belong to committee A and 24 belong to committee B. If 3 students belong to both committees and 10 students are not in either committee, how many students are in the group?

  (A) 35   (B) 38   (C) 41

  (D) 46   (E) 51

3. At Aspen School, c students are in the chemistry class and h students are in the history class. If t is the total number of students that are in either the chemistry or history class, which of the following represents the number of students in both classes?

  (A) $t-(c+h)$

  (B) $2(c+h)-t$

  (C) $(c+h)-t$

  (D) $2t-(c+h)$

  (E) $(c+h)-2t$

	Members under 30	Members 30 or older	Total
Male	3		12
Female			20
Total	8	24	32

4. The table above, categorizing the members of a tennis club, is partially filled in. During a tennis tournament, each member of the club plays exactly one game with each of the other members. How many games are played between a female under 30 years old and a male 30 years or older during the tournament?

  (A) 15

  (B) 20

  (C) 25

  (D) 40

  (E) 45

Status	Business	Education	Total
Male		16	
Female	12		44
Total	32		80

5. The table above, categorizing the faculty members of a certain college, is partially filled in. What is the probability that a faculty member chosen at random will be female and in the Education Department?

  (A) $\dfrac{1}{5}$ (B) $\dfrac{1}{4}$ (C) $\dfrac{3}{10}$

  (D) $\dfrac{7}{20}$ (E) $\dfrac{2}{5}$

6. How many different two-letter codes can be made from the letters *A*, *B*, *C*, *D*, and *E*, if no letter can be used more than once?

    (A) 8

    (B) 10

    (C) 12

    (D) 20

    (E) 25

7. How many different four-letter patterns can be formed from the word MATH if the letters cannot be used more than once?

    (A) 12

    (B) 24

    (C) 36

    (D) 48

    (E) 72

8. There are 4 roads from Town *A* to Town *B*, and 3 roads from Town *B* to Town *C*. If a person travels from Town *A* to Town *C* and back, passing through Town *B* in both directions, how many different routes for the trip are possible?

    (A) 14

    (B) 24

    (C) 36

    (D) 72

    (E) 144

Questions 9-10 refer to the following information.

A bag contains 15 marbles, numbered 1 through 15.

9. What is the probability of selecting, at random, a number that is odd <u>or</u> a multiple of 5?

    (A) $\dfrac{7}{15}$ (B) $\dfrac{8}{15}$ (C) $\dfrac{3}{5}$

    (D) $\dfrac{2}{3}$ (E) $\dfrac{11}{15}$

10. A marble is to be selected at random then replaced in the bag. A second selection is then made. What is the probability that the first number is a prime number <u>and</u> the second number is a multiple of three?

    (A) $\dfrac{3}{25}$ (B) $\dfrac{2}{15}$ (C) $\dfrac{7}{45}$

    (D) $\dfrac{1}{5}$ (E) $\dfrac{11}{15}$

11. Five cards – Ace, King, Queen, Jack, and Ten – are placed in an empty box. If three cards are randomly drawn from the box, what is the probability that both King and Queen will be among the three cards?

    (A) $\dfrac{3}{20}$ (B) $\dfrac{1}{5}$ (C) $\dfrac{3}{10}$

    (D) $\dfrac{2}{5}$ (E) $\dfrac{3}{5}$

12. What is the probability that $x^2 + bx + 24$ will factor completely, if b is an integer and $1 \le b \le 25$?

(A) $\dfrac{4}{25}$ (B) $\dfrac{1}{5}$ (C) $\dfrac{8}{25}$

(D) $\dfrac{2}{5}$ (E) $\dfrac{12}{25}$

13. A bag contains five cards, numbered 1 through 5. If two cards are selected at random without replacement, what is the probability that their sum will be at least 6?

(A) $\dfrac{9}{20}$ (B) $\dfrac{1}{2}$ (C) $\dfrac{11}{20}$

(D) $\dfrac{3}{5}$ (E) $\dfrac{7}{10}$

14. In a certain martial arts tournament, each of the 5 competitors spars exactly once with each of the other four competitors. The tournament lasts for one hour, with only 2 competitors sparring at any given time. If the total sparring time for each competitor is the same, what is the total number of minutes that each competitor spars during the one-hour tournament?

(A) 24

(B) 20

(C) 18

(D) 12

(E) 10

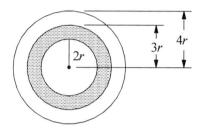

15. The figure above shows a dart board with three concentric circles of radii $2r$, $3r$, and $4r$. If a dart is randomly thrown at the dart board, what is the probability that it will hit the shaded region of the board?

(A) $\dfrac{3}{16}$ (B) $\dfrac{1}{4}$ (C) $\dfrac{5}{16}$

(D) $\dfrac{1}{3}$ (E) $\dfrac{3}{8}$

If 3 times a number, increased by 9, is 15 then the number is 2.

16. Which of the following statements is equivalent to the statement above?

I. If a number is 2, then 3 times a number, increased by 9, is 15.

II. If a number is not 2, then 3 times a number, increased by 9, is not 15.

III. If 3 times a number, increased by 9, is not 15, then the number is not 2.

(A) I only

(B) II only

(C) I and II only

(D) II and III only

(E) I, II, and III

If $a \le b$, then $a \le c$.

17. Which of the following statements is equivalent
     to the statement above?

I.   If $a > b$, then $a > c$.

II. If $a \le c$, then $a \le b$.

III. If $a > c$, then $a > b$.

(A) I only

(B) II only

(C) III only

(D) II and III only

(E) I, II, and III

18. If the second Friday in some month is the 8th, what
     date is the third Monday of the same month?

(A) 11th

(B) 17th

(C) 18th

(D) 19th

(E) 25th

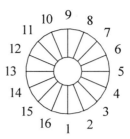

19. A 16-seat Ferris wheel, shown above, is rotating
     in a counter-clockwise direction. If seat 3 of the
     16-seat Ferris wheel is rotated and moved to the
     seat 14 position, what is the measure of the angle
     of rotation?

(A) $135°$

(B) $202.5°$

(C) $225°$

(D) $247.5°$

(E) $270°$

1. There are 150 elements in set A. Of these, 52 also belong to set B. Altogether, 320 elements belong to at least one of the two sets. What is the total number of elements belonging to set B?

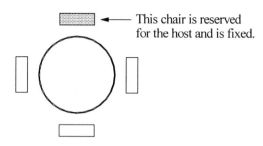

This chair is reserved for the host and is fixed.

4. In the figure above, 4 chairs are around a table. If one chair is reserved for the host, how many seating arrangements are possible for the 3 guests?

2. Four students enter a meeting room where there are 6 chairs in a row. How many different ways can the four students be seated?

$$S = \{ -5, -2, -1, 4 \}$$
$$T = \{ -2, 3, 7 \}$$

3. A product $p = s \cdot t$ is formed from the two sets above, where s is a number from set S and t is a number from set T. What is the probability that the product $s \cdot t$ will be a positive number?

5. In a survey of stock market investors, 450 people owned shares in IBM, 270 people owned shares in Intel, and 120 people owned shares in both companies. If an investor is selected at random, what is the probability that he owns shares in only one of the companies?

6. A bag contains 7 white colored balls and 5 orange colored balls. If Raymond randomly picks out one ball at a time, without replacement, how many balls must he pick out to be certain to have a white colored ball?

7. A bag of marbles contains 9 red marbles and 27 blue marbles. How many red marbles must be added to the bag to double the original probability of drawing a red marble?

8. In the equation $f(x) = 2x^3 - x^2 + 5x + 6$, if p is a factor of 6 and q is a factor of 2, how many different values of $\pm \dfrac{p}{q}$ are possible?

9. Saint Mary's Hospital has 500 volunteers. Of these, 54% are female, 62% are under age 16, and ninety volunteers are males 16 years or older. If a volunteer is selected at random, what is the probability that the volunteer is a female under 16 years of age?

10. A positive integer is called a palindrome if it reads the same forward as it does backward. For example, 747 is a palindrome. If the next two palindromes greater than 1991 are m and n, what is the value of $m + n$?

Answer Key

<u>Multiple Choice Questions</u>

1. C	2. D	3. C	4. E	5. E
6. D	7. B	8. E	9. C	10. B
11. C	12. A	13. D	14. A	15. C
16. B	17. C	18. C	19. D	

<u>Grid-In Questions</u>

1. 222	2. 360	3. 5/12	4. 6	5. 4/5
6. 6	7. 18	8. 12	9. 0.34	10. 4114

Answers and Explanations

<u>Multiple Choice Questions</u>

1. C

   The number of students on the basketball team is
   $12 + 5 + 3 + x$.
   $\Rightarrow \ 12 + 5 + 3 + x = 24 \ \Rightarrow \ x = 4$

   The number of students on the volleyball team is
   $14 + 7 + 3 + x$.

   $14 + 7 + 3 + x = 24 + x = 24 + 4 = 28$

2. D

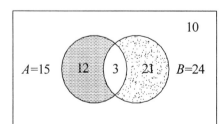

The number of students who belong to at least one of the two committees is $15 + 24 - 3 = 36$.

The total number of students in the group is $36 + 10 = 46$.

3. C

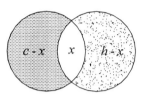

Let $x = $ the number of students in both classes, then $(c - x) = $ the number of students in the chemistry class only,
and $(h - x) = $ the number of students in the history class only.

Based on the diagram, we conclude that
$(c - x) + x + (h - x) = t$
$\Rightarrow \ c - x + h = t$
$\Rightarrow \ x = c + h - t$

4. E

   The number of females under 30 years old is
   $8 - 3 = 5$.
   The number of males 30 years or older is
   $12 - 3 = 9$.
   The total number of games played between females under 30 years old and males 30 years or older is $5 \times 9 = 45$.

5. E

   The number of female faculty members in the Education Department is $44 - 12$, or 32.

   $$\frac{\text{number of females in the Education Department}}{\text{total number of faculty members}}$$
   $$= \frac{32}{80} = \frac{2}{5}$$

6. D

Method I : Use a diagram.

AB	BA	CA	DA	EA
AC	BC	CB	DB	EB
AD	BD	CD	DC	EC
AE	BE	CE	DE	ED

There are $5 \cdot 4$, or 20, different two-letter codes.

Method II : Use $_nP_r$ (since order is considered).

$_5P_2 = 20$ (Use calculator.)

7. B

Method I : Use a diagram.

AHMT	HAMT	MAHT	TAHM
AHTM	HATM	MATH	TAMH
AMHT	HMAT	MHAT	THAM
AMTH	HMTA	MHTA	THMA
ATHM	HTAM	MTAH	TMAH
ATMH	HTMA	MTHA	TMHA

There are $4 \cdot 3 \cdot 2 \cdot 1$, or 24, different 4-letter patterns.

Method II : Use $_nP_r$. (since order is considered).

$_4P_4 = 24$ (Use calculator.)

8. E

$A \to B$ 4 different routes
$B \to C$ 3 different routes
$C \to B$ 3 different routes
$B \to A$ 4 different routes

Therefore there are $4 \times 3 \times 3 \times 4$, or 144, different possible routes for the trip.

9. C

There are 8 odd numbers. (1, 3, 5, 7, 9, 11, 13, and 15)
There are 3 multiples of 5. (5, 10, and 15)

There are 9 numbers which are either odd or a multiple of 5.

$P \text{ (odd or a multiple of 5)} = \dfrac{9}{15} = \dfrac{3}{5}$.

10. B

There are 6 prime numbers. (2, 3, 5, 7, 11, and 13)
There are 5 multiples of 3. (3, 6, 9, 12, and 15)

Since the first marble is replaced, the selection of the second marble does not depend on the result of the first selection. The event is independent.

$P \text{ (prime)} = \dfrac{6}{15}$

$P \text{ (multiple of 3)} = \dfrac{5}{15}$

$P \text{ (prime, then multiple of 3)} = \dfrac{6}{15} \times \dfrac{5}{15} = \dfrac{2}{15}$

11. C

Method I : Make a drawing.

$\boxed{A\ K\ Q}$ $A\ K\ J$ $A\ K\ 10$ $A\ Q\ J$ $A\ Q\ 10$ $A\ J\ 10$

$\boxed{K\ Q\ J}$ $\boxed{K\ Q\ 10}$ $K\ J\ 10$

$Q\ J\ 10$

There are 10 possible outcomes if three cards are randomly drawn from the box. Only three of them have both King and Queen showing.

$P \text{ (both King and Queen)} = \dfrac{3}{10}$

Method II : Use $_nC_r$ (since order is not considered).

The number of combinations of 5 cards taken 3 at a time is $_5C_3 = 10$.

The number of ways that both King and Queen can be chosen from 3 cards is $_3C_2 = 3$.

$P \text{ (both King and Queen)} = \dfrac{_3C_2}{_5C_3} = \dfrac{3}{10}$

12. A

$$24 = 1 \cdot 24 \quad \rightarrow \quad 1 + 24 = 25$$
$$= 2 \cdot 12 \quad \rightarrow \quad 2 + 12 = 14$$
$$= 3 \cdot 8 \quad \rightarrow \quad 3 + 8 = 11$$
$$= 4 \cdot 6 \quad \rightarrow \quad 4 + 6 = 10$$

There are 4 positive numbers (10, 11, 14, and 25) for b for which the quadratic equation will factor completely.

$$P = \frac{\text{success}}{\text{total outcome}} = \frac{4}{25}$$

13. D

Make a diagram of the possible choices.

1, 2	2, 3	3, 4	4, 5
1, 3	2, 4	3, 5	
1, 4	2, 5		
1, 5			

There are 10 possible outcomes if two cards are selected at random without replacement. Six of them have a sum of at least 6.

$$P \text{ (the sum is at least 6)} = \frac{6}{10} = \frac{3}{5}$$

14. A

Represent the 5 competitors with letters A, B, C, D, and E. The list of all the sparring combinations is

AB	BC	CD	DE
AC	BD	CE	
AD	BE		
AE			

Since there are 10 different match-ups, each match-up is given $60 \div 10$, or 6, minutes. Each competitor spars 4 times. Therefore each competitor spars for a total of 6×4, or 24, minutes.

15. C

Total area of the dart board $= \pi(4r)^2 = 16\pi r^2$
The area of the shaded region of the board
$$= \pi(3r)^2 - \pi(2r)^2 = 9\pi r^2 - 4\pi r^2 = 5\pi r^2$$

P (dart will hit the shaded region)
$$= \frac{\text{area of the shaded region}}{\text{total area}} = \frac{5\pi r^2}{16\pi r^2} = \frac{5}{16}$$

16. B

A statement and its contrapositive are logically equivalent.

Given statement : If 3 times a number, increased by 9, is 15 then the number is 2.

Contrapositive : If the number is not 2, then 3 times a number, increased by 9, is not 15.

17. C

Given statement : If a is less than or equal to b, then a is less than or equal to c.

Contrapositive : If a is greater than c, then a is greater than b.

18. C

Make a calendar of the month.

S	M	T	W	T	F	S
					1	2
3	4	5	6	7	8	9
10	11	12	13	14	15	16
17	18	19				

The third Monday is the 18th.

19. D

The angle between each seat is $360° \div 16$, or $22.5°$.

The measure of the angle of rotation
$$= 22.5 \times 11 = 247.5$$

Grid-In Questions

1. 222

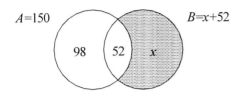

$A=150$ 98   52   x $B=x+52$

Let x = the number of elements which belong to B but not A,

then $150 + x = 320$. $\Rightarrow$ $x = 170$

The total number of elements which belong to B
$= 170 + 52 = 222$.

2. 360

When a group of objects or people is arranged in a certain order, the arrangement is called a permutation.

The number of permutations of 6 chairs, taken 4 at a time, is

$_6P_4 = \dfrac{6!}{(6-4)!} = 360$

3. $\dfrac{5}{12}$

Make a table of the possible products $p = s \cdot t$.

$(-5) \cdot (-2) = 10$ $(-5) \cdot 3 = -15$ $(-5) \cdot 7 = -35$
$(-2) \cdot (-2) = 4$ $(-2) \cdot 3 = -6$ $(-2) \cdot 7 = -14$
$(-1) \cdot (-2) = 2$ $(-1) \cdot 3 = -3$ $(-1) \cdot 7 = -7$
$4 \cdot (-2) = -8$ $4 \cdot 3 = 12$ $4 \cdot 7 = 28$

P (product is a positive number)
$= \dfrac{\text{success}}{\text{total outcome}} = \dfrac{5}{12}$

4. 6

Make a drawing of the possible outcomes.

A ☐ ◯ ☐ C B ☐ ◯ ☐ A C ☐ ◯ ☐ A
B C B

A ☐ ◯ ☐ B B ☐ ◯ ☐ C C ☐ ◯ ☐ B
C A A

5. $\dfrac{4}{5}$

The number of investors who own shares in only IBM is $450 - 120$, or 330.

The number of investors who own shares in only Intel is $270 - 120$, or 150.

The number of investors who own shares in only one of the companies is $330 + 150$, or 480.

Total number of investors $= 330 + 150 + 120 = 600$.

P (an investor owns shares in only one of the companies)
$= \dfrac{480}{600} = \dfrac{4}{5}$

6. 6

Raymond cannot be certain that he will pick a white colored ball until all of the orange colored balls have been removed from the bag. After he has picked out all 5 orange balls, the 6th ball he picks must be white. So he must pick out 6 balls in order to be certain he'll have a white colored ball.

7. 18

The total number of marbles is $9 + 27$, or 36.

P (drawing a red marble) $= \dfrac{9}{36} = \dfrac{1}{4}$

Let $x =$ the number of marbles that must be added to the bag to double the original probability.

$\dfrac{\text{number of red marbles}}{\text{total number of marbles}}$

$= \dfrac{9+x}{36+x} = 2(\dfrac{1}{4})\;\leftarrow$ double the original probability

$\Rightarrow\; \dfrac{9+x}{36+x} = \dfrac{1}{2}$
$\Rightarrow\; 2(9+x) = 36+x$
$\Rightarrow\; 18 + 2x = 36 + x$
$\Rightarrow\; x = 18$

8. 12

Given the equation $f(x) = 2x^3 - x^2 + 5x + 6$, p is a factor of 6 and q is a factor of 2.

The possible values of p are ± 1, ± 2, ± 3, and ± 6.
The possible values of q are ± 1 and ± 2.

So all the possible values of $\pm \dfrac{p}{q}$ are as follows:

$\pm \dfrac{1}{2}$, ± 1, $\pm \dfrac{3}{2}$, ± 2, ± 3, and ± 6.

There are 12 different values.

9. 0.34

The total number of volunteers $= 500$.

The total number of females $= 500 \times 0.54 = 270$.

The total number of volunteers under age 16
$= 500 \times 0.62 = 310$.

The total number of males 16 years or older $= 90$.

Use a categorized table.

	under age 16	16 years or older	total
male	(b)	90	(a)
female	(c)		270
total	310		500

(a) The number of males $= 500 - 270 = 230$.

(b) The number of males under age 16
$= 230 - 90 = 140$.

(c) The number of females under age 16
$= 310 - 140 = 170$.

P (volunteer is female under 16 years of age)
$= \dfrac{\text{\# of females under age 16}}{\text{total}}$
$= \dfrac{170}{500} = 0.34$

10. 4114

The next two palindromes greater than 1991 are 2002 and 2112.
Therefore $m + n = 2002 + 2112 = 4114$.

Part B
Practice Tests

PSAT Practice Test

PSAT Answer Sheet

SECTION 1

1 (A) (B) (C) (D) (E)	6 (A) (B) (C) (D) (E)	11 (A) (B) (C) (D) (E)	16 (A) (B) (C) (D) (E)
2 (A) (B) (C) (D) (E)	7 (A) (B) (C) (D) (E)	12 (A) (B) (C) (D) (E)	17 (A) (B) (C) (D) (E)
3 (A) (B) (C) (D) (E)	8 (A) (B) (C) (D) (E)	13 (A) (B) (C) (D) (E)	18 (A) (B) (C) (D) (E)
4 (A) (B) (C) (D) (E)	9 (A) (B) (C) (D) (E)	14 (A) (B) (C) (D) (E)	19 (A) (B) (C) (D) (E)
5 (A) (B) (C) (D) (E)	10 (A) (B) (C) (D) (E)	15 (A) (B) (C) (D) (E)	20 (A) (B) (C) (D) (E)

SECTION 2

21 (A) (B) (C) (D) (E)	26 (A) (B) (C) (D) (E)
22 (A) (B) (C) (D) (E)	27 (A) (B) (C) (D) (E)
23 (A) (B) (C) (D) (E)	28 (A) (B) (C) (D) (E)
24 (A) (B) (C) (D) (E)	29 (A) (B) (C) (D) (E)
25 (A) (B) (C) (D) (E)	30 (A) (B) (C) (D) (E)

Grid-in answer boxes numbered 31 through 40, each with columns for fractions and decimals and digit bubbles 0–9.

Directions : In this section, solve each problem, decide which is the best answer choice, and then darken the corresponding oval on the answer sheet.

Notes:
1. The use of a calculator is permitted. All numbers used are real numbers.
2. All figures are drawn to scale EXCEPT when it is stated that the figure is not drawn to scale.
3. All figures lie in a plane unless otherwise indicated.

Reference Information

  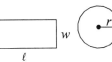

$A = \frac{1}{2}bh$ $c^2 = a^2 + b^2$ Special Right Triangles $A = \ell w$ $A = \pi r^2$ $C = 2\pi r$ $V = \ell wh$ $V = \pi r^2 h$

The number of degrees of arc in a circle is 360.

The measure in degrees of a straight angle is 180.

The sum of the angle measures of a triangle, in degrees, is 180.

1. If $\dfrac{x}{6} + \dfrac{x}{2x} = 3$, what is the value of x?

(A) 10

(B) 12

(C) 15

(D) 18

(E) 20

2. If n is an integer such that $-2 < n + 2 \le 6$, which of the following is NOT a possible value of n?

(A) 4

(B) 2

(C) 0

(D) −2

(E) − 4

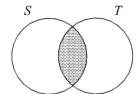

3. In the figure above, circle S represents multiples of 4 and circle T represents multiples of 6. Which of the following is represented by the shaded region?

(A) Multiples of 2

(B) Multiples of 3

(C) Multiples of 6

(D) Multiples of 12

(E) Multiples of 24

4. If one-half of a number n is five less than n, what is the value of n?

(A) 5

(B) 9

(C) 10

(D) 12

(E) 15

5. If a equals 120 percent of a number, then 40 percent of the number is

(A) $0.48a$

(B) $\dfrac{1}{3}a$

(C) $3a$

(D) $4.8a$

(E) $0.75a$

6. In a school election, 680 students voted for one of two candidates for president of the student body. If the winner received 120 more votes than the loser, how many votes did the winner receive?

(A) 340

(B) 370

(C) 400

(D) 430

(E) 460

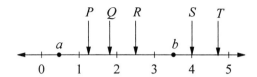

7. On the number line above, which of the following lettered points is most nearly equal to the result of multiplying the coordinate of a by the coordinate of b?

(A) P

(B) Q

(C) R

(D) S

(E) T

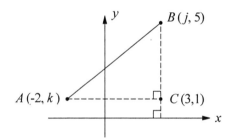

8. In the coordinate system above, what is the value of $j + k$?

(A) 1

(B) 2

(C) 4

(D) 6

(E) It cannot be determined from the information given.

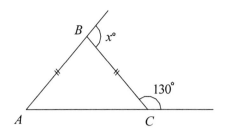

9. In the figure above, if $AB = BC$, what is the value of x?

(A) 100

(B) 90

(C) 80

(D) 70

(E) 60

10. In a certain classroom, the ratio of boys to girls was 11 to 20. One week later 5 boys and 4 girls were added to the class. What is the ratio of boys to girls after the 5 boys and 4 girls are added to the class?

(A) $\dfrac{2}{3}$

(B) $\dfrac{27}{44}$

(C) $\dfrac{19}{32}$

(D) $\dfrac{7}{12}$

(E) It cannot be determined from the information given.

Note: Figure not drawn to scale.

11. In the figure above, if $\ell \parallel m$ and $t \perp \ell$, what is the value of $x + y$?

(A) 50

(B) 60

(C) 62

(D) 66

(E) 72

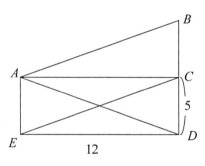

Note: Figure not drawn to scale.

12. In the figure above, $ABCE$ is a parallelogram and $ACDE$ is a rectangle. What is the perimeter of $\triangle ABD$?

(A) 20

(B) 24

(C) 28

(D) 32

(E) 36

13. If $3^x = 5$, then $3^{x+2} =$

(A) 7

(B) 10

(C) 15

(D) 25

(E) 45

16. Let $f(x) = \sqrt{ax - 1}$, where $ax - 1 \geq 0$. If $f(2) = 3$, what is the value of $f(10)$?

(A) 5

(B) $\sqrt{30}$

(C) $\sqrt{35}$

(D) 7

(E) 15

14. The average (arithmetic mean) of a set of 5 numbers is x. If the number 12 is added to the set, what is the average of the new set of numbers, in terms of x?

(A) $x + 2$

(B) $\dfrac{x}{5} + 2$

(C) $\dfrac{5x}{6} + 2$

(D) $5x + 2$

(E) $\dfrac{x}{6} + 2$

17. If $a - 1 \neq 0$, $2 - \dfrac{a-3}{a-1} =$

(A) $\dfrac{2}{a-1}$

(B) $\dfrac{5}{a-1}$

(C) $\dfrac{a}{a-1}$

(D) $\dfrac{a+1}{a-1}$

(E) $\dfrac{a-5}{a-1}$

15. How many different four-digit patterns can be formed using the digits 0, 1, 2, and 3, if the digits can be used more than once but the first digit cannot be 0?

(A) 24

(B) 108

(C) 144

(D) 192

(E) 256

18. If $x^2 + y^2 = 18$ and $xy = 7$, what is the value of $(x - y)^2$?

(A) 4

(B) 11

(C) 20

(D) 25

(E) 32

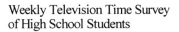

Weekly Television Time Survey
of High School Students

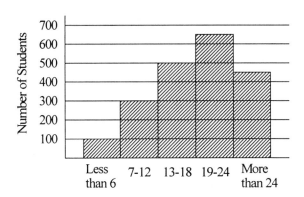

Number of Hours of Television
Watched Each Week

19. According to the graph above, which of the
following is the closest approximation to the
percentage of high school students who watch
at least 19 hours of television each week?

(A) 33%

(B) 38 %

(C) 45 %

(D) 50 %

(E) 55 %

20. If p and r are two different prime numbers, which
of the following cannot be true?

(A) $(p+r)$ is prime.

(B) $(p+r)$ is not prime.

(C) $(p+r) \times p$ is even.

(D) $p \times r$ has three different integer factors
greater than 1.

(E) p^2 has three different integer factors
greater than 1.

Directions : In this section, solve each problem, decide which is the best answer choice, and then darken the corresponding oval on the answer sheet.

Notes:
1. The use of a calculator is permitted. All numbers used are real numbers.
2. All figures are drawn to scale EXCEPT when it is stated that the figure is not drawn to scale.
3. All figures lie in a plane unless otherwise indicated.

Reference Information

$A = \frac{1}{2} bh$ $\qquad$ $c^2 = a^2 + b^2$ $\qquad$ Special Right Triangles $\qquad$ $A = \ell w$ $\qquad$ $A = \pi r^2$ $\qquad$ $V = \ell wh$ $\qquad$ $V = \pi r^2 h$
$\qquad\qquad\qquad\qquad\qquad\qquad\qquad\qquad\qquad\qquad\qquad\qquad\qquad\qquad$ $C = 2\pi r$

The number of degrees of arc in a circle is 360.

The measure in degrees of a straight angle is 180.

The sum of the angle measures of a triangle, in degrees, is 180.

21. If $a = -2$, $\dfrac{36}{24 \div (a)^2 \cdot 3} =$

   (A) 2
   (B) −4
   (C) 8
   (D) −12
   (E) 18

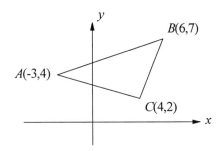

22. What is the smallest integer greater than 6 that leaves a remainder of 2 when divided by any of the integers 4, 5, and 6?

   (A) 32
   (B) 42
   (C) 52
   (D) 62
   (E) 122

23. In the rectangular coordinate system above, the vertices of $\triangle ABC$ are $A(-3,4)$, $B(6,7)$, and $C(4,2)$. If $\triangle A'B'C'$ (not shown) is the image of $\triangle ABC$ shifted 3 units right and 4 units down, what is the coordinate of each vertex of $\triangle A'B'C'$?

   (A) $A'(-6,0)$, $B'(3,3)$, $C'(1,-2)$
   (B) $A'(0,0)$, $B'(9,3)$, $C'(7,-2)$
   (C) $A'(0,8)$, $B'(9,11)$, $C'(7,6)$
   (D) $A'(-7,7)$, $B'(2,10)$, $C'(0,5)$
   (E) $A'(4,3)$, $B'(13,6)$, $C'(11,2)$

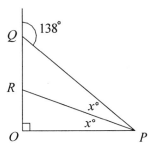

24. In the figure above, $\overline{OP} \perp \overline{OQ}$ and $\overline{PR}$ is the bisector of $\angle OPQ$. What is the measure of $\angle PRO$?

(A) 56

(B) 60

(C) 66

(D) 70

(E) 74

25. A person travels home from work at a constant speed. 20 minutes after leaving work he is 50 miles from home, and 44 minutes after leaving work he is 20 miles from home. Which of the following equations gives y, the distance in miles from home, in terms of x, the number of minutes passed since leaving work?

(A) $y = \dfrac{5}{4}x + 25$

(B) $y = \dfrac{4}{5}x + 34$

(C) $y = -\dfrac{5}{4}x + 75$

(D) $y = -\dfrac{4}{5}x + 66$

(E) $y = -\dfrac{5}{4}x + 50$

26. The cost of a telephone call between two cities is c cents for the first 3 minutes and d cents for each additional minute. If the total cost of a call that lasts x minutes is y dollars, which of the following represents y in terms of c, d, and x?

(A) $y = c + (x - 3)d$

(B) $y = 3c + dx$

(C) $y = cx + dx$

(D) $y = (x - 3)c + dx$

(E) $y = 3c + (x - 3)d$

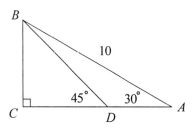

Note: Figure not drawn to scale.

27. In the figure above, $AB = 10$, $m\angle BAC = 30$, $m\angle BDC = 45$, and $\overline{AC} \perp \overline{BC}$. What is the length of AD?

(A) 5

(B) $5\sqrt{2}$

(C) $5(\sqrt{2} - 1)$

(D) $5(\sqrt{3} - 1)$

(E) $5(\sqrt{3} + 1)$

28. If $x = -2$ is a solution of the equation $ax^2 - 2x - 20 = 0$, what is another solution of the equation?

(A) -4

(B) -1

(C) 2

(D) $\dfrac{5}{2}$

(E) 4

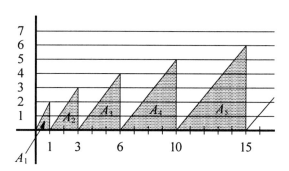

29. A cubic meter of a certain material weighs 128 kilograms. How much will 15,625 cubic centimeters of the same material weigh, in kilograms?
(1 meter = 100 centimeters)

(A) 2

(B) 20

(C) 200

(D) 2,000

(E) 20,000

30. In the sequence of triangles shown above, if A_n represents the area of the nth triangle, which of the following would equal 105?

(A) A_{11}

(B) A_{12}

(C) A_{13}

(D) A_{14}

(E) A_{15}

Directions for Student Produced Response Questions:

For each of the remaining 10 questions below, solve the problem and enter your answer by darkening the ovals in the special grid, as shown in the example below.

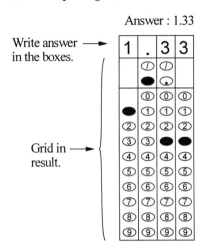

Write answer in the boxes.

Grid in result.

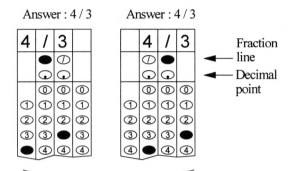

Fraction line

Decimal point

Either position is correct.

Note: You may start your answers in any column, space permitting. Columns not needed should be left blank.

- It is recommended that you write your answer in the boxes at the top of the columns to help you fill in the ovals accurately.

- Mark no more than one oval in any column.

- You will receive credit only for darkening the ovals correctly.

- Some problems may have more than one correct answer. In such cases, grid in only one answer.

- No question has a negative answer.

- Mixed numbers such as $1\frac{3}{4}$ must be gridded as 1.75 or 7/4. (If $1\ 3\ /\ 4$ is gridded, it will be interpreted as $\frac{13}{4}$, not $1\frac{3}{4}$.)

- Decimal Accuracy : Decimal answers must be entered as accurately as possible. For example, if you obtain an answer such as 1.666..., you should record the results as 1.66 or 1.67. **Less accurate values such as 1.6 or 1.7 are not acceptable.**

Acceptable ways to grid $\frac{5}{3} = 1.666...$

31. If $\dfrac{x}{10} + \dfrac{x}{100} + \dfrac{x}{1000} = 1.11$, what is the value of x?

32. If $a = 5$ and $b = 3$, $(ac - 6) + a(b - c) =$

33. If $1 < n < 2$, what is $(5 - \frac{1}{2}n)$ rounded to the nearest whole number?

35. If $\sqrt[3]{x-1} + 2 = 5$, what is the value of x?

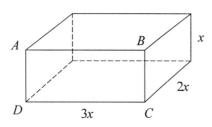

34. In the figure above, if the area of rectangle $ABCD$ is 12, what is the volume of the rectangular solid?

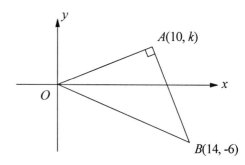

36. In the figure above, if O, A, and B are the vertices of an isosceles right triangle with equal sides $\overline{OA}$ and $\overline{AB}$, what is the value of k?

37. If $|3 - 2x| - 5 = 8$ and $x > 0$, what is the value of x?

39. In a certain music store, 25% of the compact discs are classical, and out of these 60% are on sale. If not more than 450 classical CDs are on sale, what is the maximum number of CDs in the store?

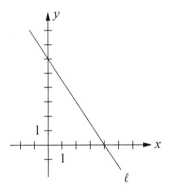

38. A line (not shown) that passes through the points with coordinates $(m, 4.5)$ and $(3, n)$, is parallel to line ℓ in the figure above. What is the value of $\dfrac{m}{n}$?

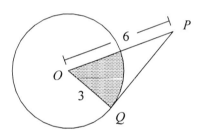

40. In the figure above, the radius of circle O is 3, $OP = 6$, and $\overline{PQ}$ is tangent to the circle. If the area of the shaded region is $k\pi$, what is the value of k?

Answer Key

<u>Multiple Choice Questions</u>

(Section 1)

1. C	2. E	3. D	4. C	5. B
6. C	7. B	8. C	9. A	10. E
11. A	12. E	13. E	14. C	15. D
16. D	17. D	18. A	19. E	20. E

(Section 2)

21. A	22. D	23. B	24. C	25. C
26. A	27. D	28. D	29. A	30. D

<u>Grid-In Questions</u>

31. 10	32. 9	33. 4	34. 48	35. 28
36. 4	37. 8	38. 2/3	39. 3000	40. 3/2

Answers and Explanations

<u>Multiple Choice Questions</u> (Section 1)

1. C

$$\frac{x}{6}+\frac{\cancel{x}}{2\cancel{x}}=3 \Rightarrow \frac{x}{6}+\frac{1}{2}=3 \Rightarrow \frac{x}{6}=3-\frac{1}{2}=\frac{5}{2}$$
$$\Rightarrow x=15$$

2. E

$-2<n+2\le6$ Original inequality
$-2-2<n+2-2\le6-2$ Subtract 2 from each side.
$-4<n\le4$ Simplify.

Therefore n cannot be -4 or less.

3. D

Multiples of 4: 4, 8, $\boxed{12}$, 16, 20, $\boxed{24}$, 28,...
Multiples of 6: 6, $\boxed{12}$, 18, $\boxed{24}$, 30,...

Therefore the shaded region represents the multiples of 12.

4. C

one half of a number $\frac{1}{2}n$ = five less than n $n-5$
$$\frac{1}{2}n-n=n-n-5$$
$$-\frac{1}{2}n=-5 \Rightarrow n=10$$

5. B

Let n = the number.

120% of a number
$$a=1.2n$$
$$\frac{a}{1.2}=\frac{1.2n}{1.2} \Rightarrow n=\frac{a}{1.2}=\frac{5}{6}a$$
40% of the number
$$\frac{40}{100}n=\frac{40}{100}\cdot\frac{5}{6}a=\frac{1}{3}a$$

6. C

Let x = the number of votes the loser received.
Then $x+120$ = the number of votes the winner received.

$$(x+120)+x=680$$
$$2x+120=680$$
$$2x=560$$
$$x=280$$
$$x+120=280+120$$
$$=400$$

7. B

Since the number line is drawn to scale, we can approximate the values of a and b.
a could equal 0.5 and b could equal 3.5.

Then $ab = (0.5)(3.5) = 1.75$.
Choice B is correct.

8. C

Notice that $\overline{AC}$ is parallel to the x-axis, and $\overline{BC}$ is parallel to the y-axis. The x-coordinates of the points B and C should be the same, and the y-coordinates of the points A and C should be the same. Therefore $j = 3$ and $k = 1$.

$j + k = 3 + 1 = 4$

9. A

$m\angle BCA = 180 - 130 = 50$
$AB = BC \implies m\angle BCA = m\angle BAC = 50$

$x = m\angle BCA + m\angle BAC = 50 + 50 = 100$
(Exterior Angle Theorem)

10. E

Suppose there were initially 11 boys and 20 girls, before 5 boys and 4 girls were added to the class. Then the new ratio would be
$\dfrac{11+5}{20+4} = \dfrac{16}{24} = \dfrac{2}{3}$.

Suppose, instead, there were initially 22 boys and 40 girls, before 5 boys and 4 girls were added to the class. Then the new ratio would be
$\dfrac{22+5}{40+4} = \dfrac{27}{44}$.

Therefore the new ratio of boys to girls, after the 5 boys and 4 girls are added, cannot be determined from the information given.

11. A

$\ell \parallel m \implies$ Consecutive interior angles are supplementary.

$\implies (5x + 8) + (3x - 4) = 180$
$\qquad 8x + 4 = 180 \implies 8x = 176 \implies x = 22$

$\ell \parallel m$ and $t \perp \ell \implies t \perp m$
$\implies y + (3x - 4) = 90$
$\implies y + (3 \cdot 22 - 4) = 90$ (Substitution)
$\implies y + 62 = 90 \implies y = 28$

$x + y = 22 + 28 = 50$

12. E

$AE = CD = 5$ (Opposite sides of a $\square$ are $\cong$.)
$BC = AE$ (Opposite sides of a $\square$ are $\cong$.)
$BC = 5$ (Substitution)

$CE^2 = CD^2 + DE^2 = 5^2 + 12^2$
$\qquad = 25 + 144 = 169 \implies CE = 13$

$AD = CE = 13$ (Diagonals of a $\square$ are $\cong$.)
$AB = CE = 13$ (Opposite sides of a $\square$ are $\cong$.)

Perimeter of $\triangle ABD = AB + BD + AD$
$\qquad\qquad\qquad\quad = 13 + (5 + 5) + 13 = 36$

13. E

$3^x = 5$
$3^{x+2} = 3^x \cdot 3^2 = 5 \cdot 3^2 = 45$

14. C

If the average of a set of 5 numbers is x, then the sum of the 5 numbers is $5x$.
If the number 12 is added, then the sum of the new set, in which there are 6 numbers, is $5x + 12$.

New average $= \dfrac{5x + 12}{6} = \dfrac{5x}{6} + \dfrac{12}{6} = \dfrac{5x}{6} + 2$

15. D

$$\boxed{3} \quad \times \quad \boxed{4} \quad \times \quad \boxed{4} \quad \times \quad \boxed{4}$$

3 choices for   4 choices for   4 choices for   4 choices for
the first digit   the second digit   the third digit   the fourth digit

$$= 3 \times 4 \times 4 \times 4 = 192$$

16. D

$$f(x) = \sqrt{ax-1} \text{ , where } ax-1 \ge 0$$
$$f(2) = \sqrt{a \cdot 2 - 1} = 3$$
$$(\sqrt{a \cdot 2 - 1})^2 = 3^2 \qquad \text{Square both sides.}$$
$$2a - 1 = 9 \ \Rightarrow \ 2a = 10 \ \Rightarrow \ a = 5$$

$$f(x) = \sqrt{5x-1}$$
$$f(10) = \sqrt{5 \cdot 10 - 1} = \sqrt{49} = 7$$

17. D

$$2 - \frac{a-3}{a-1}$$
$$= 2 \cdot \frac{a-1}{a-1} - \frac{a-3}{a-1}$$
$$= \frac{2a-2}{a-1} - \frac{a-3}{a-1}$$
$$= \frac{(2a-2)-(a-3)}{a-1} = \frac{a+1}{a-1}$$

18. A

$$x^2 + y^2 = 18 \text{ and } xy = 7$$
$$\Rightarrow \ (x-y)^2 = x^2 - 2xy + y^2$$
$$= (x^2 + y^2) - 2xy = 18 - 2(7) = 4$$

19. E

Total number of high school students surveyed
$= 100 + 300 + 500 + 650 + 450 = 2,000$.

Total number of students who watch at least 19 hours of television each week $= 650 + 450 = 1,100$.

$$\frac{\text{number of students who watch at least 19 hours}}{\text{total number of students}}$$
$$= \frac{1100}{2000} = \frac{55}{100}$$

20. E

Pick two different pairs of prime numbers for p and r, say $p = 2$ and $r = 3$, or $p = 5$ and $r = 7$.

Try each answer choice.

(A) If $p = 2$ and $r = 3$, then $p + r = 2 + 3 = 5$.

     5 is prime.   True.

(B) If $p = 5$ and $r = 7$, then $p + r = 5 + 7 = 12$.

     12 is not prime.   True.

(C) If $p = 5$ and $r = 7$, then
     $(p+r) \times p = (5+7) \times 7 = 84$.

     84 is even.   True.

(D) If $p = 2$ and $r = 3$, then $p \times r = 2 \times 3 = 6$.
     Factors of 6: 1, 2, 3, 6
     There are three different integer factors
     greater than 1.   True.

(E) If $p = 2$, then $p^2 = 2^2 = 4$.
     Factors of 4: 1, 2, 4
     There are two different integer factors
     greater than 1.   Not true.

     If $p = 3$, then $p^2 = 3^2 = 9$.
     Factors of 9: 1, 3, 9
     There are two different integer factors
     greater than 1.   Not true.

21. A

$$\frac{36}{24 \div (a)^2 \cdot 3} = \frac{36}{24 \div (-2)^2 \cdot 3}$$

$$= \frac{36}{24 \div 4 \cdot 3} = \frac{36}{6 \cdot 3} = \frac{36}{18} = 2$$

22. D

The least common multiple of 4, 5, and 6 will be the smallest integer greater than 6 that leaves no remainder when divided by any of the integers 4, 5, and 6.

Find the prime factorizations of 4, 5, and 6.

$$4 = 2^2$$
$$5 = 5$$
$$6 = 2 \cdot 3$$
$$LCM = 2^2 \cdot 5 \cdot 3 = 60$$

Add 2 to the LCM to arrive at the answer.
$$60 + 2 = 62$$

23. B

If $\triangle ABC$ is shifted 3 units right and 4 units down, then the image of (x, y) becomes $(x + 3, y - 4)$.

$$A(-3, 4) \;\rightarrow\; A'(-3 + 3, 4 - 4) = A'(0, 0)$$
$$B(6, 7) \;\rightarrow\; B'(6 + 3, 7 - 4) = B'(9, 3)$$
$$C(4, 2) \;\rightarrow\; C'(4 + 3, 2 - 4) = C'(7, -2)$$

24. C

$$m\angle PQO = 180 - 138 = 42$$
$$m\angle PQO + m\angle QPO = 90$$
$$42 + m\angle QPO = 90$$
$$m\angle QPO = 90 - 42 = 48$$

$$x = \frac{1}{2} \cdot m\angle QPO = \frac{1}{2} \cdot 48 = 24$$

$$m\angle PRO + x = 90 \;\Rightarrow\; m\angle PRO + 24 = 90$$
$$\Rightarrow\; m\angle PRO = 90 - 24 = 66$$

25. C

Start with a linear equation $y = mx + b$, where y is the distance in miles from home, and x is the time in minutes.

$$50 = 20m + b \quad (x = 20, \; y = 50)$$
$$- \;\underline{\;20 = 44m + b} \quad (x = 44, \; y = 20)$$
$$30 = -24m$$

$$\Rightarrow\; m = -\frac{5}{4}$$

Substitute the value of m into the first equation.

$$50 = 20(-\frac{5}{4}) + b \;\Rightarrow\; 50 = -25 + b$$
$$\Rightarrow\; b = 75$$

Therefore the equation is $y = -\dfrac{5}{4}x + 75$.

26. A

y = the total cost of the call.

x = the total number of minutes.

total cost	cost for first 3 minutes of call	the number of additional minutes	cost of each additional minute
$\overbrace{}$	$\overbrace{}$	$\overbrace{}$	$\overbrace{}$
$y \;=$	c $+$	$(x - 3)$ $\cdot$	d

$$y = c + (x - 3)d$$

27. D

$\triangle ABC$ is a 30°-60°-90° triangle.

In a 30°-60°-90° triangle, the hypotenuse is twice as long as the shorter leg.
Therefore $BC = 5$.

In a 30°-60°-90° triangle, the longer leg is $\sqrt{3}$ times as long as the shorter leg.
Therefore $AC = 5\sqrt{3}$.

$\triangle ABD$ is a 45°-45°-90° triangle.
Therefore $BC = CD = 5$.

$$AD = AC - CD = 5\sqrt{3} - 5 = 5(\sqrt{3} - 1)$$

28. D

$$ax^2 - 2x - 20 = 0$$
$$a(-2)^2 - 2(-2) - 20 = 0 \qquad (x = -2 \text{ is a solution.})$$
$$4a + 4 - 20 = 0$$
$$4a - 16 = 0$$
$$a = 4$$

$$4x^2 - 2x - 20 = 0$$
$$2(2x^2 - x - 10) = 0$$
$$2(2x - 5)(x + 2) = 0 \implies x = \frac{5}{2} \text{ or } -2$$

Therefore $\frac{5}{2}$ is another solution of the equation.

29. A

$$1 \text{ m} = 100 \text{ cm}$$
$$(1 \text{ m})^3 = (100 \text{ cm})^3$$
Therefore $1 \text{ m}^3 = 1,000,000 \text{ cm}^3$.

Set up a proportion.

$$\frac{1 \text{ m}^3}{128 \text{ kg}} = \frac{15,625 \text{ cm}^3}{x \text{ kg}}$$
$$\implies \frac{1,000,000 \text{ cm}^3}{128 \text{ kg}} = \frac{15,625 \text{ cm}^3}{x \text{ kg}}$$

Use cross products.
$$1,000,000x = 128 \times 15625$$
$$\implies x = 2$$

30. D

Area of a triangle $= \frac{1}{2} \cdot \text{base} \times \text{height}$.

$$A_1 = \frac{1}{2}(1)(2)$$
$$A_2 = \frac{1}{2}(2)(3)$$
$$A_3 = \frac{1}{2}(3)(4)$$
Area of the nth triangle is
$$A_n = \frac{1}{2}(n)(n+1)$$

$$A_n = 105$$
$$\frac{1}{2}(n)(n+1) = 105 \implies n(n+1) = 210$$
$$\implies n^2 + n - 210 = 0$$

You can either factor or use the quadratic formula to solve this equation.

$$\implies (n-14)(n+15) = 10$$
$$\implies n = 14 \text{ or } -15$$

Since n is a positive number, $n = 14$ is the solution.

<u>Grid-In Questions</u> (Section 2)

31. 10

$$\frac{x}{10} + \frac{x}{100} + \frac{x}{1000} = 1.11$$

$$\Rightarrow x(\frac{1}{10} + \frac{1}{100} + \frac{1}{1000}) = 1.11$$

$$\Rightarrow x(0.1 + 0.01 + 0.001) = 1.11$$

$$\Rightarrow 0.111x = 1.11$$

$$\Rightarrow x = 10$$

32. 9

$$(ac - 6) + a(b - c)$$

$$= ac - 6 + ab - ac$$

$$= -6 + ab$$

$$= -6 + 5 \cdot 3 = 9$$

33. 4

$$1 < n < 2$$

$$\frac{1}{2}(1) < \frac{1}{2}n < \frac{1}{2}(2)$$

$$\frac{1}{2} < \frac{1}{2}n < 1$$

$$(-1)\frac{1}{2} > (-1)\frac{1}{2}n > (-1)1 \quad \text{(Change the direction of}$$

the inequality symbol when you multiply each side
by a negative number.)

$$-1 < -\frac{1}{2}n < -\frac{1}{2}$$

$$5 - 1 < 5 - \frac{1}{2}n < 5 - \frac{1}{2} \quad \text{(5 is added on each side.)}$$

$$4 < 5 - \frac{1}{2}n < 4.5$$

Therefore, $(5 - \frac{1}{2}n)$ rounded to the nearest whole
number will be 4.

34. 48

Area of rectangle $ABCD = CD \cdot BC = 3x \cdot x = 3x^2$

$3x^2 = 12$ (Area of rectangle $ABCD$ is 12.)

$$\Rightarrow x^2 = 4 \Rightarrow x = 2$$

Volume of the rectangular solid
$$= \ell \cdot w \cdot h = 3x \cdot 2x \cdot x = 6x^3 = 6(2)^3 = 48$$

35. 28

$$\sqrt[3]{x-1} + 2 = 5$$

$$\sqrt[3]{x-1} = 3$$

$$(\sqrt[3]{x-1})^3 = 3^3 \qquad \text{(Cube both sides.)}$$

$$x - 1 = 27$$

$$x = 28$$

36. 4

Method I: Use the distance formula.

$$OA = \sqrt{(10-0)^2 + (k-0)^2} = \sqrt{100 + k^2}$$

$$AB = \sqrt{(10-14)^2 + (k-(-6))^2} = \sqrt{16 + (k+6)^2}$$

$$= \sqrt{k^2 + 12k + 52}$$

Since $OA = AB$, $\sqrt{100 + k^2} = \sqrt{k^2 + 12k + 52}$.

$$\Rightarrow 100 + k^2 = k^2 + 12k + 52$$

$$\Rightarrow 100 = 12k + 52 \Rightarrow 12k = 48$$

$$\Rightarrow k = 4$$

Method II: Use the slope of the line.

Since the two lines are perpendicular, their slopes
are negative reciprocals.

Slope of line $OA = \frac{k-0}{10-0} = \frac{k}{10}$

Slope of line $AB = \frac{k+6}{10-14} = \frac{k+6}{-4}$

$$(\frac{k}{10})(\frac{k+6}{-4}) = -1 \Rightarrow k(k+6) = 40$$

$$k^2 + 6k - 40 = 0 \Rightarrow (k+10)(k-4) = 0$$

$$\Rightarrow k = -10 \text{ or } 4$$

Since point A is in the first quadrant, k is positive.
Therefore $k = 4$.

37. 8

$$|3-2x|-5=8$$
$$|3-2x|=13$$
$$3-2x=13 \text{ or } 3-2x=-13$$

$$3-2x=13$$
$$-2x=10$$
$$x=-5$$

or

$$3-2x=-13$$
$$-2x=-16$$
$$x=8$$

Since $x>0$, the answer is $x=8$.

38. $\dfrac{2}{3}$

Line ℓ passes through points $(0,6)$ and $(4,0)$.
Therefore, the slope of line $\ell = \dfrac{6-0}{0-4}=\dfrac{6}{-4}=-\dfrac{3}{2}$.

The slope of the line which passes through the
points $(y,4.5)$ and $(3,n)$ is $\dfrac{n-4.5}{3-m}$.
Since the two lines are parallel, their slopes are
the same.

$$\frac{n-4.5}{3-m}=-\frac{3}{2}$$
$$\Rightarrow\ 2(n-4.5)=-3(3-m)$$
$$\Rightarrow\ 2n-9=-9+3m$$
$$\Rightarrow\ 2n=3m$$
$$\Rightarrow\ \frac{m}{n}=\frac{2}{3}$$

39. 3000

Let $x=$ the total number of CDs in the store, then
$0.25x=$ the number of classical CDs, and
$0.6\times 0.25x$, or $0.15x$, classical CDs are on sale.

Since no more than 450 classical CDs are on sale,
$0.15x \le 450$.
$\Rightarrow\ x \le 3000$

40. $\dfrac{3}{2}$

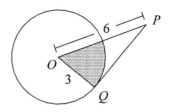

Since $\overline{PQ}$ is tangent to the circle, $\overline{PQ} \perp \overline{OQ}$.

Method I : Use the cosine ratio.
In a right triangle OPQ, $\cos\angle O = \dfrac{OQ}{OP}=\dfrac{3}{6}=\dfrac{1}{2}$
$\Rightarrow\ m\angle O = 60°$

Method II : Use the $30°$-$60°$-$90°$ triangle ratio.

In a $30°$-$60°$-$90°$ triangle, the hypotenuse is
twice as long as the shorter leg.

$$\frac{OQ}{OP}=\frac{3}{6}=\frac{1}{2}\ \Rightarrow\ m\angle POQ = 60$$

Area of the shaded region
$$= \text{area of circle } O \times \frac{60}{360}$$
$$= \pi(3)^2 \times \frac{60}{360}$$
$$= \frac{3}{2}\pi = k\pi$$
$$\Rightarrow\ k = \frac{3}{2}$$

SAT Practice Test 1

SAT Answer Sheet

SECTION 1

1 Ⓐ Ⓑ Ⓒ Ⓓ Ⓔ	6 Ⓐ Ⓑ Ⓒ Ⓓ Ⓔ	11 Ⓐ Ⓑ Ⓒ Ⓓ Ⓔ	16 Ⓐ Ⓑ Ⓒ Ⓓ Ⓔ
2 Ⓐ Ⓑ Ⓒ Ⓓ Ⓔ	7 Ⓐ Ⓑ Ⓒ Ⓓ Ⓔ	12 Ⓐ Ⓑ Ⓒ Ⓓ Ⓔ	17 Ⓐ Ⓑ Ⓒ Ⓓ Ⓔ
3 Ⓐ Ⓑ Ⓒ Ⓓ Ⓔ	8 Ⓐ Ⓑ Ⓒ Ⓓ Ⓔ	13 Ⓐ Ⓑ Ⓒ Ⓓ Ⓔ	18 Ⓐ Ⓑ Ⓒ Ⓓ Ⓔ
4 Ⓐ Ⓑ Ⓒ Ⓓ Ⓔ	9 Ⓐ Ⓑ Ⓒ Ⓓ Ⓔ	14 Ⓐ Ⓑ Ⓒ Ⓓ Ⓔ	19 Ⓐ Ⓑ Ⓒ Ⓓ Ⓔ
5 Ⓐ Ⓑ Ⓒ Ⓓ Ⓔ	10 Ⓐ Ⓑ Ⓒ Ⓓ Ⓔ	15 Ⓐ Ⓑ Ⓒ Ⓓ Ⓔ	20 Ⓐ Ⓑ Ⓒ Ⓓ Ⓔ

SECTION 2

1 Ⓐ Ⓑ Ⓒ Ⓓ Ⓔ	6 Ⓐ Ⓑ Ⓒ Ⓓ Ⓔ	11 Ⓐ Ⓑ Ⓒ Ⓓ Ⓔ	16 Ⓐ Ⓑ Ⓒ Ⓓ Ⓔ
2 Ⓐ Ⓑ Ⓒ Ⓓ Ⓔ	7 Ⓐ Ⓑ Ⓒ Ⓓ Ⓔ	12 Ⓐ Ⓑ Ⓒ Ⓓ Ⓔ	17 Ⓐ Ⓑ Ⓒ Ⓓ Ⓔ
3 Ⓐ Ⓑ Ⓒ Ⓓ Ⓔ	8 Ⓐ Ⓑ Ⓒ Ⓓ Ⓔ	13 Ⓐ Ⓑ Ⓒ Ⓓ Ⓔ	18 Ⓐ Ⓑ Ⓒ Ⓓ Ⓔ
4 Ⓐ Ⓑ Ⓒ Ⓓ Ⓔ	9 Ⓐ Ⓑ Ⓒ Ⓓ Ⓔ	14 Ⓐ Ⓑ Ⓒ Ⓓ Ⓔ	19 Ⓐ Ⓑ Ⓒ Ⓓ Ⓔ
5 Ⓐ Ⓑ Ⓒ Ⓓ Ⓔ	10 Ⓐ Ⓑ Ⓒ Ⓓ Ⓔ	15 Ⓐ Ⓑ Ⓒ Ⓓ Ⓔ	20 Ⓐ Ⓑ Ⓒ Ⓓ Ⓔ

SECTION 3

Grid-in answer boxes numbered 1 through 15, each with columns for digits 0–9, fraction bars (/) and decimal points (.).

Directions : In this section, solve each problem, decide which is the best answer choice, and then darken the corresponding oval on the answer sheet.

Notes:
1. The use of a calculator is permitted. All numbers used are real numbers.
2. All figures are drawn to scale EXCEPT when it is stated that the figure is not drawn to scale.
3. All figures lie in a plane unless otherwise indicated.

Reference Information

  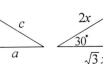   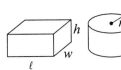

$A = \frac{1}{2} bh$ $c^2 = a^2 + b^2$ Special Right Triangles $A = \ell w$ $A = \pi r^2$ $C = 2\pi r$ $V = \ell wh$ $V = \pi r^2 h$

The number of degrees of arc in a circle is 360.

The measure in degrees of a straight angle is 180.

The sum of the angle measures of a triangle, in degrees, is 180.

1. If $\frac{15-x}{15} = 0$, what is the value of $\frac{15+x}{15}$?

(A) 0

(B) 1

(C) 2

(D) 3

(E) 4

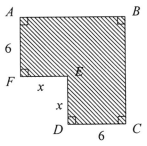

2. If a, b, and c are positive integers greater than 1, where $ab = 12$ and $bc = 21$, which of the following must be true?

(A) $b < c < a$

(B) $b < a < c$

(C) $a < b < c$

(D) $a < c < b$

(E) It cannot be determined from the information given.

3. In the figure above, if the perimeter of the shaded region is $a + bx$, what is the value of $a + b$?

(A) 14

(B) 16

(C) 18

(D) 24

(E) 28

The opposite of nine times a number, increased by four, is not more than 54.

4. Which of the following inequalities represents the statement above?

(A) $9n + 4 < 54$

(B) $-9n + 4 < 54$

(C) $-9n + 4 \leq 54$

(D) $9n + 4 \leq -54$

(E) $-9n + 4 \geq -54$

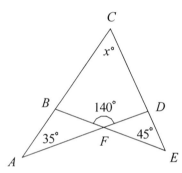

5. In the figure above, $x =$

(A) 45

(B) 50

(C) 55

(D) 60

(E) 65

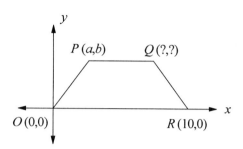

6. In the figure above, $OPQR$ is an isosceles trapezoid with equal sides $\overline{OP}$ and $\overline{QR}$. What are the coordinates of Q in terms of a and b?

(A) (b, a)

(B) $(10, a-b)$

(C) $(10 - a, a)$

(D) $(10 - b, a)$

(E) $(10 - a, b)$

7. A thermos holds 2 quarts of liquid. If $\frac{1}{2}$ tablespoon of ground coffee makes 4 cups of coffee, how many thermoses can be filled with the coffee made from 3 tablespoons of ground coffee? (1 quart = 4 cups)

(A) 12

(B) 8

(C) 6

(D) 4

(E) 3

8. $(2^x)(2^{2x})(2^{3x}) =$

    (A) 2^{6x^3}

    (B) 2^{6x}

    (C) 8^{6x}

    (D) 8^{6x^2}

    (E) 32^x

9. The sum of the numbers in a set of 40 positive numbers is S. If the eight largest numbers in the set accounted for 52 percent of the sum, what is the average of the other 32 numbers in the set?

    (A) $\dfrac{3}{500}S$

    (B) $\dfrac{3}{250}S$

    (C) $\dfrac{3}{200}S$

    (D) $\dfrac{13}{800}S$

    (E) $\dfrac{3}{20}S$

10. If $x^2 - y^2 = 4$ and $x + y = \dfrac{1}{4}$, what is the value of $x - y$?

    (A) 1

    (B) 16

    (C) $\dfrac{1}{16}$

    (D) 8

    (E) $\dfrac{1}{8}$

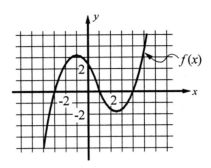

11. The figure above shows the graph of $f(x)$. For what values of x are the values of $f(x)$ positive?

    (A) $x > -3$

    (B) $x > 4$

    (C) $-3 < x < 1$ or $x > 4$

    (D) $0 < x < 3$

    (E) $x < -3$ or $x > 4$

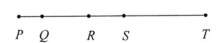

Note: Figure not drawn to scale.

12. In the figure above, $PT = 16$ and $PR = QS = 7$. If S is midpoint of $\overline{QT}$, $RS =$

    (A) 6

    (B) 5

    (C) 4

    (D) 3

    (E) 2

Questions 13-14 refer to the following circle graph, which shows the gross domestic product of country X in 1998.

The total value of goods and services produced by country X in 1998.

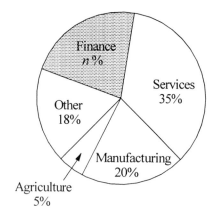

13. What is the degree measure of the central angle of the sector representing Agriculture?

(A) 5

(B) 10

(C) 18

(D) 24

(E) 30

14. If manufacturing represents 15 billion dollars, then what is the dollar amount, in billions, the finance sector represents?

(A) 11

(B) 12.5

(C) 16.5

(D) 18

(E) 22

15. If $ab \neq 0$, then $(2a^2b)^3(3ab^2) =$

(A) $6a^6b^5$

(B) $6a^7b^5$

(C) $24a^6b^5$

(D) $24a^7b^5$

(E) $24a^7b^6$

16. Stella and Min are writing addresses on invitation cards for a birthday party. If Stella can finish one card every 20 seconds and Min can do one every 30 seconds, what is the total number of cards that Stella and Min can finish in $3x$ minutes?

(A) $5x$

(B) $10x$

(C) $15x$

(D) $50x$

(E) $150x$

17. If n is divided by 4 the remainder is 3, and n is a positive integer greater than 7. What is the remainder when n is divided by 5?

(A) 1

(B) 2

(C) 3

(D) 4

(E) It cannot be determined from the information given.

18. If $x = 1 - \dfrac{n}{m}$, then $\dfrac{1}{x} =$

(A) $\dfrac{m}{1+n}$

(B) $\dfrac{m}{1-n}$

(C) $\dfrac{m-1}{n}$

(D) $\dfrac{m}{m-n}$

(E) $\dfrac{m-1}{m-n}$

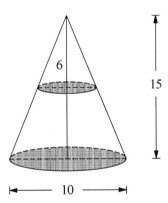

Note: Figure not drawn to scale.

19. In a circular cone, shown above, a plane parallel to the base of the cone divides the cone into two pieces. If the height of the smaller cone is 6, what is the volume of the smaller cone?

(A) 6π

(B) 8π

(C) 10π

(D) 12π

(E) 14π

20. The population P of a certain town doubles every 14 years. If the population today is 1,500, which of the following equations represents the population of the town t years from now?

(A) $P = 1500(2)^t$

(B) $P = 1500(2)^{t/14}$

(C) $P = 1500(2)^{14/t}$

(D) $P = 1500(\dfrac{14}{t})^2$

(E) $P = 1500(\dfrac{t}{14})^2$

Directions : In this section, solve each problem, decide which is the best answer choice, and then darken the corresponding oval on the answer sheet.

Notes:
1. The use of a calculator is permitted. All numbers used are real numbers.
2. All figures are drawn to scale EXCEPT when it is stated that the figure is not drawn to scale.
3. All figures lie in a plane unless otherwise indicated.

Reference Information

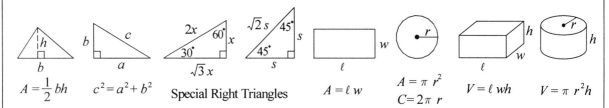

$A = \frac{1}{2}bh$ $c^2 = a^2 + b^2$ Special Right Triangles $A = \ell w$ $A = \pi r^2$ $V = \ell wh$ $V = \pi r^2 h$

$C = 2\pi r$

The number of degrees of arc in a circle is 360.

The measure in degrees of a straight angle is 180.

The sum of the angle measures of a triangle, in degrees, is 180.

1. If $1 - \left| -9 \right| = n$, what is the value of n?

   (A) 8

   (B) –8

   (C) 9

   (D) 10

   (E) –10

2. Let the function f be defined as $f(x) = x^2 - ax$. If $f(-2) = f(5)$, what is the value of a?

   (A) –1

   (B) 1

   (C) 3

   (D) 5

   (E) 7

3. The positive difference between $\frac{1}{4}$ and x is the same as the positive difference between $\frac{1}{3}$ and $\frac{1}{8}$. Which of the following could be the value of x?

   (A) $\frac{1}{9}$

   (B) $\frac{1}{12}$

   (C) $\frac{1}{16}$

   (D) $\frac{1}{18}$

   (E) $\frac{1}{24}$

4. $(\sqrt{6} - \sqrt{2})^2 =$

(A) 4

(B) $2\sqrt{2}(\sqrt{3} - 1)$

(C) $4(1 - \sqrt{3})$

(D) $4(2 - \sqrt{3})$

(E) 8

5. What is the least number x for which
$(3x - 1)(x + 1) = 0$?

(A) -3

(B) -1

(C) $-\dfrac{1}{3}$

(D) $\dfrac{1}{3}$

(E) 1

$$31, a, b, c, 59, \ldots$$

6. In the arithmetic sequence above, what is the value
of $a + b + c$?

(A) 127

(B) 129

(C) 131

(D) 133

(E) 135

Questions 7–8 refer to the following coordinate
system.

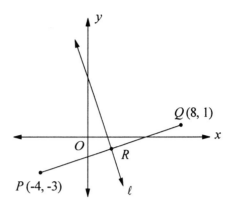

7. In the figure above, line ℓ is the perpendicular
bisector of $\overline{PQ}$. If R is the point of intersection,
what is the coordinate of R ?

(A) $(-1, 2)$

(B) $(2, -1)$

(C) $(4, -1)$

(D) $(4, 1)$

(E) $(2, -2)$

8. If line ℓ is a perpendicular bisector of $\overline{PQ}$, what
is the slope of line ℓ ?

(A) $\dfrac{1}{3}$

(B) $-\dfrac{1}{3}$

(C) 3

(D) -3

(E) $-\dfrac{3}{2}$

The number r is 8 less than 3 times the number s. When the difference of r and 3 is multiplied by the sum of s and 2, the result is 6.

9. Which of the following pairs of equations represents the statements above?

(A) $r = 8 - 3s$
$(r - 3) + (s + 2) = 6$

(B) $r = 3s - 8$
$r - 3(s + 2) = 6$

(C) $r = 3s - 8$
$(r - 3)(s + 2) = 6$

(D) $r = 3s - 8$
$(r + 3) - (s + 2) = 6$

(E) $r - 8 = 3s$
$(r - 3)(s + 2) = 6$

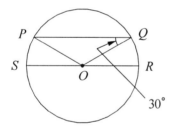

10. In circle O above, what is the value of $\dfrac{PQ}{SR}$?

(A) 0.5

(B) $\dfrac{\sqrt{3}}{3}$

(C) 0.75

(D) $\dfrac{\sqrt{3}}{2}$

(E) $\dfrac{2\sqrt{6}}{5}$

11. Jim leaves Azusa driving to Malibu at a constant speed of 60 mph. At the same time, Kay leaves Malibu driving to Azusa at a constant speed of 40 mph. If the distance between the two cities is 150 miles, which of the following graphs could represent the distance between Jim and Kay during the trip?

(A)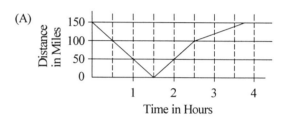

(B)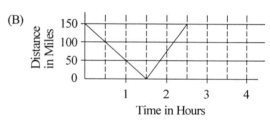

(C)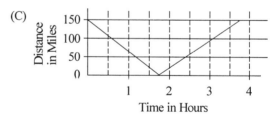

(D)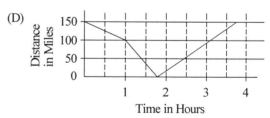

(E)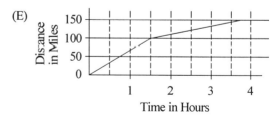

Questions 12-13 refer to the following tables.

A factory is producing aluminum and plastic storage boxes, each with small, medium, and large sizes. The table below shows the number of storage boxes produced each day, the amount of materials needed, and the cost of the materials.

Number of Storage Boxes Produced Each Day

Storage Boxes	Small	Medium	Large
Aluminum	1200	1000	800
Plastic	2400	1800	1500

Materials Needed (in pounds)

Storage Boxes	Aluminum	Plastic
Small	4	2.5
Medium	6	5
Large	10	6.5

Cost of Materials (in dollars)

	Aluminum	Plastic
Cost per Pound	$ 0.08	$ 0.03

12. What is the total amount, in pounds, of aluminum needed each day to produce storage boxes?

(A) 13,200

(B) 16,000

(C) 18,800

(D) 27,000

(E) 35,400

13. What is the total cost, in dollars, of the aluminum storage boxes produced in one day?

(A) 1,504

(B) 1,637

(C) 1,770

(D) 2,300

(E) 2,832

14. If $a > 0$, then $\sqrt{98a^3} - \sqrt{50a^3} =$

(A) $4a\sqrt{3a}$

(B) $4\sqrt{2a}$

(C) $5a^2\sqrt{2a}$

(D) $2a\sqrt{2a}$

(E) $7a\sqrt{2a}$

15. If p is 20 percent less than r, r is 20 percent less than s, and s is 20 percent less than t, then which of the following is equal to p?

(A) $0.4t$

(B) $0.4096t$

(C) $0.512t$

(D) $0.6t$

(E) $0.64t$

16. Which of the following is equivalent to $x^2 - 1 \geq 8$?

(A) $x \geq 3$

(B) $x \geq 9$

(C) $x \geq -3$ or $x \leq 3$

(D) $-3 \leq x \leq 3$

(E) $x \leq -3$ or $x \geq 3$

18. If x is positive and y is 9 more than the square of x, which of the following expressions represents x in terms of y?

(A) $x = y - 3$

(B) $x = \sqrt{y} - 3$

(C) $x = \sqrt{y - 9}$

(D) $x = \sqrt{y - 3}$

(E) $x = \sqrt{y + 3}$

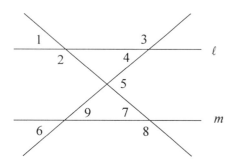

17. In the figure above, line ℓ is parallel to line m. Which of the following must be true?

I. $m\angle 1 = m\angle 7$
II. $m\angle 2 = m\angle 3$
III. $m\angle 3 + m\angle 6 = 180°$
IV. $m\angle 4 + m\angle 7 = m\angle 5$

(A) I only

(B) I and II only

(C) I and III only

(D) I, II, and III only

(E) I, III, and IV only

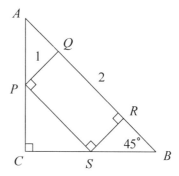

19. In the figure above, a rectangle is inscribed in an isosceles right triangle. If $PQ = 1$ and $QR = 2$, what is the area of triangle ABC?

(A) 4

(B) 4.5

(C) $4\sqrt{2}$

(D) 6

(E) 8

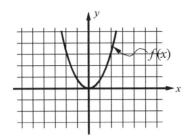

20. If the graph above represents $f(x)$, which of the
    following graphs represents $-f(x+2)$?

(A)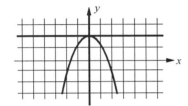

(B)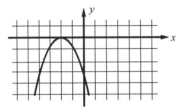

(C)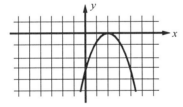

(D)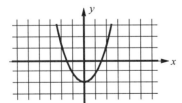

(E)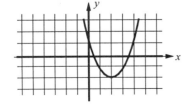

Directions for Student Produced Response Questions:

In this section, solve each problem and enter your answer by darkening the ovals in the special grid, as shown in the example below.

Answer : 1.33   Answer : 4 / 3   Answer : 4 / 3

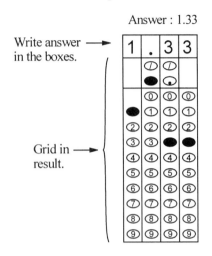

Write answer → in the boxes.

Grid in → result.

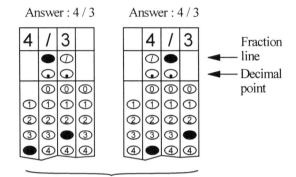

Fraction line ←

Decimal point ←

Either position is correct.

Note: You may start your answers in any column, space permitting. Columns not needed should be left blank.

- It is recommended that you write your answer in the boxes at the top of the columns to help you fill in the ovals accurately.

- Mark no more than one oval in any column.

- You will receive credit only for darkening the ovals correctly.

- Some problems may have more than one correct answer. In such cases, grid in only one answer.

- No question has a negative answer.

- Mixed numbers such as $1\frac{3}{4}$ must be gridded as 1.75 or 7/4. (If ⌊1 3 / 4⌋ is gridded, it will be interpreted as $\frac{13}{4}$, not $1\frac{3}{4}$.)

- Decimal Accuracy : Decimal answers must be entered as accurately as possible. For example, if you obtain an answer such as 1.666..., you should record the results as 1.66 or 1.67. **Less accurate values such as 1.6 or 1.7 are not acceptable.**

Acceptable ways to grid $\frac{5}{3}$ = 1.666...

Notes:
1. The use of a calculator is permitted. All numbers used are real numbers.
2. All figures are drawn to scale EXCEPT when it is stated that the figure is not drawn to scale.
3. All figures lie in a plane unless otherwise indicated.

Reference Information

  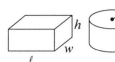

$A = \frac{1}{2}bh$ $c^2 = a^2 + b^2$ Special Right Triangles $A = \ell w$ $A = \pi r^2$ $V = \ell wh$ $V = \pi r^2 h$
                                                                                $C = 2\pi r$

The number of degrees of arc in a circle is 360.

The measure in degrees of a straight angle is 180.

The sum of the angle measures of a triangle, in degrees, is 180.

1. If $\frac{1}{x} + \frac{1}{y} = \frac{1}{5}$ and $x = \frac{15}{2}$, what is the value of y?

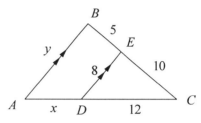

Note: Figure not drawn to scale.

4. In the figure above, if $\overline{AB} \parallel \overline{DE}$ what is the value of $x + y$?

2. On a coordinate plane, a horizontal line passes through $(-3, 4)$ and $(7, t)$. What is the value of t?

3. If $x^2 - 0.09 = (x + a)(x - a)$ and $a > 0$, what is the value of a?

5. For all positive numbers x, let f be defined as $f(x) = \frac{x+3}{x}$. What is the value of $\frac{f(3)+3}{f(3)}$?

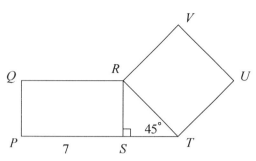

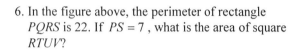

Note: Figure not drawn to scale.

6. In the figure above, the perimeter of rectangle *PQRS* is 22. If *PS* = 7 , what is the area of square *RTUV*?

7. If $x = 2y + 1$, what is the value of $(-2)^{4x-8y}$?

8. At the farmers market, *x* pounds of apples cost $3.60. If Gloria paid 4*x* dollars for 10 pounds of apples, what is the value of *x*?

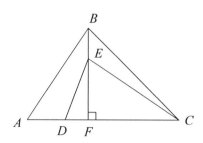

9. In the figure above, $\dfrac{BE}{EF} = \dfrac{2}{3}$ and $\dfrac{AD}{DC} = \dfrac{1}{3}$. What is the ratio of the area of $\triangle CDE$ to the area of $\triangle ABC$?

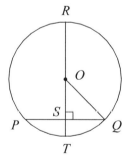

Note: Figure not drawn to scale.

10. In circle *O* above, $\overline{RT}$ is a diameter of circle *O* and $\overline{RT} \perp \overline{PQ}$. If $PQ = 12$ and $RT = 20$, what is the length of $\overline{ST}$?

11. The average (arithmetic mean) test score for all the students in a class is 78. If the average score of b boys in the class was 81 and the average score of g girls in the class was 76, what is the value of $\dfrac{b}{g}$?

12. Two spheres made of the same metal have radii of 5 inches and 10 inches. If the smaller sphere weighs 20 pounds, how many pounds does the larger sphere weigh?

13. Set S consists of all multiples of four between 1 and 99. Set T consists of all multiples of six between 1 and 99. How many numbers greater than or equal to 1 and less than or equal to 99 are not in either set S or set T?

$$a,\ b,\ \frac{4}{3},\ \frac{8}{9},\ \frac{16}{27},\ \dots$$

14. In the geometric sequence above, the ratio of successive terms is always the same. What is the value of $a + b$?

15. The figure above shows five different books on a student's desk. If the dictionary has to be at one end, how many different arrangements are possible?

Answer Key

<u>Multiple Choice Questions</u>

(Section 1)

1. C	2. B	3. E	4. C	5. D
6. E	7. E	8. B	9. C	10. B
11. C	12. E	13. C	14. C	15. D
16. C	17. E	18. D	19. B	20. B

(Section 2)

1. B	2. C	3. E	4. D	5. B
6. E	7. B	8. D	9. C	10. D
11. A	12. C	13. A	14. D	15. C
16. E	17. E	18. C	19. A	20. B

<u>Grid-In Questions</u>

(Section 3)

1. 15	2. 4	3. 0.3	4. 18	5. 5/2
6. 32	7. 16	8. 3	9. 9/20	10. 2
11. 2/3	12. 160	13. 67	14. 5	15. 48

Answers and Explanations

<u>Multiple Choice Questions</u> (Section 1)

1. C

$$\frac{15-x}{15} = 0 \implies 15 - x = 0 \implies x = 15$$

$$\frac{15+x}{15} = \frac{15+15}{15} = \frac{30}{15} = 2$$

2. B

$ab = 12$				
a	2	3	4	6
b	6	4	3	2

$bc = 21$		
b	3	7
c	7	3

From the two tables above we can conclude that
$b = 3$, $a = 4$, and $c = 7$.
Therefore $b < a < c$.

3. E

$$AB = FE + DC = x + 6$$
$$BC = AF + ED = 6 + x$$

Perimeter of the shaded region
$$= AB + BC + CD + DE + EF + FA$$
$$= (x+6) + (6+x) + 6 + x + x + 6$$
$$= 4x + 24$$
$$= ax + b$$

Therefore $a = 4$ and $b = 24$.
$a + b = 4 + 24 = 28$

4. C

the opposite of nine times a number	increased by four	not more than	
$-9n$	$+4$	$\leq$	54

5. D

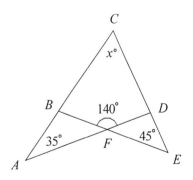

$$m\angle AFB + m\angle BFD = 180$$
$$m\angle AFB + 140 = 180$$
$$m\angle AFB = 40$$

$m\angle AFB + m\angle BAF = m\angle CBE$
(Exterior Angle Theorem)

$40 + 35 = m\angle CBE$
$m\angle CBE = 75$

$m\angle CBE + m\angle CEB + x = 180$
(Angle Sum Theorem)
$75 + 45 + x = 180$
$x = 60$

6. E

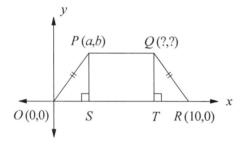

Since $OPQR$ is an isosceles trapezoid, the altitudes from P and Q form two congruent right triangles. The y-coordinate of P will be the same as the y-coordinate of Q.

Since $\triangle OPS \cong \triangle RQT$, $OS = RT = a$, and the x-coordinate of Q will be $10 - a$.

So Q will have the coordinates $(10 - a, b)$

7. E

$$\frac{1/2 \text{ tablespoon}}{4 \text{ cups of coffee}} = \frac{3 \text{ tablespoons}}{x \text{ cups of coffee}}$$

$\Rightarrow \dfrac{1}{2}x = 12 \Rightarrow x = 24$ cups of coffee

$$\frac{1 \text{ quart}}{4 \text{ cups}} = \frac{y \text{ quarts}}{24 \text{ cups}} \Rightarrow 4y = 24$$

$\Rightarrow y = 6$ quarts

If a thermos holds 2 quarts of liquid, then 6 quarts of coffee can fill 3 thermoses.

8. B

$$(2^x)(2^{2x})(2^{3x}) = 2^{x+2x+3x} = 2^{6x}$$

9. C

The sum of the numbers in a set of 40 positive numbers is S.
The sum of the eight largest numbers in the set $= 0.52S$

The sum of the other 32 numbers in the set $= S - 0.52S = 0.48S$

The average of the other 32 numbers in the set
$$= \frac{0.48S}{32} = \frac{48}{3200}S = \frac{3}{200}S$$

10. B

$x^2 - y^2 = 4$ and $x + y = \dfrac{1}{4}$
$x^2 - y^2 = (x + y)(x - y)$
$\qquad = \dfrac{1}{4}(x - y) = 4$ (Substitution, $x + y = \dfrac{1}{4}$)
$\Rightarrow x - y = 16$

11. C

The value of $f(x)$ is positive when the graph of $f(x)$ is above the x-axis.
This happens when $-3 < x < 1$ or $x > 4$.

12. E

Given: $PT = 16$ and $PR = QS = 7$.
Let $RS = x$, then $QR = QS - RS = 7 - x$.
$PR = PQ + QR \Rightarrow 7 = PQ + (7 - x)$
$\Rightarrow PQ = x$
Also, $QS = ST = 7$ since S is the midpoint of $\overline{QT}$.
$PT = PQ + QS + ST$
$\Rightarrow 16 = x + 7 + 7$
$\Rightarrow x = 2$

13. C

The degree measure of the central angle of
the sector representing Agriculture
$= 360 \times 0.05 = 18$.

14. C

$n\% + 35\% + 20\% + 5\% + 18\% = 100\%$
$\Rightarrow n = 22$

Let x = total value.
$0.2x = 15$ (manufacturing represents 15 billion)
$\Rightarrow x = 75$

$0.22 \times 75 = 16.5$ (finance sector represents 22%
of the total)

15. D

$(2a^2b)^3(3ab^2) = (8a^6b^3)(3ab^2) = 24a^7b^5$

16. C

If Stella can finish one card every 20 seconds,
then she can finish 3 cards every minute.

If Min can finish one card every 30 seconds,
then he can finish 2 cards every minute.

number of cards   number of cards
Stella can finish   Min can finish
in $3x$ minutes   in $3x$ minutes
$\overbrace{3 \times 3x}$ $\;+\;$ $\overbrace{2 \times 3x}$ $\;= 15x$

17. E

Pick numbers. Let's try $n = 11$ and $n = 15$.
(When these numbers are divided by 4 the remainder
is 3.)

If $n = 11$, the remainder when n is divided by 5
is 1.
If $n = 15$, the remainder when n is divided by 5
is 0.

Therefore the remainder cannot be determined.

18. D

$$x = 1 - \frac{n}{m}$$

$$x = 1 \cdot \frac{m}{m} - \frac{n}{m} = \frac{m-n}{m} \quad (\frac{m}{m} = 1)$$

$$\frac{1}{x} = \frac{m}{m-n}$$

19. B

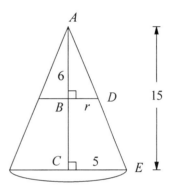

Let r = the radius of the smaller cone.
$$\triangle ABD \sim \triangle ACE \;\Rightarrow\; \frac{AB}{BD} = \frac{AC}{CE}$$

$$\Rightarrow \frac{6}{r} = \frac{15}{5} \;\Rightarrow\; r = 2$$

Volume of the smaller cone
$$= \frac{1}{3}\pi r^2 h = \frac{1}{3}\pi(2)^2(6) = 8\pi \;.$$

20. B

$$P = A(2)^{\frac{\text{the number of years elapsed since the start}}{\text{the number of years required to double the population}}},$$

where P is the population after t years and
A is the initial population count.

The population doubles every 14 years and
the initial population count is 1,500.

$P = 1500(2)^{t/14}$ is the right formula for the
time required for the population to double.

Multiple Choice Questions   (Section 2)

1. B

$$1-\left|-9\right|=n \;\Rightarrow\; 1-9=n \;\Rightarrow\; n=-8$$

2. C

$$f(x)=x^2-ax$$
$$f(-2)=(-2)^2-a(-2)=4+2a$$
$$f(5)=(5)^2-a(5)=25-5a$$

$$f(-2)=f(5) \;\Rightarrow\; 4+2a=25-5a$$
$$\Rightarrow\; 7a=21 \;\Rightarrow\; a=3$$

3. E

$$\left|x-\frac{1}{4}\right|=\frac{1}{3}-\frac{1}{8} \;\Rightarrow\; \left|x-\frac{1}{4}\right|=\frac{8}{24}-\frac{3}{24}=\frac{5}{24}$$
$$\Rightarrow\; x-\frac{1}{4}=\pm\frac{5}{24}$$

If $x-\frac{1}{4}=\frac{5}{24}$,
$$x=\frac{5}{24}+\frac{1}{4}=\frac{5}{24}+\frac{6}{24}=\frac{11}{24}$$

If $x-\frac{1}{4}=-\frac{5}{24}$,
$$x=-\frac{5}{24}+\frac{1}{4}=-\frac{5}{24}+\frac{6}{24}=\frac{1}{24}$$

4. D

$$(\sqrt{6}-\sqrt{2})^2=(\sqrt{6}-\sqrt{2})(\sqrt{6}-\sqrt{2})$$
$$=\sqrt{6}\sqrt{6}-\sqrt{6}\sqrt{2}-\sqrt{2}\sqrt{6}+\sqrt{2}\sqrt{2}$$
$$=6-2\sqrt{12}+2$$
$$=8-2\sqrt{4}\sqrt{3}$$
$$=8-4\sqrt{3}$$
$$=4(2-\sqrt{3})$$

5. B

$$(3x-1)(x+1)=0$$
$$\Rightarrow\; 3x-1=0 \text{ or } x+1=0$$
If $3x-1=0$, $x=\frac{1}{3}$.
If $x+1=0$, $x=-1$.
-1 is the answer since it is smaller than $\frac{1}{3}$.

6. E

31, a, b, c, 59, ... is the arithmetic sequence.

In an arithmetic sequence the difference between successive terms is always the same.

Therefore $a=31+d$, $b=31+2d$, $c=31+3d$, and $59=31+4d$.
$4d=59-31 \;\Rightarrow\; d=7$

Therefore $a=31+7=38$, $b=31+2(7)=45$, and $c=31+3(7)=52$.
$a+b+c=38+45+52=135$

7. B

$$R(\frac{8+(-4)}{2},\frac{1+(-3)}{2}) \quad \text{(Midpoint formula)}$$
$$=(2,-1)$$

8. D

If two lines are perpendicular, then their slopes are negative reciprocals of each other.

Slope of line $PQ=\dfrac{1-(-3)}{8-(-4)}=\dfrac{4}{12}=\dfrac{1}{3}$.

Therefore the slope of line ℓ is -3.

9. C

the number r 3 times the number s 8 less than

$$r \;\; = \;\; 3s \;\; -8$$

the difference of r and 3   multiplied by   the sum of s and 2

$$(r-3) \;\; \times \;\; (s+2) \;\; = 6$$

10. D

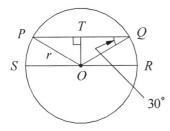

Draw a segment $\overline{OT}$, perpendicular to $\overline{PQ}$.
$\triangle OQT$ and $\triangle OPT$ are $30°$-$60°$-$90°$ triangles.

Let r = the radius of the circle.

Then $OP = OQ = r$, $OT = \frac{1}{2}r$, and

$$QT = PT = \frac{\sqrt{3}}{2}r.$$

$$PQ = PT + TQ = \frac{\sqrt{3}}{2}r + \frac{\sqrt{3}}{2}r = \frac{2\sqrt{3}}{2}r = \sqrt{3}r$$

$$\frac{PQ}{SR} = \frac{\sqrt{3}r}{2r} = \frac{\sqrt{3}}{2}$$

11. A

$$d = r \cdot t \;\Leftrightarrow\; r = \frac{d}{t} \;\Leftrightarrow\; t = \frac{d}{r}$$

Let x = time in hours before the two persons meet

the distance Jim traveled in x hours   the distance Kay traveled in x hours   the total distance

$$60x \;\; + \;\; 40x \;\; = \;\; 150$$
$$100x = 150 \;\Rightarrow\; x = 1.5$$

Therefore, after 1.5 hours the distance between the two persons is zero.
Discard answer choices (C), (D) and (E).

Jim's traveling time $= \dfrac{150}{60} = 2.5$

Jim arrives at Malibu after 2.5 hours of driving. From this point the distance between the two persons is increasing slowly.

Kay's traveling time $= \dfrac{150}{40} = 3.75$

Kay arrives at Azusa after 3.75 hours of driving. Therefore 3.75 hours later the distance between the two persons is 150.

The correct answer choice is (A).

12. C

The total amount, in pounds, of aluminum needed each day to produce storage boxes is
$1200 \times 4 + 1,000 \times 6 + 800 \times 10 = 18,800$.

13. A

The total cost, in dollars, for a day's production of aluminum storage boxes is
$18,800 \times \$0.08 = \$1,504$

14. D

$a > 0$, then
$$\sqrt{98a^3} - \sqrt{50a^3}$$
$$= \sqrt{49}\sqrt{2}\sqrt{a^2}\sqrt{a} - \sqrt{25}\sqrt{2}\sqrt{a^2}\sqrt{a}$$
$$= 7a\sqrt{2a} - 5a\sqrt{2a}$$
$$= 2a\sqrt{2a}$$

15. C

$p = r - 0.2r = 0.8r$ (p is 20 percent less than r.)
$r = s - 0.2s = 0.8s$ (r is 20 percent less than s.)
$s = t - 0.2t = 0.8t$ (s is 20 percent less than t.)

$p = 0.8r = 0.8(0.8s) = 0.8(0.8(0.8t)) = 0.512t$

16. E

$$x^2 - 1 \geq 8 \qquad \text{Original inequality}$$
$$x^2 - 9 \geq 0 \qquad \text{Subtract 8 from each side.}$$
$$(x+3)(x-3) \geq 0 \quad \text{Factor.}$$
$$x \leq -3 \text{ or } x \geq 3$$

17. E

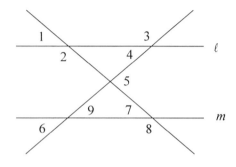

I. $m\angle 1 = m\angle 7 \qquad$ If 2 lines are ||
    corresponding $\angle s$ are $\cong$.

    True.

II. $m\angle 2 = m\angle 3$

    Not true.

III. $m\angle 3 + m\angle 4 = 180° \qquad$ A straight angle measures
    $\qquad\qquad\qquad\qquad\qquad 180°$.

    $m\angle 4 = m\angle 6 \qquad$ If 2 lines are ||
    $\qquad\qquad\qquad\qquad$ corresponding $\angle s$ are $\cong$.

    $m\angle 3 + m\angle 6 = 180° \qquad$ Substitution

    True.

IV. $m\angle 4 = m\angle 9 \qquad$ If 2 lines are || alternate
    $\qquad\qquad\qquad\qquad$ interior $\angle s$ are $\cong$.

    $m\angle 9 + m\angle 7 = m\angle 5 \qquad$ Exterior Angle Theorem
    $m\angle 4 + m\angle 7 = m\angle 5 \qquad$ Substitution

    True.

18. C

$$\underbrace{y =}_{y \text{ is}} \quad \underbrace{x^2}_{\text{the square of } x} \quad \underbrace{+9}_{\text{nine more than}}$$

$$x^2 = y - 9$$
$$x = \pm\sqrt{y-9}$$

Since x is positive, $x = \sqrt{y-9}$.

19. A

$\triangle APQ$ and $\triangle BSR$ are $45°$-$45°$-$90°$ triangles.

$$\Rightarrow \begin{cases} AQ = PQ = 1 \\ BR = SR = 1 \end{cases} \text{ and } \begin{matrix} AP = \sqrt{2} \\ BS = \sqrt{2} \end{matrix}$$

$QR = PS = 2 \qquad$ (Opposite sides of $\square$ are $\cong$.)

Since $AB \parallel PS$, $\triangle PSC$ is also a $45°$-$45°$-$90°$ triangle.

$$PS = \sqrt{2} \cdot SC \qquad (45°\text{-}45°\text{-}90° \text{ triangle ratio})$$
$$2 = \sqrt{2} \cdot SC \qquad (\text{Substitution, } PS = 2)$$
$$SC = \sqrt{2} \qquad (\text{Divide both sides by } \sqrt{2}.)$$
$$PC = SC = \sqrt{2}$$

$$AC = AP + PC = \sqrt{2} + \sqrt{2} = 2\sqrt{2}$$
$$BC = BS + SC = \sqrt{2} + \sqrt{2} = 2\sqrt{2}$$

Area of $\triangle ABC$
$$= \frac{1}{2} BC \cdot AC$$
$$= \frac{1}{2}(2\sqrt{2})(2\sqrt{2}) = \frac{1}{2}(8) = 4$$

20. B

Given: the graph of $y = f(x)$.

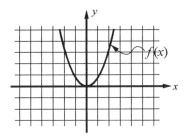

The graph of $y = -f(x)$ can be obtained from the graph of $y = f(x)$ by reflecting it about the x-axis.

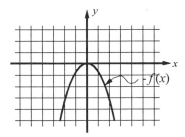

The graph of $-f(x+2)$ can be obtained from the graph of $y = -f(x)$ by shifting it 2 units to the left.

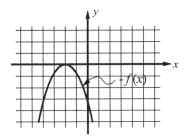

<u>Grid-In Questions</u> (Section 3)

1. 15

Given: $\dfrac{1}{x} + \dfrac{1}{y} = \dfrac{1}{5}$ and $x = \dfrac{15}{2}$.

$x = \dfrac{15}{2} \Rightarrow \dfrac{1}{x} = \dfrac{2}{15}$.

$\dfrac{2}{15} + \dfrac{1}{y} = \dfrac{1}{5}$ ($\dfrac{2}{15}$ is substituted for $\dfrac{1}{x}$)

$\dfrac{1}{y} = \dfrac{1}{5} - \dfrac{2}{15} = \dfrac{1}{5} \cdot \dfrac{3}{3} - \dfrac{2}{15} = \dfrac{1}{15}$

$\Rightarrow y = 15$

2. 4

The slope of a horizontal line is zero.

$\text{Slope} = \dfrac{y_2 - y_1}{x_2 - x_1} = \dfrac{t - 4}{7 + 3} = 0$

$\Rightarrow t - 4 = 0 \Rightarrow t = 4$

3. 0.3

$x^2 - 0.09$

$= (x + a)(x - a)$

$= x^2 - a^2$

$\Rightarrow a^2 = 0.09 \Rightarrow a = \pm 0.3$

Since $a > 0$, $a = 0.3$

4. 18

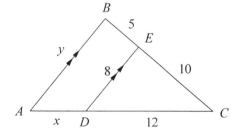

Since $\overline{AB} \parallel \overline{DE}$,

$\dfrac{10}{5} = \dfrac{12}{x} \Rightarrow 10x = 60 \Rightarrow x = 6$

$\dfrac{10}{8} = \dfrac{10 + 5}{y} \Rightarrow 10y = 120 \Rightarrow y = 12$

$x + y = 6 + 12 = 18$

5. $\dfrac{5}{2}$

$f(x) = \dfrac{x + 3}{x}$

$f(3) = \dfrac{3 + 3}{3} = \dfrac{6}{3} = 2$

$\dfrac{f(3) + 3}{f(3)} = \dfrac{2 + 3}{2} = \dfrac{5}{2}$

6. 32

Since the perimeter of rectangle $PQRS$ is 22, the length of $\overline{RS}$ must be 4.

Triangle RST is a $45°$-$45°$-$90°$ triangle. Therefore $RT = 4\sqrt{2}$.

The area of square $RTUV = (4\sqrt{2})^2 = 32$

7. 16

$x = 2y + 1 \Rightarrow x - 2y = 1$

$(-2)^{4x - 8y}$

$= (-2)^{4(x - 2y)}$

$= (-2)^{4(1)} = (-2)^4 = 16$

8. 3

x pounds of apples cost $3.60 and
10 pounds of apples cost 4x dollars.

Set up a proportion.

$$\frac{x \text{ lbs}}{3.60 \text{ dollars}} = \frac{10 \text{ lbs}}{4x \text{ dollars}}$$

$$\Rightarrow 4x^2 = 36 \Rightarrow x^2 = 9 \Rightarrow x = 3$$

9. $\dfrac{9}{20}$

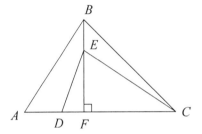

Pick numbers.
Let $BE = 2$, $EF = 3$, $AD = 1$, and $DC = 3$.

The area of $\triangle CDE = \dfrac{1}{2}(3)(3) = 4.5$.

The area of $\triangle ABC = \dfrac{1}{2}(4)(5) = 10$.

$$\frac{\text{area of } \triangle CDE}{\text{area of } \triangle ABC} = \frac{4.5}{10} = \frac{9}{20}$$

10. 2

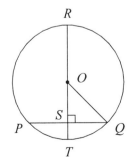

Since the diameter of circle O is 20, the radius of circle O is 10. Therefore $OT = OQ = 10$.

In a circle, if a diameter is perpendicular to a chord, then it bisects the chord. Therefore $PS = SQ = 6$.

$$OQ^2 = OS^2 + SQ^2 \text{ (Pythagorean Theorem)}$$
$$10^2 = OS^2 + 6^2$$
$$OS^2 = 64$$
$$OS = 8$$

$$ST = OT - OS = 10 - 8 = 2$$

11. $\dfrac{2}{3}$

Weighted Average of 2 groups

$$= \frac{\left\{\begin{array}{c}\text{Sum of the values}\\ \text{of group 1}\end{array}\right\} + \left\{\begin{array}{c}\text{Sum of the values}\\ \text{of group 2}\end{array}\right\}}{\text{Total number of persons}}$$

$$78 = \frac{(81 \times b) + (76 \times g)}{b + g}$$
$$78(b + g) = 81b + 76g$$
$$78b + 78g = 81b + 76g$$
$$2g = 3b \Rightarrow \frac{b}{g} = \frac{2}{3}$$

12. 160

The ratio of the radii $= 1 : 2$.
$\Rightarrow$ The ratio of the volumes $= 1^3 : 2^3 = 1 : 8$.
$\Rightarrow$ The ratio of the weights $= 1 : 8$.

Let $x =$ the weight of the larger sphere.

$$\frac{1}{8} = \frac{20}{x} \Rightarrow x = 160$$

13. 67

$S = \{4, 8, 12, 16,..., 92, 96\}$
$96 - 4 = 92$
$92 \div 4 = 23$
Add 1 to 23. There are 24 numbers in set S.

$T = \{6, 12, 18,..., 90, 96\}$
$96 - 6 = 90$
$90 \div 6 = 15$
Add 1 to 15. There are 16 numbers in set T.

$S \cap T =$ all the multiples of 12 up to 96
$S \cap T = \{12, 24, 36,..., 84, 96\}$
$96 - 12 = 84$
$84 \div 12 = 7$
Add 1 to 7. There are 8 numbers in set $S \cap T$.

Since there are multiples of 12 in both set T and set S, add the numbers of members in each set and subtract 8.

There are $24 + 16 - 8$, or 32, numbers in either set S or set T.

Therefore there are $99 - 32$, or 67, numbers that are not in either set S or set T.

14. 5

$a, b, \dfrac{4}{3}, \dfrac{8}{9}, \dfrac{16}{27}, ...$

In a geometric sequence, the ratio of successive terms is always the same. Therefore $a \cdot r = b$,
$b \cdot r = \dfrac{4}{3}$, and $\dfrac{4}{3} \cdot r = \dfrac{8}{9}$.

$\dfrac{3}{4}(\dfrac{4}{3} \cdot r) = \dfrac{3}{4}(\dfrac{8}{9}) \Rightarrow r = \dfrac{2}{3}$

$b \cdot r = \dfrac{4}{3} \Rightarrow b(\dfrac{2}{3}) = \dfrac{4}{3} \Rightarrow b = 2$

$a \cdot r = b \Rightarrow a(\dfrac{2}{3}) = 2 \Rightarrow a = 3$

Therefore $a + b = 3 + 2 = 5$.

15. 48

Make a diagram of the possible arrangements.

When the dictionary is placed at the left end
| D | 4 | 3 | 2 | 1 |
the number of permutations is $4 \cdot 3 \cdot 2 \cdot 1$, or 24.

When the dictionary is placed at the right end
| 4 | 3 | 2 | 1 | D |
the number of permutations is $4 \cdot 3 \cdot 2 \cdot 1$, or 24.

Therefore $24 + 24$, or 48, different arrangements are possible.

SAT Practice Test 2

SAT Answer Sheet

SECTION 1

1 (A) (B) (C) (D) (E)	6 (A) (B) (C) (D) (E)	11 (A) (B) (C) (D) (E)	16 (A) (B) (C) (D) (E)
2 (A) (B) (C) (D) (E)	7 (A) (B) (C) (D) (E)	12 (A) (B) (C) (D) (E)	17 (A) (B) (C) (D) (E)
3 (A) (B) (C) (D) (E)	8 (A) (B) (C) (D) (E)	13 (A) (B) (C) (D) (E)	18 (A) (B) (C) (D) (E)
4 (A) (B) (C) (D) (E)	9 (A) (B) (C) (D) (E)	14 (A) (B) (C) (D) (E)	19 (A) (B) (C) (D) (E)
5 (A) (B) (C) (D) (E)	10 (A) (B) (C) (D) (E)	15 (A) (B) (C) (D) (E)	20 (A) (B) (C) (D) (E)

SECTION 2

1 (A) (B) (C) (D) (E)	6 (A) (B) (C) (D) (E)	11 (A) (B) (C) (D) (E)	16 (A) (B) (C) (D) (E)
2 (A) (B) (C) (D) (E)	7 (A) (B) (C) (D) (E)	12 (A) (B) (C) (D) (E)	17 (A) (B) (C) (D) (E)
3 (A) (B) (C) (D) (E)	8 (A) (B) (C) (D) (E)	13 (A) (B) (C) (D) (E)	18 (A) (B) (C) (D) (E)
4 (A) (B) (C) (D) (E)	9 (A) (B) (C) (D) (E)	14 (A) (B) (C) (D) (E)	19 (A) (B) (C) (D) (E)
5 (A) (B) (C) (D) (E)	10 (A) (B) (C) (D) (E)	15 (A) (B) (C) (D) (E)	20 (A) (B) (C) (D) (E)

SECTION 3

Grid-in items 1–15, each with the following grid:

	/	/	
	.	.	
	0	0	0
1	1	1	1
2	2	2	2
3	3	3	3
4	4	4	4
5	5	5	5
6	6	6	6
7	7	7	7
8	8	8	8
9	9	9	9

1 2 3 4 5

6 7 8 9 10

11 12 13 14 15

Directions : **In this section, solve each problem, decide which is the best answer choice, and then darken the corresponding oval on the answer sheet.**

Notes:
1. The use of a calculator is permitted. All numbers used are real numbers.
2. All figures are drawn to scale EXCEPT when it is stated that the figure is not drawn to scale.
3. All figures lie in a plane unless otherwise indicated.

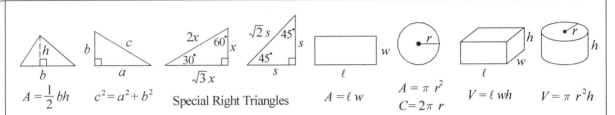

$A = \frac{1}{2}bh$ $c^2 = a^2 + b^2$ Special Right Triangles $A = \ell w$ $A = \pi r^2$ $C = 2\pi r$ $V = \ell wh$ $V = \pi r^2 h$

The number of degrees of arc in a circle is 360.

The measure in degrees of a straight angle is 180.

The sum of the angle measures of a triangle, in degrees, is 180.

1. If $n - 2 = 2 - n$, then $n =$

(A) −2

(B) −1

(C) 0

(D) 1

(E) 2

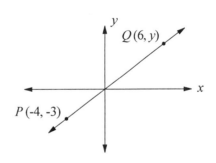

2. If $a = -2$ and $b = 3$, then $|a - b| - |a + b| =$

(A) −2

(B) −1

(C) 1

(D) 3

(E) 4

3. In the figure above, line PQ passes through the origin. What is the value of y?

(A) 4.5

(B) 5

(C) 5.5

(D) 8

(E) 10

4. Let f be defined as $f(x) = mx + b$. If $f(2) = 3$ and $f(0) = 5$, what is the value of m?

(A) −2

(B) −1

(C) 0

(D) 2

(E) 4

5. If x increased by 250 percent of x equals n, then $n =$

(A) 1.25x

(B) 2.5x

(C) 3.5x

(D) 250x

(E) 251x

6. If $abc \neq 0$, then $\dfrac{(-2ab^3c^2)^3}{4a^2b^5c^3} =$

(A) abc^2

(B) $2ab^4c^3$

(C) $-2abc^2$

(D) $-2ab^4c^3$

(E) $-2ab^2c^2$

7. If $x \neq 3$, then $\dfrac{3x}{x-3} + \dfrac{9}{3-x} =$

(A) $\dfrac{3x+9}{x-3}$

(B) $\dfrac{3x+3}{x-3}$

(C) 3

(D) $\dfrac{3x-3}{x-3}$

(E) $\dfrac{3}{x-3}$

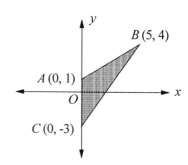

8. In the figure above, what is the area of triangle ABC?

(A) 10

(B) 12

(C) 15

(D) 18

(E) 20

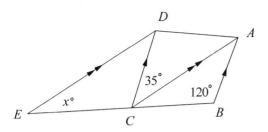

Note: Figure not drawn to scale.

9. In the figure above, $\overline{AB} \parallel \overline{CD}$, $\overline{AC} \parallel \overline{DE}$, and $\overline{BE}$ is a line segment. What is the value of x?

(A) 25

(B) 30

(C) 35

(D) 40

(E) 45

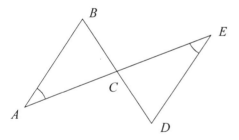

10. In the figure above, if segment BD bisects segment AE and $\angle A \cong \angle E$, which of the following must be true?

   I. $\overline{AB} \cong \overline{DE}$
  II. $\overline{AB} \parallel \overline{DE}$
 III. $\overline{BC} \cong \overline{CD}$

(A) None

(B) I only

(C) II only

(D) I and III only

(E) I, II, and III

Questions 11-12 refer to the following graph.

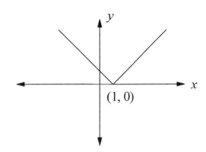

11. Which of the following could be the equation of the graph above?

(A) $y = |x|$

(B) $y = |x+1|$

(C) $y = |x-1|$

(D) $y = |x|+1$

(E) $y = |x|-1$

12. What are the domain and range of the function graphed above?

(A) Domain $\{x : -\infty < x < \infty\}$
    Range $\{y : -\infty < y < \infty\}$

(B) Domain $\{x : -\infty < x < \infty\}$
    Range $\{y : 0 \le y < \infty\}$

(C) Domain $\{x : 0 \le x < \infty\}$
    Range $\{y : -\infty < y < \infty\}$

(D) Domain $\{x : 1 \le x < \infty\}$
    Range $\{y : 0 \le y < \infty\}$

(E) Domain $\{x : 0 \le x < \infty\}$
    Range $\{y : 1 \le y < \infty\}$

(Section 1)

13. On a number line, point P has coordinate $-2\frac{2}{3}$ and point Q has coordinate 8. If point R is $\frac{2}{5}$ of the way from P to Q, what is the coordinate of R?

(A) $1\frac{3}{5}$

(B) $2\frac{1}{3}$

(C) $3\frac{3}{5}$

(D) $4\frac{1}{3}$

(E) $4\frac{4}{5}$

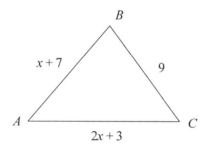

Note: Figure not drawn to scale.

14. In the figure above, if $\triangle ABC$ is isosceles, what is the least possible perimeter of the triangle?

(A) 20

(B) 22

(C) 25

(D) 28

(E) 31

Questions 15-16 refer to the following scatter plot.

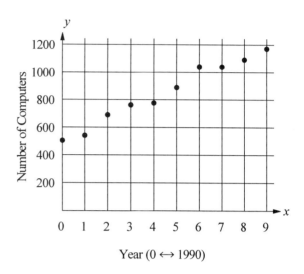

Year (0 ↔ 1990)

15. The scatter plot above shows the number of computers in use at a certain company between 1990 and 1998. In the graph x represents the year, with $x = 0$ corresponding to 1990, and y represents the number of computers. Which of the following could be the slope of the line of best fit for the data shown above?

(A) 10

(B) 25

(C) 50

(D) 75

(E) 100

16. What is the best approximation of the number of computers in use at the company in the year 2005?

(A) 1,200

(B) 1,600

(C) 2,000

(D) 2,400

(E) 2,600

17. An internet service provider offers two payment options.

Option A: Basic charge of $12.00 per month plus $3.00 per hour of use. The first 3 hours of each month are free.

Option B: Basic charge of $9.00 per month plus $4.00 per hour of use. The first 5 hours of each month are free.

After how many hours of internet service would the total monthly fee under Option A and Option B be the same?

(A) 13

(B) 14

(C) 15

(D) 16

(E) 17

18. If a wheel with a radius of r feet travels a distance of m miles, which of the following represents the number of revolutions the wheel makes, in terms of r and m?
(1 mile = 5,280 feet)

(A) $\dfrac{2640m}{\pi r}$

(B) $\dfrac{1320}{\pi rm}$

(C) $\dfrac{2640r}{\pi m}$

(D) $\dfrac{\pi r}{2640m}$

(E) $\dfrac{\pi m}{2640r}$

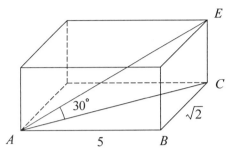

19. In the rectangular prism above, $m\angle EAC = 30°$. If $AB = 5$ and $BC = \sqrt{2}$, what is the length of diagonal AE?

(A) 6

(B) $6\sqrt{2}$

(C) $6\sqrt{3}$

(D) 9

(E) $9\sqrt{3}$

20. For all real numbers x, let f be defined as $f(x) = -x + 4$. Which of the following must be true for all real numbers x?

I. $f(f(0)) = 0$

II. $f(x+4) = f(x)+4$

III. $f(-x) = -f(x)$

(A) None

(B) I only

(C) I and II only

(D) II and III only

(E) I, II, and III

Directions : In this section, solve each problem, decide which is the best answer choice, and then darken the corresponding oval on the answer sheet.

Notes:
1. The use of a calculator is permitted. All numbers used are real numbers.
2. All figures are drawn to scale EXCEPT when it is stated that the figure is not drawn to scale.
3. All figures lie in a plane unless otherwise indicated.

Reference Information

$A = \frac{1}{2} bh$ $c^2 = a^2 + b^2$ Special Right Triangles $A = \ell w$ $A = \pi r^2$ $V = \ell wh$ $V = \pi r^2 h$
$C = 2\pi r$

The number of degrees of arc in a circle is 360.

The measure in degrees of a straight angle is 180.

The sum of the angle measures of a triangle, in degrees, is 180.

1. The sum of two numbers a and b is nine, and the number a is 5 more than b. What is the value of a?

   (A) 6
   (B) 7
   (C) 8
   (D) 9
   (E) 10

2. If $\dfrac{x^{2a+1}}{x^3} = x^{a+2}$, what is the value of a?

   (A) 2
   (B) 3
   (C) 4
   (D) 5
   (E) 6

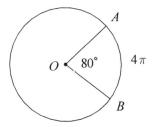

3. In circle O above, if the length of arc AB is 4π, what is the area of the circle?

   (A) 9π
   (B) 16π
   (C) 36π
   (D) 64π
   (E) 81π

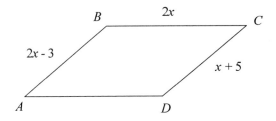

4. What is the perimeter of parallelogram *ABCD* above?

(A) 29
(B) 36
(C) 42
(D) 50
(E) 58

5. A certain company produces *d* diskettes every *m* minutes. Which of the following is the number of diskettes produced in *h* hours, in terms of *d*, *m*, and *h*?

(A) $\dfrac{60dm}{h}$

(B) $\dfrac{60dh}{m}$

(C) $\dfrac{60mh}{d}$

(D) $\dfrac{dh}{60m}$

(E) $\dfrac{dm}{60h}$

6. Let a_n be defined as $a_n = \dfrac{n}{4}$, where *n* is a positive integer. Which of the following CANNOT be a value of a_n?

(A) 0
(B) 0.025
(C) 0.25
(D) 2.5
(E) 25

7. Which of the following is the graph of $|x-3| > 4$?

(A)

(B)

(C)

(D)

(E)

8. A square piece of paper with sides of length x is cut into six pieces with areas 1, 4, 9, 9, 16, and 25. What is the value of x?

(A) 6

(B) 7

(C) 8

(D) 9

(E) 10

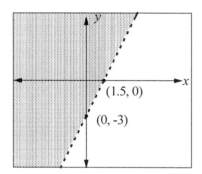

(1.5, 0)

(0, -3)

9. Which of the following inequalities represents the graph above?

(A) $x - 2y < 3$

(B) $x + 2y > 3$

(C) $2x - y < -3$

(D) $2x - y < 3$

(E) $2x + y < 3$

10. In a sequence of numbers, each term after the first is 2 times the preceding term. If a and b are two terms in the sequence and $\dfrac{b}{a}$ is 128, how many terms are there between a and b ?

(A) 4

(B) 5

(C) 6

(D) 7

(E) 8

$$P(n) = \begin{cases} 6n, & \text{if } 1 \le n \le 49 \\ 5n, & \text{if } 50 \le n \le 99 \\ 4n, & \text{if } 100 \le n \end{cases}$$

11. The equation above shows the ABC Toy Company's prices for box cars, where n is the number of box cars ordered and $P(n)$ is the price in dollars of n box cars. Which of the following is NOT true about the price of box cars?

(A) 42 box cars cost less than 50 box cars.

(B) 110 box cars cost less than 90 box cars.

(C) 96 box cars cost the same as 120 box cars.

(D) 59 box cars cost more than 49 box cars.

(E) 120 box cars cost more than 95 box cars.

12. Kim has n pounds of flour and divides it equally among s bags. Tim has the same amount of flour and divides it equally among $r + s$ bags. How many more pounds of flour are in each of Kim's bags than in each of Tim's bags?

(A) $\dfrac{n}{r+s}$

(B) $\dfrac{n}{r-s}$

(C) $\dfrac{ns}{s(r+s)}$

(D) $\dfrac{nr}{s(r+s)}$

(E) $\dfrac{nr}{r+s}$

13. The average (arithmetic mean) of 11 positive integers is 20. If three of the integers are 4, 35, and 35, which of the following must be true?

   I. The median of the integers is greater than 4.
  II. The mode of the integers is 35.
 III. There is at least one integer between 4 and 35.

(A) None

(B) I only

(C) II only

(D) III only

(E) II and III only

14. If $x^2 - bx + 25 = (x - c)^2$ and $c > 0$, for all values of x, what is the value of $b + c$?

(A) 1

(B) 5

(C) 10

(D) 15

(E) 25

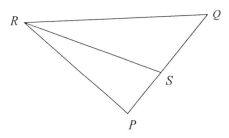

Note: Figure not drawn to scale.

15. In $\triangle PQR$ above, $PQ = 24$. If the ratio of the area of $\triangle PRS$ to the area of $\triangle QRS$ is 3 : 5, what is the length of PS?

(A) 10

(B) 9

(C) 8

(D) 7

(E) 6

16. Of a total of x pencils in a case, $\frac{1}{3}$ are blue and $\frac{1}{5}$ of the remaining pencils are red. If twice as many pencils are yellow as are red, and the remaining 8 pencils are white, what is the value of x?

(A) 24

(B) 30

(C) 36

(D) 40

(E) 45

17. It took Sara a total of 42 minutes to jog from home to the park and back again, by the same path. If she averaged 8 miles per hour going to the park and 6 miles per hour coming back, what is the distance in miles from her house to the park?

(A) 2.4

(B) 2.8

(C) 3.2

(D) 3.6

(E) 4

18. If a and b are integers and $\frac{a}{b} = \frac{4}{3}$, which of the following must be true?

   I. $a + b$ is an odd integer.

   II. ab is an even integer.

   III. $a + b$ is divisible by 7.

(A) I only

(B) II only

(C) III only

(D) I and II only

(E) II and III only

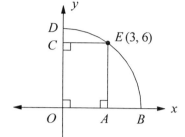

19. In the rectangular coordinate system above, BD is the arc of a circle that has center O. What is the value of $AB - CD$?

(A) $3\sqrt{3}$

(B) $3\sqrt{5}$

(C) 3

(D) $3\sqrt{3} - 3$

(E) $3\sqrt{5} - 3$

20. $\dfrac{7^x \cdot x^7}{7^7 \cdot x^x} =$

(A) 1

(B) $(x - 7)^{\frac{7}{x}}$

(C) $\left(\dfrac{x}{7}\right)^{x-7}$

(D) $(x - 7)^{\frac{x}{7}}$

(E) $\left(\dfrac{7}{x}\right)^{x-7}$

Directions for Student Produced Response Questions:

In this section, solve each problem and enter your answer by darkening the ovals in the special grid, as shown in the example below.

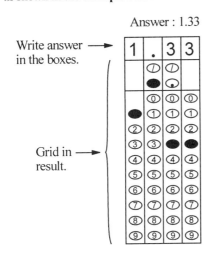

Answer : 1.33

Write answer in the boxes.

Grid in result.

Answer : 4 / 3   Answer : 4 / 3

Fraction line

Decimal point

Either position is correct.

Note: You may start your answers in any column, space permitting. Columns not needed should be left blank.

- It is recommended that you write your answer in the boxes at the top of the columns to help you fill in the ovals accurately.

- Mark no more than one oval in any column.

- You will receive credit only for darkening the ovals correctly.

- Some problems may have more than one correct answer. In such cases, grid in only one answer.

- No question has a negative answer.

- Mixed numbers such as $1\frac{3}{4}$ must be gridded as 1.75 or 7/4. (If [1|3|/|4] is gridded, it will be interpreted as $\frac{13}{4}$, not $1\frac{3}{4}$.)

- Decimal Accuracy : Decimal answers must be entered as accurately as possible. For example, if you obtain an answer such as 1.666..., you should record the results as 1.66 or 1.67. **Less accurate values such as 1.6 or 1.7 are not acceptable.**

Acceptable ways to grid $\frac{5}{3}$ = 1.666...

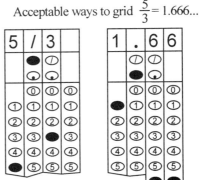

Notes:
1. The use of a calculator is permitted. All numbers used are real numbers.
2. All figures are drawn to scale EXCEPT when it is stated that the figure is not drawn to scale.
3. All figures lie in a plane unless otherwise indicated.

Reference Information

    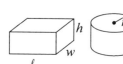

$A = \frac{1}{2}bh$ $c^2 = a^2 + b^2$ Special Right Triangles $A = \ell w$ $A = \pi r^2$ $V = \ell wh$ $V = \pi r^2 h$
$C = 2\pi r$

The number of degrees of arc in a circle is 360.

The measure in degrees of a straight angle is 180.

The sum of the angle measures of a triangle, in degrees, is 180.

1. If $x - y = -2$ and $\frac{x}{4} = y - 5$, what is the value of $x + y$?

2. If $a = \frac{1}{2}$ and $b = 2$, then $(a\sqrt{2})^b =$

3. If $a + b = 36$ and $a - b = 9$, what is the value of $\sqrt{a^2 - b^2}$?

4. What is the least positive integer k for which $24k$ is the square of an integer?

5. If $f(x) = 9^x - 4^{-x}$, then $f(\frac{1}{2}) =$

3, 7, 11, 15, ...

6. In the sequence above, each term after the first is 4 more than the preceding term. What is the 49th term of the sequence?

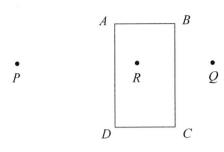

7. In the figure above, *ABCD* is a rectangle and line *PQ* (not shown) is parallel to side $\overline{AB}$. Points *P* and *Q* are symmetric about line *AD*, and points *Q* and *R* are symmetric about line *BC*. If $PQ = 24$ and $QR = 10$, what is the length of side $\overline{AB}$?

10. In the figure above, if $\dfrac{PS}{QS} = \dfrac{3}{2}$ and $\dfrac{PS}{PR} = \dfrac{5}{3}$, what is the value of $\dfrac{QR}{RS}$?

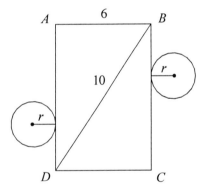

8. The mass *m* required to stretch a spring is directly proportional to the distance *d* that the spring is stretched from its original length. If a mass of 15 g stretches a spring 8 cm, what mass is required to stretches the spring 20 cm?

11. The figure shown above is a net for a right cylinder. If the net is folded without overlap to form a cylinder, the volume of the cylinder will be $\dfrac{k}{\pi}$. What is the value of *k*?

9. If $7r - 2s = 5$ and $4t - 14r = 6$, then $t - s =$

12. For the numbers a, b, and c, the average (arithmetic mean) is two more than twice the median. If $a < b < c$ and $c = 5b$, what is the value of a?

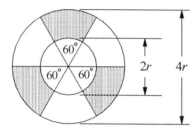

13. The figure above shows a dart board with two concentric circles of diameters $2r$ and $4r$. If a dart is randomly thrown to the dart board, what is the probability that it will hit the shaded region of the board?

14. In a bookstore, hardcover copies of a certain book are priced at $16 each and paperback copies of the same book are priced at $9 each. Last week, the total amount collected in the sales of the hardcover and paperback copies was the same as if every book sold had cost $10.40. If 30 hardcover books were sold, what was the total number of books sold?

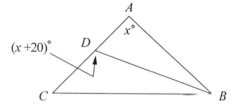

Note: Figure not drawn to scale.

15. In $\triangle ABC$ above, $AB = AC$ and $\overline{BD}$ bisects $\angle ABC$. What is the value of x?

Answer Key

Multiple Choice Questions

(Section 1)

1. E	2. E	3. A	4. B	5. C
6. D	7. C	8. A	9. A	10. E
11. C	12. B	13. A	14. C	15. D
16. B	17. B	18. A	19. A	20. B

(Section 2)

1. B	2. C	3. E	4. E	5. B
6. B	7. D	8. C	9. D	10. C
11. A	12. D	13. A	14. D	15. B
16. B	17. A	18. E	19. C	20. E

Grid In Questions

(Section 3)

1. 10	2. 1/2	3. 18	4. 6	5. 5/2
6. 195	7. 7	8. 75/2	9. 4	10. 2/3
11. 96	12. 6	13. 3/8	14. 150	15. 100

Answers and Explanations

Multiple Choice Questions   (Section 1)

1. E

$$n - 2 = 2 - n$$
$$n - 2 + n = 2 - n + n$$
$$2n - 2 = 2$$
$$n = 2$$

2. E

If $a = -2$ and $b = 3$, then
$$|a - b| - |a + b|$$
$$= |-2 - 3| - |-2 + 3|$$
$$= |-5| - |1|$$
$$= 5 - 1 = 4$$

3. A

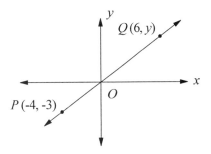

The slope of $\overline{PO}$ equals the slope of $\overline{OQ}$, since points P, O, and Q are on the same line.

$$\frac{0 + 3}{0 + 4} = \frac{y - 0}{6 - 0} \implies \frac{3}{4} = \frac{y}{6} \implies 4y = 18$$
$$\implies y = 4.5$$

4. B

$$f(x) = mx + b$$
$$f(0) = m(0) + b = 5 \implies b = 5$$
$$f(2) = m(2) + b = 3 \implies 2m + b = 3$$

$$2m + 5 = 3 \qquad \text{Make a substitution } (b = 5).$$
$$m = -1$$

5. C

the number x increased by 250 % of x equals n
$$x \qquad\qquad +2.5x \qquad\qquad = n$$
$$x + 2.5x = n$$
$$3.5x = n$$

6. D

$$\frac{(-2ab^3c^2)^3}{4a^2b^5c^3} = \frac{(-2)^3 a^3 b^9 c^6}{4a^2b^5c^3} = -2ab^4c^3$$

7. C

$$\frac{3x}{x-3}+\frac{9}{3-x}$$
$$=\frac{3x}{x-3}+\frac{9}{-(x-3)}$$
$$=\frac{3x}{x-3}-\frac{9}{x-3}$$
$$=\frac{3x-9}{x-3}=\frac{3(x-3)}{x-3}=3$$

8. A

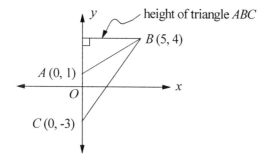

From point B draw an altitude to the y-axis. Then the height of the triangle is 5 and the length of the triangle's base, which is $\overline{AC}$, is 4.

Area of $\triangle ABC = \frac{1}{2}\cdot 4 \cdot 5 = 10$

9. A

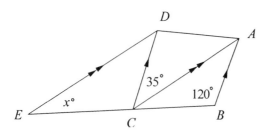

If $\overline{AB}\parallel\overline{CD}$, then $m\angle ACD = m\angle BAC$. (Alternate Interior Angles Theorem)

Therefore $m\angle BAC = 35$.

If $\overline{AC}\parallel\overline{DE}$, then $m\angle DEC = m\angle ACB$. (Corresponding Angles Postulate)

Therefore $m\angle ACB = x$.

In $\triangle ABC$, $m\angle ACB + m\angle ABC + m\angle BAC = 180$.
$x + 35 + 120 = 180$
$x = 25$

10. E

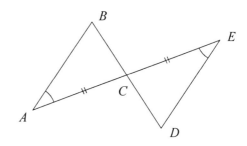

$AC = EC$	Definition of segment bisector
$\angle A \cong \angle E$	Given
$\angle ACB \cong \angle ECD$	Vertical angles are $\cong$.
$\triangle ABC \cong \triangle EDC$	ASA

I. $\overline{AB}\cong\overline{DE}$ — cpctc (corresponding parts of congruent triangles are congruent)

True.

II. $\overline{AB}\parallel\overline{DE}$ — Alternate Interior Angles Theorem

True.

III. $\overline{BC}\cong\overline{CD}$ — cpctc

True.

11. C

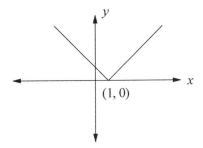

The vertex of the graph of the absolute value function is $(1,0)$.

Substitute $x = 1$ and $y = 0$ into each answer choice.

(A) $y = |x|$ $0 \neq |1|$ Discard.

(B) $y = |x+1|$ $0 \neq |1+1|$ Discard.

(C) $y = |x-1|$ $0 = |1-1|$ True.

(D) $y = |x|+1$ $0 \neq |1|+1$ Discard.

(E) $y = |x|-1$ $0 = |1|-1$ True.

Discard answer choices (A), (B), and (D).

Next, check the y-intercept of the graph. To find the y-intercept, let x equal 0.

(C) $y = |x-1|$ If $x = 0$, $y = |0-1| = 1$

(E) $y = |x|-1$ If $x = 0$, $y = |0|-1 = -1$

The graph shows that the y-intercept is positive, so (C) is the correct answer choice.

12. B

The domain is the set of all real numbers, and the range is the set of all numbers y such that $y \geq 0$.

13. A

$$PQ = 8 - (-2\tfrac{2}{3}) = 10\tfrac{2}{3}$$

Since point R is $\dfrac{2}{5}$ of the way from P to Q,

$$PR = 10\tfrac{2}{3} \times \tfrac{2}{5} = \tfrac{32}{3} \times \tfrac{2}{5} = \tfrac{64}{15} = 4\tfrac{4}{15}.$$

The coordinate of R is

$$-2\tfrac{2}{3} + 4\tfrac{4}{15} = -2\tfrac{10}{15} + 4\tfrac{4}{15} = 1\tfrac{9}{15} = 1\tfrac{3}{5}.$$

14. C

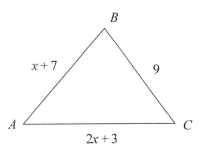

If $AB = BC$, then $x + 7 = 9$. $\Rightarrow$ $x = 2$. So $AB = BC = 9$, and $AC = 2x + 3 = 2(2) + 3 = 7$. Perimeter $= 9 + 9 + 7 = 25$

If $AC = BC$, then $2x + 3 = 9$. $\Rightarrow$ $x = 3$. So $AC = BC = 9$, and $AB = x + 7 = 3 + 7 = 10$. Perimeter $= 9 + 9 + 10 = 28$

If $AB = AC$, then $x + 7 = 2x + 3$. $\Rightarrow$ $x = 4$. So $AB = AC = 11$, and $BC = 9$. Perimeter $= 11 + 11 + 9 = 31$

15. D

Choose two points from the graph. The two points are $(0,500)$ and $(8,1100)$. Here the y-values are rounded to the nearest hundred.

The slope of the line of best fit

$$= \frac{1100 - 500}{8 - 0} = \frac{600}{8} = 75.$$

If you choose the points $(2,700)$ and $(8,1100)$,

$$\text{slope} = \frac{1100 - 700}{8 - 2} = \frac{400}{6} \approx 67.$$

Choice (D) is correct.

16. B

Let y = the expected number of computers in the year 2005.
$x = 15$ represents the year 2005

The slope of the line passing through the points $(0, 500)$ and $(15, y)$ should approximate 75.

$$m = \frac{y - 500}{15 - 0} = 75 \implies y - 500 = (15)(75)$$
$$\implies y - 500 = 1125 \implies y = 1625$$

Answer choice (B) is the best choice.

17. B

Let x = the number of hours of internet service at which the total monthly fee is the same

Total charges under Option A

$\underset{\substack{\text{\$3.00 per hour} \\ \text{of use}}}{3} \cdot \underset{\substack{\text{the number of} \\ \text{hours charged}}}{(x - 3)} + \underset{\substack{\text{basic} \\ \text{charge}}}{12}$

Total charges under Option B

$\underset{\substack{\text{\$4.00 per hour} \\ \text{of use}}}{4} \cdot \underset{\substack{\text{the number of} \\ \text{hours charged}}}{(x - 5)} + \underset{\substack{\text{basic} \\ \text{charge}}}{9}$

Therefore
$$3(x - 3) + 12 = 4(x - 5) + 9$$
$$3x - 9 + 12 = 4x - 20 + 9$$
$$3x + 3 = 4x - 11$$
$$x = 14$$

18. A

The distance traveled by a wheel
$= 2\pi r \times$ the number of revolutions.

Let n = the number of revolutions.

m miles $= 2\pi r \times n$
$5280m$ feet $= 2\pi rn$ (1mile = 5280ft)
$$n = \frac{5280m}{2\pi r} = \frac{2640m}{\pi r}$$

19. A

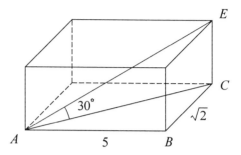

$$AC^2 = AB^2 + BC^2$$
$$AC^2 = 5^2 + (\sqrt{2})^2 = 25 + 2 = 27$$
$$AC = \sqrt{27} = 3\sqrt{3}$$

$\triangle AEC$ is a $30°$-$60°$-$90°$ triangle, therefore $EC = 3$ and $AE = 6$.

20. B

$$f(x) = -x + 4$$

I. $f(0) = -(0) + 4 = 4$
$f(f(0)) = f(4) = -(4) + 4 = 0$
True.

II. $f(x + 4) = -(x + 4) + 4 = -x - 4 + 4 = -x$
$f(x) + 4 = -x + 4 + 4 = -x + 8$
Therefore $f(x + 4) \neq f(x) + 4$.
Not true.

III. $f(-x) = -(-x) + 4 = x + 4$
$-f(x) = -(-x + 4) = x - 4$
Therefore $f(-x) \neq -f(x)$.
Not true.

Multiple Choice Questions   (Section 2)

1. B

$a+b=9$ and $a=b+5$

$(b+5)+b=9$ Substitution $(a=b+5)$
$2b+5=9 \Rightarrow b=2$

$a=b+5=2+5=7$

2. C

$\dfrac{x^{2a+1}}{x^3}=x^{a+2}$
$x^{(2a+1)-3}=x^{a+2} \Rightarrow 2a+1-3=a+2$
$\Rightarrow 2a-2=a+2 \Rightarrow a=4$

3. E

The length of arc $AB=2\pi r\times\dfrac{80}{360}$.

$2\pi r\times\dfrac{80}{360}=4\pi \Rightarrow \dfrac{4}{9}\pi r=4\pi$
$\Rightarrow r=9$

Area of the circle $=\pi(9)^2=81\pi$

4. E

$AB=CD$ Opposite sides of a $\square$ are $\cong$.
$2x-3=x+5$
$x=8$
$\Rightarrow AB=CD=13$
$\Rightarrow BC=AD=2x=2(8)=16$

Perimeter of $ABCD=2(13)+2(16)=58$

5. B

Let $x=$ the number of diskettes produced in h hours.

Set up a proportion.

$\dfrac{d \text{ diskettes}}{m \text{ minutes}}=\dfrac{x \text{ diskettes}}{h \text{ hours}}$

$\Rightarrow \dfrac{d \text{ diskettes}}{m \text{ minutes}}=\dfrac{x \text{ diskettes}}{60h \text{ minutes}}$
(1 hour = 60 minutes)

Use cross multiplication.
$d\cdot 60h=x\cdot m \Rightarrow x=\dfrac{60dh}{m}$

6. B

Given: $a_n=\dfrac{n}{4}$.   Check each answer choice.

(A) If $a_n=\dfrac{n}{4}=0$, then $x=0$, which is an integer.

(B) If $a_n=\dfrac{n}{4}=0.025$, then $x=0.1$, which is not

an integer.

(C) If $a_n=\dfrac{n}{4}=0.25$, then $x=1$, which is an integer.

(D) If $a_n=\dfrac{n}{4}=2.5$, then $x=10$, which is an integer.

(E) If $a_n=\dfrac{n}{4}=25$, then $x=100$, which is an

integer.

7. D

If $|x-3|>4$, then $x-3>4$ or $x-3<-4$.
$x-3>4 \Rightarrow x>7$ or
$x-3<-4 \Rightarrow x<-1$

Answer choice (D) is correct.

8. C

Adding the areas of the six pieces gives us the area of the original square.

Area of square $=1+4+9+9+16+25$
$x^2=64$
$x=8$

9. D

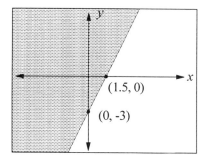

First find the equation of the dotted line.

The slope of the line is $m = \dfrac{0+3}{1.5-0} = \dfrac{3}{1.5} = 2$.

The y-intercept is -3 .
The slope-intercept form of the line is $y = 2x - 3$.
The standard form of the line is $-2x + y = -3$ or
$2x - y = 3$.

Let's use point $(0,0)$ as a test point to see whether
the point belongs to the inequality $2x - y < 3$.

Substitute $x = 0$ and $y = 0$ into the inequality.
$2(0) - 0 < 3$, which is true.

Therefore $2x - y < 3$ represents the graph above.

10. C

$$\frac{b}{a} = 128 \implies b = 128a = 2^7 \cdot a$$

The terms of the sequence can be written as
$a,\ 2a,\ 2^2 a,\ 2^3 a,\ 2^4 a,\ 2^5 a,\ 2^6 a,\ 2^7 a \ldots$

Since $b = 2^7 \cdot a$, there are 6 terms between a and b .

11. A

$$P(n) = \begin{cases} 6n, & \text{if } 1 \le n \le 49 \\ 5n, & \text{if } 50 \le n \le 99 \\ 4n, & \text{if } 100 \le n \end{cases}$$

Check each answer choice.

(A) The cost of 42 box cars $= \$6 \times 42 = \$252$.

The cost of 50 box cars $= \$5 \times 50 = \$250$.

42 box cars cost more than 50 box cars.

Choice (A) is correct.

(B) The cost of 110 box cars $= \$4 \times 110 = \$440$.

The cost of 90 box cars $= \$5 \times 90 = \$450$.

Discard.

(C) The cost of 96 box cars $= \$5 \times 96 = \$480$.

The cost of 120 box cars $= \$4 \times 120 = \$480$.

Discard.

(D) The cost of 59 box cars $= \$5 \times 59 = \$295$.

The cost of 49 box cars $= \$6 \times 49 = \$294$.

Discard.

(E) The cost of 120 box cars $= \$4 \times 120 = \$480$.

The cost of 95 box cars $= \$5 \times 95 = \$475$.

Discard.

12. D

The amount of flour in each of Kim's bags $= \dfrac{n}{s}$

The amount of flour in each of Tim's bags $= \dfrac{n}{r+s}$

The difference is $\dfrac{n}{s} - \dfrac{n}{r+s}$.

$$\frac{n}{s} - \frac{n}{r+s}$$
$$= \frac{n(r+s)}{s(r+s)} - \frac{ns}{(r+s)s}$$
$$= \frac{n(r+s) - ns}{s(r+s)}$$
$$= \frac{nr + ns - ns}{s(r+s)}$$
$$= \frac{nr}{s(r+s)}$$

13. A

The following example of 11 positive integers, whose average is 20, shows that none of the Roman numerals I, II, or III is true.

1, 1, 1, 1, 2, 2, 3, 4, 35, 35, 135

The median of the integers is 2.
The mode of the integers is 1.
There is no integer between 4 and 35.

14. D

$$x^2 - bx + 25 = (x - c)^2$$
$$x^2 - bx + 25 = x^2 - 2cx + c^2$$

In a quadratic equation if
$ax^2 + bx + c = px^2 + qx + r$,
then $a = p$, $b = q$, and $c = r$.
Therefore $b = 2c$, and $25 = c^2$.

$\Rightarrow$ $c = \pm 5$, but $c > 0$. Therefore $c = 5$,
and $b = 2c = 2 \cdot 5$, or 10.

$$b + c = 10 + 5 = 15$$

15. B

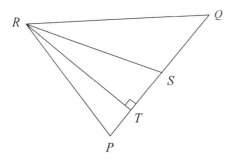

Draw $\overline{RT}$ perpendicular to $\overline{PQ}$.

Area of $\triangle PRS = \dfrac{1}{2} \cdot PS \cdot RT$

Area of $\triangle QRS = \dfrac{1}{2} \cdot QS \cdot RT$

$$\frac{\text{area of } \triangle PRS}{\text{area of } \triangle QRS} = \frac{\frac{1}{2} \cdot PS \cdot RT}{\frac{1}{2} \cdot QS \cdot RT} = \frac{3}{5}$$

$\Rightarrow \dfrac{PS}{QS} = \dfrac{3}{5} \Rightarrow PS = 3x$ and $QS = 5x$

$PS + QS = PQ$
$3x + 5x = 24 \Rightarrow 8x = 24 \Rightarrow x = 3$

$PS = 3x = 3(3) = 9$

16. B

Let the total number of pencils $= x$, then
the number of blue pencils $= \dfrac{1}{3}x$, and

the remaining number of pencils $= x - \dfrac{1}{3}x = \dfrac{2}{3}x$.

The number of red pencils $= \dfrac{1}{5} \times \dfrac{2}{3}x = \dfrac{2}{15}x$, and

the number of yellow pencils $= 2 \times \dfrac{2}{15}x = \dfrac{4}{15}x$.

the number of blue pencils	the number of red pencils	the number of yellow pencils	and the remaining number of pencils	is equal to the total number of pencils
$\dfrac{1}{3}x$	$+\ \dfrac{2}{15}x$	$+\ \dfrac{4}{15}x$	$+\ 8$	$= x$

$\dfrac{1}{3}x + \dfrac{2}{15}x + \dfrac{4}{15}x + 8 = x$

$\Rightarrow \dfrac{11}{15}x + 8 = x$

$\Rightarrow \dfrac{4}{15}x = 8$

$\Rightarrow x = 30$

17. A

Let d = the distance in miles from Sara's house to the park.

$$d = rt \implies t = \frac{d}{r}$$

$$\underbrace{\frac{d}{8}}_{\substack{\text{the time it took to jog} \\ \text{from home to the park}}} + \underbrace{\frac{d}{6}}_{\substack{\text{the time it took to jog} \\ \text{from the park to home}}} = \underbrace{\frac{42}{60}}_{\substack{\text{the total time} \\ \text{in hours}}}$$

$$\implies \frac{d}{8} + \frac{d}{6} = \frac{7}{10}$$

By multiplying 120 on both sides, we have

$$15d + 20d = 84 \implies 35d = 84$$
$$\implies d = 2.4$$

18. E

a and b are integers and $\frac{a}{b} = \frac{4}{3}$.

I. If $a = 8$ and $b = 6$, then $a + b = 8 + 6 = 14$, which is not an odd integer.
Not true.

II. If $a = 4$ and $b = 3$, then $ab = 4 \cdot 3 = 12$.
If $a = 8$ and $b = 6$, then $ab = 8 \cdot 6 = 48$.
ab is always an even integer.
True.

III. If $a = 4$ and $b = 3$, then $a + b = 4 + 3 = 7$.
If $a = 8$ and $b = 6$, then $a + b = 8 + 6 = 14$.
$a + b$ is always divisible by 7.
True.

19. C

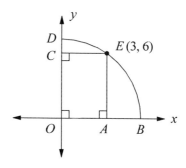

Let r = the radius of circle O, then $OB = OD = r$.

Since $OAEC$ is a rectangle, $OA = 3$ and $OC = 6$.

$$AB = OB - OA = r - 3$$
$$CD = OD - OC = r - 6$$

$$AB - CD = (r - 3) - (r - 6) = 3$$

20. E

$$\frac{7^x \cdot x^7}{7^7 \cdot x^x} = \left(\frac{7^x}{7^7}\right)\left(\frac{x^7}{x^x}\right) = 7^{(x-7)} \cdot x^{(7-x)}$$

$$= 7^{(x-7)} \cdot x^{-(x-7)} = 7^{(x-7)} \cdot \frac{1}{x^{(x-7)}}$$

$$= \frac{7^{(x-7)}}{x^{(x-7)}} = \left(\frac{7}{x}\right)^{(x-7)}$$

Grid-In Questions (Section 3)

1. 10

$$x - y = -2 \implies x = y - 2$$

$$\frac{x}{4} = y - 5 \implies x = 4(y - 5) \implies x = 4y - 20$$

By making a substitution, we have
$$y - 2 = 4y - 20$$
$$\implies 18 = 3y \implies y = 6$$

$$x = y - 2 = 6 - 2 = 4$$

$$x + y = 4 + 6 = 10$$

2. $\frac{1}{2}$

$a = \frac{1}{2}$ and $b = 2$.

$$(a\sqrt{2})^b = (\frac{1}{2}\sqrt{2})^2 = (\frac{\sqrt{2}}{2})^2 = \frac{(\sqrt{2})^2}{2^2} = \frac{2}{4} = \frac{1}{2}$$

3. 18

$a + b = 36$ and $a - b = 9$.

$$\sqrt{a^2 - b^2} = \sqrt{(a+b)(a-b)}$$
$$= \sqrt{(36)(9)} = \sqrt{36} \cdot \sqrt{9}$$
$$= 6 \cdot 3 = 18$$

4. 6

Find the prime factorization of $24k$.
$$24k = 2^3 \cdot 3 \cdot k$$

If $24k$ is the square of an integer, then all the exponents in the prime factorization must be multiples of 2, e.g. if $24k = 2^4 \cdot 3^2$ then $24k$ is the square of an integer.

The least positive integer value for k occurs when $24k = 2^3 \cdot 3 \cdot k = 2^4 \cdot 3^2$.

Therefore $k = \frac{2^4 \cdot 3^2}{2^3 \cdot 3} = 6$.

5. $\frac{5}{2}$

$$f(x) = 9^x - 4^{-x}$$

$$f(\frac{1}{2}) = 9^{1/2} - 4^{-1/2} = 9^{1/2} - \frac{1}{4^{1/2}}$$

$$= \sqrt{9} - \frac{1}{\sqrt{4}} = 3 - \frac{1}{2} = \frac{5}{2}$$

6. 195

The nth term of an arithmetic sequence is
$$a_n = a_1 + (n-1)d.$$

3, 7, 11, 15, ... is a sequence with $a_1 = 3$ and $d = 4$.

$n = 49$ for the 49th term.
$$a_{49} = 3 + (49-1) \cdot 4 = 195$$

7. 7

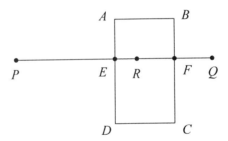

Draw line PQ. Let E and F be the points of intersection of $\overline{PQ}$ and $\overline{AD}$, and $\overline{PQ}$ and $\overline{BC}$, respectively.

Since points P and Q are symmetric about line AD, and $PQ = 24$, $PE = QE = 12$.
Since points Q and R are symmetric about line BC, and $QR = 10$, $RF = QF = 5$.

$$RE = QE - QR = 12 - 10 = 2$$
$$AB = RE + RF = 2 + 5 = 7$$

8. $\dfrac{75}{2}$

$m = k \cdot d$ (m is directly proportional to d.)

$15 = k \cdot 8$ (A mass of 15g stretches the spring 8cm.)

$\Rightarrow k = \dfrac{15}{8} \Rightarrow m = \dfrac{15}{8}d$

$m = \dfrac{15}{8}(20) = \dfrac{75}{2}$

9. 4

$7r - 2s = 5$ First equation
$4t - 14r = 6$ Second equation

Multiply the first equation by 2, then add it to the second equation.

$2(7r - 2s) = 2(5) \Rightarrow 14r - 4s = 10$

$\begin{array}{l} \cancel{14r} - 4s = 10 \\ + 4t - \cancel{14r} = 6 \\ \hline 4t - 4s = 16 \Rightarrow 4(t - s) = 16 \\ \qquad\qquad \Rightarrow t - s = 4 \end{array}$

10. $\dfrac{2}{3}$

$\begin{array}{cccc} \bullet & \bullet & \bullet & \bullet \\ P & Q & R & S \end{array}$

Let's pick a number for the length of $\overline{PS}$.
Let $PS = 30$. (30 is a multiple of 3 and 5.)

Then $\dfrac{PS}{QS} = \dfrac{3}{2} \Rightarrow \dfrac{30}{QS} = \dfrac{3}{2} \Rightarrow QS = 20$,

and $\dfrac{PS}{PR} = \dfrac{5}{3} \Rightarrow \dfrac{30}{PR} = \dfrac{5}{3} \Rightarrow PR = 18$.

$RS = PS - PR = 30 - 18 = 12$
$QR = QS - RS = 20 - 12 = 8$
$\dfrac{QR}{RS} = \dfrac{8}{12} = \dfrac{2}{3}$

11. 96

$ABCD$ is a rectangle whose length, AD, equals the circumference of the cylinder's base, $2\pi r$.

$BD^2 = AB^2 + AD^2$
$10^2 = 6^2 + AD^2$

$AD^2 = 64 \Rightarrow AD = 8$

$2\pi r = AD = 8 \Rightarrow r = \dfrac{8}{2\pi} = \dfrac{4}{\pi}$

$V = \pi r^2 h = \pi(\dfrac{4}{\pi})^2 \cdot 6 = \pi \cdot \dfrac{16}{\pi^2} \cdot 6 = \dfrac{96}{\pi}$

$\dfrac{k}{\pi} = \dfrac{96}{\pi} \Rightarrow k = 96$

12. 6

If $a < b < c$, then b is the median.

$\underbrace{\dfrac{a+b+c}{3}}_{\substack{\text{the average of}\\ a, b, \text{ and } c}} = \underbrace{2b + 2}_{\substack{\text{2 more than twice}\\ \text{the median}}}$ and $c = 5b$.

$a + b + c = 3(2b + 2) \Rightarrow a + b + c = 6b + 6$
$a + b + 5b = 6b + 6$ (5b is substituted for c.)
$a + 6b = 6b + 6 \Rightarrow a = 6$

13. $\dfrac{3}{8}$

Total area of the dart board $= \pi(2r)^2 = 4\pi r^2$
Area of the shaded region

$= [\text{Total area} - \text{Area of inner circle}] \times 3(\dfrac{60°}{360°})$

$= [4\pi r^2 - \pi r^2] \times \dfrac{180}{360}$

$= 3\pi r^2 \times \dfrac{1}{2} = \dfrac{3}{2}\pi r^2$

The probability that a dart will hit the shaded region of the board

$= \dfrac{\text{area of the shaded region}}{\text{area of the board}}$

$= \dfrac{3/2\,\pi r^2}{4\pi r^2} = \dfrac{3/2}{4} = \dfrac{3}{8}$

14. 150

Let x = the total number of books sold,
then $x - 30$ = the number of paperback copies
sold.

$$\$16 \cdot 30 + \$9 \cdot (x - 30) = \$10.40 \cdot x$$
$$480 + 9x - 270 = 10.4x$$
$$210 = 1.4x$$
$$x = 150$$

15. 100

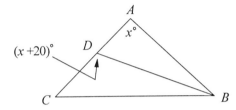

Since $AB = AC$,

$$m\angle C = m\angle ABC = \frac{1}{2}(180 - x) = 90 - \frac{1}{2}x.$$

Since $\overline{BD}$ bisects $\angle ABC$,

$$m\angle ABD = \frac{1}{2}(m\angle ABC) = \frac{1}{2}(90 - \frac{1}{2}x) = 45 - \frac{1}{4}x.$$

$$m\angle ADB = 180 - (x + 20) = 160 - x$$

The sum of the angles in $\triangle ABD$ equals 180.

$$x + (45 - \frac{1}{4}x) + (160 - x) = 180$$

$$-\frac{1}{4}x + 205 = 180$$

$$-\frac{1}{4}x = -25 \implies x = 100$$

Order *Acing the New SAT I Math* today!

To order online, visit our website at http://greenhallpublishing.com.

To order by phone call (805) 241-2500.

To order by mail, fill out the form below and send it to:
Greenhall Publishing
463 Pennsfield Place #102
Thousand Oaks, CA 91360

- -

I want _____ copies of *Acing the New SAT I Math*, at $18 each plus $2 shipping and handling per book. (California residents please add 7.25% sales tax – $1.31 per book.)

Payment Option:

☐ *My check or money order for $_____.___ is enclosed.*
   (payable to Greenhall Publishing)

☐ *Please charge my credit card:*
   ○ *American Express*   ○ *Discover*   ○ *MasterCard*   ○ *Visa*

Card Number _____   *Expiration Date* _____

Cardholder Name (as appears on card) _____

Cardholder Signature _____

Delivery Address:

Name _____

Address 1 _____

Address 2 _____

City/State/ZIP _____

Phone _____   *E-mail* _____